Community Development Strategies

George J. Washnis

Published in cooperation with
the Center for Governmental Studies

The Praeger Special Studies program—utilizing the most modern and efficient book production techniques and a selective worldwide distribution network—makes available to the academic, government, and business communities significant, timely research in U.S. and international economic, social, and political development.

Community Development Strategies

Case Studies of Major Model Cities

PRAEGER SPECIAL STUDIES IN U.S. ECONOMIC, SOCIAL, AND POLITICAL ISSUES

Praeger Publishers New York Washington London

Library of Congress Cataloging in Publication Data

Washnis, George J
    Community development strategies.

    (Praeger special studies in U.S. economic, social,
and political issues)
    "Published in cooperation with the Center for Govern-
mental Studies."
    Includes bibliographical references.
    1. Urban renewal—United States—Case studies.
2. Cities and towns—Planning—United States—Case
studies. 3. Community development—United States—
Case studies. I. Title.
HT175.W37   309.2'62'0973   72-92471

PRAEGER PUBLISHERS
111 Fourth Avenue, New York, N.Y. 10003, U.S.A.
5, Cromwell Place, London SW7 2JL, England

Published in the United States of America in 1974
by Praeger Publishers, Inc.

Printed in the United States of America

For more than a third of a century, the federal government has given aid to cities to make improvements in older, rundown neighborhoods. The Housing Act of 1937 began a public housing program with the triple purpose of new housing for the poor, jobs for the unemployed, and demolition of slums. The Housing Act of 1949 started a redevelopment program with federal subsidies for a slum clearance that led to a variety of new land uses. The Housing Act of 1954 introduced urban renewal to the lexicon, provided assistance for neighborhood rehabilitation, and required cities to have a workable program for community improvement.

The 1960s saw greater emphasis upon social renewal of the inner city through a set of demonstration projects funded by the President's Committee on Juvenile Delinquency and then through the Community Action Program. By the mid-1960s, city and federal officials became convinced of the necessity of marrying programs of social and physical improvement, and this notion was embodied in the Demonstration Cities and Metropolitan Development Act of 1965, which created what became known as the Model Cities Program. It took a year to select cities and another year or more to plan local programs and obtain federal funding, but now a few cities are in their fifth action year and many more in their fourth. As the demonstration period draws to a close, Congress is considering consolidating Model Cities, urban renewal, and several other programs into an even more comprehensive community development program.

As this newest stage of evolution occurs, it is important to assess what has been learned from the Model Cities Program. This is what George J. Washnis does in this report, which looks at the program in its totality and at the experience of eight cities in detail. His conclusions about planning processes, management and coordination techniques, citizen participation, and the product expressed in terms of program results, all of these are relevant to the design and implementation of a nationally supported, locally administered community development program. As a former city administrator, he adds his practical knowledge of how to get things done.

In the conduct of this study, Camille Cates made a significant contribution to the case studies, and Judy Chavkin served as an editorial assistant. Local reporters provided valuable information from the eight cities studied: Elliot Friedman (Boston), William Hood and Thomas Gray (Chicago), Denise Goodman (Dayton), Jim Hetherington (Indianapolis), Larry Hall and Peter Bridge (Newark),

Josh Friedman and Wayne Barrett (New York), Neal Baker (Savannah), and Hilda Bryant (Seattle).

Financial support for this study came from the Ford Foundation. However, the conclusions and recommendations reflect the views of the author and are not necessarily those of the Ford Foundation or the board of directors of the Center for Governmental Studies.

Howard W. Hallman
President
Center for Governmental Studies
Washington, D.C.

This study focuses on eight cities in the Model Cities Program and the effects of the program on national urban policy and the ability of cities and counties to cope with urban problems. The cities (Boston, Chicago, Dayton, Indianapolis, Newark, New York, Savannah, and Seattle) were chosen not only for their geographic and population representativeness but also because they were reported to be making some noticeable impact on their communities, whether positive or negative in nature. However, these few cities have been used only as a base for an analysis of the full program. Findings of studies conducted by the U.S. Department of Housing and Urban Development (HUD) and others (plus other studies by the author), involving as few as one city and as many as all 147 cities in the Model Cities Program, are used for comparative purposes, to confirm or qualify some points.

The body of the manuscript is in the form of six case studies and deals with the major components of the Model Cities Program and what impact they have had on relieving urban problems in each area. Its focus is on the operation of local general government and how this has been affected by the objectives, organization, and methods imposed by the Model Cities Program.

Two case studies—Indianapolis and Dayton—have been omitted from the body of the manuscript (but not the analysis) because these cities have been covered extensively in other reports and because their inclusion would have made this report too lengthy. However, these full case studies can be obtained by contacting the Center for Governmental Studies, 1701 K Street, N.W., Washington, D.C.

The overall analysis is a synthesis of experiences of all eight cities and how they have measured up to the program's main objectives, which include such things as program demonstration and innovation, coordination and comprehensive planning, concentration and commitment of resources, citizen involvement, and service improvement. The evaluation and effect of new programs—Planned Variations, special revenue sharing, Better Communities, block grants—are compared to Model Cities, which we believe has been the genesis for many of the new ideas.

CONTENTS

	Page
FOREWORD by Howard W. Hallman	v
PREFACE	vii
LIST OF TABLES AND CHARTS	xvii

PART I: THE MODEL CITIES
PROGRAM—AN ASSESSMENT

Chapter

1 OVER-ALL ASSESSMENT	3
Origins	3
Decisions: A Local Responsibility	4
Commitment: Never There	5
Concentration and Comprehensiveness	8
Concentrating in Target Areas	8
Comprehensive Planning	9
Experience of Cities	10
Coordination	11
Techniques Used to Improve Coordination	12
A-95 Process	12
Chief Executive Review and Comment	13
Annual Arrangements	13
Demonstration and Innovation	14
Institutional Change	15
Health Centers	15
Model Schools	16
Manpower Centers	16
Semiindependent Corporations	16
Management Capacity	17
Increasing Responsibility and Capacity	17
Change of Emphasis	18
Citizen Participation	19
General	19

Lessons   19
Model Cities Product   20
     Process vs. Product   20
     Measurement of Product   21
     Level of Service   21
     Efficiency   22
     Quality of Service   22
     Concluding Comment   23
Notes   23

2   CHARACTERISTICS OF MODEL NEIGHBORHOODS   25

Size and Severity   25
Health Crisis   26
Overcrowding   26
Educational Achievement   27
Unemployment   27
Other Factors   27

3   ASSESSMENT OF THE PRODUCT   30

Seattle's Success   31
Health Projects   32
     Seattle   32
     Indianapolis and Boston   32
     Newark   33
     Dayton   34
     Chicago   34
     New York   35
Education Programs   35
     Chicago   35
     Dayton, Savannah, Seattle, and Indianapolis   36
     Boston   36
     Newark   37
Manpower and Economic Development   37
     Newark's Goals Vis-à-vis Its Problems   38
     Seattle's Modest Success   38
     Dayton's Progress   39
     New York City's Multiple Problems   40
     Chicago First in Innovation and State Coopera-
        tion in Manpower Centers   41
     Savannah Needs Prodding   42
     Indianapolis—Leadership from the Top   42

Chapter   Page

Other Model Cities Projects   42
   Housing   42
   Public Facilities and Social Services   44
   Law and Justice   44
Conclusion   45
Notes   46

4   CITIZEN PARTICIPATION   47

Using Helpful Nomenclature   47
Overview of Eight Cities   48
Chicago: Staff Dominance   48
Indianapolis   49
   Staff Dominance or Parity   49
   Planned Variations   50
Savannah: Staff Dominance   51
Newark: Staff Dominance   52
Dayton: Resident Dominance   53
New York: Resident Dominance Vis-à-vis Staff
   Influence   55
Boston's System of Parity   57
Seattle's Parity   58
Conclusions   59
Notes   63

5   STATE ACTION AND PRIVATE RESPONSES   65

State Role   65
Model Cities Emerges as a Catalyst   65
The Power of the State   65
The Level of State Participation   66
   Newark Gained   66
   Chicago Unresponsive   67
   New York Sidetracked   68
   Seattle Benefited   69
   Boston: Passable Assistance   70
   Dayton: Standard Assistance   70
   Indianapolis and Savannah: Minimum As-
     sistance   70
Local Strategies and State Plans   71
Private Response   72

Chapter   Page

6   FEDERAL ROLE IN THE FUTURE   74

    Block Grants   76
        Planned Variations as a Block Grant   76
        Model Cities: Block Grants and Com-
            mitment   77
        Pending Legislation   78
        Commitment   81
    Notes   82

            PART II: THE INDIVIDUAL APPROACHES
                      OF SIX CITIES

7   SUCCESS IN SEATTLE   87

    The City   87
    The Government and Power Structure   88
        The Government   88
        Departmental Organization   89
        Power Structure   91
        Urban Renewal   92
    Model Cities   93
        Background   93
        Characteristics of the Model Neighborhood   94
        Administration of the Agency   95
        Citizen Participation   99
    Model Cities Programs   105
        Manpower and Job Development   106
        Recreation and Culture   110
        Health   111
        Crime and Delinquency   112
        Social Services   114
        Education   116
        Economic and Business Development   118
        Housing   120
        Transportation   122
        Relocation   123
        Community Facilities   123
        Environmental Protection and Development   124
        General Impressions of the Program   124
    Planned Variations   126
    Analysis and Recommendations   130

        Judging Program Success   130
        Private Response   131
        Accomplishments   132
        Administrative Direction   133
        Citizen Participation   133
        Migration Hurts the Model Neighborhood   135
    Conclusion   136
    Notes   136

8   UNUSUAL PROBLEMS IN NEWARK   137

    The City   137
        General   137
        Too Many Tax Exemptions   138
        High Tax Rate   139
        Education   140
    The Government   140
        Politics   140
        Organization   142
        Government Performance   144
        Improving City Government   144
    Model Cities   148
        The Model Neighborhood   148
        Administrative Structure of the Model Cities
            Program   150
        Departmental Coordination and Financial
            Integration   153
        State and Federal Assistance   156
        Citizen Participation   157
        Congressional Hearing on Newark Model
            Cities   163
        Projects   165
        Councilmanic Perceptions About Model
            Cities   180
    Planned Variations   182
    Analysis and Recommendations   184
        A Poor Start   184
        The Need to Reorganize   185
        Improved Coordination and Integrated
            Financial System   186
        Confusion and Disarray Still Present   186
        The Role of the Business Administrator   187
        The Role of the Mayor   188

The Role of City Council   189
Conditions That Hinder Progress   190
Summary of Management Problems   190
Model Cities Project Analysis   191
Summary   195
Citizen Participation   195
Citywide Orientation an Improvement   197
Notes   197

9   A NEW BEGINNING FOR SAVANNAH   199

The City   199
Government   200
Structure and Politics   200
City Service Effectiveness   204
Model Cities   205
History of Model Cities   205
The Model Neighborhood   209
Administrative Structure and Coordination   211
Citizen Participation   214
Programs   218
Education   219
Employment and Economic Development   220
Health   221
Crime and Juvenile Delinquency Prevention   221
Resident Programs   221
Recreation and Cultural Activities   222
Municipal Services   223
Analysis   223
Accomplishments   223
Coalition of Interests Needed   225

10 CHICAGO DEMONSTRATES EFFICIENCY   226

The City   226
General   226
Fiscal Accountability   227
Population and Race   228
Employment   229
Board of Education   232
City Housing   233
Welfare   235
City Health   236

Chapter   Page

          The Mayor and City Council   237
          Patronage   239
          Power Structure   240
          City Service   241
          Department Effectiveness   242
     Model Cities   243
          Model Cities Administration   243
          Federal, State, and Local Views of the
               Program   246
          Demography of the Four Model Neighbor-
               hoods   249
          Citizen Participation   250
          The Woodlawn Organization Experience   258
          Programs   259
          Institutional Change   272
     Critique and Analysis   273
          Mayor Adopts Model Cities   273
          Strengths   274
          Weaknesses   276
          The Need for a New Commitment   279
     Notes   280

11 COMPETENCE IS BOSTON'S HALLMARK   282

     The City   282
          Demography   283
          Economics and Taxes   283
          Capital Improvements   285
     The Government and the Power Structure   286
          The State and Independent Agencies   286
          The Mayor   288
          City Council   291
          Civil Service   293
          Political Power   294
          Business Power   295
     Boston's Model Cities   295
          History   295
          Structure and Demography   296
          Organization of Model Cities Administra-
               tion   298
          CDA Staff   300
          Federal Government and Model Cities   300
          State Government and Model Cities   301

Chapter   Page

        Local Relationships   302
        Citizen Participation   303
    Model Cities Programs   313
        Community Services   313
    The Start of Citywide Decentralization   320
    Analysis and Recommendations   321
        The Government   321
        Model Cities   322
    Notes   327

12   NEW YORK FALLS BEHIND   328

    The City   328
        The National Center   328
        Fiscal Crisis   329
    Government   331
    Power Structure   333
        Political Power   333
        City Planning Commission   334
        The State   334
        Business   335
        Unions   336
    Administering the Bureaucracy   337
        Deputy Mayors   338
        Superagencies   340
        Model Cities as a Superagency   340
        Model Cities and Service Agencies   341
        Model Cities and Superagencies   343
        Decentralization   344
    Model Cities   346
        Demography   347
        History   348
        Citizen Participation in Model Cities   354
        Administration   359
    Model Cities Projects   370
        General   370
        Brooklyn   371
        The Federation of Addiction Agencies and
          Brooklyn Model Cities   381
        Harlem-East Harlem   385
        Bronx   389
    Analysis and Recommendations   391
        Reasons for Delay of Program   391
        Projects   393

Chapter   Page

Model Cities as a Superagency   398
Citywide Orientation and Need for a
   Genuine Coalition   399
Model Cities Administration Unnecessary   401
Decentralization   402
Improving General Government   405
Lessons of Model Cities   406
Notes   407

PART III: SUMMARY

13   CONCLUSIONS AND RECOMMENDATIONS   411

ABOUT THE AUTHOR   416

LIST OF TABLES AND CHARTS

Table		Page
1	Original Model Cities Participants	6
2	Population Ranges of Model Communities	7
3	Demography of Model Neighborhoods	28
4	Annual Funding for Planned Variations Cities	75
5	Member Organizations of Interagency Directors Committee, Seattle Model Cities	96
6	SMCP Planned Variations Budget Allocations Summary	128
7	Deaths per 1,000 Population for Certain Diseases, 1969, Newark	149
8	Funds Generated and Expended, Newark, October 1971	158
9	Functions and Responsibilities of Model Area Councils	256
10	Brooklyn Model Cities Cost to Beneficiary Analysis	366

Chart		
1	Organization Chart, City of Seattle	90
2	Organization Chart, City of Newark	143
3	Functional Organization of the City of Savannah	202
4	City Demonstration Agency Organizational Chart, Savannah, Georgia	213
5	Organization of Boston's City Government	289

Chart   Page

6   Organization Chart, Boston Model City
            Administration   299

7   Boston Model Neighborhood Board—Structure-
            Staff, Path of Decision Making   305

8   The Government of the City of New York   339

9   Model Cities Organizational Chart, New
            York, New York   360

THE MODEL CITIES PROGRAM—
AN ASSESSMENT

Origins

Many of the principles that have formed the basis of the Model
Cities Program have been a natural extension of past urban programs,
and many of these concepts will be continued in new programs. The
idea for the Model Cities Program came out of a Presidential Task
Force on Urban Problems, appointed in 1965 and chaired by Robert C.
Wood (who later became undersecretary of HUD). This task force
drew on lessons learned in such urban programs as urban renewal,
juvenile delinquency, community action, and others but also sought
significant program innovation. Congress enacted the legislation in
the fall of 1966, and at the bill-signing ceremony President Lyndon
Johnson conferred the name Model Cities on the new program.

Compared to previous programs, there would be greater emphasis on basic management concepts, such as planning and coordination, evaluation, and demonstration of new techniques. The most
important additions were ideas of program comprehensiveness, meaningful citizen involvement, and flexible money—the last of which could
be used for almost any purpose. And as lessons were learned from
Model Cities, they were adopted or proposed for community development and special revenue sharing legislation.

Yet, in practice, the urban mind has not changed very much
from the desire to tinker with basic management principles, regardless
of how programs have been designed. The most significant bottleneck
has always been finding the right sets of people with the right motivations to make things work.

3

Decisions: A Local Responsibility

Contrary to the belief of many, the Model Cities Program has worked well in a great number of cities. One of the reasons it has succeeded where it has is because the right sets of people have come together, properly motivated and willing to compromise yet preserve the program's principles. It is important to note that the success or failure of the program has always rested with local officials, inasmuch as they were given the decision-making authority to develop their own strategies and priorities.

Indeed, there was plenty of federal red tape, requirements for voluminous reports, monthly evaluations, and time-consuming citizen participation. In spite of this, numerous cities moved directly ahead to design their own organization and programs in order to meet the needs of their communities as best they could with the resources available, as the legislation intended. Procedural requirements were just another step that had to be coped with. While many cities complained about federal intervention, others (including most cities in this study) found their way through the bureaucratic muddle to the real purposes of the program. And having mastered the federal process, these cities were content to live with it and even stop griping, although they would all have naturally preferred greater simplicity.

Nevertheless, it is important to recognize that the complex process did not seriously impede programing in well-administered cities. Administrative costs turned out to be considerably higher than normal, and an additional bureaucracy was created at the central levels; yet the operation of services has taken place rather independently in the field, much as it does in any other program. This is no argument for complexity, but we do believe that it should not be used as an excuse for the failure of a whole Model Cities Program.

Early in 1972, Floyd Hyde, then head of the federal Model Cities and Community Development Programs and now undersecretary of HUD, emphasized the local role by declaring to a group of mayors, "Let me make it clear, priority setting was yours."[1]

Model Cities has always given local officials the responsibility to determine their own programs, who would run them, and how they would be operated. There is no indication that under special revenue sharing, now being considered as a replacement for Model Cities, better decisions will be made. Some programs may be consolidated and emphasis changed, but a great deal of this has already occurred under the Planned Variations and Model Cities Programs. In fact, the new decision-making could very well be less concerned about doing things for the disadvantaged, in housing and human resources particularly.

Commitment: Never There

Neither the Congress nor the federal bureaucracies ever really committed the necessary resources to the Model Cities Program. For the most part projects could only be funded piecemeal, with only part of the problem addressed. Washington politics also hurt Model Cities.

The original intention was to limit the experiment to six or eight cities in order to heighten the impact of the money to be spent. However, political reality meant that a larger number of cities would have to be chosen, enough to award one to almost every state, to some small cities, and to rural-oriented congressmen. Moreover, many of the cities and counties were selected to gain political support for the administration rather than for the quality of their proposals. And a few cities were required to spend only a few weeks in preparing their applications of acceptance, in contrast to the majority, which had to labor for a year or more in a tedious, qualifying planning process.

The political process expanded the Model Cities Program to 150 cities (See Tables 1 and 2 for cities and population ranges), seriously diluting the impact that funds would have on each city and immeasurably increasing the responsibility and scope of the federal supervisory role, which would add to the program's delay.

There were not enough funds for the problems of even a small number of cities, let alone 150, to be addressed seriously. Moreover, the bulk of money was supposed to come from existing programs in other federal agencies, with Model Cities supplying the basic working capital needed to tie programs together in complete packages for each functional area and at the same time fill all the gaps. HUD's assistant secretary at that time, H. Ralph Taylor, recognized the funding problems but characterized Model Cities as an experiment to test the will and competence of communities to meet the problems of slums, in spite of the irrationality of the pipeline through which federal funds were poured. The new flexible financing—performing much like a block grant—was designed to grease the federal pipeline and at the same time make mayors "bolder and freer" in attacking human and physical blight. In some ways this happened, but the impenetrable federal bureaucracy was never fully cracked, and each agency participated only to the extent it had to. Jealousies and tradition prevailed, and no agency was willing to give up a great deal of funds or control to any new program. The Department of Health, Education and Welfare (HEW) was the principal exception to this, but it, too, held tightly to its reins.

As the years wore on, federal and local officials in many parts of the country angrily attributed the immobility of Model Cities to the lack of commitment and fancied what could have taken place if

TABLE 1

Original Model Cities Participants

ALABAMA	**INDIANA**	**NEW JERSEY**	**PUERTO RICO**
Huntsville	Gary	East Orange	San Juan
Tuskegee	Indianapolis	Hoboken	
	South Bend	Jersey City	**RHODE ISLAND**
ALASKA		Newark	Pawtucket
Juneau	**IOWA**	Paterson	Providence
	Des Moines	Perth Amboy	
ARKANSAS		Plainfield	**SOUTH CAROLINA**
Little Rock	**KANSAS**	Trenton	Rock Hill
Texarkana	Kansas City		Spartanburg
	Wichita	**NEW MEXICO**	
ARIZONA		Albuquerque	**TENNESSEE**
Gilla River Indian	**KENTUCKY**	Santa Fe	Chattanooga
Community	Bowling Green		Cookeville
Tucson	Covington	**NEW YORK**	Nashville—
	Pikeville	Binghamton	Davidson County
CALIFORNIA		Buffalo	Smithville
Berkeley	**LOUISIANA**	Cohoes	DeKalb County
Compton	New Orleans	Mt. Vernon	
Fresno		New York City	**TEXAS**
Los Angeles City	**MAINE**	Central and	Austin
Los Angeles County	Lewiston	East Harlem	Eagle Pass
Oakland	Portland	South Bronx	Edinburg
Pittsburg		Central Brooklyn	Houston
Richmond	**MARYLAND**	Poughkeepsie	Laredo
San Diego	Baltimore	Rochester	Texarkana
San Francisco	Prince Georges	Syracuse	San Antonio
San Jose	County		Waco
		NORTH CAROLINA	
COLORADO	**MASSACHUSETTS**	Asheville	**UTAH**
Denver	Boston	Charlotte	Salt Lake County
Trinidad	Cambridge	High Point	
	Fall River	Winston Salem	**VERMONT**
CONNECTICUT	Holyoke		Winooski
Bridgeport	Lowell	**NORTH DAKOTA**	
Hartford	Lynn	Fargo	**VIRGINIA**
New Haven	New Bedford		Norfolk
New London	Springfield	**OHIO**	
Waterbury	Worcester	Akron	**VIRGINIA**
		Cincinnati	Norfolk
DELAWARE	**MICHIGAN**	Cleveland	Richmond
Wilmington	Ann Arbor	Columbus	
	Benton Harbor	Dayton	**WASHINGTON**
DISTRICT OF COLUMBIA	Detroit	Martins Ferry	Tacoma
	Genesee County	Toledo	Seattle
FLORIDA	(Flint)	Youngstown	
Dade County	Grand Rapids		**WISCONSIN**
Tampa	Highland Park	**OKLAHOMA**	Milwaukee
	Lansing	Lawton	
GEORGIA	Saginaw	McAllister	**WYOMING**
Alma		Tulsa	Cheyenne
Athens	**MINNESOTA**		
Atlanta	Duluth	**OREGON**	
Gainesville	Minneapolis	Portland	
Savannah	St. Paul		
		PENNSYLVANIA	
HAWAII	**MISSOURI**	Allegheny County	
Honolulu	Kansas City	Bradford	
	St. Louis	Erie	
IDAHO		Lancaster	
Boise	**MONTANA**	Philadelphia	
	Butte	Pittsburgh	
ILLINOIS	Helena	Reading	
Carbondale		Scranton	
Chicago	**NEW HAMPSHIRE**	Wilkes Barre	
East St. Louis	Manchester		
Rock Island			

Note: As of June 20, 1972, $1.7 billion was received by the 147 cities in the program and $866 million expended. The administration proposes that unexpended funds from fiscal years 1972 and 1973 be carried over into fiscal year 1974 to fill the gap of a zero 1974 appropriation.

Source: National League of Cities/U.S. Conference of Mayors, June 1971.

TABLE 2

Population Ranges of Model Communities

Population Range	Cities	Cities Approved
Over 1,000,000	6	6
750,000 to 1,000,000	5	4
500,000 to 750,000	17	15
250,000 to 500,000	27	20
100,000 to 250,000	94	37
50,000 to 100,000	232	29
25,000 to 50,000	476	15
10,000 to 25,000	1,165	16
5,000 to 10,000	1,171	4
1,000 to 5,000	15,054	1
Total		147

Source: Community Development, Department of Housing and Urban Development, 1973.

only a small number of cities had received the funds. Cities like New York got $65 million annually from Model Cities compared to its 1973 $10 billion city budget; Boston $7.7 million compared to a $486 million city budget; Chicago $38 million compared to a $899 million city budget. The medium-sized cities fared better, getting as much as a third or more of their regular city budgets. At least two small cities received more than their city budgets and were able to make considerable progress. Alma-Bacon County, Georgia, has been one of these cities. With a population of a little over 8,000, it is an example of a real success story, largely due to the catalytic action of some $1.2 million of Model Cities funds given annually.[2]

Most cities never received the necessary funds to overturn urban blight. Nor have many of these cities been able to maintain what they started. In many cases, mini-parks sit in disrepair among scattered debris and broken equipment; Head Start is bogged down over lack of funds to carry the learning experience into higher grades; new housing sits in the middle of a sea of destitution and deterioration; and job training is tagged useless without jobs at the end. There is no question that the failure of many individual programs is due to poor management; on the other hand, there are successful programs that have fallen by the wayside, submerged in other massive need. There are also programs that continue to be successful.

7

Concentrating in Target Areas

The Model Cities administrators at HUD believed that comprehensive programing and the effects of commitment could best take place with a requirement to concentrate Model Cities efforts in small areas of each city, usually containing about 10 percent of the population or 15,000 inhabitants, whichever was greater. But this had the effect of sowing many seeds of disaffection and weakening HUD's initial hopes for strong mayoral involvement in and support for the program.3 Many mayors refused to participate actively because they felt it was an invitation to political suicide to have to choose one area of the city over another—even having to favor one poor area over another poor area.

When in 1971 Planned Variations gave 20 cities an opportunity to develop a citywide strategy of urban development and to double Model Cities funds, the chief executives reacted favorably. This has enabled these mayors to treat almost all disadvantaged areas, to reach the community at large with some programs, and to gain necessary support for bond issues and tax increases and other community development objectives.*

The Planned Variations cities in this study—Seattle, Dayton, Indianapolis, and Newark—have all experienced favorable citizen acceptance for dealing with problems on a citywide basis and in a more realistic way. Moreover, the majority of funds are still being invested in the disadvantaged areas, but this is the case mainly because the Model Cities mandate for dealing with the poor is still in effect. An emphasis away from the poverty areas could very well take place under special revenue sharing or some form of block grants. In the Planned Variations cities, for example, there is already a shift away from programs that deal primarily with the disadvantaged and a change to physically oriented projects as opposed to human resource programs. In order to maintain a concentration of effort on the poor, any new legislation should stipulate that a certain percentage of funds would have to be used in disadvantaged areas.

---

*Much earlier, in 1968, Boston's Mayor Kevin White launched a municipally funded citywide Little City Halls Program for much the same reason but particularly to improve communication and reduce alienation throughout the city. (See George J. Washnis, Municipal Decentralization and Neighborhood Resources [New York: Praeger Publishers, 1973], p. 72.)

Comprehensive Planning

By concentrating efforts, there has been at least some visibility
of projects in the target areas. Furthermore, such concentration allowed some money to be spread in almost every major functional area
to fulfill the requirements of comprehensive treatment. However, it
turned out that not enough money could be allocated across the board
to carry out the goals established by residents and planners or to reach
the threshold in individual functions where a noticeable and permanent
difference could be made.

Although an excellent planning tool, comprehensiveness caused
too great a diffusion of resources. As it happened, citizen committees
were set up in major functional areas (usually 10 or 12), and each
had to have its share of the pie, even though a particular function might
have had lower priority than other functions. To illustrate, in one
case a $3 million Model Cities grant was split into 12 parts of about
$200,000 each and there were 6 to 10 projects under each function.
There was not enough money in any area to make a meaningful impact,
but the grant satisfied citizen groups by giving them all something.
The number of projects in most cities proliferated irrationally, which
meant that instead of having 20 or 30 projects, cities turned up with
over 50 (as in Dayton and Newark) and in some cases over 100 (in
New York City, 300). In a positive sense, comprehensiveness was
serving its purpose as a planning tool; in a negative way, there was
little impact on a visible product in the Model Neighborhoods. Lessons
have been learned, however, and in the past two years, many cities
have cut their projects in half and concentrated funds in high-priority
areas.

The whole Model Cities planning process was likely the most
extensive ever in the analysis of urban problems in a manner that
has required action and solutions at the end. It meant analyzing root
causes and the reasons why they originated. However, local interpretation of the planning process was perhaps as confusing as its
understanding of the citizen participation process. Some officials
envisioned it as traditional land-use planning, which usually produces
loads of material to sit on shelves. But fortunately, much of the local
distrust for planners and plans was dispelled because community
people were eventually included in the process and because there was
money to deal with problems after analysis. The physical planners
began to consider social concepts in greater depth and to integrate
human and physical amenities into a single plan. In some cases, social
planning divisions were added to once sterile, physically oriented departments. And HUD made a point of emphasizing the importance of the
interrelationships of problems and causes and the past failures of
trying to deal with one-problem (urban renewal, welfare, housing)

solutions. It was soon obvious that the planning process was highly complex and that a comprehensive plan was not achievable in one year. Its work would have to be spread out over several years of planning.

The planning process has had mixed effects. The results of the first year of planning were judged a modest success by Marshall Kaplan, Gans and Kahn Associates, who were assigned the responsibility of studying the Model Cities Program almost from its inception to the present. At the same time, they enumerated the problems that held up planning: (1) there was an immediate escalation of citizen participation, which diverted attention away from planning; (2) comprehensiveness was less the result of an organized process and more a post facto rationalization on paper (a kind of stitching together); (3) the pressure of deadlines kept everybody straining at project development and provided little time for studying and perfecting the process; and (4) HUD was unable to understand that innovative process does not necessarily bring about innovative product.[4]

In its concluding studies of the Model Cities Program, Kaplan Associates were still not convinced that the concept of comprehensive planning was achieved. Most cities still have several planning systems in operation, and traditional planning departments are still too physically oriented. To help correct this, they believe that the details of comprehensive planning should not be dictated by federal agencies; rather, federal assistance should be in the form of money or staff for localities to develop their own systems and capability. The authors express particular disenchantment that the use of private consultants, who were hired to do a large part of the local planning, has not increased the capacity of local government to perform on its own. They advocate the continuation of comprehensive planning through an improved local management system and a stronger role for the chief executive and his staff.[5]

Experience of Cities

Our study of eight cities concludes that progress has been made in comprehensive planning. Cities like Dayton and Seattle have come a long way in five years, progress that would unlikely have taken place without the Model Cities and Planned Variations Programs. Even Newark, in spite of its unusual problems, has made significant strides in bringing all planning elements together and developing an over-all city policy in human and physical development. Chicago has developed a citywide social planning division, has combined the resources and planning capacities of the Model Cities and Community Action Programs, and for the first time has given serious consideration to the integration of human and physical planning in most city programs. Comprehensive planning has been extremely difficult to achieve under

New York's complex governmental structure and is only in its initial stages in Savannah and Boston (with the possible exception of the Dorchester area in Boston).

Indianapolis has proceeded the furthest because of its own aggressiveness and also because federal agencies have given it invaluable assistance. The city is attempting to consolidate all its planning functions and to treat problems comprehensively through a Unified Planning System under the Department of Community Services. An important element is the integrated information flow (Unified Management Information System), which passes data from its origins of federal, state, city, and neighborhood units through systems of collection, processing, retrieval, analysis, decision-making, display, and dissemination. The management system includes the consolidation of all funding and the research and evaluation of all functions and programs. A team of Community Services Program professionals with multidisciplinary backgrounds (planning, economic, sociology, and political science) performs most of the evaluation. Potential trouble spots are treated quickly. And the basic planning staff deals across the board with all disciplines—human and physical—and also receives input from a structure of neighborhood councils. Even at the present time, only one common work program is necessary to meet the requirements of each federal agency, and only one contract is prepared for each agency. The city hopes that eventually it will be necessary to prepare only one city document for all programs, much as it would be under special revenue sharing or block grants. Already Washington requires only one annual audit for Indianapolis.

Other cities have benefited from the general reduction of red tape. Shortly after assuming office, Floyd Hyde substantially reduced requirements for paper work by permitting cities to submit simplified statements on strategy and objectives, on the planning process, and on neighborhood conditions and other regulations. He also ordered his own staff to cut HUD directives by more than half, or he would simply throw out every other page. These changes clearly show up in the Planned Variations Program, where the size of applications has been reduced as much as 75 percent, living proof that the executive branch can make programs eminently more simple for localities and still demand that congressional mandates be carried out. Of course, block grants would simplify the process further.

Coordination

Improving coordination has been one of Model Cities' most difficult objectives, but at least the first steps have been taken. It has been particularly hard to do much about coordinating government

11

units while working from one small target area. To achieve success in the coordination of programs and agencies it appears a citywide approach and strong chief executive involvement are prime requisites. Planned Variations has taken the next few steps by moving in this direction.

Model Cities experienced a number of difficulties in its attempts to integrate programs and reduce duplication. Agencies and special government units had no intention of giving up power, and, in most cases, chief executives were too far removed to be able to influence groups outside of local government. James Sundquist's Making Federalism Work points out that mayors have been expected to undo 50 years of work of the good government groups that succeeded in isolating large segments of government from the influence of chief executives and the "evils" of partisan politics.[6] Normally, cities have been only one of a dozen or more independent government units in the same geographic area, with little responsibility over education, manpower health, transit, urban renewal, and housing. And in many governments, the mayor finds himself in a weak position under a complex system of boards and commissions. Model Cities tried to by-pass many of these traditional problems by dealing directly with the agencies.

Techniques Used to Improve Coordination

The program's most powerful resource has been the ability to "buy into" other agencies in order to gain some degree of cooperation. Even the powerful Richard Daley in Chicago admitted he was unable to move certain agencies in the direction of meeting city objectives until he was able to offer them supplemental Model Cities funds. Almost all the cities have used the "buy in" technique. They also established intergovernmental task forces and hired special staff. Through the catalyst of HUD money, the states were encouraged to cooperate more than usual by employing state personnel for coordinating purposes and setting up Model Cities offices to assist local governments.

A-95 Process

The Model Cities Program demonstrated a need to formalize and strengthen coordinating procedures. One such device was the A-95 Project Notification and Review System, which was devised by the Office of Management and Budget (OMB), in 1969. For those programs under A-95, federal agencies require applicants to submit brief descriptions of their projects to state and areawide clearing houses, which in turn are required to clear appropriate projects with cities and counties. Local governments can make their own review

12

and request the clearing house to pass the comments on to the federal agencies.

Although the process has helped, it has been less than successful. Some of the difficulties have been (1) inadequate review staff, (2) too little "clout," (3) too few federal and state agencies ready to participate, and, (4) time limitations, which have made the process rather mechanical. Clearing houses have been so understaffed that they have been little more than large "stapling machines," and their boards of directors (mostly elected officials from the region) have been too busy with other matters.

On the other hand, local chief executives have been more effective. For example, Mayor Richard Lugar of Indianapolis has used Planned Variations money to increase staff capacity and to improve his review system. He has also devised a questionnaire that other agencies are obligated to use to secure city approval for projects. This review system, like any other, functions only as well as the abilities of the people administering it. Indianapolis has had both the will and the resources to develop a satisfactory system.

Chief Executive Review and Comment

To improve upon the A-95 process, the Chief Executive Review and Comment (CERC) strategy was introduced by OMB in 1972 for the Planned Variations Program. CERC extends the philosophy of the A-95 process by strengthening the role of the chief executive, giving him adequate staff and authority, and adding policy development to the office. Mayor Kenneth Gibson in Newark, for example, has created a Mayor's Office of Policy and Review and has placed CERC under its director. Indianapolis has located CERC under a deputy mayor in charge of the Community Services Department. CERC has not only given chief executives courage to deal with outside agencies, it has also given them the resources to be able to make some meaningful changes.

Annual Arrangements

Another system designed to facilitate coordination is HUD's Annual Arrangements. It is simply a negotiation process between federal regional officials and local officials to establish realistic city priorities, based on the actual amount of federal funds available during the year. The process takes about as long as negotiations for grants have always taken, but the important thing is that it is designed to save time and frustrations over the long run. Cities avoid going through the tedious process of applying for funds that are not there, and communication between the different levels of government is considerably improved.

13

In any event, it is fair to attribute the development of these new management techniques largely to the experiences realized under Model Cities.

Demonstration and Innovation

Two additional purposes of Model Cities have been demonstration and innovation. These are usually closely linked, since almost any demonstration is either a new idea (innovation) or funding for an old idea in a new city. Usually, however, when programs are simply expanded to increase existing services, they are more demonstrations of impact than anything else.

On the whole, Model Cities has not been the catalyst for a great many untried projects. However, the program has made it possible to demonstrate how existing concepts can be applied and what effect they will have in ghetto areas. Making certain projects available in disadvantaged areas has been an innovation in itself. And by implementing programs areawide, some new results have taken place that were not achieved when the programs were applied to a smaller population group, including such things as more effective community organization, the necessity for agencies to cooperate and avoid duplication, and the serious analysis of community problems.

Innovations have been of large and small varieties. Model schools—composed of adult evening classes, intensive remedial courses for slow learners, parents in the classrooms, and citizen advisory councils—were introduced for the first time in Boston, Seattle, and Chicago, for example. Semiindependent satellite corporations—which operate manpower, health, housing, and social services in competition with established agencies—were created in Dayton. And the introduction of ideas such as boy scouts, ballet, camp, day care, and neighborhood health centers to ghetto children have all been new. Coordinating task forces, unprecedented state involvement in model neighborhoods, and the combination of social and physical planning are new concepts to many sections of the country. Indeed, having the poor sit on policy-making boards with elected officials is an innovation.

Yet there has been a paucity of ideas from all quarters, including the professionals and consultants, many of whom contributed to the plans. Not many new ways have been found to do things, but at least there is a greater understanding that once ideas are formulated and community concurrence is achieved, it takes skilled help to operate programs successfully. In many quarters, that realization too is novel.

14

Institutional Change

Some innovations have led to institutional changes. But altering the basic ways agencies and governments operate is not easy. As we have already indicated, stone walls exist between most agencies and change agents who wish to improve coordination, acquire additional resources, improve services, or make agencies more responsive to local general government and/or residents. What tends to happen is that once agencies get established in their ways, with comfortable civil service positions and salaries and stable operating procedures, they pay more attention to internal mechanics than servicing clients. At least this is what the Model Cities Program—with the help of inquisitive residents—found to be true in most cases.

The likelihood of turning around this seemingly normal bureaucratic tendency is greater under a system of external (impartial) evaluation, determined citizen groups, and a chief executive who is interested. Some of the "new breed" mayors (a majority of those in this study) have been just as determined to change the way public agencies and city departments operate as citizens have, and they have succeeded in many instances. It is this combination that will most likely continue to succeed. Strengthening the chief executive as the main actor (through CERC, Annual Arrangements, and so on) might give him sufficient responsibility whereby he will have to produce. It appears that only with the in-depth involvement of local general government will cities experience rapid and significant institutional change. So far, the more independent Model Cities programs have not been highly successful in this respect; yet there are examples of change.

Health Centers

Model Cities acted as the catalyst for the development of neighborhood health centers in seven cities in this study (and for a large percentage of the 147 cities in the nationwide program). Clinics providing free service to entire geographic areas of the poor have changed the traditional ways health departments operate, and it appears the new system is most likely to remain, particularly in light of the fact that this country's chief health dilemma is its inability to deliver quality health service (preventive and emergency) to the neighborhood level.

For example, Boston not only changed the way traditional health institutions operate, it has also been the catalyst for incorporating the latest health care philosophy of treating all family problems at one source. And Newark Model Cities can take credit for permanently changing a backward city health department to one actively engaged in treating a broad range of health problems.

Model Schools

Model schools have created institutional changes in at least three cities in this study. The experiment has been successful enough in Chicago, for example, that the Board of Education would like to extend the demonstration in the nine Model Neighborhood schools to the entire system.

Manpower Centers

Improving manpower programs has largely been the task of the Labor Department, but Model Cities has used much of its own funds to make additional headway in the target areas. Funding manpower centers—as has occurred in Seattle—for purposes of agency coordination, client convenience, and comprehensive treatment of individual problems (health, grooming, counseling, education, and testing and interviewing techniques) has been a major change in the usual way of doing business. Getting state employment service personnel out of their offices and into the neighborhoods and streets to search for the unemployed has certainly changed the outlook of these once rather staid agencies. Although the Community Action agencies were first to make changes in the manpower field, Model Cities agencies instituted similar practices in their own neighborhoods.

Semiindependent Corporations

A number of cities have established nonprofit corporations incorporated by the state. Some of the more effective semiindependent corporations will most likely continue; others will probably be eliminated in favor of operation by established agencies.

The chief criticism is that they are competing units that have not materially changed the way established agencies operate. Much of this is because they are too far removed from the internal operations of the system. It is still too early to tell whether agencies will adopt Dayton's satellite corporations. On the other hand, corporations in certain other cities have included agency people in their operations, encouraging them to make changes. Multiservice centers in Chicago, Savannah, Norfolk, Kansas City, Mo., and many other cities, for example, have been particularly adept at getting the agencies into target areas, handling clients differently, and forcing some permanent changes.

One of the purposes of the Model Cities Program was to test new delivery systems and to encourage the continuation of effective operations and the elimination of others. Hopefully, one of the lessons we have learned is not to abandon all programs, but to pick from the good and bad. We must also hope that block grants will not discourage the use of federal money for experimentation.

Management Capacity

Increasing Responsibility and Capacity

The Model Cities Program has served as a measuring tool for
management needs, and it has demonstrated the wisdom for local
officials to deal with a wide variety of human and physical functions.
In many cases, it has exposed the lack of management capacity in
local general government and made obvious the need for additional
professional staff. The program's planning objectives made it necessary for mayors to deal with problems not traditionally in their scope
of concern, such as education, health, economic development, welfare,
and jobs. In order to deal effectively with these mostly human services,
it has been necessary to recruit from professions with which chief
executives have not been entirely familiar. But recruiting, communicating, and developing policy with these new management types has
had the effect of teaching city officials about the problems of other
agencies and how the latter influence the course of city development.
Chief executives have come a long way in understanding the need for
coordination, comprehensive planning, review, and evaluation of public
agency proposals and above all the necessity to have competent staff
of their own in all functional areas. In this manner, other professionals
and politicians might be willing to follow local government's lead.

However, it has been difficult to use a great deal of these funds
to improve the chief executive's capacity. Too much Model Cities
money has been consumed by sources such as City Demonstration
Agency (CDA) staffs and their need to respond to excessive federal
requirements, the training of subprofessionals, and a pure lack of
sound organization in many cases. Administrative expenses have run
as high as 20 percent (as was the case in New York City). Most local
officials believe that costs for training are justified and will be rewarding in the long run, but they clearly feel other expenses can be
drastically reduced. This is one of the objectives of special revenue
sharing, to cut red tape and administrative expenses by starting fresh
or at least to shift qualified personnel from the more independent
CDAs to the chief executive's staff.

Streamlining the organization of Model Cities into a more directly
responsible city department, such as Community Services in Indianapolis and Urban Affairs in Kansas City, Mo., is a natural step to
improving government as long as basic objectives of the program are
maintained, including innovation, coordination, comprehensiveness,
and citizen involvement. Furthermore, much confusion and duplication
can be eliminated through the consolidation of Community Action,
Model Cities, and other overlapping bureaucracies into single city
urban affairs departments (as has been done in Chicago). It must be

made clear, however, that the objectives of Model Cities need to be retained and that independent citizen groups should actually be strengthened, partly with government funds. At least several of the cities in this study are proceeding to do this, realizing that proper local organization and the retention of the most competent staff from social programs should make an immediate and marked improvement on local government capacity.

In addition to reorganization, almost all local general governments now realize the need for additional staff capacity. But in regards to hiring additional staff, local government officials are very realistic in their appraisal of the lack of will of city councils to approve general tax money (including community development and other broad federal funds) for increased professional staff. Because of taxpayer criticism, funds for this purpose will most likely have to come from a special federal source. Indianapolis, for example, is using over $1 million of its Planned Variations funds for this very purpose, to hire whatever number and quality of staff are necessary to get the total management job done. It is doubtful that they would have used substantial local tax funds for this purpose.

In fact, the fastest way to improve local government may be the use of a special fund to hire and train the best possible administrators in the nation to help solve urban problems, much as was done when the best minds were engaged to meet the nation's aerospace objectives. Comprehensive Planning and Management Act (once known as "Section 701 grants") funds might be increased to $400 million annually so that all communities and the nation could realize the act's benefits immediately. Instead, it looks as if Congress may go in the other direction, cutting funds from $100 million to $75 million. On the other hand, the Nixon Administration's Responsive Government Act may pick up some new money for purposes of improving management, but the commitment of resources is not anywhere near the same level this nation has made to other high-priority goals.

Change of Emphasis

Too many people expected too much from the Model Cities experiment. Indeed, we overestimated the will and competence of cities and counties to meet the urban crisis. Local administrators were undertrained or not available, and HUD was just as ill-prepared to meet Model Cities objectives. The process was as new to federal people as it was to local technicians. At this stage, a lot of the problems have been worked out, and there are more competent professionals to deal with them. But now local project directors worry about the shift in emphasis, believing that there is too much stress on better government and too little on the goals of quality of life. Nevertheless,

HUD officials believe that improved management will help local government reach these goals. Floyd Hyde believes that they are complementary. In his words, "We are on the right track on how to make this government system work."[7]

Citizen Participation

General

Perhaps the most controversial requirement in the Model Cities Program has been citizen participation. The intent of its designers was to tone down participation from the highs of the Community Action Program to something closer to the urban renewal experiences yet not go as far as to "plan for" people but rather to "plan with them." To the surprise of many, citizen participation developed so strongly in many cities that the original conception of the mayor's role—as one of unquestioned control—was far more uncertain than the role for citizens. The resident's role developed so strongly in a few cases that established government was actually threatened and programs were delayed.

Under the Nixon Administration's New Federalism, roles were redefined. A stronger role was stressed for the chief executive, and later an even stronger one was conceived under the proposed Better Communities Act. In a number of the citywide Planned Variations experiments, roles of the citizens declined to an advisory position, while in others, they have remained at about the same strength. In the eight cities in this study, most of the original resident councils have remained at the same level of power. But there seems to be little question in the minds of residents and elected officials that citizen power will be considerably diluted without a legislative mandate to sustain it.

An increasing number of local officials see the value in citizen involvement, and some express incredulity that we still need a federal mandate to ensure that it continues. On the other hand, there have been good and bad experiences. In some cases, cities have had little problem; in others, a hard core of self-interested resident spokesmen have delayed progress. On the whole, the experience has been worthwhile as cities have ironed out the kinks.

Lessons

There are a number of lessons to be learned from the various citizen participation processes. First, we should not accept the experience of any one city as typical. Too often the chief executive is willing to use his single experience to judge a whole complex process. There is too great a variety of conditions, social and physical, which may bring about success or failure. These include the degree of mayoral leadership, skills of the chief administrative officer, competence of Model Cities staff, leadership and cooperative nature of the citizen board chairman, factional conflicts on the board, self-interests of a few, lack of balanced interests on the board, little authority or purpose for the board, poor facilities and inadequate citizen staff, and the immensity of problems and shortage of resources.

Yet in spite of difficulties, effective leadership from both the mayor and board can overcome most problems. In essence, the success of the citizen process—quite aside from its formal structure—depends largely on the leadership ability of city officials and how much time they are willing to devote to it. In the end, it may involve disbanding the original structure or structures and starting anew until the right mix of ingredients is found. In almost all cases, the correct mixture can be found.

But why even begin a process fraught with potential conflict? Many observers admit that there has not been a great deal of progress with or without citizen participation. But there are purposes for citizen participation that have been especially learned through the Model Cities process: (1) to develop an education and training process so that the average and poor American can become honestly involved in the understanding and operation of local government and in making decisions that might affect his life, (2) to improve communication and trust between city hall and residents, (3) to develop new leaders from a class of people who otherwise might never have such an opportunity, (4) to get early agreement on the kinds of projects citizens want so that progress would not later be held up, (5) to provide citizens with an effective process by which they can effectively criticize and evaluate services, and (6) to formalize participation structures so that they may become a genuine part of government.

Model Cities Product

Process vs. Product

In the Model Cities Program, it is difficult to distinguish between product and process because one of Model Cities' products has been to improve government processes. Some observers point out that there has been considerable success in process but not in product. Yet a large part of what we have described so far is as much product as process. Such things as innovation, institutional change, improved management, and more effective citizen involvement are products of the Model Cities process and represent in themselves a higher quality of government and life. Product and process are very much inter-related.

Measurement of Product

Product can be measured in a number of ways. We have looked at it in three ways: level of service, efficiency, and quality of service. In all of the Model Neighborhoods in this study, quality of service has naturally improved for those thousands of citizens who have never received such services in the past. In most of the neighborhoods, the quality of services has been improved for all citizens through addition of staff and equipment and improved techniques. For many projects, efficiency is equal to or better than that in agencies providing similar services; for other projects, efficiency, productivity, and the best use of the tax dollar are far below standard.

This study did not include an evaluation of all projects in the eight cities and was not meant to. Conclusions are based on a review of the principal projects in each city, direct observation, and inter-views with staff and clients. We believe that most of the cities have reached a point where major projects are providing at least standard services as stipulated in individual contracts but that considerable improvement can be made with more highly trained staff, better facili-ties, more resources (in some cases), and more effective evaluations.

Importantly, although individual projects may perform satis-factorily, it is difficult to see any measurable improvement in the over-all quality of life for entire Model Neighborhoods. For the most part, housing and streets are still in a deteriorated state, unemploy-ment is high, and survey after survey show citizens' discontent with their lot and a remarkable lack of understanding about the objectives of Model Cities. The elimination of outdoor toilets, the paving of a few streets, and the construction of some scattered homes have not been enough to raise the spirits of the mass of people. Yet, in spite of this, there are improvements in some quality-of-life goals.

Level of Service

A simple declaration of the level of service is not indicative of costs or quality, but it does demonstrate new efforts in poor neigh-borhoods. It is an indicator of how many people are being served at a particular period of time, almost all of whom were never receiving such services before. A later section entitled "Assessment of Product" describes the types of services in more detail and gives figures of service levels where available. In many instances in this study, pro-grams were only in their beginning stages, and sometimes data were not kept in the cities. However, as projects finish their fourth and fifth years, such data should be more readily available and also more valuable for comparative purposes.

Efficiency

The level of increase in services in proportion to costs is one measure of efficiency. In this study we have primarily used this method to judge increases in productivity. We have not made comparisons of basic costs with other public or private enterprises. However, it was determined that in some cases costs were higher and in others lower than with other agencies. Our concern was whether productivity was improving or not. Of course, conditions vary from city to city and also with the kind of service. A health care program in one city can serve as an example.

The three Model Cities health centers in Boston served only 18,000 clients in 1971. This increased to 68,000 in 1972 and has continually increased during 1973 with the same number of centers and approximately the same basic costs exclusive of supplies. This increase has been indicative of several factors: (1) greater resident trust in the system, (2) improved communications (including the use of several media) with residents, and (3) the fact that many citizens have accustomed themselves to using the centers with the same regularity that higher-income groups visit their family doctors or local hospitals. Although use of the centers is lower than officials would like in relationship to the outlay of funds, it is increasing at a fairly rapid rate. As a consequence, productivity and efficiency are up because of a substantial increase in work load and the maintenance of quality and costs. Furthermore, since these services are available to all Model Neighborhood residents whenever they need them, community health care—as one measure of quality-of-life factors—is higher in general. It could be improved further by using the highest-quality physicians and by increasing chief executive interest. The point is that this project (and others like it) ought to be preserved and strengthened, for it has demonstrated a sound base for improving quality and lowering per capita costs.

Quality of Service

Quality (or effectiveness) of services is more difficult to measure. In Boston's health centers, inasmuch as more people are getting approved health care from licensed medical personnel than ever before, quality of care is better—and so is the delivery system. Usually the strongest complaints against neighborhood operations are leveled at the inexperience or inability of the director and/or staff. Facilities,

22

location, and equipment have been generally adequate or are such that they can be corrected in a very direct way. On the other hand, personnel actions take more time because of human sensitivities, politics, or the unwillingness of boards to act. Furthermore, it is especially difficult to find competent persons who want to work in poor areas at lower salaries and in less favorable conditions than private practice offers elsewhere. In spite of these pitfalls, the personnel in Boston's centers are rated highly satisfactory by their fellow medical workers in private practice and by residents of the model neighborhood. And as the quality of care is recognized by more citizens, attendance should increase further.

Concluding Comment

The Model Cities Program has only taken the first few steps toward quality-of-life goals, but at least it has moved us a little closer to an understanding of the problems of the poor and has taught us a great deal more about what is needed to solve some of the most serious problems. The program has gone through what it had to go through first, showing residents and city officials alike all the elements of a rational planning process. Citizens had to learn almost from scratch about government processes, the inventories of plans and policies, and how to get local officials to think about priorities most important to residents. And government officials learned more about the importance of the all-encompassing management needed to deal with the new priorities. So far, both citizens and officials have benefited, and the quality of life for a large number of disadvantaged citizens has improved as well.

Notes

1. Model Cities-Planned Variations Conference sponsored by the National League of Cities/U.S. Conference of Mayors, Tucson, Arizona, February 24-25, 1972.
2. Robert E. Nipp, The Alma-Bacon County Story—A Model for Rural America, U.S. Department of Agriculture and Forestry, U.S. Senate (Washington, D.C.: Government Printing Office, July 24, 1973).
3. Fred Jordon, "Model Cities in Perspective," Model Cities— A Report on Progress, Special Issue, National League of Cities/U.S. Conference of Mayors, June 1971, p. 4.
4. Marshall Kaplan, Gans and Kahn Associates, The Model Cities Program: A History and Analysis of the Planning Process in Three Cities, 1969, pp. 90-92.

5. Marshall Kaplan, Gans and Kahn Associates, The Model Cities Program: A Comparative Analysis of City Response Patterns and Their Relation to Future Urban Policy, Spring 1973.

6. James L. Sundquist and David W. Davis, Making Federalism Work (Washington, D.C.: Brookings Institution, 1969).

7. Planned Variations Seminar, Indianapolis, Sponsored by the Department of Housing and Urban Development and the National League of Cities/U.S. Conference of Mayors, August 2, 1973.

2

CHARACTERISTICS
OF MODEL NEIGHBORHOODS

Size and Severity

The characteristics of neighborhoods served by the Model Cities Program can be illustrated by the eight cities where we conducted case studies: Seattle, Chicago, Indianapolis, Dayton, Savannah, Newark, New York, and Boston. In all cases, the cities selected target areas because of their extreme deterioration and depression. But the cities vary in the degree of blight, from most severe in New York, Newark, and Chicago to lesser degrees of oppressiveness in the other cities. In fact in Seattle's case, observers have asked, "Where are the slums?" Yet hidden behind a facade of fairly sound structures are depressed human souls.

Most of the smaller cities have pockets of blight, such as in Savannah, but these pockets are physically as bad as the larger areas in the big cities. But for the most part, the human problems in the smaller cities are somewhat less severe than those in the larger cities because problems of crime, drugs, youth gangs, congestion, and the like are not as intense. In most cases, knowingly or unknowingly, citizens of smaller cities are already better off than their counterparts in big cities.

The Model Cities Program has been able to make a greater impact in smaller communities because the level of funding has been more commensurate with the problems. Therefore, proportionately more people have been served and results have been more visible. We believe it would not take an excessive national commitment of resources to wipe away the problems of slums in cities under 200,000 population. The larger cities and counties would need special programs.

The seriousness of the problem in the Model Neighborhoods is still not recognized by some. Whether it be a large or small community, the problems each family faces—discrimination, inadequate education, and lack of opportunity—are as important as any set of problems anywhere else. The statistics of blight in all the Model Neighborhoods points out the severity of individual problems. Although Model Cities, in conjunction with other programs, has improved the physical and social environments some percentage points, conditions still remain severe. Model Cities has taken only the first few steps.

Health Crisis

In all the cities, health care facilities were inadequate and doctors have been leaving the inner city in vast numbers. The development of neighborhood health centers has improved conditions immeasurably, and some doctors have been encouraged to come back to the ghettos. But health indices are appalling. Newark's death rate, for example, is 35 percent above the national average. In New York's Model Neighborhoods, infant mortality is more than twice that of the rest of the city, drug addiction is five times greater, and alcoholism four times as high. Savannah too has problems—infant mortality rate in the Model Neighborhood is one-third higher than the county as a whole, the tuberculosis rate more than twice the county rate, and infectious syphillis four times the county figure. None of the Model Neighborhoods in the eight cities were found immune from these types of glaring deficiencies.

Overcrowding

Of course, overcrowding is not only a major health factor but results in poor conditions in general. In Newark, 85 percent of the housing units in the model area were built prior to 1940 and 74.3 percent are deficient. Remarkably, although 10,000 housing units were demolished in the city between June 1969 and June 1972, no single-family units or public housing were built during this period, and only 14 two-family and 682 multifamily units were constructed. In New York's model areas, only about 20 percent of the housing is sound, compared to 64 percent citywide. In Savannah, more than 60 percent of the Model Neighborhood housing was constructed prior to 1930, and only 4 percent of it is considered standard; outside toilets flourish, and so far, there are no public or federally subsidized housing in the model area. Substandard housing in Seattle's model neighborhoods is considerably higher when compared to the city as a whole.

Educational Achievement

Education too has been sorely inadequate. Ten of Newark's 14 permanent Model Neighborhood elementary schools were constructed before 1901 and generally operate at 112 percent of capacity, with some having 51 percent more pupils than originally planned. During this review, 10 of Savannah's 11 model neighborhood schools were reported to have mental maturity, reading, and arithmetic norms one and two grades below the national average. In Seattle's Model Neighborhood, one-half of household heads did not finish high school, while in Savannah, 53 percent of adults over 25 years of age had less than an eighth grade education. And in almost every one of the Model Neighborhoods, most students do not go beyond high school, and drop-out rates are as much as twice as high as for the rest of the school system.

Unemployment

Unemployment and welfare are well out of proportion in all of the Model Neighborhoods. In 1972, Newark registered 17 percent unemployment and 36,000 persons on some form of public assistance. At the same time in the New York Model Neighborhoods, unemployment was twice the national average, twice as many residents had unskilled jobs, and three times as many were on welfare compared to the city as a whole. Seattle has been experiencing a severe grip of unemployment primarily because of aerospace industry cutbacks. It has ranged from 13 to 18 percent during 1972 in the city as a whole and as high as 28 percent in the Model Neighborhood. It is typical for the Model Neighborhoods to have unemployment rates two or three times the city's average as well as an unusually high percentage of the city's welfare case loads. When youth and females and those who have temporarily given up looking for work are included, unemployment figures in most Model Neighborhoods reach as high as 30 percent. If one adds the underemployed, these figures rise to 50 percent in some areas — certainly a tragic condition.

Other Factors

Other services are rated just as poorly. Crime figures in the Model Neighborhoods are considerably higher than for the cities as a whole, sometimes as much as double. Youth gangs are prevalent in the larger cities and law enforcement is less effective. Recreation facilities and supervision are grossly inadequate, multiservice centers

TABLE 3

Demography of Model Neighborhoods

City	Population	Model Neighborhood Population	Model Neighborhood Demography (percent)
Newark	384,000	76,087	Black 77 Spanish-speaking 15 Italian and other 8
Indianapolis	792,299	50,000	Black 75
Savannah	118,000	21,500	Black 70
Seattle	530,831	38,581	Black 68
Dayton	243,601	35,000	Black 98
Boston	641,071	57,000	Black 67.8 White 19.3—Spanish 11.3 Indian and Asian 1.6
New York	7,894,862	1,000,000 total	
South Bronx		260,000	Black 32 Puerto Rican 61 White 7
Central Harlem		240,000	Black 98
East Harlem			Puerto Rican 80 Italian and other 20
Central Brooklyn		500,000	Black 60 Puerto Rican 30 Italian and other 10
Chicago	3,580,400	326,823 total	
Woodlawn		60,030	Black 99
Near South		115,877	Black 99
Lawndale		96,916	Black 99
Uptown		54,000	Appalachian whites 29 Indian, black, oriental 29 Puerto Rican and other 42

Source: Center for Governmental Studies, U.S. Census Bureau, Local Model Cities reports, 1972 data.

almost nonexistent, transportation is ineffective in carrying residents to jobs and service centers, day-care facilities are inadequate, and many city services poorly delivered. Housing code enforcement, street construction and repair, refuse collection, and recreation and park space have been the prime areas of complaint. Encouragingly, the Model Cities Programs have begun to make progress in some of these areas.

One of the key factors in the creation of slums is discrimination. This means a wide range of discrimination encompassing such things as services, schools, housing, jobs, social contacts, and political acceptance. The demography of the Model Neighborhoods clearly shows segregated patterns. Most of the neighborhoods are mainly black. One of the four Chicago areas is predominantly white, and one of the three New York areas is about 60 percent Puerto Rican, while another New York area has a large Puerto Rican and Italian population (See Table 3). There are concentrations of ethnic groups in most of the Model Neighborhoods; however, they are small in comparison to the total populations.

Some citizens have described Model Cities as a program for blacks. Block grants or some scheme of citywide orientation could very well erase this connotation. But of course the discouraging statistics of the Model Neighborhoods show that the nation still needs to concentrate resources in these severely depressed zones. And even with possible errors in statistics—10 percent unemployment rather than 12 percent, or 50 percent more crime rather than double—there appears to be a clear mandate that special efforts need to be taken in the Model Neighborhoods and other areas like them.

3

ASSESSMENT
OF THE PRODUCT

Improving the quality of life and achieving concrete program results have been fundamental to the Model Cities Program. Yet little has been done to assess the product of these goals, for almost all evaluations have concentrated on process. In fact, there is no over-all federal compilation showing in which detailed categories the money was spent (such as street lighting or street repairs), let alone an evaluation of the effectiveness of expenditures. In most cases, when federal officials describe the lack of results in product they can cite little of substance to back up their allegations. On the other hand, many localities have conducted specific program evaluations that are very useful in providing an estimate of progress.

This study's direct assessment of eight cities—plus the utilization of local evaluation reports—has resulted in conclusions that we feel offer a useful picture of the program's progress. However, because of the extensive number of projects, only major ones were reviewed and only through part of the fourth action year. Meanwhile, with the apparent phasing out of Model Cities, it seems there should be more concern about the product, what chance there still is for success, and what needs to be done to make improvements. Such analysis should take place regardless of the way the federal government plans to funnel money to local government.

This review has found that, not only in these eight cities but also in every other city we have looked at, product success has depended primarily on the caliber of each project's staff, as long as adequate resources were present. Chief executive leadership, citizen interest, and other factors—although important—have always been secondary. A competent staff usually proceeds straightaway and does its job, many times regardless of the political and social climate. Of course, better leadership from the top, efficient procedures, and citizen support make the job easier.

In the following pages, an assessment is made of major functional areas—health, education, manpower and economic development, housing, social services, and law and justice—and results cities have had in dealing with many of the projects within these broad categories. There are many successes and failures; but even with limited successes, there are notable changes in the quality of life. Several conclusions are drawn: (1) each project should be judged on its individual merits and not totally disparaged because the rest of the function did not succeed; (2) it is illogical and wasteful to throw out whole programs simply to try new ideas; good programs should be saved; and (3) we should benefit from past mistakes by making improvements in those projects that have a reasonable chance of succeeding. Many times only one or two needed elements will make the difference.

Seattle's Success

When looking at whole programs in the eight cities, Seattle's is the most impressive. This is due to competent staffing, good relations between city hall and residents, and executive leadership. Little energy has been expended fighting over roles, and there have been few delays or serious conflicts. Priorities were readily agreed upon, the projects were implemented expeditiously, and both internal and external mechanisms were created to monitor and correct programs from the very first year. Meanwhile many other cities let their evaluation components start up late on the theory that there was not anything to evaluate so early in the program. The administrators in these cities discounted the importance of early evaluation of ideas, plans, facilities, and staff. Too many of their monitors were obsessed with numbers, waiting for client lists to grow and failing to analyze personnel and policies.

On the other hand, Seattle learned its lesson well. It was not content with its own impressions of programs; it hired impartial consultants with special expertise in each function to make evaluations. With few exceptions, other cities did not wish to do this for fear negative reports might hurt their funding, and besides they were not used to evaluating regular city programs in this fashion—at least not across the board. But this evaluation paid off for Seattle because recommendations were followed in most instances.*

_____

*Seattle and other cities have improved upon their evaluation technique. Some cities would like to extend this experience of in-depth evaluation to other city departments as a regular procedure of local government—in contrast to the more superficial annual budget review process. One or 2 percent of the city budgets spent for this purpose could do much to improve the caliber of local government.

But even with its major components working well, Seattle's success has not been overwhelming. Resources have been short, unemployment has been high, experience in the human resource field has been minimal, and in plain words, it has been simply too much to expect economic and social conditions to change in a few years. But let us look at the principal functions in all the cities.

Health Projects

Seattle

In health programs, Seattle Model Cities has made substantial headway in prepaid health insurance, representative community health councils, and general health planning. Although prepaid health for 1,350 low-income families is comparable to standard health insurance, highly desirable services of transportation and child care have been added. The Community Health Board, Inc.—composed of five Model Neighborhood residents, five professionals, and five mayoral appointees—advises on all local health matters and is developing a comprehensive health care system. This board represents an institutional change and there are several others: (1) the system of neighborhood health centers (plus a successful mobile dental component), (2) a community-based mental health center (over 6,000 monthly visits), and (3) an alcoholic rehabilitation center. Under Planned Variations, these projects have been expanded to three other disadvantaged areas in the city, and King County, which takes in the suburbs, has been sufficiently impressed to emulate parts of Seattle's Model Cities health program.

Indianapolis and Boston

Neighborhood health centers have been particularly successful in most cities. Although Indianapolis was having a problem filling health clinics to capacity in 1972, its dental and eye care services were considerably overtaxed. Boston, too, found its three health centers underutilized in the first two years; but it did not take long to go from 18,000 clients in 1971 to 68,000 in 1972. In fact, this program, which offers comprehensive family care in a simple, coordinated fashion under one roof—where you can deal with a headache and the anxiety that caused it and the unemployment problem that caused the anxiety in the first place—is perhaps Boston's most successful effort.

Boston's program has demonstrated two particular things: (1) a model of cooperation between public and private sectors and (2) the training and creative use of community people. For the first time, physicians and hospitals are deeply involved in and sincerely trying to solve community health care problems. And trained resident technicians are helping other residents. On the other hand, even greater private commitment and resources are needed. There are suggestions that the mayor, too, needs to get more deeply involved, to encourage greater participation by the private sector, and to sell the program. For example, effective advertising is needed to reach the mass of people on the benefits of preventive care; pay incentives are needed to attract and retain skilled physicians. None of these problems is impossible to solve. Furthermore, only a small increase in the budget for these items could preserve this program for the long-range future.

Interestingly, these same types of problems are manifest in other health programs as well—that is, lack of adequate funding, understaffing and underpay, secondhand equipment, less than ideal facilities, and, rather than assistance, usually nonconstructive criticism from the established medical societies about the quality treatment. This is true in Indianapolis, where residents nevertheless prefer the neighborhood centers to the almost inaccessible private doctors' offices or Marion County General Hospital, where a visit involves a difficult bus ride and long waits. In spite of the problems, public health administrators there feel that neighborhood centers not only are vital but also show the way to more effective methods of treating the entire population.

Newark

Newark has had an especially difficult time developing an effective health program; yet it has made impressive progress since 1972. A report by the Center for Analysis of Public Issues at Princeton[1] points out how clients must go to a multitude of institutions (mostly long-established, traditional agencies) for health care and, in many instances, not receive any treatment. It argues that the same amount of public health money can buy effective care merely by reshuffling priorities and using neighborhood centers. Model Cities is supporting the recommendations and has proceeded to develop health centers. The first, the Gladys Dickinson Health Station, served over 7,500 clients in the first year and will function as a model for what Model Cities hopes will be "seven to ten additional health centers." However, this will never happen without the use of general revenue sharing funds and other new sources, and revenue sharing is already scheduled for budget balancing and for cutting an excessive property tax rate.

Another major health program is the Interim Direct Dental Care Project, which provides dental insurance and ear and eye testing to 8,000 children in five model schools. However, even with this service, surveys show the need is so great that tens of thousands of school children receive no dental care at all during their elementary school years. Traditional health care institutions are practically moribund. But recognizing the seriousness of the problem, Mayor Kenneth Gibson gave the city's health program a shot in the arm by appointing a new director of health and welfare. In Newark's case, Model Cities has been instrumental in providing much of the resources to help the city; however, there would be little progress without the assistance of some private institutions and the election of a new mayor interested in the cause.

Dayton

The Comprehensive Health Center in Dayton is one of four non-profit corporations. The contract for renovation of the center was awarded through a negotiated bid process so that the door was opened for the first time to minority contractors by means of alleviating some of the experience requirements. The center started with serious administrative difficulties, including the necessity of dismissing its first director, but new staffing has been its salvation. Because it has been in operation only since October 1971, it has not had sufficient time to work out all the kinks; however, city officials feel it is a successful project.

Chicago

In Chicago, Model Cities funds have been used to start four health centers: remodeling of the Epstein Clinic at Providence Hospital to serve the Near South; building a center uptown designed to handle 25,000 persons; and two centers under development in the Mid-South area to handle 11,000 clients each. In spite of this dramatic increase in facilities, these centers will only be able to handle about 10 percent of those needing care.

In addition to the centers, the city has instituted an innovative and effective ambulance project, which serves over 7,000 patients annually.

As a result of the health programs, several institutional changes have occurred: (1) medical professionals have accepted the neighborhood center concept, (2) citizens are now involved on boards running the centers, and (3) for the first time, an over-all citizen board is advising the commissioner of the Board of Health.

However, the city's program still faces difficulties because Board of Health leadership remains docile—even after Model Cities convinced Mayor Daley to appoint a new health director. The new director has relegated the advisory board to a largely meaningless position, a situation not much different, however, from that of other advisory boards in Chicago.

There are other problems too: (1) a short supply of technical help and (2) less than the best available care to the poor because the system is not integrated with private health care and the most effective, latest techniques. Nevertheless, several giant steps have been taken to provide decent health care for the poor. Further incentives to attract top-quality physicians and the best private health care could substantially improve the program.

New York

In New York, health programs have been less successful. Model Cities was not able to get its health centers started until the fourth action year because of delays in renovating facilities and general bureaucratic hangups. Its most successful health projects have been in training paraprofessionals, establishing an alcoholic center in Harlem, and providing free ambulance service to model area residents.

Education Programs

Model Cities education projects have experienced less success than health projects for a number of reasons: (1) difficulty of establishing model schools comparable to model health centers due to the extraordinary personnel costs per capita attached to education; (2) greater independence of school systems and their sensitivities to interference by local government officials; (3) difficulty of measuring educational achievement levels; and (4) persistent arguments among scholars and technicians about which programs do the most good.

Many of the Model Cities communities developed projects in areas that they felt would make immediate improvements, such as more training for teachers; greater number of quality teachers; special programing for the slow and fast learners, involvement of parents; a voice for citizens; and opening the schools to adult education and other community programs.

Chicago

Of the education programs in Chicago, the impact of the Schomes (amalgam of school and home) community school project—operating in seven schools—has been felt throughout the school system. This Model Cities program has demonstrated to the Board of Education the value of various educational techniques, such as resident aides, increased teacher training, citizen advisory boards, adult education, better learning environments (for 10,000 children), free meals (for 20,000), and parental involvement. In some instances, results have been better than expected. The Educational Testing Service of Barton-Aschman Associates, Inc. believes that citywide achievement test scores of pupils in these schools reported during the Model Cities third action year "give rise to the hope that the steady downward trend in academic achievement has been halted." In fact, the Board of Education would like to institutionalize the program citywide as a regular part of the system, but it lacks the funds. The director of Model Cities, Erwin France, describes the program as an excellent example of "buying into the system" to create institutional change, but he admits that there are still problems in the program. Not enough parents have gotten involved in an in-depth way, and it is still difficult to get widespread community support for Schomes. On the other hand, impressive advances have been made.

Dayton, Savannah, Seattle, and Indianapolis

Many of the cities have developed various components of the community school concept, although none as comprehensively or as successfully as Chicago. Dayton, Savannah, Seattle, and Indianapolis, for example, have all extended regular school hours to adults for evening classes, involved parents to a greater extent in the schools than previously, provided funds for teacher training, and developed special courses for dropouts and slow students. Of these cities, Seattle has probably progressed further because of its intense efforts on individualized instruction, continuous progress curricula, innovative teaching techniques, and related health and social welfare services. Furthermore, over 200 Seattle parents are actively involved in classroom activities (as instructors and testers) and in community development, fund raising, and project evaluation. Indianapolis has had serious problems in getting adults to attend classes and in stimulating residents to participate in academic and vocational curricula as opposed to recreational programs. However, parental advisory councils have been added in eight of the model schools, and elaborate programs have been designed to raise the achievement levels of Model Neighborhood students to the citywide level. Results of these efforts will have to wait for later evaluation.

Boston

In Boston, the most visibly successful education programs have been for adults. Most impressive has been the stimulation of a consortium of colleges to unite for the first time to provide unusual and exceptional educational services to the community. Important inroads for institutional change have occurred through the placement of low-income adults in college, changing curricula to suit the needs of the population, and making credit-gaining policies more flexible.

Newark

Newark too has developed some innovative education programs, including model schools. Of moderate success are five model schools that are concentrating on improving reading and math skills for 8,000 students. Each school has an elected joint faculty-community advisory committee, plus psychological and guidance services for pupils. The Model Cities Office of Program and Staff Development (OPSD)—funded by Model Cities but responsible to both the superintendent of schools and the CDA—is attempting to focus on the important issues. It believes, for example that the schools cannot be upgraded unless the fundamental system is changed, teachers are taught the skills necessary to teach well, more positive attitudes prevail, and teachers receive monthly evaluations to improve their performance. But leadership in the school system is weak, and there are too many things left to be done in this program to call it successful. City officials believe it is still not much more than a "Title I Project" or a block grant of $100 per pupil. It has not attacked the fundamental problems it believes to be so important. Model Cities money could be used more wisely here as a catalyst.

Manpower and Economic Development

Training and job development have had but limited success in Model Cities programs. Although considerable funds were committed for manpower programs in some of the cities, there were few results. A major difficulty has been the high unemployment rates in the nation's cities and the much higher rates in the Model Neighborhoods. Experience has demonstrated that training does little good if there are no jobs at the end.

The Model Cities economic development programs have not helped much in creating employment because they have involved only a small number of businesses, and with few exceptions there are the types that employ few people, the "Mom and Pop" stores. Furthermore, since initial concentration was in the target areas instead of the region, chances for success were considerably reduced. Special problems were raised by such narrow concentration: ineffective or improper zoning for commercial and industrial development, too narrow a market, insufficient capital or outside investment interests, limited technical skills and business experience within the area, and a shortage of existing facilities in which to locate larger businesses. Many of these problems have been alleviated as cities have proceeded to go citywide with their programs. But the Model Cities experience has demonstrated that it is to the disadvantage of the target area to try to confine economic development to an area short of resources and technical assistance.

Newark's Goals Vis-à-vis Its Problems

The total job money in Newark was an impressive $30 million in 1972. Mayor Gibson's two major job goals are impressive also: (1) to employ 12,000 residents and (2) to enforce the city's affirmative action plans, which stipulate that 50 percent minority apprentices and 30 percent minority journeymen must be employed in all construction trades. (In 1972, there were only 70 blacks out of 11,350 construction trade union members.) But with cutbacks in manpower funds, it will be even more difficult for Gibson to achieve his goals. However, he has made substantial progress in gaining minority hiring concessions from six airlines in the development of Newark's new international airport, and the airline industry has agreed to finance a $2 million basic construction skills training program for minorities. Nevertheless, the lack of other major construction jobs will hurt. And Model Cities, with its limited economic development funds, could hardly be expected to make an impact in this regard.

Furthermore, the city has been unable to operate its federal Public Employment Program (PEP) successfully, largely because it has treated the jobs as meaningless part-time employment, with political patronage as the prime motivator (for example, each city councilman was given a quota of people he could hire for the program.)*

Seattle's Modest Success

Most Model Cities are still in the process of developing one-stop comprehensive employment centers, and results have been mixed. Seattle's Employment Unicenter is one of the most successful nationally; yet it too has had its share of difficulties. A joint board—comprised of state and city officials and model neighborhood residents—

---

*PEP is not a Model Cities program, but it has had considerable effect on what Model Cities was able to do with the unemployed from the target areas. New York and Newark failed miserably, for example, while Seattle and St. Louis were highly successful—proving once again that failure is usually not due to program design but to the administration of it.

has made it possible to get the participation of all the principal manpower agencies; however, it has not yet resulted in the kind of coordination necessary to avert duplication of effort and build a system
responsive to the disadvantaged. Its major components are only in
the early stages of development. These include a unified management
information system, a Minority Skill Bank, common referral forms,
and a health services plan. The most crucial difficulties appear to
be the lack of a single, strong administrative unit and the hesitancy
on the part of individual agencies to relinquish their autonomy for the
benefit of a unified system. The apparent needs are for the participating agencies to commit themselves first to the actions and policies
of the board and second to a single administrator with responsibility
to direct all personnel in the center.

In spite of these difficulties, the Unicenter has elicited more
coordination and cooperation out of agencies than existed before.
Moreover, Model Cities and city officials are taking concrete steps
to correct the deficiencies by following up on evaluation reports.
However, more time is needed to correct mistakes, and there must
be a strong effort from state officials to simplify their own manpower
structure and direct their agencies to cooperate.

As already indicated, Model Cities manpower programs have
been vitally concerned about hiring minorities. Seattle is one of the
few cities that has succeeded in establishing a fair record, particularly
in the hiring of minorities in the construction industry. In 1972, it
had 454 minority persons (or 17.5 percent of the city's total) in construction jobs. One of Model Cities' accomplishments includes
approval by the Seattle Board of Workers to allow various project
staff to hold preaward conferences with contractors on city jobs. In
the past, conferences were held after contracts were awarded. The
new scheme has resulted in project staff approving 39 contracts and
turning down four.

In economic development—even though most of Seattle's efforts
have resulted in "Mom-and-Pop"-type businesses—12 minority construction contractors have been financed with Model Cities backing,
and several large performance bonds (one for $748,000 and another
for $1 million) have been obtained in support of the contractors. Also
a number of businesses have been developed in such fields as printing,
shopping centers, frozen foods, and specialty food processing.

Dayton's Progress

Dayton has had its share of problems with manpower programs.
One of its most serious difficulties has been with the Manpower Center
—a nonprofit corporation and its major employment project. The
first two directors were fired for incompetence and the center never

succeeded in developing "one-stop" (all agencies under one roof) objectives. The Concentrated Employment Program (CEP), working in conjunction with Model Cities, has had even greater problems. It fired four directors, lost important records, and has been faced with general administrative inadequacies from the beginning. Nevertheless, with all its faults, each year some 400 to 500 persons have received training, and records show that as many as 85 percent of these have been placed in jobs. The CDA believes most of the problems have finally been worked out.

Although economic development projects have not advanced very far, there are some notable exceptions. Perhaps the most highly successful example is the Unity State Bank. a black enterprise supported by Model Cities. It received almost no assistance from other lending institutions of the business community; nevertheless, it is prospering and now plans to open a downtown branch. In respect to progress in other economic projects, the city feels it may be able to show considerably more success as it proceeds to develop enterprises citywide under Planned Variations.

New York City's Multiple Problems

Manpower programs in New York have been ineffective almost across the board. Of all the projects, health career training has shown the greatest potential for success because it was designed to train for meaningful jobs—ones where openings actually exist. Yet even here only 50 percent of the enrollees have stayed in the program. And by the middle of 1972, only 100 persons had been graduated—a small effort in solving this great city's unemployment problems.

Clerical training, operated by the Chamber of Commerce, also was provided built-in potential for success because it practically guaranteed job placement for those who completed the course; yet in 1972 only 94 remained out of the 842 who had entered the program.

The biggest training project, Job Training, was less successful. Its budget for the first two years was $7,917,000; but by the end of the first year, it graduated less than 400 trainees and placed fewer than 150 in jobs—an unusually high cost-benefit ratio. Furthermore, the program has had difficulty in finding and keeping a reliable operator. On the other side, a much smaller job training program operated by the Urban Coalition in Harlem is reported by the CDA evaluation unit as operating efficiently and effectively.

One of the unfortunate aspects of New York's Model Cities manpower program has been too heavy a reliance on trying to develop career ladders (permanent city job slots where employees have a chance to advance) in municipal departments. The problems started when the unions rebelled and then the courts upheld them against what they called favoritism to get Model Neighborhood residents on the civil service lists. The unions called it discrimination in reverse. As a consequence, millions of dollars have been spent on jobs for Model Cities residents in mostly useless and unproductive training slots, almost all of which will end as soon as Model Cities' money dries up. Not all has been wasted, however, because a sizable segment of the unemployed were hired for jobs and a good portion of the money —$17 million—was used for special sanitation and clean-up programs. But it looks like no one will come out with permanent jobs from this effort.

On the other side, the community service officers, hired to work in Housing Authority projects, are in a useful program, highly regarded by residents and the police. The fire inspector's training program is also rated above average by residents and fire department employees, who appreciate extra inspection help. However, there has been little pressure to break down the traditional hiring processes or lower the qualifications for recruiting police and firemen; these unions are too powerful.

As far as intervening to get jobs for minorities in the outside construction unions, Model Cities has not even tried. On the other hand, the city has been no more successful. Mayor John Lindsay and the Building and Construction Trades Council agreed to the New York Plan, calling for 800 trainees annually, but by the end of the first year less than half that number were in training and only 22 persons were permitted to join unions.

Chicago First in Innovation and State Cooperation in Manpower Centers

Chicago reached agreement early with the Illinois State Employ- ment Service and other agencies to locate manpower offices in the city's Community Action (OEO) funded multiservice centers. In fact, it was ahead of the federal government in these innovations. Instead of creating separate manpower or health centers, large comprehensive centers were developed to handle all social services. (The negative aspect of the program is the size of the centers. In some cases, the centers have turned into additional bureaucracies—the very thing the program was trying to avoid.) In 1972, Model Cities appropriated funds for four additional but smaller multiservice centers to serve each Model Neighborhood, and they will include manpower programs.

Model Cities has played a minor role in helping to get minorities into the construction trades. The city made an effort to do something about the problem in the Chicago Plan, which called for 4,000 minority trainees. But this plan fell apart. By July 1972, a new plan was being developed.

41

Savannah Needs Prodding

Savannah has been successful in bringing together manpower agencies under one roof, such as the Georgia Department of Labor State Office of Rehabilitation Services, and Savannah-Chatham Board of Education. However, not all agencies are cooperating, and there is no single effective administration. In Savannah, there were no major breakthroughs in minority hiring in the construction trades well into 1973. And there were no signs that any would take place.

Indianapolis—Leadership from the Top

Indianapolis's Comprehensive Manpower Center has had serious difficulties. Evaluation of the center by the city's Community Services Program in 1972 reported that "internal disorders resulting from lack of staff communication, and top administrative disinterest, reflected upon the poor achievement of project objectives." Ever since, improvements have been under way, including staff restructuring, new lines of authority of the Metropolitan Manpower Commission, and realistic project objectives. Here the mayor and his top administrators are proving that they can turn a less than successful venture into a successful one without dismantling the entire program.

In regards to minority hiring in the construction trades, Model Cities has mostly taken a back seat, mainly because this type of activity takes collective bargaining and leadership from a wide variety of people, including elected officials, business and unions, and residents. On the other hand, the city has made progress in its Indianapolis Plan (rated by the Office of Federal Contract Compliance as one of the two best in the nation in 1971) because of its ability to pull the collective leaders together.

Other Model Cities Projects

Although this review cannot discuss all the numerous Model Cities projects, a brief look at the highlights of some of the remaining programs should serve to portray the extent of the Model Cities Program and what was expected of it.

Housing

Housing and neighborhood conditions are the first thing the eye sees, and it is from this physical appearance that many judge the quality of life. But if one were to assess improvements from this alone, he probably would not get very far from a zero score, for there have been few physical changes in the Model Neighborhoods. The occasional new multiservice center or paved street is hidden amongst massive housing deterioration. And housing programs seem to take the longest to develop, about three to four years from planning to building. Some urban renewal projects took 10 to 15 years to develop, and many cleared acres still sit idle, so it is hardly fair to expect that Model Cities would revolutionize this process.

Construction and rehabilitation of housing are more costly than any other function. Model Cities could have spent all its money in this way with nothing left for other programs and thus would have made little impact on neighborhood appearance. Cities, therefore, simply decided to demonstrate possibilities and act as catalysts for not-for-profit housing development corporations. But too few houses were built to make a difference.

By the middle of the fourth action year, almost all cities in this study had only 50 or 100 houses under new construction and not many more under rehabilitation. In new construction, Seattle had 38 units, Boston 129, Chicago 25, Indianapolis a development loan for 65 units, Savannah none, Dayton 137, Newark was still in the planning stage, and New York had the largest number, over 1,200, mainly because it got an early start with other HUD housing money. Model Cities acted as the catalyst.

In New York, by January 1971, there were 9,993 low-income units and 669 moderate-income units under construction, and another 4,100 units of low-income and 7,300 units of moderate-income in planning; but these could not be attributed to the Model Cities Program. In the Brownsville Model Cities area, often described as the "slum of slums," there had not been a single housing start by January 1972.

Newark has taken two big steps in housing: (1) in rehabilitation and (2) in planning of a proposed $389 million new-town-in-town in the eastern end of the Model Neighborhood, for which Model Cities has already allocated $4,077,497. There are 500 homes under rehabilitation and 2,000 more assigned to private developers. The Housing Development and Rehabilitation Corporation established by Model Cities is perhaps the program's most successful component. At one time the city was assured of receiving $50 million for its rehabilitation program, but federal budget cuts have reduced this drastically.

In rehabilitation, except for Boston and New York, the cities in this study are not doing much. By early 1972, Boston had 719 housing units in the pipeline and New York had 1,031 units under rehabilitation and another 2,400 in planning. New York's biggest housing tragedy has been the Emergency Repair Program (which Model Cities entered after the program was in operation for several years under the city's Housing and Development Administration), which ended up in bribes, kickbacks, and millions of wasted dollars. This same type of program has also experienced difficulty in several other cities (not covered in this study); however, this does not reduce the need for the program or the ability of well-managed cities to operate it properly.

Public Facilities and Social Services

Most of the cities put money into community facilities. Seattle was particularly proficient at this. It built over 15 parks and playgrounds, added $85,000 of new street lighting, $66,000 of underground wiring, and $225,000 of utility upgrading, and completed many other projects for the Model Neighborhood. It is now developing a series of multiservice centers and other socially oriented facilities.

Almost all of the cities have constructed or plan to construct elaborate community facilities. Chicago is proceeding to build four $2.5 million multiservice centers in the four Model Neighborhoods; Indianapolis already has four centers; Dayton is building a million-dollar comprehensive social service center; and Savannah has rehabilitated an old building for this purpose.

Newark has placed a large share of its funds in new street lighting, new street signs, tot lots, improved refuse collection, and four Action Now centers. It has also allocated over $1 million for three multipurpose centers. The city's biggest problem has been its inability to select competent and dedicated people to run these programs properly. The right programs have been selected, but few function well and maintenance and follow-up are poor (typical, however, in most cities). Playgrounds and certain other facilities have been allowed to deteriorate to the point of nonuse and community disgrace, largely because of the hurry to spend money and build things and the lack of concern for providing ongoing, long-range funds to keep the facilities in decent condition.

Law and Justice

All the cities have developed projects designed to reduce crime. Perhaps the most comprehensive is Newark's law and justice program. In June 1972, Eugene Doleschol, director of the Information Center at the National Commission on Crime and Delinquency (NCCD), stated that Newark is one of three cities that stands out above all other when its Model Cities criminal justice projects are examined from a city point of view rather than project by project. He stated that Newark administers the most well-rounded program, outstanding "because of the comprehensiveness of its approach, its planning and coordination, the sophistication of its programs, and its fiscal skill in using Model Cities seed money to attract . . . other funds."[2]

An idea of the program's comprehensiveness may be derived from an outline of projects. As a master project, Newark's Comprehensive Law Enforcement and Criminal Justice Planning Project coordinates subprojects. The Comprehensive Law Enforcement and Criminal Justice Planning Project coordinates subprojects. The Comprehensive Juvenile Delinquency Strategy Program consolidates existing and new juvenile delinquency projects. The Youth Service Agency plans, operates, and coordinates community-based youth services that operate from youth centers. The Pilot Project in Pre-Adolescent Services is part of a national strategy of the Youth Development and Delinquency Prevention Administration (YDDPA), in which Newark and 15 other cities have been selected to develop and implement comprehensive demonstration programs. Another body, the Narcotics Advisory and Rehabilitation Council, consolidates five narcotic prevention and treatment programs. Legal services for residents, three police storefronts, safety lighting, miniature teletype units in patrol cars, walkie-talkies for the Police Tactical Squad, and an electronic stenographic system are all part of the program. As is indicative of these projects, funds for Newark's programs have not all gone to hardware, a common complaint about law enforcement projects in many other cities.

Certain other cities have done fairly well with their Model Cities criminal justice money also. Seattle has developed an outstanding Public Defender Program under a nonprofit corporation, which is attending annually to 45,000 needy cases never before serviced. Most of the cities have developed halfway houses for ex-convicts, drug addicts, alcoholics, and youth offenders. Chicago has developed six police community centers and two youth correction service centers. It also has 486 police-community aides who assist the police in minor duties. They have mainly, however, succeeded in developing better police-community relations and calmer neighborhoods. The quality of centers and the performance of police-community aides in the cities are mixed. In many cases, for example, aides have not been fully trained or integrated into police departments. And too often they are given unproductive and unrewarding assignments.

Again, to emphasize the importance of sound management, when there is good administration and leadership from the top, programs run better. Where there is not, it is difficult to see where greater local discretion to make decisions will help.

Conclusion

In order to reach its quality-of-life goals, the Model Cities Program believed it needed to attack all problems, and at the same time. This has had the effect of diluting funds so that it has been difficult to show an impact in any one function. On the other hand, the wide range of programs has provided valuable demonstrations of what the urban areas need and what might work. This latter experience has probably been more worthwhile than what would have been derived from a concentration of funds in only a few functions, for then Model Cities would have been much like categorical grants without the benefit of flexible and innovative monies.

As stated previously, we believe that smaller amounts of money should have been used in many of the questionable, experimental areas, with larger doses applied to the top priorities. In any event, there was never enough money to reach the critical mass—to substantially solve problems—in any function. And now, to the detriment of cities and counties, the debate has unwittingly switched from the need for resources to the structure of the revenue process. Nevertheless, the nation will shortly have to think seriously about the level of resources needed to solve its problems.

This study shows that very few cities have been able to achieve success in all service areas. On the other hand, it reveals examples of individual project successes that could very well be expanded city-wide or of experiences that if transferred to other jurisdictions might benefit these latter. In this respect, one must not lose sight of the importance of trying to make specific projects in the neighborhoods successful, where the potential exists. In this way residents may continue to receive services they need, regardless of some failures in the services. In the meantime, further improvements can come about through additional federal incentives, local leadership, better city management, and a concerned citizenry.

Notes

1. Center for Analysis of Public Issues, The Doctor is Out; A Report on the Newark, New Jersey Division of Health (Princeton, N.J., March 1972).
2. Eugene Doleschol, "Criminal Justice Programs in Model Cities," Crime and Delinquency Literature 4, 2 (June 1972): 318-321.

4

Citizen participation has been perhaps the most controversial feature of the Model Cities Program. It has had successes and failures. And although Model Cities was designed to be the mayor's program, the unexpected determination of residents to have a strong voice in the program changed the scope of priorities: Ever since, HUD has been trying to return the program to the chief executives while maintaining a meaningful and effective system of citizen participation.

Using Helpful Nomenclature

A useful classification of the relationships among citizens, staff, and city officials was developed by Marshall Kaplan, Gans and Kahn in a study of the Model Cities planning process.[1] They placed planning in the context of five basic possibilities (with the likelihood of numerous variations): (1) staff dominance: strong control by staff, sustained chief executive interest, and citizen involvement primarily to legitimize the process; (2) staff influence: some staff involvement, minimal chief executive interest, and weak (noncohesive and not politically integrated) resident involvement; (3) parity: acceptable levels of staff involvement, sustained chief executive interest, and cohesive, turbulence-free citizen involvement; (4) resident influence: minimal staff and chief executive involvement, and usually a non-cohesive, mostly turbulent resident group; and finally (5) resident dominance: support from the chief executive and staff, and strong and cohesive—not necessarily politically integrated or turbulent— resident involvement. It is natural for these variables to interchange frequently, as political and social climates change.

47

Overview of Eight Cities

In the eight cities examined in this study, the range of diversity has varied from one extreme to another. Parity has been the case for both Seattle and Boston, and resident dominance—for much of the time—in both Dayton and New York. Staff dominance has existed in four cities: Chicago, Indianapolis, Savannah, and Newark.

Indianapolis emerged from a strong resident position to one of parity and then to staff dominance, as the professionals began to initiate, plan, and manage almost all programs. There is a feeling now that it may have again moved to a position of parity.

Until recently, Newark's staff dominance did not mean mayoral or city hall control but rather the overpowering elusiveness, independence, and secrecy of the CDA director and a few staff members. In Chicago and Savannah, staff dominance has never been questioned.

Dayton is another story. Many observers would call this system resident dominance because of a powerful, rather independent citizen's board, which has had veto power over any action in the Model Neighborhood. Yet the city staff has been influential enough to prevent things from getting completely out of control.

In New York the dominance of residents was countermanded by a much stronger staff role. The resident groups are presently noncohesive and nonturbulent.

Chicago: Staff Dominance

Under the powerful leadership of Mayor Daley, citizens in Chicago have been unable effectively to challenge city hall control. In the early days of Model Cities—when HUD was pushing for greater citizen involvement—Mayor Daley sternly warned HUD Secretary George Romney and Regional Director Francis Fisher that the federal government was not going to tell him how to run his city. But after some federal pressures and a recommendation from a blue-ribbon committee he appointed, the Community Improvement Advisory Committee (used as the Workable Program Advisory Committee), he agreed to the concept of citizen involvement and declared that 50 percent of Model Cities Board members would be elected and 50 percent appointed, as long as he made the appointments. In Chicago's one-sided, politically dominated system, this meant the Democratic organization would win almost all elective seats and Daley would need to make only one or two appointments in each area to control the board; only in the Woodlawn area did the anti-Daley forces gain a significant voice.

This obsession by city hall for control led to one of the highest votes of any Model Cities program in the nation. Daley marshaled precinct workers and his whole political machinery to "get out the vote"; consequently, over 30 percent of eligible voters participated, compared to 5-10 percent in most cities.

In spite of the unfavorable odds against citizen control, residents have been given more power than ever before and more than any other official body in the city. For example, the city's war-on-poverty program—Chicago Committee on Urban Opportunity (CCUO)—has always been a city operation without citizen control, symbolically guided by a blue-ribbon board appointed by the mayor. The CCUO local boards have dealt mainly with less important problems revolving around neighborhood centers. But in the Model Cities program, local political analysts believe that Mayor Daley's strategy—to appoint half of the Model Cities membership—was designed to provide broader participation rather than to gain control. If all board members had been elected, Daley's political apparatus could have easily won the majority, if not all members in three of the areas. The appointment process has allowed the Model Cities director, Erwin France, to recommend qualified persons to the mayor from a wide variety of sources. And although there is little question that all major decisions are made in Daley's office, a good deal of what the boards recommend is accepted. For the first time, citizens are actually contributing ideas and determining neighborhood priorities. As a result, the pendulum of success or failure for citizen participation in Chicago has swung to the positive side.

Indianapolis

Staff Dominance or Parity

Indianapolis has a program that is strongly oriented to the staff but that also has considerable input from citizens. Citizens assume mostly a secondary role because of lack of staff for the Model Cities Board and because the city hall staff is exceptionally competent and far ahead in its planning. The substance of plans and new program ideas are generated mainly from city hall. Indeed, some key residents feel that the neighborhood task force proposals, as restructured by technicians, distort their views. In the second and third action years, Model Cities Board members continued to express a belief that they were receiving only token recognition from the mayor's office. They particularly resented strong city hall control over fiscal, personnel, and policy matters.

Part of the problem stems from the fact that the board itself has been split most of the time. There have been serious factional disputes, and, moreover, there are questions about whether the board fairly represents the community. For example, when elections were due in the spring of 1971, the board balked, pointing out that there was not enough time to show program effectiveness and, therefore, this might hurt their chances for reelection. Mayor Richard Lugar finally threatened to cut off the $75 monthly stipend paid to neighborhood members if an election were not held. It finally took place February 4, 1972, resulting in a more cohesive, less turbulent board.

Although the program is characterized by staff dominance, program administrators in Indianapolis have nurtured channels of communication and participation. For example, the city requires program approval by both the neighborhood planning councils and the CDA board. In explaining the effectiveness of this process, David Meeker, former deputy mayor of Community Services (the department under which Model Cities falls), stated that all past board proposals have been accepted by Lugar and that the mayor insists he will support any program receiving substantial citizen acceptance—not merely board endorsement. This philosophy is designed to encourage greater participation. Furthermore, there is a community feeling that city officials are genuinely attempting to develop an acceptable process, even though it is one designed by city hall. On the whole, in spite of past difficulties, the system is operating successfully.

Planned Variations

Under Planned Variations, although the Model Neighborhood continues to enjoy the special position as an impact area (with the same level of funding), Indianapolis has taken steps to include other disadvantaged areas in its redevelopment plans. A Mayor's Task Force on Community Services is engaged in making recommendations for additional areas to be included in the plan based on two major criteria: (1) availability of resources so that the required impact can be achieved and (2) existence of a viable citizen participation organization within the community and completion of a sound planning process. The relationship to the city's over-all strategy is taken into consideration in designing the plan. This includes a policy of expansion until the central business district is largely surrounded and the entire "inner city" is designated as Model Neighborhoods.

Initial expansion is taking place in the Highland-Brookside neighborhood, which has a subarea plan approved in 1969 by a local citizen participation structure—the Near East Side Community Organization (NESCO). NESCO was selected by a Neighborhood Congress, which is comprised of 140 formal representatives appointed by 70

50

different citizen groups. In February 1972, $3 million in projects was approved for Highland-Brookside and $3.75 million set aside for all other neighborhoods in the Inner Need Area. The city has committed itself to an effective citizen participation program and certification of recognized citizen units on a citywide basis.

Savannah: Staff Dominance

Another system dominated by the CDA staff and city officials is Savannah's. There was little history of citizen involvement prior to the Model Cities or Community Action Programs. Apathy and alienation have been the rule, with residents laboring under the belief that their ideas would be of little value and probably would not be considered anyway. It was not surprising that there was no clamor from residents to bring Model Cities to Savannah. Indeed, it was up to the city manager to initiate the planning and convince an overly conservative city council (there is now another, more liberal council) that the money would be an economic advantage to the city—much like a new industry. It was the Model Cities planning process, the workshops and resident training (the latter, conducted by Savannah State College and the University of Georgia), that led to the active involvement of once passive residents. Former City Manager Picot Floyd even today is highly impressed with this successful mobilization, declaring the active development of the Model Cities Neighborhood Council is the most significant accomplishment of the Savannah program. Although he feels this new political maturity will continue to grow, there are those who are skeptical of the intentions of certain elected officials to nurture this rather successful development process. As one alderman put it, "It would be no great loss if Model Cities fell." Responsible local observers believe that a "no-strings-attached" special revenue sharing package would very likely let it fall, along with five years of citizen growth and motivation.

Like other programs, this one has had its problems. The Model Cities Neighborhood Council was legitimately elected through a community convention process of several meetings, which drew as many as 1,000 persons. But factional disputes disrupted the board during the various periods of its history, and arguments about not hiring enough residents slowed the program. The board's executive director was fired for mismanagement and unethical practice. Eventually, the city was forced to place tighter controls on operations, and ever since, things have run more smoothly.

The Savannah experience, like many others, points out the need for city guidance through growth periods. With this kind of administrative leadership, this program continues to improve, projects are operating near capacity, and participation is growing, a sense of community is apparent, and (as observed by a local official) there are more blacks in local government (many in key positions) than would have been employed 10 to 15 years hence without Model Cities.

Although Savannah was not fortunate enough to fall under the Planned Variations Program, the CDA staff (in anticipation of revenue sharing) proposed that the city extend citizen participation citywide and expand resources to all 11 poverty areas outside the Model Neighborhood. They recommended that one representative be elected to a Community Advisory Council for each 1,000 residents living in the poverty areas. However, until more is learned about the status of revenue sharing, the city council has postponed any decisions on this plan. In brief, many believe that without a requirement for citizen participation, the city fathers may drop the idea even though it is judged to be perhaps the city's most important accomplishment.

Newark: Staff Dominance

Newark started out under city hall control and practically no citizen influence. With the election of Kenneth Gibson, it turned to a staff-dominant program, but still with executive leadership and weak citizen involvement. The CDA not only controlled the citizen participation process but also, to the annoyance of city officials, remained almost completely independent of city operations, proceeding to create a "shadow government." The director during this period, Junius Williams, believed that citizen participation would be more effective by employing Model Neighborhood residents in key positions rather than developing a strong citizen board—in direct disregard of a management philosophy that supports a clear distinction between elected policy-makers and staff. Some local people were employed in important positions, but many principals were not city residents, anyway. Most damaging, the approach resulted in a weak citizen board—one that was unable to develop legitimacy, influence city policies, or even keep tabs on what the director was doing.

From the beginning in 1968, Williams led a dissident group called Newark Area Planning Association (NAPA). They held an independent election outside federal guidelines that nearly cost Newark its first-year funding. However, HUD merely nullified the election. A second election was held that drew about 6,000 voters and used regular city voting machines. But the second council was too big (52 members) and was afflicted with severe racial splits and calculated control from city hall—directed by then Mayor Hugh J. Addonizio. Addonizio moved decisively to gain control of the Model Neighborhood Council by offering jobs to its members and loading the entire agency with patronage employees. Naturally, citizen participation never got off the ground.

When Kenneth Gibson won election as mayor in 1970, he replaced almost all patronage employees with Model Neighborhood residents and committed himself to operating a "clean ship." However, the Model Neighborhood Council never developed any strength, even though it was granted veto power by the city council. Its powers were diluted because everything it did was treated in a negative way. The CDA staff immersed it in the review of previous activities rather than concentrating its attention on new programs. Its decisions turned out to be untimely and unimportant. And by fall 1972, the Model Neighborhood Council was not having any more success than it had had in the beginning in controlling programs or influencing the largely independent CDA. Block clubs and district assembly meetings turned out to be the main source of citizen involvement. As time passed, the community appeared even less motivated to improve itself, and citizen enclaves were battling among themselves. Gibson had to do something.

Planned Variations gave the mayor that chance. He began to plan and program citywide, and he also developed one citywide citizens advisory council of 27 members—18 appointed by the mayor and 9 by the city council. The Model Neighborhood Council has been abandoned, but the district assemblies continue to meet as a source of additional input. Moreover, although the new citywide council is merely advisory, some of the city staff believe it may become fairly influential if it can help to diffuse the highly volatile mix of mayor and city council. It could also assist in bringing some of the independent administrative units together under a strong mayor or business administrator. In effect, it could act in a capacity that the city council is unable to fulfill at this time because of its differences with the mayor.

Although the new citizen body has been given some staff, its lack of formal power might very well hurt its legitimacy and effectiveness over the long run. Newark has been fooled so many times—by the selfish interests of some leaders, by official incompetence, and now by black nationalism and white reaction—that it is running scared. It looks as if no substantial authority will be given to any citizen group until some of the major issues are resolved.

Dayton: Resident Dominance

Dayton's citizen structure could very well be the strongest in the country. This is because of an "equal partnership" agreement that is respected by the residents and the city but that has not been passed into law, mainly because it would be illegal to give this much power away to a resident group. For a long time, the Model Cities Planning Council (MCPC—policy board) was almost as powerful as the city commission in Model Cities affairs. This local board has had a four-man staff, has developed its own programs, and has had virtual veto power over any proposal intended for the Model Neighborhood. Realizing that it had gone too far, the city commission was anxious to pull back when Planned Variations came in by declining to give the same latitude to five other citizen councils it had developed on its own initiative for the rest of the city. It justified giving extensive power to the mostly black Model Neighborhood because of historic inequities against minorities and the need for them to catch up. Despite the genuineness of this reasoning, the city fathers were also trying to find a way out of diffusing their authority any further, for perhaps there would be no need for the city commission. They believe they have found a middle ground in the new councils.

Nevertheless, the Model Cities Planning Council has been a valuable demonstration in power and organization. The system utilizes a pure election process and regular voting machines. The Planning Council's 27 members are elected from nine neighborhoods. During the first year, it had to fight for its legitimacy with city hall and groups from West Dayton that challenged it. For instance, the West Dayton Area Council, an umbrella group of organizations with a long history of involvement in the area, attacked the MCPC for not truly representing all the area's constituents but preferred not to get involved itself because it believed the Planning Council to be dominated by a few spokesmen. Other groups complained that despite the high degree of organization and nine paid community organizers, citizen participation never did become widespread. It largely relied on leaflets and the "grapevine" for its communication. And the lack of participation was compounded by the chairman, Roger Prear, who surrounded himself with black militants who frightened poor and middle-class blacks and whites.

By the second year, a much more open chairman, George Washington, was elected, and the atmosphere improved, though it was still clouded by the presence of fear. During the whole period of development, middle-class blacks continually charged the city with racism for allowing the MCPC openly to ignore sound and honest rules so that the city could eventually claim control by default. However, from the city's point of view, officials did not want to intervene for fear of violating their "equal partnership" agreement. Nevertheless, it became apparent that some form of city intervention would have to take place; yet it came only when additional resources from Planned Variations allowed MCPC to go citywide. But the city commission has still not defined precise roles between itself and the Planning Council.

In spite of its problems with the Planning Council, for a long time the city had recognized the value of creating meaningful citizen structures in all sections of the community. Well before Planned Variations, it allocated $200,000 of city funds for this purpose. And under Planned Variations, an additional $2 million has been distributed to five elected councils on the basis of community need. Their less extensive power tends to balance that of the Planning Council but includes such important things as developing a comprehensive plan and determining priorities for the use of money allocated to them. They also channel a great deal of attention to over-all city goals and objectives, although each council meets directly with the city commission on its own problems. Staff assistance is provided by a "super CDA" under the direction of an assistant city manager.

New York: Resident Dominance Vis-à-vis Staff Influence

Taking its cue from the Community Action Program, Model Cities in New York fell under resident dominance immediately. Initial feelings were that resident power was supposed to be on the same level for both programs. As the program ran into delays of up to a year or more and in light of the inability of the city to spend half of its Model Cities money, the city blamed the residents and the residents blamed the city for the problems. But blame can be placed both on factional conflicts in the local boards and on the shoulders of city officials who refused to resolve problems and move the program along early enough.

To begin with, Mayor Lindsay placed Model Cities under a weak executive secretary and a committee of powerless and uninterested city commissioners, who ended up sending their subordinates to meetings. Policy decisions were really made by the three local directors and three Model Cities Policy Committees from the three different boroughs affected. Although the committees did not possess final decision-making authority, they had informal veto power through their ability to hold up projects they did not like, and the city usually gave them their way. What was called Model Cities "partnership" turned out to be local board dominance and demands for things the city did not want. And there was a general concern that Model Cities might get as independent and powerful as the Community Action corporations, with little room for city participation.

Well into the first action year, the program dragged along. Lindsay finally had to face up to the fact that it was necessary to move control in the direction of city hall, confront community opposition, and direct the bureaucracy to cooperate. It was at this stage that the bureaucracy was holding up progress as much as anybody else, particularly such departments as Budget, Real Estate, and Personnel and Investigations. The delays prompted the Brooklyn Policy Committee to stage a two-day sit-in in December 1969, charging that the system had allowed it to spend only a fraction of its allotted $29 million, while the first action year was nearly half over. The other two Model Neighborhood groups were even in worse shape in the area of operating programs and spending agency money. The city decided it was time to follow a report of reorganization prepared by the McKinsey consulting firm of New York.

Lindsay issued an executive order making Model Cities an administration and placing it under the direction of a strong administrator and a newly appointed central board of citizens. The administrative arrangements seemed to work well, but the new board was underutilized and consistently by-passed. The program's administrator, Joseph Williams, called the board into session only twice in two years; it was a defunct operation for all practical purposes. On the other side, Williams has proved to be an effective and strong administrator, managing key aspects of the program himself and unafraid to make unpopular decisions even in the face of community opposition. And local Policy Committees have continued to be the source for citizen input, although their powers have been largely diluted.

As it happened, most people behind the Policy Committees never truly represented their communities. To correct this, new elections were called in 1972, with the guidelines designed to include representation from the young and aged and a limit on the number of "povertycrats" (those in the OEO poverty programs) who could serve, so that a few "professional spokesmen" would not be able to control the boards. The elections corrected some of the abuses, but even today there are overlapping controlling memberships with a few people dominating the Policy Committees. In any event, dual elections and dual structures—the antipoverty corporations and Model Cities Committees—have created two power structures in the poor communities, a duplication of services, and a great deal of wasted citizen effort. This system has merely diffused power and caused frustrations. Model Cities has been able to achieve the degree of coordination and cooperation necessary to improve neighborhood organization.

To create some harmony out of the proliferation of neighborhood groups and to develop an effective participation structure, Lindsay proposed a citywide system of neighborhood government in 1972. Later that year, the Scott Commission, appointed by Governor Nelson Rockefeller, recommended a system of neighborhood government with even greater power than Lindsay had proposed. And now a newly appointed Charter Commission is looking into the possibilities of decentralization, hoping to come out with a report by 1974. The city is presently engaged in a pilot project in eight districts, designed to demonstrate the effects of decentralized administrative control under a district manager and single responsible citizen body in each area. To a large extent, these moves toward neighborhood government have come about because of the experiences of the Community Action and Model Cities Programs.

Boston's System of Parity

A system of parity—that is, meaningful, nondisruptive citizen participation and acceptable levels of staff and chief executive involvement—exists to a larger extent in Boston and Seattle than the other cities in this study.

In Boston, the Model Neighborhood Board has been given considerable power yet works well with the city. The genesis of effective citizen participation here, in sharp contrast to many other communities, was the Community Action Program, more specifically the Area Planning Action Council (APAC). Four APAC corporations function in various parts of the Model Neighborhood, and they have been unusually cooperative in assisting Model Cities administrators.

The Model Neighborhood Board has developed into a position of strength. However, it has been difficult for it to assimilate a feeling of areawide interest because of its elongated doughnut shape and three distinct neighborhoods. But after some internal power struggles of its own and the resignation of its first chairman, the board was able to establish its primacy among local resident groups. Its prestige has evolved far enough along to have developed an "aura of sanctity," and the legitimacy of its decisions is seldom questioned. While other local bodies have had advisory or review powers delegated to them by administrative agreements, the Model Neighborhood Board was uniquely given important decision-making authority by city ordinance. These powers include authority over all Model Cities plans, programs, proposals, and contracts and have made it into a powerful body.

The CDA administrator is obligated to follow the wishes of the majority of the board. If he disagrees he may submit disputes to binding arbitration before three arbitrators—one chosen by the board, one by the administrator, and one by agreement between the two. Surprisingly, no issue has yet had to go as far as arbitration. Usually, consensus is reached through a rational discussion of differences in community workshops.

Many believe that a principal reason for success is that rhetoric from the board is well-chosen, careful, and seldom publicly critical of city government or the CDA. The most frequent outbursts have been against the federal government and the Nixon Administration's "cynical lack of support" for the Model Cities effort. It shuns radicals. When one black activist organization, RAP, attempted to win some board seats, the group lost badly because it "scared people." Yet, the CDA has assisted groups like the Black Panthers and the National Welfare Rights Organization when it felt their projects were justified. It repeatedly states it purpose as "planned constructive social change within the existing political structure." The CDA administrator, Paul Parks, believes that working within the system may be the "main reason this board is more effective than Dayton's"—which has operated too independently.

On the other hand, the board's effectiveness is limited in a number of ways. Its staff is small, and the CDA overwhelms it with expertise, making it difficult for members to influence programs and priorities. But it is respected, mostly seeing itself as a change agent and evaluator, not an operator of programs. This role may be its most important purpose anyway.

The success of the Model Neighborhood Board may encourage the city to go further. In 1968, Mayor Kevin White appointed a Home Rule Commission, which eventually came forth with recommendations for a system of elected community councils for the entire city—still under consideration by the city and state legislature. And since 1968 the city has had 14 Little City Halls, which cover the entire city. The mayor would like to see citizen boards developed alongside all the Little City Halls.

Seattle's Parity

Seattle too has a system of parity. Although the Model Cities Citizen Advisory Council has little formal power, it has significant influence. The residents and staff get along well, and the mayor has shown a sustained interest in the program. Perhaps much of this is so because of an ever present interest in improving the area. For example, the Model Neighborhood has never suffered from lack of organization, with over 100 groups operating there long before Model Cities. Furthermore, residents and the city agreed on their roles from the beginning, and the city made a conscious effort not to oversell the program. The Model Cities Council has been given more power than its name suggests. It can create policy, and it can approve plans before submission to the mayor and city council. But city hall has made it clear that it has final control over the program. Instead of wasting time and energy fighting over roles, residents and city hall have concentrated on getting the most out of the role assigned to each.

While in most places boards are elected, in Seattle local organizations choose the racially mixed, 100-member body. Although no one suggests that such a large board is the best way to operate, its chairman, Judge Charles Johnson, believes the system is satisfactory because a lot of the work gets done through smaller committees. He also feels this board is more effective than that of the local Community Action Program because it has broader representation and is more convincing to the power structure. On the other hand, groups have criticized it for a number of reasons: for not electing at least some members, for being too large and unwieldy, for involving too few disadvantaged citizens, and for not legitimizing the structure for long-range permanence.

However, some of these things have occurred in other ways. A Model Cities Land Use Review Board, composed of Model Neighborhood residents, has been given the final decision-making authority on all zoning changes and land-use policy in the Model Neighborhood. There is consensus that "nothing gets done in the Model Neighborhood without the approval of this board." And under Planned Variations, there has been an expansion of Citizen Advisory Councils to three other Model Neighborhoods. In addition, an elected Advisory Council— from the four neighborhood councils—has been empowered to consider broader questions.

Meanwhile a Mayor's Task Force is examining the possibility of creating citizen (district) councils in all neighborhoods of the city— to advise the city on general policies, city budget, legislation, and comprehensive development plans submitted by each city department. Besides the neighborhood councils, the mayor and business community are in favor of a citywide (central) council, with representation from all district councils. Little City Halls are also being developed to assist the work of neighborhood councils.

In summary, citizen participation has been healthy for Seattle and for its programs. It has developed new leadership, made citizens more productive, and created a more positive image of government and its officials.

Conclusions

Although measuring the results of citizen participation is difficult, there are some clear indications of progress. We have indicated a number of them in the discussion of product in this report. But beyond that, citizen participation has sought and found new resident leadership, forced some important changes in government, brought democracy and decision-making closer to the people, and involved at least some of the poor in the actual workings of government. Most importantly, it has created a feeling in large segments of our population that government really cares. As this study shows, there have been successes and failures. Where successes have occurred, the people involved believe their experience to be worthwhile personally and valuable for better government. In the failures, most officials are treating them as temporary and are attempting to find the right mix of ingredients for their particular city or county. Some have given up or are trying to submerge the process so that it is largely meaningless. But one has only to look at cities where residents are actively participating in the processes of government to feel a spirit and interchange that has never existed before. It is surely a closer step to the democratic principles of this nation.

Some important lessons have been learned about developing the citizen participation mechanism.

Council Size. When one reviews the cities in this study, as well as some others, a consensus emerges that the most effective citizen board size is a small grouping—usually less than 20 members—because it is more manageable and responsive and members tend to retain greater interest. Naturally, some larger councils succeed, but most experience unnecessary delays, tedious rules and procedures, and greater chance for disruption. Usually, large bodies have to be broken down into rather specialized committees anyway, with small executive committees doing most of the work. The main argument for a large body is that broader community representation may be obtained; however, the negative points tend to outweigh this advantage.

Compensating Members. In regards to compensating members for their services and time, the question is less clear. Citizen councils, like city councils and other boards can be effective with or without pay. Usually other motivations are more important, such as dedication, interest in one's work, and the authority and meaning given to the job. Nevertheless, feelings are strong in favor of paying ordinary residents for their services, especially in a society that pays elected officials, private corporate board members, and others. At the very least, meeting expenses should be reimbursed for low-income persons.

Authority and Staff. Experience shows that citizen participation will be largely meaningless and short-lived if the system does not include genuine purpose and authority. It is best that the extent and limit of power be officially established by ordinance, including a clear explanation of the chain of command so that there is no question of how plans and policies originate and pass from residents to city hall and on to elected officials. The range of authority should not only include the ability to create specified policies but the flexibility to operate programs where necessary. Decision-making may involve city budgets, zoning, comprehensive planning, capital improvements, evaluation of services, and other matters important to each neighborhood.

Operations may include multiservice center projects, information and referral, or any service that a citizen group might improve. We have witnessed too many citizen groups that have deteriorated because they did not have project operating responsibilities. First, James L. Sundquist, in his Making Federalism Work, advocated that Model Cities neighborhood resident organizations be nonoperating because he believed their planning and coordinating responsibilities to be incompatible with operations.[2] HUD has pursued the same policy, although some Model Cities resident groups are operating programs anyway. This policy was more appropriate when there were only single neighborhood councils, but under a citywide system, operating projects seems to come naturally. We find that certain neighborhood groups are more effective and long-lasting if they are able to operate at least some programs. In any event, coordination is achieved at this level largely through the staffs of agencies in one-stop multi-service centers. It has been difficult for neighborhood councils to achieve areawide coordination from smaller target areas. The most meaningful coordination has occurred at the chief executive level and under the auspices of a citywide citizen body, much different from neighborhood operations. As a practical matter, neighborhood councils should be allowed to operate programs suitable to them; otherwise, many of them will not have much reason to exist.

Boards should be provided the resources to hire some staff— either part-time or full-time and in relation to their responsibilities.

Citywide Vis-à-vis Target Area Orientation. The community as a whole should be involved in the participation process if a city expects to reduce alienation and gain support for bond issues and other matters requiring majority approval. There are also good reasons for target area concentration—to allocate resources where they are most needed and to develop leadership where it was nonexistent before. However, concentrating resources should not obviate the need to organize and carry on citywide programs. Furthermore, it is nearly impossible to develop comprehensive plans and achieve interagency coordination without dealing with problems and issues on a citywide basis.

Citywide Citizen Board. In addition to neighborhood councils functioning in all area of the city, one central body—to influence directly city departments—is desirable for most large jurisdictions. For cities with few neighborhood councils, a central board may not be appealing; yet an effective mechanism is needed to give citizens the opportunity to influence plans and policies right at their inception. Already there are federal requirements for citizen participation in workable (urban renewal) programs, Annual Arrangements, revenue sharing proposals, and in most other federal grants. Placing the citizen participation responsibility for all these programs in the hands of one representative board makes sense because it reduces duplication and a good deal of confusion.

Preferably, the majority of the central body should come from the neighborhood councils and the rest from appointments by the chief executive so that an atmosphere of partnership is created. This body too should have some staff but, unlike the neighborhood groups, should be nonoperating. It should concentrate on developing citywide plans and assisting the city council by helping to create community consensus on city goals and objectives. It should be involved in such areas as conducting periodic neighborhood workshops and monitoring and evaluating city services on a day-to-day basis. It should not be a competitor of the city council. On the contrary, it should be a complement, doing the kinds of things city council outlines as appropriate to assist the council and at the same time getting the average citizen actively involved.

Various city departments, in addition to being involved in community development and human resources, ought to be made responsive to the citywide board. It is no longer enough that citizen groups have impact only on Model-Cities-type activities. Community development in fact involves all departments; therefore, all departments should be brought into a more formal system of relating directly with residents.

Selection Process. How neighborhood councils should be selected is a much more complicated process. In the case of councils with extensive authority, the pure election process may be the best; for others, the combination of election and appointment may be most suitable. In most cases, the decision may very well be left up to each neighborhood; and neighborhoods should have the right not to participate if they so choose. The combination of election from the neighborhoods and appointment by the chief executive has developed a sense of partnership in many cities. However, where organizations are permitted to choose council members, it is important that opportunity be provided for other residents—who are not organization members—to choose nominees also. Furthermore, it is appropriate that the majority of members be chosen by the residents of the area, that an impartial observer be chosen to oversee the election, and that the entire process be publicized widely.

Voter participation has not been good. A few cities in the Model Cities Program have approached 25 percent turnout for elections, two were higher, but on the whole, voting has been poor. However, it has been better than the OEO Community Action Program, which has averaged less than 5 percent over the life of its program. Critics enjoy pointing to these low vote percentages to support their arguments for resident lack of interest and apathy. Yet, to a large extent, residents simply have not been encouraged by the city's leadership to vote or have had little reason to vote for boards delegated little authority. In many instances, local officials had no intention of encouraging massive resident involvement, for fear it might compete with their own political careers. For many it was better to see the process wither away, unless they could control the new system, too. It has not been the habit of political figures to encourage the use of television or newspaper publicity, and furthermore, there was little public service time available for neighborhood elections. In addition, elections have been too confining. They have only involved a small section of the community, and few major organizations or the mass media took them seriously. It is more likely that a system of citywide participation would encourage greater interest. It is also desirable that one day be set aside for all neighborhood elections so that a maximum amount of publicity could be obtained.

Leadership from City Hall. Widespread participation is more likely to come about with official city leadership. A principal fault of most of the Model Cities programs has been the lack of mayoral or administrative leadership—usually due to fear of getting involved with activist citizens of different points of view. Yet to avoid wasteful and unusable creations, election officials should help in molding the system, participate themselves, publicize the purposes, legitimatize the process, and provide leadership and assistance when the program is in trouble.

Furthermore, the cause of responsive government is not helped by officials who persistently point out that they are the ones elected by the citizens to run the city and that others are not needed. Elections normally come in four-year cycles. Meanwhile, citizens need to be involved in important, almost day-to-day decisions of government; otherwise, democracy and responsiveness turn out to have little meaning for the average person. Waiting to get back at officials in the next election is not what most people would call citizen participation. More and more chief executives have recognized this and are exercising leadership genuinely to involve citizens.

Notes

1. Ten Model Cities: A Comparative Analysis of Second Round Planning Years, July, 1973. Marshall Kaplan, Gans and Kahn

63

Associates also completed studies of 21 Model Cities in 1972 and a survey of 147 Model Cities in 1973, making use of the same terminology. They have concluded that findings in the later studies are essentially the same as those in the earlier work.

2. James L. Sundquist and David W. Davis, Making Federalism Work (Washington, D.C.: Brookings Institution, 1969), p. 120.

5

State Role

Model Cities Emerges as a Catalyst

The Model Cities Program has demonstrated the need for assistance from other levels of government, including the states and regions.
It has been criticized for an inability to coordinate and demand performance of other agencies; yet cities and states with considerably
more stature and power have experienced virtual impotence in the
same area, and for a longer period of time. For the most part, regular
government has been unable or unwilling to streamline structures,
consolidate programs, establish coterminous service districts, or
reassign programs to the most effective operating levels. In most
cases it was not until Model Cities personnel and citizen task forces
caused certain issues to emerge that state and local officials realized
the immensity of the problem. Moreover, although there have been
some changes, delivery in health, employment, and social services
is still the weakest government link. Model Cities brought to the surface the problem of the lack of intergovernmental response but has
never been the appropriate body to do much about the problem. Nevertheless, state and local cooperation reached its highest peak during
the Model Cities Program. It remains for the more powerful to take
the next steps.

The Power of the State

There appears to be little question that the states need to take
a stronger role in the development of intergovernmental cooperation
and more effective local governments. They already have the power.
In most cases, an act of the legislature can bring consolidation or

strong regional government. The legislature can abolish special districts and transfer their power and indebtedness to city, county, or regional governments. It can designate councils of governments (COGs) as operating agencies for such things as mass transit, water and sewer control, air pollution abatement enforcement, housing development, or regionally oriented functions. Legislatures of two or more states can enter into compacts to give combined power to the regional council of government. The governor, by executive order, can direct his cabinet heads or department directors to meet in the form of regional bodies to coordinate functions and consolidate staff and facilities. He can appoint one of these persons in each region as chairman (to whom others report) and he can use state funds or federal monies (which pass through the state) as incentives to encourage local government cooperation. Furthermore, the federal government can help the states by using a large block of incentive money to be awarded to the regions and localities that show the most progress. Washington should also consider awarding special grants similar to that proposed for local government to increase state government capacity. Attaching specific performance requirements to revenue sharing bills for both the states and localities would be helpful, but this has been proposed before in Congress and has not seen the light of day.

In recent years, states have begun to do something about their own problems. Many have created planning districts throughout the state and have given new authority to state regional officials to act. California, for example, has established planning councils in every section of the state. Texas has gone one step further by giving the councils the authority to allocate resources. Many of the states where there are active Model Cities programs have established task forces and commissions to help solve coordinating problems. But the whole question of reorganization and consolidation is still on fertile soil. Meanwhile, some states are helping their Model City communities in other ways.

The Level of State Participation

Most states contributed at least technical assistance to Model Cities communities. Some gave extra resources through various means, such as increasing the number of state workers in the model area, awarding extra grants, and building additional facilities, which ordinarily would have gone elsewhere.

Newark Gained

In Newark's case, because of the city's generally depressed condition, the state doubled urban aid to the city to $7.4 million annually. It also has been providing $9.25 million annually for the operation of Martland Hospital, a city-owned facility. Legislation was also passed to allow the city to impose new taxes of its own. And New Jersey's Community Affairs Department has been particularly helpful. It awarded $60,000 in initial Model Cities planning funds and $100,000 for the first action year. State specialists have been assigned to Newark's program full-time. Moreover, the city received technical assistance and planning grants from the State Law Enforcement Planning Agency (SLEPA) and the Regional Medical Program.

In addition, New Jersey has assisted the city by (1) beginning construction of the New Jersey College of Medicine and Dentistry (a project delayed since 1967); (2) transplanting an entire public health staff to Newark to assist in the construction of a public health system; and (3) picking up much of the local share on projects that it administered itself but that would never have functioned if Newark had had to provide the funds. However, even with this involvement, actual coordinating mechanisms between the state and city are lacking and formal links have been not established that can stand on their own and carry on for the long term.

Chicago Unresponsive

In Illinois, it has been somewhat different. With a Republican administration in control of the State House during most of the life of Chicago's Model Cities Program and a strong city Democratic organization, state and local relationships were held to a minimum. Mayor Daley would not tolerate any "interference" from state or federal officials. Nevertheless, he was particularly disturbed about not getting a "fair share" of state tax distributions to the city. In 1972, he estimated that although Chicago residents and businessmen paid half of the state income tax, only 2.6 percent was returned to the city. (Mayor Lindsay and other big-city mayors have presented similar arguments.) However, the aid to Chicago has increased dramatically in the last several years—from $68.6 million in 1968 to $139 million in 1972—because of the state income tax and increased returns on water, fuel, and sales taxes.

During Governor Richard Ogilvie's administration, attempts were made to assist Chicago in a number of areas—including Model Cities—but intervention was difficult in Daley's Chicago. Yet aid has been channeled to some city programs. Two Model Cities projects— Day Care and Police Community Services—receive funds on a three (state) to one (city) matching basis. Also, Chicago received most of the $19 million in state aid made available in 1972 throughout Illinois to Model Neighborhoods and public housing projects. Without state aid, several Chicago Model Cities projects and many other Model Cities projects throughout the state could not continue.

Without question, the state of Illinois was attracted to doing a great deal more about urban problems because of the investment of the federal government in the Model Neighborhoods. This involvement consisted of financial aid, technical assistance, and organizational improvements. Although organizational changes, such as joint local and state coordinating task forces, were not developed in Chicago, they were created in other Model Cities communities in Illinois and at least reached the first plateau of success, largely because the governor wanted them to be successful and because he directed his regional directors to participate actively.

There was a substantial amount of money and other forms of state assistance invested in the Model Cities communities in Illinois. This would not have occurred without federal intervention, which created the necessary resource base and guaranteed the federal government's sharing in local urban adventures.

New York Sidetracked

On the other side, New York City has been considerably less successful in getting state assistance. Political differences between Governor Nelson Rockefeller and Mayor John Lindsay have not helped matters. Rockefeller maintains Lindsay is an incompetent administrator and has brought disaster to New York; Lindsay attributes similar incompetence to the governor. Unfortunately, this careless display of politics has hurt service and hampered the flow of resources to the city, as one politician has tried to undermine the other. Naturally the clients have been hurt the most.

Having felt itself being left behind, the city began to take steps to help correct the situation. Model Cities established a division of Federal/State Relations because of evidence that the city was not getting its fair share of state funds. For example, in 1970 the city only received $2.5 million (or 18 percent) of $23,952,948 in HEW money distributed by the state, yet it had 90 percent of the state's educationally disadvantaged, 62 percent of the economically disadvantaged children, 58 percent of all high school dropouts, and 50 percent of all jobs in the state. And of the total state and federal allotment of $74 million, the city was getting only 10 percent. The state's justification was that the city had not developed the necessary administrative apparatus to operate sound programs. Nevertheless, the city's efforts paid off. Because of the leadership of the Model Cities division of Federal/State Relations and important local congressional assistance, the city's share of HEW money was increased to $4.5 million in fiscal 1971, a substantial improvement.

State distrust of the Lindsay Administration has been further demonstrated by the creation of the New York State Urban Development

Corporation, which has taken the initiative away from the city in the development of housing and economic projects. For example, it is developing one of the nation's largest and most publicized projects, the $325 million Welfare Island apartment and commercial complex in the heart of New York City. Clearly, state aid is coming in forms that give credit to the state and not to Lindsay. Moreover, the state legislature, which has veto power over every city budget expenditure, has cut many health and education programs aimed at the city's poor neighborhoods. Thus, in the last two years, Model Cities money has become more important for filling gaps created by reduced appropriations, with the city merely trying to maintain ongoing programs. This naturally has had the effect of limiting the choices for the use of Model Cities funds and has seriously hurt the program's ability to demonstrate innovative results, even with a new source of flexible money.

Seattle Benefited

Seattle has received strong response from the state, even though it has been mainly in the form of technical assistance. At the beginning of Model Cities, Governor Daniel Evans appointed six principal Washington state officials—from Employment Security, Public Assistance, State Planning, State OEO, and from Evans's personal staff—to assist the city in developing the program. As a result, Seattle was able to develop the Model Cities/State Interagency Team and certain other coordinating mechanisms, such as the City Interdepartmental Team, Seattle-King County Economic Opportunity Board Liaison, and the Advisory Council Resource Committee. In turn, this led Model Cities to develop a Department of Governmental Relations, designed to consolidate efforts at cooperation, and an Interagency Directors Committee, to involve agencies more closely in local project planning and implementation.

Although far from ideal, coordination and cooperation between the state and city have improved immeasurably over the past several years. For example, Model Cities and the State Department of Social and Health Services staffs prepared joint grant applications for integrated services to Seattle's Skid Road area; and the governor's State Model Cities Office was instrumental in the award of a federal grant to the State Child Care Coordination Committee for technical assistance to Model Cities for the development of a comprehensive plan for child care. Agency after agency has provided assistance to the city; moreover, Seattle Model Cities has been praised for its ability to motivate other agencies and institutions to help it. Finally, the creation of the State-City Task Force (which includes county and private agencies) has advanced coordination even further and among more organizations.

Boston: Passable Assistance

Some states have limited their participation. The State of Massachusetts' involvement in Model Cities has been very sporadic. The State Department of Community Affairs has offered only peripheral technical assistance to Boston, and most state funds to the city have simply consisted of the formal pass-through type. There has never been a single effective point at which the CDA could approach the state; therefore, Model Cities Director Paul Parks has had to negotiate trade-offs with state officials to gain assistance—a game at which he is very adept. The hope for improved coordination and cooperation lies in the city's Office of Planning and Program Coordination, which has profited from Model Cities experience and is now assuming much of the city's coordinative role.

Dayton: Standard Assistance

Ohio too has not participated in an integral way. Dayton has received only minor assistance from the state. However, the lessons of Model Cities and Planned Variations are changing this. Through the creation of a State-City Task Force, the state now plans to use Dayton as a model for demonstrating maximum coordination of state programs in an urban area. Also the State Department of Urban Affairs and the Ohio Law Enforcement Planning Agency are providing important funding to Dayton. Nevertheless, financial assistance has been limited to a few functional areas. Mostly on its own, Dayton has been able to achieve modest success in coordinating social service agencies. The Model Cities head of social services, for example, now chairs the Health and Welfare Planning Council's Comprehensive Coordinated Child Care body. But employment agencies—in particular State Bureau of Employment Services, National Alliance of Businessmen, Opportunities Industrialization Center—continue to experience major problems associated with red tape and bureaucratic defenses. On the other hand, the Model Cities Planning Council has established good relationships with two other planning bodies—the Miami Valley Regional Planning Commission and the Transportation Coordinating Committee. Prior to Model Cities, little headway had been made with these bodies.

Indianapolis and Savannah: Minimum Assistance

The states of Indiana and Georgia have participated in a minimal way. In Indianapolis, the state has limited itself to giving technical endorsement and operating a few programs in the Model Neighborhood. Private agencies also have not been enthusiastic about assisting the Model Cities Program.

In Savannah, the A-95 review process has forced the state to become more deeply involved. However, at least one problem—coordination—is not nearly as serious in this region as elsewhere because there are only eight communities in the metropolitan area to coordinate. And greater state participation is beginning to take place under Governor Jimmy Carter, who has committed himself to the concept of areawide planning and community action and who is taking the lead in increasing state funding and technical assistance to Model Neighborhoods in the state.

Local Strategies and State Plans

The scope of problems associated with the Model Cities communities clearly indicates the need for cities to develop intergovernmental relations techniques. Cities need to develop adequate staffs and input into the state system. Some Model Cities communities have developed such capacity, passing it on to local government. In any case, staffs (which may consist of as little as one person) should become thoroughly familiar with those state, regional, and local plans that are normally required for most federal programs. In order to develop an effective level of cooperation, state and local staffs, usually by means of the State's Community Affairs Department, should see that state plans and legislation include the following items:* (1) State notification of all units of local government about the availability of formula grant money and how to apply for it (a simple point of entry for federal money to the states would also be helpful); (2) distribution of funds based on need factors, such as urban and rural geography, poverty, welfare clients, unemployment, aged, youth, and other matters peculiar to disadvantaged areas; (3) establishment of specific criteria for funding priorities, and the passing of a fixed percentage of state funds to local governments so that the latter can better plan their own strategies; (4) requirements that matching fund criteria be flexible enough so that financially strapped communities can meet them; (5) legislative provision permitting localities to challenge provisions they believe unfair; (6) state control of the informational process in order to keep localities fully informed of all programs affecting them, and the authority for localities to review and sign off on such projects; (7) legislative mandate for local (regional and/or city-county) and

---

*HUD gives an explanation of some of the main elements of state-local cooperation in its Community Development Evaluation Series No. 3, Local Strategies to Affect State Plans Allocation of Federal Funds (Washington, D.C., January 1972).

state coordinating commissions (fully staffed) in principal functional areas, such as employment, social services, criminal justice and corrections, finance, and government organization; and (8) incentive (or discretionary) funding to localities based on performance, improved government organization, and greater regional cooperation.

Private Response

The solution to urban problems involves more than the need for federal and state government action. It also requires private response, which has been lacking in almost all Model Cities communities. The participation of business and union interests has been extremely poor. Too often these interests have not wanted to get involved in local conflicts and what they thought were strictly government problems. On the other hand, the behavior of private service agencies has been somewhat different. Since many were already involved in urban matters, they readily accepted Model Cities money, which they badly needed and which intensified their involvement.

The lessons of Model Cities indicate that few urban problems will be solved without the genuine participation of businessmen and union leaders and private agency heads. However, it is unlikely they will get involved unless the local chief executive is able to motivate them and state officials particularly the governor and key legislators, are able to demonstrate sincerity and leadership in establishing formal mechanisms for coordination, cooperation, and investment. Furthermore, it seems clear that both federal and state funds are necessary to create the proper investment base and incentives on which private interests will chance their money.

Private investment is likely to come about in the urban ghetto if certain things occur. Local government needs to take steps to develop a comprehensive plan, city goals, and a mechanism to pass bond issues. In this study, the most successful example of private initiative is Seattle's Forward Thrust. This is a group of business and civic leaders who have been instrumental in getting millions of dollars in bond issues approved and legislation important to the city passed. It has received over $529,999 in private contributions from more than 1,000 businesses and individuals. Its impressive record of accomplishments includes assisting in passage of 20 measures through the state legislature on highways, mass transit, pollution control, and strengthened city and county finances; helping to pass seven major city and county bond issues totaling $333.9 million and two state bond issues for $65 million for local capital improvements; helping to pass state legislation for revenue sharing to localities; and developing numerous joint planning projects and more efficient methods of operating local government. It is now pushing for 25 community centers, neighborhood library facilities, and other human resource projects.

Although not a part of this study, the Hartford Process—a coalition of concerned metropolitan area (Hartford, Connecticut) business and civic leaders who have contributed financial resources and talent for the development of comprehensive community goals and growth plans—is another excellent example of the mobilization of private forces. If cities were able to combine such movements as Forward Thrust and the Hartford Process with community development strategy, a giant step would be taken in solving our most pressing urban problems. At least, many cities now realize the significance of combining these processes. Furthermore, the experiences gained through the trials and errors of Model Cities have pinpointed many of the ingredients necessary for success.

6

FEDERAL ROLE
IN THE FUTURE

There will always be a federal role in local and state government affairs. Public employment policies, environmental laws, civil rights legislation, mortgage assistance, and so on will make the federal government's presence felt. Nevertheless, although the cities and counties expect continued federal involvement, they are not particularly pleased with increased state intervention for fear it may create another bureaucratic nightmare. Yet we have described areas where cooperation is essential; otherwise little progress will occur. As it happens, most localities are willing to work with the federal government because of the increased funding and the prodding they receive to engage in policies they would not ordinarily want or dare to assume responsibility for at home. The states can probably work themselves into similar positions in respect to local government by increasing state aid and improving their own organizations. Meanwhile if the federal government intends to maintain or increase its credibility, it will have to simplify its procedures and offer greater technical and financial assistance.

We have already discussed some newer federal methods for improving local government capacity, including Annual Arrangements, Chief Executive Review and Comment, Federal Regional Councils, and other assistance. The effectiveness of these devices would be improved significantly by a more streamlined flow of funds and less diffused direction from both the federal and state levels. The block grant system is one way of doing this. In addition, the commitment of an effective level of national revenue for community development is needed, as is support, both financial and civic, from the public.

TABLE 4

Annual Funding for Planned Variations Cities
(millions of dollars)

Region	City	Regular MC Funding	PV Increases of MC Funding	Total MC Funding
II	Newark	5.7	7.0	12.7
	Paterson	2.1	4.1	6.2
III	Erie	1.6	2.9	4.5
	Norfolk	4.5	8.0	12.5
IV	Tampa	4.1	7.1	11.2
	Winston-Salem	1.9	3.3	5.2
V	Dayton	2.9	5.2	8.1
	East St. Louis	2.1	3.8	5.9
	Indianapolis	6.2	8.5	14.7
	Lansing	1.9	3.3	5.2
VI	Waco	2.6	4.6	7.2
VII	Des Moines	2.1	3.7	5.8
VIII	Butte	1.7	1.5	3.2
IX	Fresno	2.8	4.9	7.7
	Tucson	3.1	5.5	8.6
X	Seattle	5.2	5.2	10.4
II	Rochester (CERC only)	3.0	.2	3.2
III	Wilmington (CERC only)	1.7	.2	1.9
VI	Houston (CERC only)	13.4	.2	13.6
IX	San Jose (CERC only)	3.1	.2	3.3
	Totals	71.7	79.4	151.1

Source: U.S. Department of Housing and Urban Development, Community Development Evaluation Series No. 7 (Washington, D.C., October 1972).

Block Grants

Perhaps the most effective way to improve coordination is to consolidate programs. Block grants might best be able to do this from the federal to the state and local levels. Numerous federal and local administrators as well as principal city and county service organizations have endorsed this approach.

Recently the International City Management Association (ICMA) advocated the adoption of block grants because of the almost impossible task of coordinating and scheduling federal projects at the local level.[1] For example, under categorical grants, for a project that involves urban renewal, open space, and water and sewer grants, a city or county needs to follow three different application procedures dealing with three sets of HUD officials, three sets of technical requirements, three piles of paper, and three different time schedules. ICMA would like to see this nightmare eliminated and postcontrol instituted, the latter having the further effect of reducing red tape and yet providing needed safeguards.

Planned Variations as a Block Grant

Both the Model Cities and Planned Variations Programs offer some valuable experience about what may be expected from block grants and other relatively new ideas. Planned Variations was designed to correct many of the faults of the Model Cities Program and at the same time serve as an introduction to special revenue sharing. It resulted from a review of the Model Cities Program early in 1970 by the President's Domestic Council and closely followed the administration's efforts to reorganize federal agencies. Sixteen cities have been receiving funds that will total $157.2 million over a two-year period or longer and are participating in three variations, which include (1) extending programing citywide, (2) minimizing red tape and federal reviews, and (3) providing stronger mayoral coordinating power through CERC process. Table 4 shows annual funding for Planned Variations cities.

In a HUD first-year study of Planned Variations, the findings indicate a number of changes from the original Model Cities Program: (1) Federal restraints have been reduced, most resource allocation has been placed in the hands of the chief executive, and priorities have changed from social to physical programing (43 percent in physical programs compared to 21 percent under Model Cities). (2) Federal response has mostly been aimed at simplifying procedures.*

---

*The Federal Assistance Review (FAR) program, begun in March 1969, aimed at improving federal response by (1) placing greater reliance

Handbooks have been simplified and the average size of applications
has been reduced by 75 percent (399 pages in Model Cities, compared
to 102 in Planned Variations); however, processing time has remained
unchanged from one-and-a-half to three months. Only four cities have
used the "waivers" process, created to allow cities to identify unnecessary administrative requirements in categorical programs.
And the Federal Regional Councils have only moderately supported
the program. But more than anything else it has been the "hands-
off" policy of the area physical offices that has resulted in greater
local discretion and control. (3) CERC has stimulated the development
of citywide strategies, and as a result, some cities have had major
departmental reorganizations. Intergovernmental task forces have
only been partly successful in gaining state and county support. The
involvement of the counties has been minimal because they prefer
that more money and influence be given directly to them. (4) Citizen
participation has taken on a different character, becoming more advisory and taking on a more traditional "blue ribbon" air in about
half the cities, over the protests of existing Model Neighborhood
groups. The chief executives now appoint a greater percentage of
Model Cities board members.[2]

Model Cities: Block Grants and Commitment

Although new problems may arise in the administration of block
grants, the wisdom of the flexible use of funds has already been
demonstrated. In the Model Cities Program, officials have been able
to use funds for almost any purpose to meet broad goals and objectives
developed through comprehensive planning. It has been primarily
through this system that city officials have been able to look seriously
at the totality of community problems and spend money as they see
fit. The ability to use funds broadly has encouraged city officials to
tackle unusual problems in formerly "restricted" areas. The desir-
ability of continuing this motivating catalyst seems obvious. If it is
not done through some system of special revenue sharing or block
grants, strong arguments can be made for continuing the Model Cities
or Planned Variations approach to maintain the momentum for governmental improvement and responsiveness.

_____

on state and local governments; (2) increasing interdepartmental coordination; and (3) reducing red tape and speeding services, but it had
only modest success. Apparently, more drastic measures were needed.

Pending Legislation

There have been a number of bills introduced to consolidate categorical grants for community development purposes. The latest administration bill is the Better Communities Act (BCA, introduced in the House of Representatives as HR 7277, April 19, 1973 and in the Senate as S 1743, May 8, 1973), which differs considerably from 1971 special revenue sharing proposals. The new bill includes the following major differences: (1) A poverty factor is now included in the formula. This is similar to the 1972 House and Senate block grant bills; however, BCA does not include "past performance" or "housing condition" factors, which congressional leaders would like to see included. (2) Counties over 200,000 and cities over 50,000 population (or designated center city) are now automatically included. This means that many jurisdictions will be included that have little or no need for this type of funding, which will simply decrease the amount of money high-priority areas need. (3) Hold harmless protection (maintenance of present level of funding) for cities now participating would be phased out over four years, and new communities would be phased in over three years. This means many communities in dire need would be getting less money after hold harmless runs out. (4) States are automatically entitled to funds for which cities under 50,000 population would be eligible to apply.

There are other differences and controversial elements. The new bill does not require a formal application from cities or counties, nor does it require the spending of funds in matters of national priority. This is in sharp contrast to both 1972's and 1973's congressional bills, which require a plan and an application designed to eliminate and prevent blight, to facilitate additional housing opportunities, and to provide community facilities. BCA does require an annual statement of community development objectives, past-performance statements, and an evaluation of effectiveness. However, the chief complaint from congressional critics is that without a specific plan, no work will get done toward meeting national or local priorities. Furthermore the Congress and the General Accounting Office (GAO) are afraid that the Nixon Administration's requirements for performance evaluation are weak and unenforceable.

There are other difficulties as well. The Better Communities Act proposes to terminate seven categorical programs, while Congress wishes to leave some of these programs alone. The 1972 congressional bills did not consolidate Model Cities; also the Senate bill excluded Section 312 rehabilitation grants and the House bill excluded water and sewer programs. Another major criticism by congressional leaders is that BCA does not contain any linkage between community development and housing programs. Finally, BCA has no requirement for local financial sharing, no citizen participation, no A-95 review, and no workable program.[3]

In spite of these difficulties, there appears to be general agreement from all sources that a more simplified method of channeling federal funds to the states and localities is needed. Most officials feel that the need for grantsmanship should be reduced and that cities and counties should be allocated funds based on real needs. Let us look in more detail at three aspects of the proposed Better Communities Act that would severely hurt community development: (1) funds for many cities would be cut; (2) there would be fewer incentives for local officials to face up to poverty and discrimination; and (3) citizens would not be effectively involved.

The Distribution Formula. The distribution formula needs changing if the most disadvantaged areas are to benefit. The proposed formula—based on (1) size of population, (2) extent of housing overcrowding, and (3) extent of poverty—does not truly reflect neighborhood deterioration and poverty in most cases. The size of population bears no relationship to the poverty population. Secondly, figures on overcrowding and substandard units in poverty areas of the 100 largest standard metropolitan statistical areas (SMSA's) reveal no direct correlation between the "extent of overcrowding" and physical condition.[4] In fact, say Richard T. LeGates and Mary C. Morgan in a recent issue of the Journal of the American Institute of Planners, the most deteriorated urban areas do not have high incidences of overcrowding. Furthermore, they indicate that although the "extent of poverty" is a valid measure of need and "double weighting" of this indicator is useful, these advantages makes little difference because of the nature of the formula. The wide range of population ratios in the various SMSA's minimize the significance of double weighting the poverty indicator.[5] Because of the formula's automatic nature, most of the largest deteriorated urban areas will most likely receive less money than under the categorical system. Moreover, comprehensive planning and quality-of-life goals would probably be even less meaningful than under Model Cities without the necessary funds to implement programs.

Maintenance of Effort. Because the Better Communities legislation does not require local matching or maintenance of local effort, it is likely many communities will simply use federal funds as a substitute for local money already allocated for some of these services. Therefore, urban areas may not only experience an eventual loss of funds but less incentive to use money in the disadvantaged areas. LeGates and Morgan point out that many of the programs now administered with federal funds would not be carried out if local officials and communities had to decide the priorities by direct vote. Certainly, the poverty areas would suffer.

Citizen Involvement. Citizen participation requirements in the Better Communities Act are very similar to the past rather poor experiences with public hearings in transportation and urban renewal programs. Minorities fear that revenue sharing funds will be given right back to the very officials, in many cases, who have been "racist in the first place" and disinterested in improving the lot of the poor. As we have pointed out for example, the Annual Arrangements process has demonstrated only minimal and infrequent citizen involvement and many of the Planned Variations cities have changed their citizen participants from policy-makers to advisors.

The Congress and community groups do not want to take any chances about leaving the idea of resident participation up to local officials. The Senate more than the House has taken a leading role in this, adding amendments to the proposed special revenue sharing legislation. For example, language in Senate Bill 3248, passed March 2, 1972 (but left out by the House), is believed by federal Community Development officials to be stronger than the original Model Cities language. It reads as follows in regards to the cities' obligation to carry out the bill's mandates:

> [A certification that the applicant] has afforded adequate
> opportunity for citizen participation in the development
> of the annual application and has provided for the meaning-
> ful involvement of the residents of areas in which com-
> munity development activities are to be concentrated in
> the planning and execution of these activities, including
> the provision of adequate information and resources.[6]

The bill is stronger for two reasons: (1) it provides for meaningful resident involvement in all areas (not just the model area) of the city where any significant community development activities are to take place, and (2) it calls for adequate information and resources to enable citizens to do their part. (Original Model Cities legislation did not specifically call for the provision of adequate resources.)

Providing adequate resources may be the most important element because it gives citizens the ability to develop technical and political know-how to carry out strategies. Moreover, if residents are to be given resources, it is all the more important that local officials devise participation plans that are meaningful and workable so that funds will be used to the best advantage. Federal encouragement to do nothing about citizen participation can only cause frustration and further alienation among local groups. It would be foolhardy to dictate plans of participation to localities; however, guidelines of successful experiences would be helpful. Furthermore, if genuine and widespread local decision-making is to take place, there is an obligation on the part of the nation's leaders to encourage more effective democratic processes and also to indicate the desirable levels and kinds of participation.

Commitment

Even with block grants, it seems probable that Congress will continue to appropriate funds for projects to meet special congressional objectives. Thus, a system of block grants (in all major functional areas) could provide the basis for a coordinated, more simplified method for dealing with the cities' problems at the same time other funds are used as incentives and for expediting programs. As a practical matter, categorical funding in our political system seems here to stay. Possibly, the best we can hope for is the consolidation of some categorical grants or funding of a variety of grants through multiapplications.

Furthermore, because of the minimal level of funding requested for community development and its wide dispersal to over 1,200 cities and counties, urban pressures will mount for the executive branch and the Congress to approve separate blocks of funds in order to make goals and plans realistic. The magnitude of these demands might very well be double what is now being spent in the urban areas, or an additional $35 or 40 billion annually. For example, the preliminary comprehensive plan in Dorchester (a district within Boston of about 130,000 residents) projects a minimum expenditure of $50 million annually for the 10 years from 1973 to 1983, exclusive of housing mortgages.[7] This can be effectively multiplied 700 to 800 times in the United States, taking into account large and small areas of need. We know that under Model Cities the commitment of funds never approached the threshold necessary to cope with the extent of the problem. Proposed funding under block grants does not either; therefore, special purpose grants and different formulas will most likely emerge. This will be especially true if Congress demands that the cities and counties prepare realistic applications and that evaluations be sufficiently stringent to enable the federal government to initiate penalties and enforce compliance.

Under conditions where local officials demonstrate adequate performance, the federal government and the taxpayer will be more likely to pass on the vast amounts of money needed to solve the urban crisis. Performance will not necessarily improve merely by giving local officials greater discretionary authority, even though allowing the city to devise its own process of implementation is a good idea. Strengthening the chief executive through the devices already discussed and designing policy and information systems that make city councils cooperative partners, not antagonists, are important. Setting up a "talent bank" on the scale, for example, used to recruit the best skills available for the nation's aerospace programs is needed for the cities. And further, consideration ought to be given to sending teams of experts (both government and private) into cities for long periods of time (two or three years or longer) to solve special problems and complete troubled projects, and then pass on to other cities.

The nation cannot afford to let even one city fail. On the other hand the withholding of assistance will be necessary to secure compliance in many cases, even if only temporarily. The fears of government leaders (and GAO monitors) are real in regard to nonperformance, political interference, and favoritism. The way that we can face up to matters of performance and reaching goals is to bring them to public attention and then concentrate full efforts on achieving them. Community participation, management capacity, and new organizational techniques are all necessary elements for improving performance. However, in the past, many of the deficiences found in Model Cities and other community development programs have been generated by feelings of failure and lack of national purpose and general public interest. This need to be changed.

There are many local and federal leaders who feel confident about the nation's technical ability to solve the urban crisis. Assuredly, the problems are complex—full employment, crime reduction, meeting housing needs, gaining community support, and so on. Nevertheless, the only way they will be solved is by focusing leadership on the problems and persistently trying alternative solutions. In short, there needs to be a national pledge to reach goals, a willingness to accept failures, make corrections, and move ahead again, regardless of the differences in political styles and governmental processes. As yet we have not made the necessary commitments, either in purpose or resources. Model Cities provided initial momentum in small geographic areas. This could very well dissolve away, and the investment with it, if we fail to appreciate the significance of the Model Cities experiment.

Notes

1. U.S. Senate, Banking, Housing and Urban Affairs Committee, Subcommittee on Housing and Urban Affairs, statement by Hugh McKinley on behalf of International City Management Association, July 19, 1973.

2. U.S. Department of Housing and Urban Development, "Planned Variations First Year Survey," Community Development Evaluation Series No. 7, (Washington, D.C.: October 1972), pp. 1-58.

3. Most of the above major points of discussion were derived from John Maguire, director, National Association of Housing and Redevelopment Officials Information Center for Community Development, "Better Communities Act—HR 7277," Journal of Housing, 5 (May 1973): 222-223.

4. U.S. National Commission on Urban Problems, Building the American City (New York: Praeger Publishers, 1969) Table 8, pp. 14-18.

5. Richard T. LeGates and Mary C. Morgan, "The Perils of Special Revenue Sharing for Community Development," Journal of the American Institute of Planners 39, 4 (July 1973): 257-258.

6. Senate Bill S. 3248, Housing and Urban Development Act of 1972, passed March 2, 1972, Sec. 307(a) (3) (c), pp. 151-152.

7. Dorchester Area Planning Action Council, Doris Graham, executive director, Dorchester Comprehensive Community Project, January 24, 1973.

THE INDIVIDUAL APPROACHES
OF SIX CITIES

The City

Seattle is a boom town in trouble. She enjoys prominence as the industrial, commercial, and shipping center of the Northwest. The University of Washington is located here. The city's general education levels are above the national average, and the cultural facilities of the 1962 International Exposition are available to all residents. Since the city is situated between Puget Sound, Lake Washington, the Cascades, and the rain forests of the Olympic Peninsula, scenic beauty is another Seattle asset, one that the citizens go to great lengths to protect.

But with all her cultural and scenic riches, the city has severe problems. Her economic base is crumbling. She had 530,831 people (7 percent black) in 1970, a decline of 27,000 from 1960. King County had a 1970 population of 1,067,216 (4 percent black). In Seattle, the aerospace industry laid off 5,000 people per month in 1970 and averaged 1,000 layoffs per month throughout 1971. In 1972, official unemployment figures reached 13 percent, with unofficial estimates going to 18 percent and as much as 28 percent in the Model Cities area. (It was less than 2 percent over-all in 1969.) From 1968 to 1970 the case load for Aid to Families with Dependent Children increased from 8,000 to 16,000. With the defeat of the SST (supersonic passenger carrier) in Congress, her economic and employment status worsened. Applicants now total more than 100 for some city government jobs that used to attract five or ten. Apartment vacancies are as high as 30 percent in some residential areas, particularly where many aeronautical engineers used to live (although there is still overcrowding in the Model Cities area). And the city-owned electric-power and water companies report an unprecedented number of service shut-offs because of failure to pay bills—in a city whose utility rates are among the lowest in the nation.

Other events have hurt the city. The police department was shaken by accusations, resignations, and firings triggered by a federal grand jury investigation of organized crime and racketeering. And in May 1970 voters rejected the second Forward Thrust (a countywide private funding and planning organization described below) principal recommendations for a package of bond issues, including rapid transit and a domed, multipurpose stadium near the downtown.

Despite these setbacks, Seattle has sold herself on manageability. She has been able to maintain a balanced budget despite adverse economic conditions, but only with severe cuts in 1972. The property tax is relatively low compared to other big cities, kept down by the sales tax and other state aid. The city still lays claim to forward-looking leadership. Mayor Wes Uhlman is earning a reputation as a progressive leader, although he is criticized in Seattle for his many out-of-town trips and has drawn hostility from the Nixon Administration. Jim Ellis, a businessman, was the force behind Forward Thrust. But even the leaders find it takes ingenuity just to provide general services. It is in this setting that the Model Cities Program is placed. It, like many other aspects of the city, is recognized as a well-managed program. And, like other aspects of the city, it is going through changes that should be examined.

The Government and Power Structure

The Government

Mayor and City Council. A few years ago the City of Seattle switched from a weak-mayor/strong-council to a strong-mayor/strong-council system, which has resulted in a near impasse between the mayor and council because of their different philosophies and approaches to solving problems. The previous mayor had developed excellent rapport with the city council, primarily because he was a former city councilman and head of the important finance committee. But both mayors have strengthened the office. And organizational changes, such as transfer of the budget function from the council to the mayor's office, have reinforced it. The mayor now appoints the city planner; previously this responsibility belonged to the Planning Commission. The comptroller and treasurer are still elected, a drain on mayoral strength. The power of the mayor, as in most cities, tends to be technically not socially oriented—education, welfare, and manpower do not fall directly under his control. So it is more difficult to coordinate and to develop unified plans that might benefit the area as a unit. The nine-member city council chooses its own president, who is then legal successor to the mayor. Councilmanic positions are full time, and there tends to be little turnover. Councilmen are elected at large, are paid $21,000 a year, and meet daily. In the last election, two liberals were elected to the council largely due to efforts of a young, aggressive group formed a few years ago, called Committee to Elect an Effective City Council (CEECC).

In 1971-72, the county also changed its governmental structure, going from a county commissioner system to a strong-county-executive/strong-county-council system. Here, too, there have been a number of impasses, but most of the time the new system has been effective. The county executive is a Republican and the mayor a Democrat, a situation that causes some difficulties between these two levels; but Seattle is full of political "mavericks" who very often vote across party lines.

Departmental Organization

The Department of Community Development was in existence when Uhlman took office. It consolidates the functions of social and physical planning and provides liaison between the city and neighborhood groups. Uhlman is attempting to reorganize some departments and has asked for a referendum on charter amendments that would abolish the office of city comptroller and create a finance department directly responsible to the mayor; establish a general service administration, combining building and code enforcement departments; and develop a department of transportation in place of the transit commission. The mayor believes too many services have been compartmentalized as a reaction to political corruption in the early 1900s, and that now city government must update its own delivery system to fit more properly federal programing.

There are 10 professionals in the mayor's office. Each of two deputy mayors are in charge of either the "foreign office" or the "internal office." The former deals with the county, Council of Governments (COG), the state, and the federal government. Its programs involve rapid transit, urban renewal, housing, and press relations. The internal office consists of 20 department heads who deal with the other city functions. Since the conception of Planned Variations in the fall of 1971, a Policy Planning Committee has been created to develop plans and effect citywide coordination of departments and agencies. A policy-planning cabinet, composed of key agency heads, is the focal point now for planning and policy development. The city structure is shown in Chart 1.

The Seattle Model Cities Program (SMCP) is directed from the mayor's office. For this purpose, the mayor uses a policy coordinating team consisting of one of his special assistants, the director of the Department of Community Development, and the Model Cities director. The latter reports directly to the mayor.

89

CHART 1

Organization Chart, City of Seattle

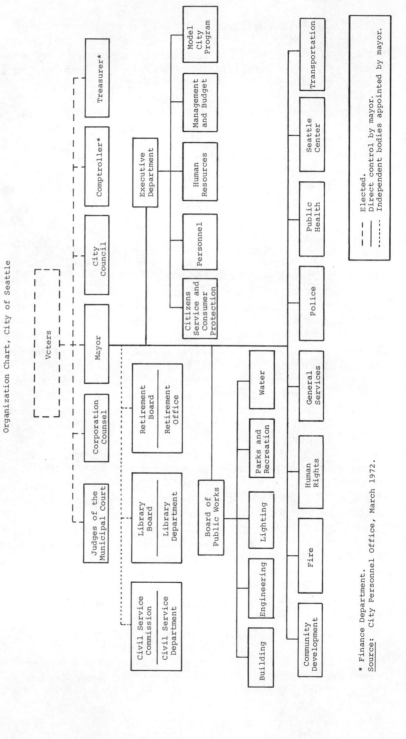

* Finance Department.
Source: City Personnel Office, March 1972.

90

A successful organizational innovation is the use of management teams. The Department of Community Development uses teams for special projects that can be moved rapidly from planning to implementation. A team consists of members from several divisions or departments and the captain of the team changes as the project progresses into each stage, that is, planning, programing, development, and so on. The captain may be on contract if special skills are required. And projects can be generated by the mayor, city council, citizen groups, or a city department. Members of the team still report directly to their division heads, but the captain is given maximum latitude and independence in direction of the team. The city feels the management team approach has been extremely successful in improving the capacity of local government to do its job and in assisting Model Cities in many of its programs.

Power Structure

Business and Unions. The power structure, outside of government, consists primarily of the Central Association, downtown big business. This group lost politically to Mayor Uhlman but is still powerful. Unions are a second strong element of the power structure, as Seattle has historically been a strong union town.

Forward Thrust. To some degree Forward Thrust has become a third element of power. Started in 1966 under the leadership of James Ellis, Forward Thrust is an association of business and civic people from the city and county who seek to achieve organized civic improvements. Over its life span, it has received $529,000 in private contributions from more than 1,000 businesses and individuals. Although not all of its proposals have been realized, it has compiled an impressive record:
    1. It helped get 20 measures passed during three legislative sessions for such things as highways, public transit, water pollution control, and strengthened city and county finances.
    2. It helped pass seven major bond issues for the city and county totaling $333.9 million and two state bond issues for $65 million for parks and open space, water pollution, neighborhood playgrounds, tennis courts, golf courses, the zoo, aquarium, boat ramps, tree planting, 14 Seattle fire stations and equipment, street widening and paving, alley paving, curbs and sidewalks, street lighting, sanitary sewers and separation of combined services, underground wiring, airport improvements, and a number of other capital improvement items.
    3. It developed the first comprehensive joint capital planning for King County and its cities, established design commissions and an Urban Arterial Board, and started public reporting of bond expenditures.

4. It developed a countywide credit system to finance planned improvements (inside or outside cities), convinced legislators to reserve city borrowing capacities for local needs, got state funds applied to mass transit and urban arterials (one-half of Seattle's operating deficit is met by the state), helped to increase county and city debt capacity to 10 percent of assessed valuation, helped establish the office of county executive to Metro Council, and helped pass legislation for revenue sharing for localities (Seattle receives about $10 million annually from the state).

It has also pushed human development projects. However, its prize human resource program has so far failed to gain approval of the voters—a system of 25 community centers, a regional center and library facilities tailored to meet community needs as "defined by residents of each community to prevent personal isolation and loss of identity of communities." Services would include recreation, meeting room, arts, day-care, counseling, adult education, health, foster care, employment counseling, legal aid, senior citizen projects, and other local, state, and federal assistance programs.

Forward Thrust itself represents an areawide approach to improved community services. Some feel it should be directly linked to Model Cities and that Seattle Model Cities cannot hope to succeed without such citizen involvement. Solving fundamental problems that affect the entire city and the participation of all residents in their solution appear essential to the success of Model Cities.

Urban Renewal

The city has had some successful federal-city ventures as well. One example is the rather successful urban renewal project (in an area that was plagued with deterioration, dust, and floods) called the South Seattle Project, which has produced a 1,300 percent increase in jobs in the area and is now an attractive industrial park. Annual tax revenues have gone up in the area 322 percent—from $55,000 to $245,000—and private investment came to $9 for every $1 of city expenditure. More than 2,000 employees work in the 78-acre area, where only 140 persons were formerly employed.

Four other projects are under development, including a residential renewal project in central city, a 37-acre project to provide additional land for the University of Washington, 110 acres of residential rehabilitation in various stages of development, and the Pike Plaza Project, which will rehabilitate an existing farmers' market and provide sites for office and apartment buildings on the edge of the central business district.

Model Cities

Background

Long before her general employment problem arose, Seattle took the initiative in solving some of the special, chronic problems hurting her growth. She started planning for Model Cities in autumn 1966. And in April 1969, the city council approved Mayor J. D. Braman's 200-page document requesting $375,000 of federal Model Cities funds. Edward J. Devine of the mayor's office (later deputy mayor) headed the planning. Citizen participation started after the planning grant was received, and the first grass-roots planning meeting was held November 22, 1967 at the Mount Zion Baptist Church Community Hall (a black church in the inner city), with more than 200 organizations invited. About 350 central area residents (evenly divided between blacks and whites) met, with some discord from black power militants. Over the next several months, blacks expressed objections that the Model Cities Program was being misrepresented, that Braman had the last say, and that it should be the voters who have final authority. A new organizational structure was developed. HUD asked for revisions, and finally agreement was reached.

Governor Dan Evans named six principal Washington State officials (from Employment Security, Public Assistance, State Planning, state OEO, and two from Evan's personal staff) to assist Seattle in its efforts with the federal government. And black attorney Charles Johnson was named chairman of a 100-member Model Cities Citizen Advisory Council. Johnson, now a municipal court judge, was formerly an official of the local NAACP and is a personal friend of Walter Hundley, who was appointed Model Cities director by Braman in December 1967. The council and its numerous task forces continued meeting three nights a week throughout the entire year. Specialists from the University of Washington (mostly the Graduate School of Social Work) helped.

The federal government rated the completed 335-page plan the "best in the Nation," and it was approved November 21, 1968. The plan listed 29 first-year projects costing $57.5 million. And the program's slogan, inspired by the birdlike shape of the target area, was "Make It Fly."

In the same month, the Model Cities Task Force on Education agreed in principle to a 13-point program to be referred to the Model Cities Advisory Council, which would decentralize control of central area schools. The 13 predominantly black schools of the central area have operated under their own nearly autonomous, community-elected school board for more than a year—perhaps the most successful such experiment in the nation.

During 1969, citizen participation task forces were strengthened. And in April 1969, 1,000 persons voted at mobile polling places for a Model Cities Citizen Health Advisory Board, which was to coordinate local health services. One of its duties would be to decide which 1,000 needy families in the Model Neighborhood would receive free prepaid hospital-medical and dental care with Model Cities funds under a national experiment with Group Health and Blue Cross.

Other federal grants continued to come. Comprehensive health care and programs for the aged were later regarded as national models by federal officials who reviewed them. And Mayor Uhlman disclosed that Seattle would be used as a "model" Model City. On January 4, 1970, the city entered its second action year with 40 projects under way. The third action year started July 1, 1971 and included a $5.2 million Planned Variations Program, and three additional Model Neighborhoods, described below. The fourth action year started in the fall of 1972.

Characteristics of the Model Neighborhood

The original Model Neighborhood consists primarily of the central area of the city, but is gerrymandered to include Pioneer Square (the nation's original Skid Row, called Skid Road here) and the international district, which is primarily Oriental. The largest area encompasses a number of varied problems without becoming the exclusive territory of any particular group. Altogether these three areas border the downtown section on the east and south.

Driving through the Model Neighborhood, a stranger would be hard pressed to find slums. Housing is mostly single family and looks sound. However, many houses have been converted to multifamily dwelling units, and close inspection shows them to be inadequate and unsafe. Their physical appearance is deceptively cheery and masks the same social, economic, and physical problems common to all big cities. The Model Neighborhood is similar to many others in the nation:

Substandard housing—24.0 percent
Incomes under $3,000—17.9 percent
Infant deaths per 1,000—36.0 percent
Unemployment—three times higher than rest of city
Welfare families—3.6 percent
Education—half of heads of household did not finish high school
De facto school segregation is seen in schools whose populations
  range from 45 percent to 95 percent black
School dropout rate—45 percent higher than city average

There are 20 areas in the city defined as poverty districts. The original Model Cities area covers eight of these with a combined population of 38,581, of which about 68 percent are black (these figures may represent some undercounting of black men). The original Model Neighborhood represents 85 percent of the city's black population.

SMCP staff believe that the Model Neighborhood is probably in worse shape than it was in the first year because of the general increase in unemployment. However, the change in the rate of unemployment is less severe than it otherwise would be because fewer Model Neighborhood residents (compared to other areas) worked in the aerospace industry and other firms that were mostly affected by the layoffs and also because many government-funded jobs in the area remain.

Administration of the Agency

Structure. Model Cities administrative structure was changed in the second action year to give the director more administrative help in consolidating functions and to create a Department of Governmental Relations because of the increased need to maintain strong working relationships with all agencies. An Interagency Directors Committee was established in November 1969 to involve agencies more closely in project planning and implementation. Table 5 lists the many agencies and illustrates the complexity involved in the process of coordination and communication.

Other formal coordinating mechanisms during the first two years included the Model Cities-State Interagency Team, the City Interdepartmental Team, the Seattle-King County Economic Opportunity Board (SKCEOB) Liaison, and the Advisory Council Resource Committees.

Involvement of State Government and Other Agencies. State government has been responsive and has developed strong cooperative relationships with local Model Cities officials. For example, SMCP staff and the State Department of Social and Health Services prepared a joint grant application for integrated services to Seattle's Skid Road area. The State Model Cities liaison in the governor's office was instrumental in the award of a federal grant to the State Child Care Coordination Committee for technical assistance to Seattle Model Cities in development of a comprehensive plan for child care. And the Model Cities representative in the State Office of Planning and Community Affairs has assisted in obtaining and classifying information helpful to Seattle. Nevertheless, there is a feeling common to most Model Cities communities in the nation that greater state financial aid is preferable to technical assistance.

In general, agency involvement has been genuine in Seattle's program. As Simpson Lawson pointed out in an article in City

TABLE 5

Member Organizations of Interagency Directors Committee
Seattle Model Cities

American National Red Cross
Atlantic Street Center
Central Area Committee for Peace
and Improvement (CAPI)
Central Area School Council
Central Seattle Community Council
Concentrated Employment Program
(CEP)
Cherry Hill Baptist Church
Community School for Unwed
Mothers
Extended Services Project for
Low-Income Elderly
Family Counseling Service
First Avenue Service Center
Francis House
Harborview Medical Center
Seattle Public Schools Head Start
Program
Seattle Housing Authority (SHA)
Seattle Park Department
Seattle Police Department
Community Psychiatric Clinic
Community Services for the Blind
Council of Planning Affiliates
(COPA)
Council on Aging for Seattle-King
County
Income Maintenance Project
Foster Homes for the Elderly
HUD-Northwest Area Office
Seattle Human Rights Commission
Indian Center
International District Improvement
Association
Seattle Model City Program (SMCP)

Jewish Family and Child Service
Job Therapy, Inc.
Juvenile Court and Youth Service
Center
Seattle-King County Health Depart-
ment
King County Youth Corps
Legal Services Center
Malden Rehabilitation Centers, Inc.
Medina Children's Service
Multi-Service Center
Seattle Neighborhood Youth Corps
Planned Parenthood
OEO Liaison
Pioneer Cooperative
Providence Hospital
SCORE
Family Life Education
Seattle Day Nursery
Seattle Engineering Department
Seattle Mental Health Institute, Inc.
Seattle Public Schools Pupil Personnel
Seattle Urban League
Senior Centers Inc.
Seattle-King County Economic Oppor-
tunity Board, Inc. (SKCEOB)
Seattle Opportunities Industrialization
Center (SOIC)
South Center Day Care
Travelers Aid Society
Urban Affairs Offices
United Good Neighbors (UGN)
Seattle Urban Renewal
Volunteer Bureaus of America
Yesler-Atlantic Urban Renewal
Washington Association for Retarded
Children
Washington State Employment Security
Department

Source: Model Cities Program, City of Seattle, Washington, 1969.

(October-November 1970), ". . . the genius of the Seattle Model Cities program lies less in its geographic makeup and more in its capacity for motivating other agencies and institutions to be responsive to the needs of area residents." Cooperation and coordination with agencies have continued right into the fourth action year, and many local officials believe it has improved with the creation of the State-City Task Force (including county and private groups) and additional funding of agencies to operate programs.

Importance of Competent Directorship. The effectiveness of any program depends on the quality of the director. A mayoral-appointed personnel committee of 10 chose Walter Hundley from among 40 applicants. At the time, he was director of the Central Area Motivation Program, one of Seattle's largest Community Action projects. Before that he was a minister and a director in the Congress of Racial Equality and worked for the State Department of Public Assistance. He has brought considerable administrative skill to the job and firsthand knowledge of the county and local area. And he has been successful in dealing with two different mayors and administrators, although relations are strained between him and Uhlman over program emphasis in the expanded Planned Variations Program. Former deputy mayor Edward J. Devine, of Devine and Associates (a local consulting firm), believes Hundley is both strong and weak; he feels Hundley's consistent competence and soft-spoken leadership have discouraged wider delegation of authority and that overdependence on him has tended to retard leadership development among staff and citizens. From the start, Hundley played a strong role in creating policies and was the chief architect of the final citizen participation structure, a structure reflecting his own philosophy that residents be actively involved but primarily as advisers, helping city councilmen by taking them "off the hook." He fears neighborhood planning encourages narrow self-interests and cites several housing projects as examples. He leans more toward community-wide citizen planning and councils. In short, while Hundley advocates citizen participation, he does not favor a strong level of authority for residents, as experienced in programs in Dayton and Boston, for example.

Recommended Administrative Improvements. Administrative improvements are still being weighed, and some are being put into effect. Devine and Associates, in a May 1971 report to the local CDA, proposed recommendations, some of which follow:[1]

    1. Program planners should be involved with less administrative detail; they should be Program Advocates, working more closely with Citizen Task Forces to improve quality.

2. A central core of planners should be created (separate from Program Advocates) to prepare final plans and to better correlate projects and achieve uniformity.

3. A monitoring function should be established to report on special areas of interest directly to the administrative assistant in the Office of the Director. This would conserve the director's time and pinpoint matters of great concern.

4. Project evaluations should be reviewed by department heads and by a special monitoring team to improve evaluation and better identification of pressing issues.

5. Procedures should be established for review of final applications and plans by appropriate staff, task forces, and others who participated in preparation. This would improve morale, make citizen work more relevant, and contribute to the education and development of people in the program.

6. Each task force should review other programs to broaden understanding of the total program and increase interest and the ability to carry out their own assignments.

7. Incentives and awareness of opportunities for advancement should be strengthened. Educational and training programs, career ladders, and the transfer to regular city and agency jobs should be utilized.

The Devine study believes too many decisions, often petty ones, are made at the highest levels by the director and administrative assistant. It says that the system has excellent leadership but has produced a good deal of disgruntlement at lower and middle staff levels, limiting the ultimate effectiveness of the program; that task forces and citizens do not even have enough information to vote intelligently on issues, while program administrators have free access to information, giving them a natural edge in decision-making capability. In this regard, the impression that decisions are made quite independently of staff seems to be more the product of their being ultimately made without much communication with staff than of their being made without considering staff recommendations.

Though the director makes most decisions in Model Cities, he gets cut out of normal decision-making with city officials because of the special status of the program. Instead of affecting the way services are delivered to the Model Neighborhood as a matter of course, most things must be done on a special basis. On the other hand, Planned Variations, with its city approach, may reduce this tendency to isolate the Model Neighborhood.

In addition to the above comments, Devine Associates feel the comprehensiveness of Model Cities has been worthwhile but has placed too much responsibility on the director—there appears to be more concern with the way the operation fits together as a whole than concern

with whether the services are reaching the people. Yet this comprehensive concern is necessary and has resulted in unusual success in
acquiring federal funds. The director in some ways has been forced
to act like an extension of every concerned regional office, responding
to key questions as they arise, and being sure that federal agencies
have faith that he has everything under control.

In short, the program has developed a personal and informal
approach; for example, the director is known by his first name, and
many staff members have developed their own personal styles. While
"personal style" has achieved some success, it has also contributed
to some of the problems mentioned above: lack of proper delegation
of authority; too much involvement of top management in subordinate
tasks; and confusion over who is supposed to do what and when. Staff
is dedicated to accomplishment, but goals are seen differently by each
member. Moreover, differences must be resolved before the staff
can work together effectively.

On the other hand, the federal government takes a more positive
view of the program when looking at end results. In approving the
third action year plan, HUD observed that it is "one of the best plans
we've seen. . . . The planning holds together, with the different projects and activities supporting each other in a comprehensive and
systematic manner. . . . Seattle Model Cities has been successful in
developing umbrella groups and organizations in aging, child care,
health, law and justice, etc. . . . Coordination, control, management,
and financial systems are generally good. . . . Evaluation activities
have been generally adequate; however, there is a tendency for evaluation reports to be weak in assessing the quality of services and impact
of projects and activities." HUD has approved the fourth action year
as well.

Seattle's program appears to be meeting its goals. It is perfecting coordination and achieving results better than other large
cities. Since much of its success is due to the strong leadership of
the director, second-level management will necessarily have to be
made more effective and responsible, otherwise, the program could
be seriously hurt by a change in this "singular leadership."

Citizen Participation

Sometimes, strong administrative leadership may result in weak
citizen participation. But Seattle has a tradition of doing things for
herself. Forward Thrust is typical of this kind of resident initiative,
and in this respect Model Neighborhood citizens are not much different
from others in the city. Indeed, the model area never suffered from
a lack of organization. The 100 or more organizations that already
existed caused difficulties in creating unity. Yet this high degree of

social awareness and citizen mobilization increased the degree of participation.

Citizens always knew what their role would be. From the beginning, city hall made it clear that it would have final control over the program and made a conscious and constant effort not to oversell the program. Instead of wasting time and energy fighting over roles, residents and city hall concentrated on getting the most out of the functions each was to assume.

Participation Structure. The Citizens Advisory Council has more power than its name suggests. It can create policy, and it can approve plans before submission to the mayor and city council. The 100-member Advisory Council consists of representatives appointed by organizations within the Model Neighborhood and those outside whose concerns are relevant to the area. Hundley states that residents themselves chose this method over elections. And it appealed to the regional HUD office because all elements, including the radical and unorganized, were invited to participate. Board membership is acceptable because it reflects the racial mix of the neighborhood: about 60 percent black, 30 percent Caucasion, 10 percent Oriental, 87 percent Model Neighborhood residents. Officers are also selected to represent the racial composition of the area. The steering committee consists of officers of the Advisory Council and chairmen of task forces.

There are six task forces (similar to general assemblies) representing functions of major concern; they are allocated $5,000 each for expenses and incidentals; and their members receive in-depth training on the governmental system and how citizens can make an impact on services and institutions. A 36-week training course was held in 1971 for 78 members. In conjunction with this, residents were trained and took part in educational workshops. The participation philosophy of Seattle Model Cities is that the program cannot really belong to the people without their complete involvement. Hundley states they are involved throughout all stages of planning but do not sit in on the signing of contracts with agencies. He says any substantive changes recommended at top levels must be brought back to the citizens for approval or modification.

The second action year plan particularly emphasized quality rather than quantity in resident involvement. To do this, it eliminated contracts with community organizers (mostly with the local CAP) and reduced the citizen participation staff. The citizen participation project is now administered by the Model Cities Department of Citizen Participation and a deputy director who reports to the Model Cities director and Citizen's Advisory Council. In the third action year, it expanded into three other neighborhoods, and an areawide citizen structure was created. The fourth action year plan considers the possibility of extending citizen participation citywide.

Funded Citizen Participation Projects. There are a number of citizen participation projects. A brief description of those funded provide valuable insight into the program. Model Cities and other sources of annual funding are shown.

   1. Citizen Participation Project (MC, $220,447). Involves residents in planning, monitoring, and directing public service activities. Citizen task force roles have been refined, and in 1971 the staff established a Task Force Planning Coordinating Committee, which has greatly improved coordination among city planners, citizen staffs, and citizens.

   Under this program, numerous Spanish-Americans have been taught fluent English, and 180 have been enrolled in the Seattle Community College. Several Spanish-speaking residents have been employed in the Model Cities Program, and more Spanish-speaking citizens have become involved with the task forces.

   A Central Seattle Community Council (CSCC) is funded under this project to expand existing community organizations and increase meaningful citizen involvement in the Model Cities process.

   A community organizing committee is composed of representatives from each neighborhood community council and is engaged in developing black leadership. Its priorities have been land use planning and employment. It formed an Employment Coalition, which advocates establishment of food banks and free health clinics, prevention of mortgage foreclosure and utility rate hikes, city purchase of the Seattle Center Food Circus, and declaration of a disaster area in the State of Washington. Because of a difference in methods and emphasis, it has been difficult for Model Cities to support CSCC. Central Council's efforts have been directed toward coalition-building and confrontation, whereas Seattle Model Cities has focused on program planning. Expressing this difference but not discouraging it, Model Cities states, "Issue-oriented activities directed at short-term goals have a specific role in community organization, but are inappropriate for long-term planning because high expectations are developed with few positive problem solutions."

   Model Cities believes CSCC has been instrumental in amplifying issues and expanding the size of community organizations. On the other hand, much work remains to be done to increase the number of low-income persons on existing councils and to develop new community councils where none exist.

   Another citizen group funded by Model Cities is the International District Improvement Association (INTER-IM). It has developed citizen review for land use and a community-funded Drop-In Center for the elderly and has obtained involvement of some highly skilled community-minded individuals. In 1971, it received an award from the Seattle Municipal League for outstanding achievement in community organization.

2. <u>Leschi NDP-Project Area Council</u> (MC, $48,000). Involves residents in a redevelopment program, which has gotten approval for underground street wiring and a number of other local improvements.

3. <u>Citizen Trainees</u> (MC, $3,000; other, $71,000). Prepares residents for informal decision-making through formal training and allows them to monitor over 32 Model Cities projects.

These funded projects are designed particularly to make task forces more effective but have not yet been fully successful.

<u>Citizen Participation in Welfare Programing</u>. One analysis prepared for the CDA explains that citizen participation in welfare programs is grossly inadequate.[2] It states that participation is "surely in need of redesign and repair. Citizens participating in the (welfare) task force are relatively few in number, and, although they are clearly dedicated to the program, they are better described as meeting-goers than representatives of the numerous communities that make up the Model Neighborhood." The report says that members are outside the decision-making process, and even their monitoring role is largely dictated to them. Attendance is low, and some participants are motivated more by the fee ($10 for two meetings per month) and babysitting expenses than by interest in improving the program. The task force has been divorced from the divisions of planning, program review, and funding. Some projects have been terminated without task force approval or knowledge. The report indicates that the problem is not that the task force is paid but that it is paid to do things that have ultimately not affected the program, and communication between staff and citizens is poor. It further states:

> Another factor affecting not only the task force but every aspect of the program is the blind identification of Model Cities' programs with the black community, sometimes to the extent of focusing on that one community need to the detriment of others. <u>The task force membership reflects disproportionately many blacks to their current proportion of the Model Neighborhood's population—just under 60 percent</u>. The role played by the task force is clearly affected. It has questioned the Comprehensive Services for the Elderly project on whether it is serving enough blacks despite the finding of Model Cities own survey that less than 10 percent of the Model Neighborhood's needy elderly population is black, and the program's caseload is over 40 percent black. More basically, the viewpoints and needs of non-black communities cannot get fair representation without broader participation.

Further Evaluation of Citizen Participation. Another report completed in April 1971 by Pro Bono Publico, a local consulting firm, reviewed Seattle Model Cities citizen participation.[3] Assessing the difference between Community Action and Model Cities citizen involvement, it said that the assumption of many in the poverty program was that institutions had to change to be more responsive to the poor, but that the assumption in Model Cities is that people have to change to take their places on boards that govern those institutions. A review of Pro Bono Publico's principal conclusions follows:

1. Participation will be believable to people when it can result in new projects and different divisions. It must reach a point where it will be self-operating and self-perpetuating.

2. Task force members have little influence, which has led to cynicism and resentment. Attendance is poor. And few return because usually the issue that brought them to the meeting is not discussed or the meeting is dominated by several spokesmen. There is little planning and decision-making. And task forces are not representative of the community. There are few middle class, young, Oriental, American Indian, or Spanish-speaking. For many attendees, their relationship approaches that of a "client." And little organization and assistance is given task forces. (To improve task force effectiveness, Devine and Associates recommended in May 1971 that the task forces be given the responsibility for collecting hard data in the Model Neighborhood and that some of the paid interviewer jobs be given to task force members, in order to increase their interest and contribution to the program.)

3. The link between task forces and the Model Cities Advisory Council is so weak that the council is unable to play its coordinating role. (Devine and Associates recommend that at least two members from each task force attend Advisory Council meetings to improve communication.) The Advisory Council appears not to share any responsibility for the ultimate decision to fund a project. This decision is made almost unilaterally by Model Cities staff. The council is not representative of the community, in part because of the way it originated and because it has no methods to attract "new blood." The council and the task forces represent divergent but equally narrow constituencies.

Model Cities citizen involvement should be institutionalized. More and better public information is needed. Training should be increased. The link between task forces and the Advisory Council should be strengthened. This might be done by electing the task force members. And task forces should meet as a whole only once every two or three months. The Central Seattle Community Council and similar groups should be encouraged to increase their involvement.

4. The inability of Model Cities to foster citizen participation or to take a leadership position around important issues has led to alienation in some sectors.

5. Three Model Cities citizen participation projects are providing important and useful services and should be built upon: Equal Opportunity for Spanish-speaking Americans, Central Seattle Community Councils, and Project Area Council.

6. Model Cities planners concerned with citizen participation must develop it with little support. Most planners find it more efficient (especially with project deadlines) not to expend the effort or not to work with small groups of citizens or professionals. Since there is no apparent demand from the Model Cities administration to expend the extra effort, most planners do not.

More Forms of Participation. Perhaps the most successful citizen participation component and the one that gives Model Neighborhood residents the greatest degree of decision-making authority is the Model Cities Land Use Review Board composed of Model Neighborhood residents. The board recommends zoning changes to the city and is guided under a cooperation agreement with the Planning Division of the City of Seattle's Department of Community Development. There is general feeling that "nothing gets done in the Model Neighborhood without the approval of this board." It is an institutional change for which Model Cities can take credit.

Moreover, states Walter Hundley, the mayor and city council will not approve any program that does not originate through the citizen participation structure—and, so far, this has held true. Hundley believes citizen satisfaction might be diminished if residents completely controlled the program because they would have less influence within the system. This middle-ground arrangement between Model Cities and the city council has resulted in at least temporary "institutional change" by providing heretofore unrealized decision-making power in the neighborhood.

In support of this system, Judge Charles Johnson, chairman of the Advisory Council, believes Model Cities citizen participation is probably more effective than that of the local CAP (he served in both) because it has broader representation and is more convincing to the power structure. Its method of choosing members by appointments from neighborhood organizations guarantees representation from welfare mothers and other poor families, whereas, he says, "elections sometimes shut-out these people in favor of a few spokesmen." Johnson believes the Model Cities Council is more representative of the people than even the elected Central Area Schools Council and that it has raised the level of citizen participation in other areas of the city. "The Model Cities structure has given hope to other Seattle communities, as well. It has aroused interest in white areas, where it has been lacking," he says. Nevertheless, CAP disagrees with Model Cities' method of selection, believing elections are the purest and most positive way to legitimize boards and make them effective over the long run.

As important as the question of representation is the authority of the Advisory Council and its task forces. Public defender John Darrah and Gordon Wilcox (of Devine and Associates) believe the council's role should be strengthened, particularly in its responsibility to evaluate and in the definition of task force duties. Wilcox feels the Health Task Force ought to be used as a model for others because of its effectiveness and very specific duties. He states that, in general, task forces wallow in broad policies, receive little monitoring information, and are unaware of Model Cities' impact on other agencies.

Furthermore, citizen participation may be considered in the form of resident employment. About 63 percent of employees in the program are residents of the Model Neighborhood and its fringes. It is generally believed that this involvement has created a safety valve for racial tensions. It has kept many belligerents too busy being productive to "raise hell," and it pays "embarrassingly high" salaries so that "they can barely afford to be militant."

In brief, Model Cities citizen participation has been healthy for Seattle. It has developed new leadership, made citizens more productive, and created a more positive understanding of government and city officials. Much of policy initiation stems from top administrative leaders, but residents at least have more voice than they ever had before. More effective task force deliberation, more interest in programs, and improved communication would accelerate participation.

Model Cities Programs

The programs listed below are placed into 12 broad categories—manpower and job development; recreation and culture; health; crime and delinquency; social services; education; economic and business development; housing; transportation and communication; relocation; community facilities; and environmental protection and development—and are described over three years of progress, continuing into the fall of 1972. However, the major emphasis is on the first two years of performance, when more finalized figures were available. The amount of funding from Model Cities and other sources is shown for the third action year (except when programs were funded only for earlier years) and is not an attempt to give a full picture of finances, but rather to give the reader an idea of the level of money needed to operate various kinds of programs. (In descriptions of programs for some of the cities in other case studies, funding amounts may be omitted for ease of reporting or because money allocations may not contribute to the discussion.)

Manpower and Job Development

1. Employment Unicenter (MC, $63,000). A one-stop delivery system for all job-related services. The Employment Unicenter is considered by Hundley and other Model Cities officials as an important success and certainly the beginning of much-needed coordination of manpower programs. It brings together many programs under one roof so the job hunter need visit only one location. A joint board of state, city, and Model Neighborhood representatives is responsible for the center. The board is composed of two Model Neighborhood residents elected from the Model Cities Employment Task Force (who are extremely vocal and contribute a great deal to the program) and a representative from each of six state agencies and four city agencies.

The program consists of finding jobs, coaching, orientation, placement, counseling, training and vocational rehabilitation, and welfare assistance (food stamps, child care, medical care, financial assistance, and homemaker services). All participants must reside in the Concentrated Employment Program (CEP) area (which includes all of the Model Neighborhood). CEP is the main intake vehicle; the coordinating staff is composed of seven professionals; and each participating agency contributes to cover costs.

Seattle CDA admitted in July 1971 that "the project has not yet been as effective as anticipated in coordinating programs. There have been problems in developing a unified management information system, and the absence of a Minority Skill Bank makes it difficult to recruit minority workers. . . . The most crucial difficulty is the lack of a single strong administrative structure . . . and agencies are hesitant to relinquish their autonomy for the benefit of the total concept of a unified system."[4] The staff felt the following was needed: a more effective team approach in providing service; a single administrator with authority over all agencies in each center; operational procedures based on function rather than on agency responsibility; common referral forms; enrollee follow-up questionnaires to evaluate the program; and a Manpower Health Service Plan to provide readily available health services to improve chances of employment. Radio spot announcements and other forms of advertising were increased to improve participation.

An August 1971 report by Booz-Allen and Hamilton consultants analyzed the control elements and problems of Unicenter's development. It concluded that state and local dissatisfaction with manpower services was a major impetus to the center's creation and that citizen participation in its planning set the stage for detailed development. A summary of findings and problems is listed below.

Findings:

1. Active support of major state and local political officials ensures the participation of key manpower agencies.
2. The city-state compact was general enough to give the Joint Board flexibility to deal with unforeseen problems in developing and operating the Unicenter. (The compact was the basis for inter-agency cooperation.) In addition, the compact provided for Joint Board composition that balanced the interests of state and local agencies as well as community residents. Lack of precision reduced conflict between potential participants and hastened establishment of the Unicenter.
3. Federal agency support is necessary to establishment of the Unicenter. Since most Unicenter programs involve federal funds, federal approval is necessary to combine these programs at the local level.
4. A full-time staff is needed to assist the Joint Board with its management activities. If adequate staff support is unavailable, the Joint Board will become overly involved in dealing with day-to-day operational problems.

Major problems:

1. The Joint Board must exercise its authority to review, approve, and coordinate all manpower programs affecting central Seattle. (To date, the board has not exercised its authority.)
2. Participating agency representatives must have the authority to commit their agencies to courses of action chosen by the Joint Board. Reduction in the individual authority of Joint Board members has resulted in the following:
   a. Agency representatives being more committed to maintenance of internal agency guidelines and regulations than Joint Board activities.
   b. A reduction in the effectiveness of the Joint Board as a policy-making body.
3. The Joint Board cannot provide detailed management of all Unicenter activities. Absence of either an over-all manager or established executive within the operating components has slowed integration of participating programs and reduced Unicenter morale. At a minimum, executive authority within each operating component must be firmly established. (The board was formed because agencies were unwilling to relinquish authority to an over-all manager.)[5]

2. City Job Trainee Project (MC, $218,860; other, $1,140). Work study program to achieve proportionate representation of Model Neighborhood residents in career priorities in city government. Out of 92

107

trainees, 70 are Model Neighborhood residents. Trainees are included on the project advisory committee, and all trainees are offered up to 20 hours per week of formal education or special tutoring. Twenty office workers have passed qualifying examinations for higher (parent) positions, and a few have been placed. The project convinced the City Civil Service Commission to delete the question "Have you ever been arrested or charged with a crime?" but retain the question "Have you ever been convicted of a crime?" in all job applications.

In addition to the efforts of this project, many government jobs have been generated by Model Cities. Model Neighborhood residents hold 1,132 jobs. Approximately 63 percent of the staff are residents of the model area or fringe, and 58 percent are black, 35 percent white, and 7 percent Oriental and other—which roughly reflects the composition of the Model Neighborhood.

In order to get Model Neighborhood residents hired in substantial numbers, Hundley believes that Model Cities has to stay away from civil service. He hires most staff himself upon recommendations from related task forces. Now, after several years of operation, he feels it is advantageous for staff to be incorporated into the city's personnel system in order to add security to Model Cities employment. (Presently, 99 percent of city employees are under civil service protection.) Recently, 10 Model Cities trainees were appointed to regular civil service positions. With renewed emphasis on minority hiring in city jobs, the project has increased leverage; however, there is continued difficulty with the Police Department, which has downgraded the Police Trainee project component.

3. Technical, Organizational, Professional Intern Training (TOP-IT) (MC, $67,860; other, $1,140). On-the-job and academic training to open lower and middle management positions to the underemployed. A cooperative agreement has been reached with school officials for academic training, about 14 interns have been placed in the private sector, and a few bank management trainee slots have opened. Early in 1971 the program was far behind its projected achievements, but it picked up substantially in the first quarter of 1972 to exceed its placement rate by 25 percent.

4. Handicapped Skills Center (MC, $48,906; other $94). A sheltered industrial workshop to train disadvantaged and socially handicapped persons in social and job skills. Expectations have not been reached. Only 15 of an expected 30 trainees are enrolled. Lack of success is blamed on inadequate funding primarily for equipment and supplies. However, a recent agreement with Western Electric Company of Sunnyvale, California and a possible subcontract with Boeing should improve the prospects of success and bring the project closer to a self-supporting position. A contract is also pending with the Air Force for plant maintenance and security. Handicapped skills projects

take long and difficult negotiation in the search for potential jobs, compared with less disadvantaged trainee projects.

5. Construction Contract Compliance (MC, $45,000; other, $7,680). Enforcement of a city ordinance requiring proportionate minority representation on all city construction projects. The project placed 145 minority workers in jobs in the construction industry in the spring quarter of 1971 and succeeded in getting 17.5 percent minority workers (454 persons) in construction jobs by the first quarter of 1972. A major accomplishment was the gaining of approval of the Seattle Board of Workers to allow the project staff to hold pre-award conferences with contractors bidding on city jobs. In the past, conferences were held after the contract was awarded. This meant that subcontracts were let and crews already hired, making it difficult to enforce minority hiring. The project approved 39 contracts through preaward conferences and recommended that four contracts not be awarded. Moreover, the Human Rights Department has been successful with the Board of Public Works in denying contracts for past noncompliance with the city's affirmative action program. The project's authority has been extended to include contract compliance on the 1-90 highway project. The staff is also working with other agencies to draft a more affirmative and viable ordinance for city adoption.

6. Intern Project (MC, $206,000). Work/study and scholarship program to aid Model Neighborhood college students and enhance the Model Neighborhood pool of managerial and governmental expertise. The project Scholarship Committee awarded a total of 123 scholarships. The deputy director worked in conjunction with the State Office of Planning and Community Affairs, Seattle University, and HUD in setting up a "university without walls" program for Model Cities employees— designed to provide BA and MA degrees at Seattle University. Thirty-two employees are in the program.

7. Construction Industry Development (MC, $458,718; other, $4,000). Management, technical, bonding, and loan assistance to minority contractors. On April 16, 1971, this project was temporarily suspended because of a boycott by the Central Contractors Association, which resulted in total project shutdown. The project was later revived. It has secured bonding of joint ventures and contract awards for minority contractors; financed 12 contractors by supporting bank loans; supports a $748,000 performance bond for Scott Electric; supports other Model Neighborhood contractors with bonds or letters of credit; and has made capital work loans of $121,500. Also, the major minority general contractors in Seattle have been assured a position on a select bid list for Operation Breakthrough's city site. This should produce a black or minority general contractor bonded for $1 million in the Model Neighborhood. Since there have been performance problems with the original project operator, the entire program is being reorganized to make it more effective and responsive.

Recreation and Culture.

   1. Yesler Neighborhood Facility (MC, $283,000; other, $605,
000). Remodeling of a former synagogue to provide 18,000 square
feet of space for a variety of social and cultural events. Construction
has been completed and agreements for operation have been finalized.
   2. Performing Arts (MC, $71,287). Outlet for the works of
African and Afro-American artists and dramatists. Theater per-
formances and workshops have been held, as well as a highly successful group showing of painting and sculpture by seven Model Neighborhood artists. Typical center monthly audience attendance totals in
1971 were as follows: April—2,446; May—3,450; June—131. The
Seattle Times (April 18, 1972) praised a recent production, Ace Bom
Coon, and indicated that the drama group has come a long way from
its orginal "amateurish" productions to more refined, sophisticated,
quality work. The project director is engaged in a pilot program for
a curriculum in Black Fine Arts Administration at Albany State College, Georgia. A grant proposal has been submitted to the Ford
Foundation for additional programs.
   3. House of Art (MC, $52,000; other, $15,000). Opportunities
for Model Neighborhood residents of all ages and ranges of ability
to express themselves via arts and crafts. This project never got
off the drawing board, but a new project, Multi-ethnics Arts and
Culture Coordination, will carry out some of the program objectives.
   4. Model Neighborhood Camp Facility (MC, $215,000; other,
$170,000). Facilities to be used by Model Neighborhood youth for
swimming, fishing, arts and crafts, and other outdoor activities.
Construction will cost about $97,000 and will include renovation of a
bunkhouse, landscaping, and converting a swimming pool for year-
round use.
   5. Youth Services (MC, $212,000). Comprehensive planning
and administration of youth-serving projects in the Model Neighborhood. The Mayor's Youth Consortium, the primary mechanism for
project coordination, has not been effective. A workshop was held
that did result in the formation of a youth worker association. Some
activities include Seattle Boys' Club in the Model Neighborhood;
United Inner-City Development Association, which has designed a
Youth-in-Business program, patterned after Junior Achievement;
The Anchor, which has been successful in consolidating activities of
drop-in centers; Filipino Youth, which has had partial success but
has not served many disadvantaged youth; Girls' Club, which serves
many young people of the Model Neighborhood; Talented Youth in the
Arts, which has been providing services to many more youth than
contracted for, especially in the field of music; Work/Study Program,
which has been a success in getting many youth placed in jobs in a

short period of time; Black Arts/West, which served 100 youth when school was in session; Black Professional Artists Program, which successfully sought out black talent; Friendly Town, a successful cultural exchange program whereby youth experienced living in different types of communities; First AME Youth Activity Center, an unsuccessful attempt to have a general program activity center; YMCA Youth Action, which serves about 25 boys a month, average age around 13, who have been given up by other agencies (works closely with the juvenile court); Swimming/Water Safety Education project, administered by the Eastside YMCA and staffed wholly by Model Neighborhood residents. A cumulative total of 5,115 Model Neighborhood youth have been served. Two hundred fifty-eight housewives have participated in the swim and trim program and baby-sitting services for low-income mothers.

Health

Of all the major components, health is perhaps the most effective administratively. Institutional change has come about through innovations in the programs of community mental health, alcoholism, neighborhood health centers, and the Health Advisory Board (community board). The board combines professionals and citizens and consists of five Model Cities Health Task Force members, five health professionals, and five members appointed by the mayor from a list submitted by Model Cities.

1. Prepaid Medical Program (MC, $205,000; other, $1,374,231). Medical coverage for low-income families, comparable to that provided by standard health insurance programs. Total enrollment is 1,350 families. Transportation to clinics and child care services are provided to those eligible. In addition, the Community Health Board, Inc. is developing a comprehensive system of health care.

2. Odessa Brown Health Station (MC, $270,829). Complete medical and dental services for Model Neighborhood children from poverty families. The project has been limited by its small budget and increased service demands brought about by the sagging economy, but staff is working out ways to use volunteer medical and dental help. Quarterly visits have reached 1,572. A major accomplishment was approval by HEW of a mobile dental component. The staff treats about 123 dental patients a month, representing 213 visits. The oral health education program was particularly successful in the McGilvra School where there has been a 20 percent improvement in oral hygiene. The project employs 23, of whom 14 are Model Neighborhood residents.

3. Community Mental Health Center (MC, $200,000; other $716, 969). Community-based treatment, detection, and prevention of mental illness. Day-care (partial hospitalization) services are provided.

111

Community consultation hours and the number of individual participants in this program continue to increase. Approximately 5,700 contacts are made in a month, and there are 35 volunteers. A major walk-in clinic operating 13 hours a day is available, as well as a resident psychiatric doctor. Ambulatory care is equivalent to 15,000 annual visits. Plans are under way for services to the Asian community of the Beacon Hill Area and to the city jail, and primary prevention services are being developed in cooperation with the school board to treat 2,000 children in eight elementary schools.

4. Herzl Neighborhood Facility (MC, $292,000). Remodeling of a former synagogue to house the Model Cities prepaid health program, Environmental Health Project, and adult health services of the county health department. This facility is nearly ready.

5. Pioneer Square Health Station (MC, $195,681; other, $21,000). Outpatient medical and supportive services designed for the special needs of low-income residents of Skid Road area, including a program for detoxification of alcoholics. This project has had a history of setbacks but is now in operation. A project director and a project administrator have been hired, a facility has been leased, equipment has been requisitioned, and other personnel are being hired. An Alcoholic Screening and Detoxification-Indigent Alcoholics Program (MC, $98,750; other $453,770) is also operating in conjunction with this project.

Crime and Delinquency

1. Community Service Officers Program (MC, $442,941). Recruitment and training of Model Neighborhood residents to increase their representation on the police force and in educational and assistance roles. The unarmed officers, wearing uniforms to distinguish them from regular officers, perform duties such as inspecting streets and alleys for safety and health hazards, assisting motorists, working with youth, and aiding the sick and injured. The program proposes to hire 35 community service officers, but only 11 were hired because of the uncertainty of future funding. These officers have performed primarily as inspectors, without much input into the police process itself.

2. Group Homes (MC, $213,180; other $337,228). Alternative living arrangements, with counseling and therapy, for dependent and delinquent teenagers in conflict with their families. Two homes have been purchased; most activity so far consists of staff training and readying facilities. A contract between the State Law and Justice Planning Office and City of Seattle was signed for $213,486 in Law Enforcement Assistance Administration (LEAA) funds.

3. Public Defender Program (MC, $198,180; other, $407,131).
Free legal assistance and detention services to indigent defendents in
criminal cases. About 325 persons charged with misdemeanors and
juvenile offenses are assisted each month, with services ranging from
jail interviews to trials. A recent local evaluation noted that judges
have been favorably impressed with the courtroom performance of
public defender attorneys and that approximately one-fourth to one-
third of misdemeanor cases litigated by staff attorneys were won.
Program cost per trial is about $143. However, when considering
the number of cases that did not go to trial but that required preliminary research and the additional work of the juvenile section, the
program's true cost per misdemeanor case is closer to $100, an
economically effective figure.

The Public Defender program represents institutional change
because it has created a basic service that did not exist previously
in Seattle-King County. It also demonstrates a new level of cooperation between the county and city (each contributes a portion of the
budget), and new relationships between citizens and lawyers. The
program is administered by the Defender Association, a nonprofit
corporation. The board consists of five Model Neighborhood residents
(members of the Model Cities Law and Justice Task Force), five
lawyers, and five members appointed by the mayor from a list provided by Model Cities.

Public Defender Executive Director John Darrah reports directly
to the board, and the Model Cities Law and Justice Task Force is kept
informed by progress reports, fiscal accounting, and minutes of board
meetings. The client work load is about 55 percent county and 45
percent city. Before this program, the county used to have about 45,000
cases each year in which legal counsel was needed but not provided.
Now the program helps at least some of the most needy clients and
is considered highly successful by most local government officials.
Darrah feels the major improvement could come with more frequent
evaluation by the board, task force, and outside teams.

Besides defending clients, the program has engaged in some
substantive matters. One is the appellate/law reform program.
Although not extensive in scope, it has had important results. In this
matter, the Public Defender appeared as amicus curiae in the case of
State ex rel. Wallin v. Noe, in which the State Supreme Court ruled
unconstitutional the municipal court practice of requiring that defendants in traffic court post bail in order to secure a trial on traffic
charges. In another case, Seattle v. Alexander, the Public Defender
office successfully persuaded the State Supreme Court to rule that
the Seattle "disorderly conduct" ordinance was unconstitutional as
applied and enforced by city police and prosecutors in tens of thousands of cases since the 1930s. This case may have major long-range

impact on the municipal court case load. Furthermore, a comprehensive law reform plan has been prepared, which identifies unjust, substantive, and procedural laws and urges their elimination.

A team from the National Legal Aid and Defender Association (NLADA) evaluated the project in 1971, concluding that the Seattle Public Defender is providing a broader range of quality service to the client group than all but a few other defender offices in the United States. Its evaluators noted that, unlike most other Public Defenders in the United States, the Seattle Public Defender provides a single lawyer for each client through all stages of the criminal process, rather than a different lawyer at each stage of the proceeding. However, the NLADA report did indicate some administrative problems. Among the most significant recommendations were the following: maintain a personnel file/manual; develop investigators' training program; develop attorneys' training program, including more varied experience for project attorneys (experienced and inexperienced) in all phases of the project's work (felonies, misdemeanors, juvenile court); use investigative staff better for factual investigations; improve data keeping; and use third-year law student interns.

4. Halfway Houses (MC, $45,360; other, $109,228). Transitional living environment, with job counseling and other supportive services, to help released felons readjust to life outside prison. The project enrolls 20-40 men per quarter. Enrollment is for 90 days of work training and personal-development education; graduates are then placed in jobs. Industrial wood and metal workshops are used for training. CDA evaluation states that a considerably higher percentage of persons in the project score better in attitude than those who merely reside in the halfway house and that there are improved changes in self-esteem for those who participate in the program. A total of 77 have been graduated, and the rearrest rate is a relatively low 17 percent. Information on the project includes social and demographic characteristics of the 121 clients served and comparisons of those who completed the project and those who did not, a valuable source for answering questions about recidivism.

5. Group Legal Services (MC, $25,000). Group coverage, similar to medical insurance plans, to provide legal assistance when needed to persons who cannot otherwise afford it. The State Supreme Court still has not acted on proposed bar association rule changes that are required before service can begin.

Social Services

1. Child Care (MC, $240,000; other, $2,700). Day-care and educational and nutritional services to model neighborhood children whose mothers work or are enrolled in job training. This project

was unable to secure licensing for 11 planned group day-care homes and therefore discarded this objective. Also, a child-care registry was disbanded because it was too difficult to find personnel. The project is now serving 258 children (46 more than were projected at the time of this review). The capacity of day-care centers, measured against total need, has increased at a faster rate in the Model Neighborhood than outside the area. Model Cities now performs the initial review and makes recommendations for the licensing of day-care homes in the Model Neighborhood. This change simplifies licensing and could substantially increase day-care homes in the area. Each center has an advisory board, and there is one central Parent Advisory Board. A new director was hired in January 1972, inheriting a fiscal crisis, low staff morale, lack of project direction, and a generally poor situation. Considerable administrative improvements have been made since then, and it appears the project will turn out satisfactorily.

2. ADC Council (MC, $22,000). Public information, problem-solving assistance, and representation for welfare recipients in the Model Neighborhood. The CDA ruled that this project was not making effective progress in reaching objectives; therefore, it was terminated. Its objectives are to be pursued through existing programs.

3. Comprehensive Services for the Elderly (MC, $93,565; other, $108,118). Drop-In Centers, homemaker/handyman assistance, and part-time employment. The number of child-service hours provided by the elderly has been more than projected, but employment of homemakers/handymen is substantially down, as is the number of senior citizens regularly attending Drop-In Centers. Model Cities says this is due to a low budget. But an evaluation done for the CDA stated the project could be improved by creating a technical advisory committee. It further stated that changes have not occurred in the delivery systems of other agencies (the project itself makes no claim on having affected other agencies) and that "there is no satisfactory medium for communicating the demonstrated services and the technical knowledge to other agencies." On the other hand, a sampling of participants shows a substantial increase in the total amount of services available to the elderly and a high opinion of the project. A monthly newsletter is helping to improve the project.

4. Special Counseling and Continuation School (MC, $90,000). High school classes, counseling, health education, and infant nursery care to allow pregnant teen-agers to receive diplomas. Total enrollment is 57 girls, three fewer than projected. Renovation is complete at the Metropolitan YWCA, which houses Onward Bound, a dormitory residence for 12 mothers and their children.

5. Pioneer Square Rehabilitation (Other, $25,000). A unified program, with participation by residents themselves, to provide social services to the Skid Road population. This project has completed its

study in defining problems and needs in the area. Meanwhile, the Skid Road Community Council (SRCC), a citizen body established by the project, has increased citizen participation effectiveness and program development input. Weekly open meetings in the SRCC office have made the organization more accessible to residents. Approximately three to five citizens per day drop by the front office to chat, get advice, or register complaints.

6. Neighborhood Social Service Centers (MC, $815,051; other, $103,664). Social service network of strategically located centers and outreach stations in the Model Neighborhood. Joint delivery of services by the State Division of Vocational Rehabilitation (DVR) and the State Division of Public Assistance (DPA), components of the Pioneer Square Center, has proceeded beyond expectations. A team is used to evaluate clients for vocational rehabilitation. First, an in-depth evaluation is made of each client and a step-by-step rehabilitation plan is devised, then each team member is assigned certain implementation tasks. Proceedings of each team meeting are recorded, and follow-up is conducted. This method enables the project to handle a larger number of clients more effectively. And to further increase efficiency, plans are under way to combine DVR and DPA files and use a joint narrative social service write-up for clients serviced by both components.

The project is in compliance with training, resident employment, and career development requirements of the Seattle Model Cities Program. The only exception to this is where staff people are hired outside the Model Neighborhood because no qualified MN residents apply.

7. Tenant Organization (MC, $38,000). Information, redress of grievances, and representation for Model Neighborhood tenants. Model Cities determined this project was not making effective progress and terminated it.

Education

1. Demonstration School (MC, $150,000; other, $210,000). Early childhood education with individualization of instruction, continuous-progress curricula, innovative teaching techniques, and associated health and social welfare services. Continuous-progress classes (progressive education) are administered for 380 enrollees from five to seven years of age. Over 200 parents are actively involved in classroom activities (as instructors, testers, preparers of audio-visual materials), community development, fund raising, and project evaluation. Racial balance is 35 percent white, 64 percent black, and 1 percent Asian and other. More white families are endeavoring to place their children in this rather effective instructional program.

2. SCOPE (Seattle Career Opportunities Program—Education)
(MC, $111,226; other, $189,980). Employment and training of Model
Neighborhood residents as career teachers and administrators in
central region public schools. There are few drop-outs in this program, which enrolls about 54. Presently, 43 SCOPE trainees are
on the job, teaching small groups, tutoring, and supervising pupils.
Some trainees are taking related courses toward a BA degree in
education at the University of Washington.

3. Occupational Skills (MC, $72,000; other, $460,302). Vocational
instruction to orient Model Neighborhood youth to the world of work,
provide them with marketable skills, and show how to break down racial
barriers to employment. Work centers for all vocational curricula
except dry-cleaning training are in effect. Additional sections had to
be added due to student interest and enrollment. The goal for the
1971-72 school year to train 500 students was slightly exceeded, and
despite the limited job market, 26 students were placed in jobs during
the school year and the rest during the summer months. Contracts
have been made with related unions and professional organizations
in an effort to assure relatedness of the occupational training to real
work and to increase employability of the students involved.

4. Extended Services (MC, $187,134; other, $800). Alternative
instructional settings, including counseling, academic instruction, and
vocational training, for Model Neighborhood youths who are emotionally
unable to function in a regular school environment. One hundred (the
project goal) students are enrolled in the six Extended Services
centers, and over 100 received counseling within the regular school
setting. Nineteen students were returned to the sender school after
receiving training from Extended Services. Five of these were
recidivists. This represents 15 percent of the student enrollees
and surpasses the 10 percent expected to be returned to their base
schools.

Five students graduated with diplomas, two with General Educational Development certificates, and 30 acquired marketable skills.
It had been projected that 50 percent of the graduating students would
go on to institutions of higher learning; actually 100 percent of the
graduates have pursued further education. Seventeen students were
trained in TV and film production, two were placed in related jobs,
and two were placed in colleges. Four films were completed, and
16 film clips for television were produced and used.

The Seattle-King County Economic Opportunity Board, Inc.
provides bus transportation for 230 pupils of the Central Region
Satellite Preschools. Twelve buses are used. Employment has been
provided for 14 Model Neighborhood residents: 1 coordinator, 1
secretary, and 12 bus drivers. Although many children have been
transported who could not otherwise have gone to the preschools,

117

the over-all transportation system is not reliable, and alternatives
are being sought.

    5. Mid School Planning (MC, $253,422; other, $800). Develop-
ment of curricula, instruction techniques, and ways to eliminate de
facto segregation in the newly organized Central Region middle schools.
All project goals and objectives to date have been met. A new instrument for measuring individual student progress was developed and
successfully tested in 1971-72.

    Human relations training for middle school desegregation was
conducted for 24 teachers (including blacks), 80 parents, and 50 students. One training session was held for school administrators.
Teaching training in continuous progress and individualized teaching
techniques was conducted for 240 teachers. Leadership training was
conducted for 20 school personnel, and transactional analysis training
was given to an additional 50 instructional personnel.

    6. Staff Training (MC, $36,200; other, $800). Staff support and
technical assistance to the decentralized Central Area School Council.
Evaluations of programs carried out in the Central Region schools
are made on the basis of responses gathered by questionnaires. Twice
a month, the council holds open meetings with the community where
Model Neighborhood residents are able to express their concerns.
Attendance varies from month to month, averaging about 75. A
Desegregation/Education Plan was completed, submitted to the school
board, and received considerable community support.

Economic and Business Development

    Economic Development Program (MC, $212,000; other, $683,000).
Loan arrangements, technical assistance, training, planning and research to promote locally owned businesses in the Model Neighborhood.
The project was operated by the United Inner-City Development Corporation (UICDF) and only expended $111,980 by April 1972.

    There were approximately 62 cases under review by the end of
the second action year. Preliminary studies in several types of
business—canvas products, molded plastics, and paints, chemicals,
and solvents—were conducted. Seventeen local businessmen currently
in business or seeking to initiate ventures were counseled by the
Industrial Development staff. Nine firms received contract counseling
assistance; two of these received contracts.

    The following is a summary of loans approved by the second
action year:

Type of Business	Amount	Financial Sources
Pet shop	$54,000	MESBIC of Washington
Women's clothing	20,000	Liberty Bank

Type of Business	Amount	Financial Sources
Laundry/dry cleaning	19,000	SBA (direct)
Beauty school	25,000	SBA/Liberty Bank
Construction	15,500	SBA/Liberty Bank
Heating oil and fuel	86,000	SBA/Liberty Bank
Trucking	25,000	SBA/Liberty Bank
Skating rink	25,000	SBA
Total	$270,000	

Not much progress was made during the third action year, there were serious organizational problems between the UICDF board and staff, and the project failed to institute an effective Community Development Corporation (CDC). OEO discontinued its support early in 1972, followed by similar action of SMCP on June 30, 1972. Although UICDF failed to perform, the city believes economic development is one of the most serious problems facing Seattle; therefore, a considerable amount ($565,000) of Planned Variations funds has been allocated to economic development, and administration of the project will most likely be undertaken by the city's Office of Economic Development. Eventually, a series of public corporations would be created to carry out specific projects.

Evaluation of Employment and Economic Development. A number of resources are available for developing employment and the economy in the Model Neighborhood. Principal ones are Department of Labor manpower and training programs and various Small Business Administration (SBA) projects. Both economic development and manpower programs have been allocated substantial sums of Planned Variations money to carry out the objectives of this goal. A review of some of the basic problems in this area of endeavor may be helpful.

In an April 1971 evaluation of employment and economic development in the Model Neighborhood, a consortium of the Seattle University Urban Affairs Institute and the Human Resources Planning Institute reported approximately 874 businesses in the MN.[6] Almost all are retail and service firms, predominantly one-man, or "mom and pop" operations, which provide little employment for residents. About 30 percent are black-owned, and about half of these had been formed within the past four years. The consortium indicates that 90 new black-owned businesses have started up and endured since 1968 and that while 60 percent of the businessmen were familiar with SBA, few had received services. Only 14 percent reported awareness of UICDF and only 9 percent of the Economic Growth Organization (EGO), both of which provide direct service and help to local businesses; 12 percent were aware of the Minority Enterprise Small Business Investment Companies (MESBIC). Model Cities is reconsidering the utility of concentrating on small businesses, which employ few and which have a high failure rate. With Seattle's economic slump, even fewer jobs have been created than originally projected.

The consortium concludes that "the objectives of the Division of Employment and Economic Development are nowhere near accomplishment." Besides the poor economy, it points to the high migration rate as a factor in economic problems. One study shows that 45 percent of Model Neighborhood families resided there for less than two-and-a-half years and that those families have a disproportionate share of social and economic problems. Many residents who receive jobs or are upgraded move out of the area. (An earlier study commissioned by OEO reported central area families average 59 moves per 100 houses—or 28 percent of families—per year in Seattle, and that about 70 percent of all moves are intraurban.)

The consortium makes two major recommendations. First, that a systematic application of services be perfected to achieve true coordination rather than an exchange of information. All components of economic development "should be considered to be integral parts of a system" rather than each going its own way. Agencies, even under contract, tend to execute their own policies. The implication is that agencies need to eliminate barriers and boundaries of operation and undertake any operation in which they have competence and that they should give assistance wherever needed.

And second, that labor-intensive, community-based (ownership and control vested locally) industries be created. They can provide a substantial number of jobs, serve as a training base, generate local cash flow, and provide an internal source of funding for community improvements. The consortium lists the following kinds of resources not now being utilized by Model Cities:

1. Title 8a preference on bids on federal procurement contracts
2. Near-cost-free leasing of federal surplus equipment
3. Department of Labor JOBS (Job Opportunities in the Business Sector) and OJT (on-the-job training)
4. Sheltered, "most-favored vendor" contracts with local or regional major industries
5. Long-term loaned technical and administrative personnel for man-on-man, over-the-shoulder technical assistance and training

Housing

1. Housing Development League (MC, $148,454; other, $348,503). Technical assistance and seed money for development of low- and moderate-income housing, both new and rehabilitated. A consolidation of the Seattle Urban League's Operation Equality and the Seattle

Housing Development League (SHDL) was accomplished, and a new organization, Seattle Operation Equality Housing Development League (SOEHDL), was formed. The corporation serves Pierce, King, and Snobomish Counties; however, Model Cities funds are used primarily for the benefit of the Model Neighborhood.

Physical development was hampered in 1972 because of HUD's freeze on all new construction in central city areas. Rehabilitation of Elnore House, a 55-unit building for the elderly, was completed; construction on Texoda, a 25-unit building for the elderly, is 70 percent completed. Thirteen new FHA 235 single-family houses are under construction, and plans have been readied for seven more.

2. Repair Service Project (MC, $87,354). Minor home repairs for low-income Model Neighborhood homeowners; training for apprentices in building trades. Approximately 27 homes are repaired each quarter. The project is meeting its objectives, but a substantial backlog of projects has developed.

3. Housing Demonstration (MC, $150,000; other, $11,650). Financial and technical assistance in construction of low- to middle-income Model Neighborhood housing that demonstrates new concepts in technology, livability, land use, and community involvement. One objective is to provide employment and training opportunities for MN residents in the construction field. It has been achieved in varying degrees with each of the demonstration projects. Seventy-five percent of all construction on FHA 235 homes using Model Cities commitments has been done by minority workmen; 90 percent have been sold through MN real estate brokers; and 51 percent have used minority loan companies. However, closer monitoring is needed during the construction process to determine that contractors are building in accordance with plans approved by the Housing Demonstration Subcommittee of the Housing and Physical Environment Task Force.

One-hundred MN residents who made use of the SMCP's FHA 235 commitments have received counseling in homeownership, 14 residents have received financial counseling, and 101 have received counseling in maintenance and repair. The counseling program has been administered by the Seattle Urban League's Operation Equality.

4. Leased Housing (Rent Subsidy) (MC, $45,000). Rent-subsidy housing, with supportive counseling and social services, for low-income Model Neighborhood families. Family counseling primarily involves advice on home maintenance, health and emotional problems, neighborhood difficulties, and child-care problems. The project has counseled or made contact with 431 residents out of 582 applicants. Although it has developed a fine counseling service, the main objective of leasing and subleasing has not been accomplished. Of the 425 allocations available, only 210 have been used. More time is required to perfect this project.

121

Transportation

1. Model Neighborhood Transportation Study (MC, $100,000; other, $108,000). Study of the transportation needs of the Model Neighborhood and recommendation of a system to best meet those needs.

A community bus system is being developed to increase mobility to jobs and social and cultural activities. The Mini-Tran system is highly experimental and innovative and is being developed in close coordination with Seattle Transit System personnel. It provides the Model Neighborhood with 12-passenger vans operating at 20-minute intervals throughout a 14-hour day, at 10-cent fares. Stops are made for passengers about every other block and augment Seattle Transit System routes to the central business district. The average daily ridership was 871 during its six-month trial period, compared to a capacity of 2,400. The cost for six months was $133,690, based on 68 cents per vehicle mile and comparable to larger systems that enjoy greater economy of scale. SMCP has decided to continue funding Mini-Tran rather than phasing it out as initially planned because of the highly visible and positive effect it has had on the community served.

In relationship to this experiment, Alan M. Voorhees and Associates, a consulting firm, is conducting a comprehensive transportation study, and Bailey Associates is concentrating on the basic type and layout of service and a management system to operate it.

Community involvement in the transportation study is made up of three interrelated components:

1. Public Information. Press releases are regularly issued to the local media, wherein study progress is explained and information about current project activity disseminated to the MN and the rest of the city.
2. Transportation Information Office. An office of Alan M. Voorhees and Associates has been established in the MN to provide information, on demand, about the study, current progress, and available transportation. Residents can call or come in to complain or express their opinions about transportation problems.
3. Home Meetings. By far the major effort is concentrated in home meetings, which provide an opportunity for staff to gain intimate and personal knowledge of resident transportation problems. Meetings are fairly well structured and held in resident homes, and each is attended by roughly 12 persons from the immediate neighborhood.

Relocation

Relocation Program (MC, $103,786). Location of replacement
housing, reimbursement of moving costs, and supportive social services
to households and businesses forced to move by Model Cities sponsored
activities. The project staff also gives service to Model Neighborhood
residents who are not regularly considered a relocation responsibility.
This service consists of assistance in finding housing, obtaining counseling in financial responsibility of homeownership, and obtaining
needed social services through referral. The Relocation Advisory
Committee, made up of Model Neighborhood residents and staff members of social service agencies working in the area, is an effective
tool for communication and education about housing and relocation.
A total of 50 relocation payments were made from 69 claims.

Community Facilities

Parks and Block Development (MC, $506,000; other, $14,000).
Acquisition, design, and improvement of park sites and recreation
facilities in the Model Neighborhood. Status of projects earmarked
for completion during the 1971 and 1972 calendar years was as follows:
Harrison Minipark: completed June 1971.
Bradner Park: HUD has agreed to acquire the land from Seattle
    Public Schools for future Park Department development in
    1974.
Powell Barnett Park: completed June 1971.
28th and Jackson Minipark: completed 1971.
Firehouse Minipark: completed April 1971 and named state's
    best public landscape design of 1971 by the Washington
    Nurserymen's Association.
Spring Street Minipark: completed 1971.
30th Avenue Minipark: pending site approval; study of alternative
    designs and bidding.
Pioneer Place Park: in design development stage.
Occidental Park: in design development stage.
Madrona Bathhouse: completed August 1971.
Garfield Playfield Improvement: Wall of Respect motif under
    review by Seattle Design Commission. Plans and specifi-
    cations sent to Board of Public Works for approval.
Miller Playfield Expansion: completed October 1971.
Spruce Minipark: completed November 1971.
Leschi Playground: completed August 1971.

Environmental Protection and Development

    1. Model Neighborhood Land Use Planning (MC, $122,000; other $5,000). Development and adoption of a comprehensive land use plan for the Model Neighborhood, to ensure that community future growth reflects wishes of the residents. Land use consultants have concluded their study with submission of a proposed land use plan for the Model Neighborhood. Community review is now taking place.

    2. Utilities Upgrading (MC, $225,000; other, $2,450). Improvement of utilities—street lighting, sewer systems, water and electric systems, street, and so on—in Model Neighborhood. Most projects are completed or being implemented:

    International District street lighting: total cost is $85,000, with Model Cities providing $22,000.

    23d Avenue undergrounding: completed spring 1972.

    Sewer separation: construction has begun.

    14th Avenue street and alley lighting: evaluation of impact on the crime rate has been completed. Construction in under way.

    Leschi NDP undergrounding: undergrounding of electric and telephone wires in the Leschi area of the Model Neighborhood at a cost of $66,000 is completed.

    Yesler undergrounding: completed September 1972.

    Bus stop shelters: designs were completed and approved for six shelters. Construction of each will be handled individually through the City Purchasing Department so as to involve small Model Neighborhood contractors. Completion is scheduled for fall 1972.

    3. Land Bank (MC, $401,000). Acquisition of undeveloped land for low-income housing and other uses in fulfillment of Model Cities project objectives.

    4. Environmental Health (Other, $500,000). Survey of sanitary conditions, clean-up campaigns, rodent control, and community education to remove environmental causes of poor health in the Model Neighborhood has been completed. Major emphasis has been on development and implementation of a systematic program of rubbish and debris removal. These services have been carried out on a scheduled basis in all Model Neighborhood districts. The major drawback has been failure to obtain civil service status for project employees who have successfully passed civil service exams. There are 27 full-time project employees and 24 temporary employees (18 with the Beautification Project and 6 with the Neighborhood Youth Corps).

General Impressions of the Program

    On the whole, the impression made by Seattle Model Cities on city and county officials is favorable. Deputy County Executive Joe McGarick States,

I'm fairly impressed with Model Cities performance for delivering health services . . . particularly the pre-paid health experiment. . . . Also their action citizen's committee which is a land development review board is being used by us as a model for a county program. It has been very effective. . . . And the Model Cities Mental Health Advisory Group has been used in a unique way to come up with a really representative community group to serve on their advisory board. It is broader and more truly representative of the community than any other advisory board I've heard about. They took a random sampling of citizens and knocked on their doors to get members and came up with really different types—it's very good. . . . I've heard that health planning is good—some doctors at the University of Washington are impressed. We, the county, would use the device of establishing community councils (initiated by Model Cities) and we'd provide them with 30 percent to 40 percent of their staff. Nobody in the country has done that. We have tested this in our Highline District and we think it's working out well. . . . Our observation of Model Cities is that it is working out and is rather exciting.

Seattle Councilwoman Phyllis Lamphere feels that evaluation of Model Cities has not yet "been put to the test." She does believe it would rate fairly high if revenue sharing were to take effect. She also points out that "good pilot programs" should be expanded citywide, such as prepaid medical care and many of the criminal justice programs.

Councilman Tim Hill believes Model Cities will continue to be funded at present levels by the council if revenue sharing takes place. On the other hand, Councilman George Cooley feels Model Cities "could get the small end of it" under revenue sharing. He goes on to say, "City council thinks Model Cities here has done a good job. Basically, I think they are accomplishing a great deal. . . . It has helped other programs, such as underground wiring, for example. . . . Citizen participation is a good concept. It's a fine idea to expand that to the entire city. . . . I think Model Cities concepts are workable and realistic—not a pie-in-the-sky experiment."

The only black councilman, Sam Smith, says, "We are almost going to be dependent on Model Cities because it has created so many job opportunities and done so many needed things. If it were yanked out of our city, [we] would be in real trouble." He feels the program should be expanded citywide but that present programs earmarked for Model Cities should continue. He also states, "Citizen participation has been successful in Model Cities. The practice has its evils, small power groups, etc., but it is a useful process. . . . The only thing to do is to extend citizen participation to the whole city. . . . I think it's healthy."

Almost all councilmen believe Model Cities is worthwhile and has made valuable contributions. The only negative expressions come from Leim Tuai (the only Oriental on council, and often conservative), who believes Model Cities "is trying to do some good but has often floundered because it has hired a lot of people who have no expertise. . . . I know of nothing visible that Model Cities has done." (There are charges that the program has discriminated against Orientals.) Tuai believes too little attention has been given to the International District (which is primarily Oriental and falls within the target area). He feels citizen participation has not worked out, yet he believes the city considers it a "useful method" to deal with residents.

Chamber of Commerce officials appear to be less enthusiastic and informed about Model Cities. Their general impression has been that Model Cities has not really accomplished very much, and they are unable to point to any specific results. The Chamber's primary concern is creating jobs for the Seattle area; therefore, it pays little attention to less visible human resource and Model Cities problems.

Planned Variations

Seattle Planned Variations in continuing the Model Cities philosophy of improving services to the poor by including all of the city's disadvantaged neighborhoods in the program and establishing Citizen Advisory Councils (represented by agencies, business, and citizen task forces) in them. It is also continuing to make agencies more responsive through catalytic programing and by not operating programs itself but rather improving the performance of others.

Administratively, the program has been improved by (1) a Policy Planning Committee, which develops, reviews, and coordinates citywide policies in a manner similar to the Model Cities Office of Program Planning and acts as a focal point for interdepartmental coordination through a policy planning cabinet, composed of key agency heads, including the deputy mayor and SMCP director; (2) increased staff capacity and strengthened federal grants review and control system (use of computer aid systems analysis) in the City Office of Management and Budget; and (3) more structured planning and coordination among city, state, county, and United Way (private united social program funding) systems through a State-City Task Force funded by $100,000 from HUD, HEW, and SMCP sources.

Additional citizen participation is funded for $135,000 and now includes a unified Advisory Council, elected by the four Advisory Councils, which considers areawide policies and programing, standards, and coordinating techniques. Meanwhile, a Mayor's Task Force is seriously examining Citizen (District) Councils for all city neighborhoods, which will advise city officials on city policies, budgets, legislation, and an annual Comprehensive Development Plan from each city department. The mayor and business community are also in favor of a citywide council with representation from all District Councils.

Supplementing the councils are four branch offices that act as nuclei and models for District Councils and for the proposed mayoral little city halls. In addition, citizen task forces (which develop, recommend, and evaluate projects) are operating in each functional area, under each council.

Projects under this expanded program were selected on the basis of two criteria: (1) constituent support from residents, SMCP and city staff, and agencies and business; and (2) program potential based on impact on institutions or on causes of major problems, visibility and numbers of people affected, long-term funding linkages with other agencies, city budget impact, short-term impact on high-priority problems of employment and economic development, and over-all performance capability on neighborhood conditions, goals, administrative procedures, and utilization of supplemental funds in conjunction with other public and private money sources.

Largely, projects follow the patterns of present SMCP programing and are expected to be matched by about $2 million of funds from other public and private agencies (See Table 6 for program categories and amount of funding):

1. Recreation, Culture, and Youth. Centers and playgrounds are being expanded and rehabilitated. Mobile playgrounds, swim instruction, camping, transportation services, handicapped programs, and youth projects (temporary residential shelter, culture, drop-in recreation, counseling, food and nutrition, and employment) are included.

2. Health. Priority project areas are neighborhood health services, environmental health, alcoholism, and drugs (an attempt to go citywide), and food and nutrition.

3. Law and Justice. The successful Public Defender program has been expanded by three attorneys to reduce the case load from 570 trials to 400 per year for each attorney. Two neighborhood legal service centers to handle civil cases are being added. Approximately six group homes will be used for rehabilitation of delinquent youth. Replacement of the obsolete Georgetown Police Precinct House is planned. Also predelinquent boys and high school student service programs are being considered.

TABLE 6

SMCP Planned Variations Budget Allocations Summary
(thousands of dollars)

| PBS No. | Type of Program | 3d Action Year | | | | PV Total |
		E	SE	SW	N	
311	Recreation/culture/youth	–	191	151	204	546
312	Health	–	100	100	100	300
313	Law and justice	–	70	70	70	210
314	Social services	–	125	125	215	465
321	Education	–	50	50	30	130
322	Economic and business development	–	188	188	189	565
323	Manpower and job development	–	165	164	74	403
331	Housing	–	170	70	50	290
332	Transportation and communications	–	27	8	8	43
333	Relocation	–	25	25	25	75
334	Community facilities	–	115	352	145	612
335	Environmental protection and development	73	70	150	450	743
392	Citizen participation	–	45	45	45	135
391/393	Information and evaluation	–	40	40	40	120
100/200	Administration (supplemental share)	–	193	192	193	578
	Totals	73	1,547	1,730	1,838	5,215

Source: Seattle Model Cities Program, Seattle, Washington.

4. Social Services. This includes development of a citywide child care project, neighborhood multiservice centers, elderly programs, comprehensive services for pregnant teen-agers, group homes for mentally retarded young adults, and a permanent shelter and food facilities for Skid Road.

5. Education. An educational Development Program will be conducted to involve to a greater degree teachers in minority concerns, deal with children who cannot adjust to the existing system, and involve residents. Also, English classes to Chinese, Filipinos, Spanish-Americans, and Indians will be provided.

6. Economic and Business Development. Seattle believes unemployment is the city's most serious problem that can be addressed by these new funds. Besides the 300 jobs to be created by implementing new projects, other economic activity will be generated, including businesses such as printing, a shopping center, frozen foods, and specialty food processing.

7. Manpower and Job Development. Priorities are job creation, basic skill training, upgrading and retraining, second-language programs, job discrimination, financial support, and social/cultural sensitivity (to train employees and counselors in special and sensitive problems).

8. Housing. This involves planning fund assistance to certain areas and rent supplement money for some residents. A Housing Action Program will provide home repairs and a housing and classification study.

9. Transportation and Communications. The project includes planning for a crosstown shuttle bus, and bus service for the handicapped, elderly, and youth.

10. Relocation. The primary effort will involve the definition and development of an expanded MN relocation program. Implementation of the Uniform Relocation Assistance and Real Property Acquisition Policies Act of 1970 will have a serious effect on the amount of local funds necessary to relocate residents, as a result of a future Comprehensive City Demonstration Program. After June 30, 1972, the 100 percent federal share of relocation costs caused by urban renewal and other federally assisted programs will drop to the level of the federal matching share (that is, two-thirds, three-fourths, and so on) for the particular program. Eight medium-sized cities, including Seattle, report costs from $500,000 to $1 million if this takes effect, seriously diluting Model Cities and Planned Variations funds. There will be strong efforts from local officials to change this.

11. Community Facilities. Substantial funds ($612,000) will be used for park development and West Seattle Reservoir Land Acquisition and will supplement efforts of Forward Thrust in this regard.

12. Environmental Protection and Development. A considerable sum of PV funds ($743,000) will be utilized here also, pointing out the heavy emphasis of new money on visible projects. Projects include utility upgrading, pedestrian overpasses, street beautification and improvement, greenbelt acquisition, and residential traffic diverters to make neighborhoods more livable.

Analysis and Recommendations

Judging Program Success

Seattle Model Cities has achieved many of its short-term project objectives. Long-range goals—to eliminate unemployment, crime, and depression—are yet to be achieved. The total program would be considerably more successful if the city were not in such a severe state of unemployment. It is difficult, if not impossible, to raise employment levels, lower welfare rolls, train people for meaningful work, stimulate economic development, and raise citizens' hopes when the area's basic economic and social forces are working the other way. No isolated program can reverse national or regional economic trends, yet much of the criticism against Model Cities in Seattle (and elsewhere) has come for just such a reason.

In order to be fair, this evaluation weighs success in narrower terms: on the basis of limited objectives and incremental changes. It means looking more at individual project success and examining accomplishments based on specific objectives. If objectives were achieved, or nearly so, projects are considered successful. Where objectives were impossible to achieve because of economic conditions, the credibility of the program is questioned only if it did not change to meet new conditions. On this basis, Seattle's program is considered one of the most successful.

The projects themselves are typical of those in other Model Cities communities. For example, they meet federal guidelines stressing comprehensiveness, operate in a ghetto setting where problems are great and solutions limited, and mostly use models tried before. The principal difference is the degree to which they fill program gaps, develop innovations, and reach program objectives. Seattle has been more successful at these than other cities. While Model Cities has not made sweeping institutional changes locally, it has made some, and others are forthcoming. In a practical setting, this is what was hoped for from Model Cities; this is what has happened here. Indeed, it would take a great deal more private and federal resources to be able to reach the ultimate goals of the program.

Private Response

The failure of private organizations to respond to Model Cities in Seattle has been one of its principal drawbacks. Acute unawareness of and noninvolvement in the program by the Chamber of Commerce and business groups and by civic groups and union organizations outside the Model Neighborhood reflect the isolated objectives of each body and the difficulty the community has in dealing comprehensively with its problems. Such narrowness makes a strong case for the citywide Planned Variations approach and its philosophy of involving the total community.

In addition to a citywide approach, smaller steps may be taken to tune diverse groups to the same channel: an honest attempt to communicate by encouraging interchange of members and information, inclusion of progress reports in each other's newsletters, and a personal effort between executive directors to meet with each other and lessen intragroup rivalry. Many believe that one of the difficulties is working up enthusiasm for blacks in particular when everybody has problems. Therefore, it may be up to the more innovative Model Cities Program to take the initiative for exchange and participation. Planned Variations may make such innovation possible.

Forward Thrust has already gained considerable areawide cooperation but has not seriously involved Model Cities. Model Cities should link itself more closely to this city-county endeavor, and in turn Forward Thrust should actively engage in the work of Model Cities by fully participating in meetings and adding influence through skills and resources. The target area cannot create lasting improvements without participation and support of the entire community because only the majority of citizens pass bond issues and only a majority of legislators pass legislation. Forward Thrust has been eminently successful in convincing the majority on many issues. On the other hand, it needs help, and there is no good reason why Model Cities (and Planned Variations) should not fill the gaps where bond issues have failed, rejuvenate some Forward Thrust programs with its funds, and mobilize citizen strength behind areawide projects (such as the areawide comprehensive community center proposal). Reasonable exchange of resources would help to achieve Model Cities as well as area goals. In this respect, Seattle is fortunate it has an effective coalition like Forward Thrust. Importantly, everything should be done to maintain the coalition's viability; otherwise, years of effort will be lost and the necessary ingredients to achieve fundamental change will go with it.

Accomplishments

A great number of citizens do not hear much about Model Cities, yet there are many who do and praise it. For example, county officials are impressed with the prepaid health experiment, health planning, and the "truly" representative community health councils. The comprehensive health care for the aging is considered by federal officials as one that could be used as a national model. And the Model Cities Land Development Review Board is being used as prototype by the county.

Model Cities also has been the fringe benefit to make other programs possible: $300,000 to Seattle public schools to fund the racial desegregation of several schools; matching funds for a variety of projects, including those for Omnibus Crime Control for the city.

It has successfully engaged as a pressure group in construction/union disputes, presentations and lobbying before the state legislature, tenant law reform, inner-city housing, health and child care, small minority businesses, and reforming education processes. On the other hand, it has been less than effective in reforming police-community relations. Although it has tried, there is huge disparity between police leadership and the black community. And there have been notable failures in target area townhouse projects. Yet almost all other projects are meeting objectives.

Moreover, new leadership has emerged, especially among minority youth. Some have surfaced on task forces, some as staff. Some have been lured away by state, city, or out-of-town employers. Some of the angriest and most militant black young men who had triggered widespread community fear (mostly in white areas) were employed by Model Cities, and their hostility was neutralized and rechanneled into positive productivity. In other cases, older men and women, who were activists and community workers before the black revolution was popular, gained long-deserved recognition through participation, and, in several cases, by employment, on citizen task forces.

It is also a measure of success, particularly in the black community, that blacks now encourage the involvement of more militant, conservative whites in the program. Though a difficult task, it is necessary to involve whites if changes are to be lasting and widespread. There are risks—risks that some blacks will resent such an "intrusion" into what has come to be considered a "black program" and risks that white ultraconservatives will attempt to undermine black leadership.

But Model Cities has always been risk-oriented, and its leadership has won many battles against what had appeared to be an intractable, white conservative establishment. Perhaps the most noteworthy example is when certain traditionalists, with much power (in this

instance, the city corporation counsel), insisted on strict adherence
to a narrow interpretation of the state constitution (which would not
permit the CDA to grant credit and loan money or create development
funds), Model Cities staff turned to the state legislature and won.

Administrative Direction

The program has been fortunate to have a competent director,
but as pointed out earlier this strength may be a program weakness
if other staff are not trained to administer the future program and if
procedures and policies are not institutionalized. It is apparent that
effective chain of command is lacking and program continuity is
ambiguous. This situation has not seriously affected morale, but
some staff are disgruntled. Fortunately, middle-level management
staff are now receiving increased training to remedy this problem.

Moreover, through the director's skill, many agencies have
been brought together in a comprehensive and systematic way.
Hundley has successfully, with agency cooperation, created many
effective umbrella groups (in aging, child care, health, manpower,
law and justice, and so on). And under his direction, precedents have
been established for dealing with needs outside the Model Neighborhood, such as the Senior Centers Program, which is expanding county-
wide. Too many cities merely talk about coordination and the elimination of duplication. Seattle has come closer to achieving it than most
others. If this process can be extended citywide, important institutional changes will take place. Hundley may be able to achieve these
changes while he is still in command. In short, obviously it is better
to have a strong and competent director who gets things done than
someone weaker who is unable to complete programs and solve issues.
Yet if the director were able to delegate authority properly, he would
be even more effective.

Citizen Participation

Citizen Advisory Council. Citizen participation in Seattle is
middle ground. It has not legitimized itself with elections, nor does
it appear Citizen Councils will develop strong partnership relations,
similar to those in Boston or Dayton, for example. Citizen power
rests mainly upon the good will of the mayor and city council at any
particular time and on any issue. Model Cities should seek an ordinance establishing more definite powers and procedures. Written
sanctity adds bargaining strength and makes it more difficult for
newly elected officials, in particular, to lessen such strength. In the
long run, however, because city hall (in all Model Cities communities)
legally retains final decision-making authority, power will be determined by the citizens' ability to lobby and bargain.

Proof of the Advisory Council's success is its ability to hold the trust of agencies and the support of city council. No major citizen project has been turned down by city council, and for the most part elected officials believe the program is a success. A good part of the Advisory Council's success with city council is because it has made an effort to avoid appearing like a "shadow" government.

One can confidently predict Walter Hundley will continue to discourage activist pressures on city officials by Model Cities residents. He prefers to leave this to the Central Seattle Community Council, the Community Action Agency, and other more independent groups. He chooses formally to disassociate himself from these groups and work through the system—which he believes is the most expedient way to get things done.

In this view, he is supported by the chairman of the board, Judge Johnson, who believes the Model Cities Advisory Council is really more effective than the elected "war on poverty" board. Johnson feels selection of Advisory Council members by organization is fairer than elections because it provides representation for all groups, including the less vocal, the nonpolitical, and those minorities too small to be effective in an election. In Model Cities, residents (not merely their representatives) are members of the Advisory Council, and appointments are made to assure representation from areas where there are no organized groups. Yet grass-roots representation is minimal. Most members represent organizations that already have the ability to make their opinions known. And it is apparent that some process, in addition to appointment, is necessary in order to increase legitimacy and to ensure a regular influx of new "blood"—now lacking— to keep the council vital and relevant.

The addition of three more citizen bodies in the Planned Variations Program is an excellent step toward developing citizen councils citywide and is already supported by key officials. But this expanded participation structure needs to be legitimized by legislation and some financial resources that are institutionalized into the system if residents are to have permanent bargaining strength.

The Unified Citizens Advisory Council may prove to be another layer of bureaucratic delay, if it is designed to approve actions of District Councils. The latter should act relatively independently of any other body, reporting directly to the mayor and city council. A Unified Citizens group, representing all community forces (business, labor, civic, District Councils), is an excellent concept for developing citywide goals and priorities and performing as a pressure group to stimulate the city into action. It should be given resources for an executive director and staff. It should not be made part of the chain of command. The mayor and city council have final responsibility and must assume the citywide decision-making role, tempered by a formal system of District Councils and a less formal Unified (Coalition) Council.

Grass-Roots Task Forces. Model Cities Task Forces are poorly organized and their duties ambiguous. It would be more appropriate to have formal, effective umbrella bodies (such as the Health Task Force) in each functional area operating citywide and with sufficient grass-roots membership. Broad-based citizen participation would best come through periodic workshops and conventions, which would also plan the interrelationships of the various functions. In addition, neighborhood workers should be trained to gather information, participate in formal planning, and lead workshop sessions. The existing task force structure involves too few residents, certainly much fewer than in workshops, and is too cumbersome to be able to carry every idea forward.

Migration Hurts the Model Neighborhood

Migration is a major difficulty in achieving participation and improvement of economic and social conditions in the Model Neighborhood. Population dropped 5,586 between 1968 and 1972, and about 27 percent of the residents move out of the area each year (many of whom have received training and employment). A smaller percentage move in but need basic Model Cities services and jobs and keep unfavorable statistics high.

Such fluctuation argues in favor of citywide development, since it is difficult to reach project goals for a continually changing clientele. And experienced citizen participation and interest are hard to maintain. Citywide Planned Variations, job training and placement for the hard-core unemployed, and participation in social and other services, regardless of residency, would be more meaningful. Of 90 planning areas in the city, 20 are hard-core depressed areas. The city's concentration of resources in the four Model Neighborhoods, which include these 20 areas, should substantially resolve the problem of migration, but not completely. As incomes are raised, residents will continue to move out, and poorer citizens from other parts of the region may move in. At some point, the problems of the poor will have to be solved areawide; otherwise, the Model Neighborhoods may continue depressed.

On the other hand, the extraordinary needs of the disadvantaged will continue for a long time; therefore, it is important that a citywide philosophy not diffuse citizen action or the comprehensiveness of programs in the Model Neighborhood. Model Cities has helped to fill the gaps in human needs, and its diversity and experimentation in programs has produced some successful innovations. This is why

135

special funds should still be concentrated in target areas. Importantly, attacking problems citywide will diminish the ghetto characterization of the Model Neighborhood and help unify the model area as well.

Conclusion

Seattle is fortunate in a number of ways. It has good leadership and community spirit, and its problems are of a size that can be solved in a reasonable time frame, given the necessary resources. Mayor Uhlman is enlightened as to the needs of disadvantaged areas, and he understands that areawide problems have to be faced at the same time. On the whole, the city council is impressed with Model Cities progress and understands the necessity for citizen participation. But improved relations between the mayor and city council are necessary in order to coalesce the forces of change. Encouragingly, the red tape, patronage, and usual sluggishness of bureaucracies have not strangled Seattle as they have so many other cities. With an improved economy and a better job market, the ingredients for success would be present.

Notes

1. Edward J. Devine and Associates, An Evaluation of the Program Administration of the Seattle Model Cities Program, Seattle, Washington, May 1971.
2. Welfare Programs, report prepared for Seattle Model Cities Program, CDA, Seattle, Washington, May 1971.
3. Pro Bono Publico, Citizen Participation in Seattle Model Cities, report prepared for Seattle CDA, May 1971.
4. Seattle Model Cities Program, SMCP Quarterly Report, July 1971.
5. Booz-Allen and Hamilton Management Consultants, A Study of the Seattle Unicenter: A Unique Local Approach to Providing Comprehensive Manpower Services, August 1971, pp. 1-67.
6. Employment and Economic Development in the Seattle Model Cities Program, a report by the Seattle University Urban Affairs Institute and the Human Resources Planning Institute to SMCP, April 1971.

8

The City

General

One of the nation's oldest cities (settled in 1666), Newark has thrived over the centuries as a manufacturing, transportation, and business center. Like most other major northern cities, however, whites began a mass exodus from the inner core after World War II. They were supplanted by a large influx of southern blacks, who were making their way to the industrial centers during the same period. Over 100,000 whites fled the city, and the population now stands at 384,000, with 60 percent black, 11 percent Spanish-speaking, and 19 percent white, predominantly Italian. The city has served as a receiving center for poor people, lately Puerto Ricans, who constitute the fastest-growing group. And one-third of the population has not lived in the city more than five years.

Today Newark stands as a prime example of historic catastrophe, with one in three dwellings substandard (an average of one building every day is abandoned in Newark); unemployment at 14 percent and much higher among the least-skilled blacks; one out of every three residents on public assistance; 10 percent of the population in public housing; 20,000 addicted to drugs; sewers, streets, and other city facilities generally run down (most of the sewer system is 100 years old, of brick construction that combines flood water and sewage waste); the crime rate one of the highest in the country, and rising; and serious fiscal problems.

Mayor Kenneth A. Gibson has said, "Wherever America's cities are going, Newark will get there first." In his plea for greater assistance from Congress, he continued, "We are not talking about saving the Newarks of America, we are talking about saving America itself."

Paradoxically, Newark, the largest city in New Jersey, is still the focal point for industry. The white-dominated, business community does over $3.5 billion worth of retail trade annually. Some of the largest and most affluent firms in the country are based here (Prudential Insurance Company and Mutual Benefit Life, for example). Nevertheless, Newark is a mere shadow of its former industrial and commercial self. The Greater Newark Chamber of Commerce indicates that for every three jobs that move into Newark, two move out. Perhaps the most serious of these moves was the closing of the major operations of Ballantine and Sons Brewery in March 1972, which may eventually mean the loss of about 2,000 jobs. It appears that Prudential is about to leave also.

Although the state is the most urbanized in the nation and ranks seventh in per capita income, it is last in per capita expenditures and, consequently, provides a low level of support to its cities. And Newark itself does not seem to fit well into the state or regional structure. It is the "accidental city," never designed to be self-supporting. Its true function is regional rather than local—250,000 people work in the city, but most do not live there, and its large number of poor can never hope to sustain it.

Too Many Tax Exemptions

Newark Airport is the oldest commercial airport in the country, with $200 million in improvements ongoing, which will make it the metropolitan area's third international airport. It will be one of the busiest, comparable to Kennedy International, and should have a profound impact on the local job market. Also, Port Newark, adjacent to the airport, is developing quickly as one of the most modern containerports on the East Coast. However, these two facilities, which dominate almost 30 percent of the entire land mass of the city (23.6 square miles), are operated by the Port of New York Authority, which pays rent to the city of only $579,000 per year (a sliding scale will raise this to $1 million in 1976)—a pittance when compared with the property's tax potential.

Newark is the seat of Essex County, but the several county buildings are also tax exempt. The same is true of a large state office building, federal building, several state highways, county roads, and miles of city streets. Rutgers, the State University, occupies a large campus in the center of town, adjacent to another large campus of Newark College of Engineering. And Essex County College has broken ground for a new campus in the same area. All are tax exempt.

These, and other tax exempt properties, plus large public housing tracts (which reimburse the city less than 20 percent of the legal tax rate), church-owned property, and tax-abated land and buildings

138

leave only 37 percent of Newark taxable. And because of a measure taken to encourage new enterprise, some commercial and industrial buildings enjoy reduced property taxes for the first 15 years. As a result, homeowners are stuck with one of the highest property tax rates in the country.

High Tax Rate

The 1972 tax rate was $9.63 (up from $9.19 in 1971) per $100 of assessed valuation. Assessed valuation has dropped 22 percent since 1962. The tax rate is based on 100 percent of market value, but the effective rate is somewhat less because it is equalized with other countries to make the base comparable.

The annual budget of over $200 million continually faces deficits. Since state law does not permit an unbalanced budget, costs must be reduced or the property tax, which has no imposed limit, raised to eliminate projected deficits. To avoid raising taxes beyond a $10 rate, city council adopted three new revenue measures in 1971 to help offset an estimated $60 million in deficits for the next two years: 1 percent tax on business payrolls (paid by the employer), 15 percent tax on commercial parking lot receipts, and a sewer service fee based on a portion of the water rates. However, the state legislature permitted the imposition of the first two measures for only a two-year period, and the city was again faced with a $65 million deficit. But continuation of the above revenue measures plus federal aid (which will bring Newark only $6 million in general revenue sharing and about $12 million in education funds) would cut this in half. The state has also been giving Newark $7.4 million in State Urban Aid and $9.25 million as a reimbursement for Martland Hospital to help it along, particularly since there is no state income tax that could be partially reimbursed to cities. These combined measures would leave a deficit of about $20 million, which Newark hopes would be made up by the state through part of its share of federal revenue sharing. City officials believe that since need factors unfairly make up one-third of the formula that determines how much federal money local governments will receive, the state ought to disburse some of its revenue sharing funds to cities in dire need based on a more equitable formula. It will take something like this because it appears impractical to raise the property tax further. Moreover, the business administrator, Cornelius Bodine, believes major budget cuts cannot be made without seriously jeopardizing the city's health and safety.

If the property tax alone were to pay for recent budget increases, it would have to climb to $13 or $14. This would most likely be self-defeating, since it would lead to more uncollected taxes and a greater number of property foreclosures and abandonments. Bodine feels the city may have reached an "optimal point of return" when further tax increases will not result in more revenue. Presently, only 88.2 percent of property taxes are collected (up slightly but still low compared to most cities, which reach 95 percent). The city relies on the property tax for 65 percent of its revenue. Taxes on a $20,000 home are $1,850. And home ownership is declining.

Education

The school budget is particularly hard on the property tax rate, and city government can do little about it because the Board of Education is independent. The total education budget can be cut by city council or the administration, but specific items cannot be cut. This has resulted in budgets being left intact. The board is appointed by the mayor for two-year terms, yet he has been unable to influence it in holding down expenditures significantly.

Most of the budget problems have been because of salary hikes. But working conditions have been at stake too. In 1971, Newark experienced the longest school strike in America's history, which had very little effect on improving benefits and which intensified hatred between board members and teachers.

The Government

Politics

Historic Perspective. Historically, the city has suffered from poor administration and improbity. In 1962, Hugh J. Addonizio, a seven-term liberal congressman, was elected mayor of Newark, ending generations of Irish dominance of city hall. Traditionally, city government served as a vast patronage resource for Newark's Irish majority. But as the more prosperous Irish moved out, Italians moved in. Under Addonizio, "patronage continued to be the main reason city government existed" but with the lucrative jobs and contracts going to Italians rather than the Irish. Addonizio and his patronage lasted eight years.

Before his defeat in 1970, Addonizio was convicted of conspiracy and extortion in federal courts and sentenced to 10 years in prison. He is now in Lewisburg Federal Prison. The pattern described during the trial was classic. It involved a flat 10 percent kickback on city-financed projects (which more often than not involved federal and state money). On the other hand, this sea of official corruption has not been unique to Newark. It has engulfed northern New Jersey for many years and in 1971-72 resulted in over 122 grand jury indictments of officeholders.

By the mid-1960s, a new political machine was being constructed by George Richardson, a Newark politician long regarded as the coming black in New Jersey politics. In 1966, he decided to run a black candidate for mayor to pave his way to the mayor's race in 1970. He chose Kenneth Gibson, whom he regarded as a respectable citizen with little political orientation and no chance to build a competing organization. Gibson wound up with only 16,200 votes and received even less support than Addonizio in the black wards.

Nevertheless, Gibson learned something of political machinery, and with this new knowledge and the tide of revulsion to corruption on his side, he was elected in 1970. A solid bloc of black votes (95 percent in the black wards), plus an unusually large outpouring of liberal white votes and the negative votes of older Italian-Americans combined to defeat the incumbent mayor. About 10 to 15 percent of the white wards went to Gibson, enough to swing the election. The older Italians did not generally like the idea of electing a black mayor but were even less tolerant of a fellow Italian American bringing dishonor to the Italian community. The solidarity evident in the mayoralty race did not, however, extend to the council election. Only two black ward councilmen were elected and one black councilman at-large was elected, for a total of three blacks and six whites. Blacks won seats in the heavily black Central and the South Wards but showed poorly in the at-large races. It is numerically possible for blacks to win all at-large seats because the majority of the population is black; however, it is not electorally possible because the majority of registered voters is white. Older Italians who voted black for mayor (and voted to throw out the three councilmen indicted with Addonizio) voted white for council. Moreover, voters were less concerned about council seats, and therefore, fewer voted for councilmen. This phenomenon tends to support the notion that it was not the black voter, despite his solidarity, that elected Gibson, but rather that decisive number of whites who rejected Addonizio.

Present. Since taking office, Gibson has sincerely tried to maintain equality in black and white relationships, in hiring, and services. He has not developed close ties with the most forceful and vociferous of black leaders who helped elect him, Imaru Baraka (the poet and playwright who changed his name from LeRoi Jones) and his "502 Crowd: (his Committee for a Unified Newark operates out of 502 North High Street). Baraka interprets the fair share of black power as 60 percent of all city jobs, and he criticizes Gibson failing to develop a patronage system that would give blacks this power, just as the Italians and the Irish before them had.

However, Gibson views the use of patronage and political machinery somewhat differently. He believes a black administration will not pull the city up by its own bootstraps any more than white administrations have. Business and state and federal resources are needed, he feels, and are more likely to assist if complete black control and a superghetto are not created. His aides picture him as trying to convince the establishment that a majority black city, with a respectable black mayor, is as good a candidate for salvation as any other city. Gibson has said that he has no plans to develop a political machine and that his constituency will develop naturally, if he does things right. He said in a 1972 speech, "We don't have party labels when we run in Newark. I am a true non-partisan. I deal with a Republican Governor, a Democratic Congress, and a Republican President."

Organization

Newark's government is of the strong-mayor/council type, with an appointed business administrator who partially assumes the role of chief administrative officer. Five of the nine-member city council are elected by wards and four at-large. The current council president holds an at-large seat, the first time this position has not been held by a ward councilman. The council appoints a city clerk who serves as their chief aide and operates a particularly strong office. The business administrator is appointed by the mayor. His appointment and removal must be confirmed by city council, but only the mayor can initiate removal proceedings. He prepares the budget and prescribes purchasing, personnel, and other administrative practices for all city departments. The mayor appoints all department heads, who must also be approved by city council. (See Chart 2.)

Administrator Cornelius Bodine, a professionally trained city manager with experience in several cities and private industry prior to his employment in Newark, has been successful in influencing only several appointments. The finance director was his choice, and he was influential in choices for directors of health and welfare and recreation. Four department heads were already in office before Bodine was appointed. He perhaps has had his greatest difficulties in keeping the lower echelon personnel system straight. By mid-1972, he was having trouble getting his recommendations for laborers through the mayor's office. This can be attributed to Assistant Business Administrator Elton Hill, a carpenter until his appointment by his boyhood friend, Kenneth Gibson. Hill is in charge of city government patronage from top to bottom. For example, he personally approved the hiring of every employee in the Public Employment Program (PEP). Bodine is especially disturbed by what has happened with PEP, a $6.3 million annual program to hire the unemployed and improve government services at the same time. The program provided 1,200 jobs for nonwelfare and 451 jobs for welfare persons. Over two years,

CHART 2

Organization Chart, City of Newark

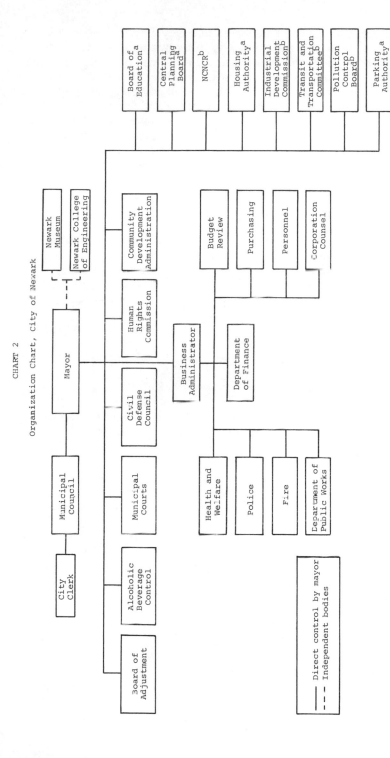

[a] Autonomous.

[b] Advisory bodies.

Source: Office of Business Administrator, Newark, New Jersey, January 1972.

143

the administration cut the 7,000-member city work force by 300. It could have made up this deficiency by selecting and training PEP people who could perform well and by using these funds like another source of revenue sharing. Many of the positions have been used wisely; however, the program has turned out to be largely patronage, spread among all ethnic groups, with little training or work performance. Unofficially, each city councilman has been allowed 10 workers of his choice, many of whom do not "show." Many assignments have turned out to be "odd jobs," and an independent class of employees has developed who do not demonstrate an equivalent sense of dedication as regular employees. This program, which could have accomplished immeasurable good for the city, if administered properly, damaged employee morale and destroyed any semblance of order and good management.

On the other side, when hiring has involved higher positions, Gibson has made sincere efforts to hire mostly competent people, reaching out of town when necessary and against the opposition of the political "noise-makers." The out-of-city appointments include those for business administrator, finance director, city engineer, health and welfare director, and recreation and parks director. Directors of police, fire, public works, and law were residents. Of these nine, there are three blacks, two Irish, three WASPS, and one Italian. With a few exceptions, appointments have been good.

Government Performance

The present administration is faced with correcting a great number of past inefficiencies and solving many problems. Traditionally, city departments have functioned far below their capacities. Police corruption was rampant, street cleaning poor, complaints were not honored, and most services simply below grade. There were no engineers in the engineering department, few qualified planners, an understaffed finance department, and poor coordination and management. Even with its decreased population (down 5 percent between 1960 and 1970), Newark has needed more city employees to take care of increased demands. The number of employees rose 6 percent between 1968 and 1970. It has been only since 1971 that the total number of regular employees has been cut, but increased federal money to Newark has kept per capita costs high.

Improving City Government

Charter Commission. The 1953 Charter Commission recognized the problems of poor management and recommended the adoption of a mayor-council government to replace the commission form. It said

this would eliminate the weaknesses of split administrative control
and create strong political leadership through an elected mayor. Home
rule, more responsive government, and sounder administration were
hoped for, but the mayor-council government never reached its anticipated potential of effectiveness and efficiency.

Touche Ross Consultants. In 1970, with Mayor Gibson's endorsement,
the business community financed a study of Newark's government by
Touche Ross and Company and arranged for Robert Smith, vice-presi-
dent of Prudential Insurance Company in Newark, to act as city business administrator until a permanent appointment could be made.[1]

Only some of the study's recommendations were politically feasible, and savings were less than expected. The report's recommendations were fairly standard but erred in comparing Newark statistically
with other cities of similar size. It did not sufficiently consider geography, historical development, politics, poverty, need, economy, and
other factors. It recommended reductions or increases in the work
force, for example, based principally on the total number of employees
in similar departments in other cities. Work load and need turned
out to be secondary factors. Perhaps its main contribution was to
stimulate the city administration into making some broad reorganization moves, such as appointment of a business administrator, expanding
the responsibility of CDA, and seriously looking at government efficiency.

Mayor-Council Relations. Mayor Gibson has been successful in dealing
with some issues and unsuccessful with others. He has managed to
hire some competent staff but has been plagued by patronage struggles
and other problems with the city council. When he tried to increase
work hours over 30 per week, the courts ruled in favor of civil service,
stating it was a matter to be negotiated. And most of his recommendations on budget cuts have been turned down. Of 450 reductions recommended by his finance director in 1971, 450 were put back in by
city council.

Gibson has been unable to establish a working relationship with
city council; the fault lies jointly with Gibson and the council, a situation created by both accident and design. Gibson's attitude is that
he is available and council members can see him any time they want.
In contrast, ex-Mayor Addonizio developed close rapport with council
and sat in on its deliberations. Under Gibson, communications are
poor, council is not consulted, informative reports to it are infrequent,
and it receives some material too late or is ill-informed on important
issues. The council has reacted by stalling projects and demanding
that it too be allowed to run programs and hire people.

Moreover, the business administrator, the mayor's staff, and Model Cities have not tried hard enough or simply have not been sufficiently effective in establishing rapport with city council. Model Cities particularly developed poor relationships with council. It placed political pressure on city council several times. When the mayor became distraught about council's refusal to enact several new taxes for which he had gained state legislative approval (after several trips to the state capital, Trenton), large groups of Model Cities workers took to the streets on foot and in several trucks to muster "community support" for the taxes to be presented to city council. A near riot ensued at the council meeting, and a deeper, more serious council distrust developed against Model Cities.

Model Cities personnel were also active during the 11-week school strike. They mustered the same kind of "community support" at a meeting of the school board that almost resulted in a riot. When the strike had outlived its political usefulness, Model Cities arranged "community support" for a plan that had been opposed six weeks earlier. This type of political pressure strained relations with most of Newark's elected officials.

Furthermore, Model Cities brought things to a near boiling point by holding back information and forwarding reports so near HUD deadlines that council did not have sufficient time to analyze them and make changes. Documents were falsified by the CDA, and the administration tried to "end run" the council by seeking direct HUD approval of Planned Variations without even the council's knowledge of the project. When this approach failed, Junius Williams, then CDA director, drew up new documents, with new dates, and forwarded them to council. Naturally, the council exploded when it discovered what had occurred.

For months the council refused to approve Planned Variations, not only because of the above action but because it wanted final approval power for programs and a voice in who would be hired to run them. Councilmen have been disturbed about Gibson's out-of-town hirings, and one member has called nonresidents "poverty pimps" because they "jump from one program to another, only trying to take care of themselves."

Relations have improved somewhat. Planned Variations was eventually approved, and a liaison position has been created to develop better mayor-council communication. More information is being sent to councilmen, and other procedures have been improved. However, even with these changes, it appears that unbridled cooperation from city council is unlikely. At least two council members have their sights on the next mayoral campaign, and it is hard to believe that they will be willing to let Gibson achieve much success.

146

Office of Newark Studies. In addition to consultant recommendations, there have been other types of private help. One is the Office of Newark Studies. This private, nonprofit operation is funded by three foundations and was established early in Gibson's administration to provide him with some expert help. The office has been engaged largely in projects for which regular city staff would have difficulty finding time and for which they would lack expertise, such as the watershed project —the study of a 50-square-mile area (almost twice Newark's size, 30 miles northwest of the city) that was purchased by the city at the turn of the century and that could turn out to be one of the city's major economic and recreational assets; executive personnel search for the mayor; staffing and implementing of the Education Task Force, which advises the mayor and Board of Education; relations with New York Port Authority; cable TV studies; management training seminars for employees; reorganization proposals for Urban Renewal and Public Housing; study of general revenue sharing; assisting in Phase I of Planned Variations proposals; and paying some city staff and supplementing some salaries from its budget in order to retain qualified personnel.

Service Improvements. As a result of organizational changes, increased staff and funding capacity, and Gibson's executive abilities, a number of achievements have taken place. For example, refuse routes have been more properly balanced, making signs for alternate street parking is under way in order to effect better street cleaning, preventive maintenance for equipment has been instituted, work crews are more effectively utilized, automated billing is in operation, license fees have been raised where appropriate, and an integrated financial and budget system for all local-state-federal funds is being instituted. The whole criminal justice system is being improved.

When Gibson first tried to make changes in the Police Department, he ran into trouble. When he recommended the appointment of John L. Redden as police chief, the council balked nine to zero. It was only after a threat by Gibson to bring the scorn of his constituents upon the council members that they finally approved. Blacks were displeased because Redden is white; whites were displeased because his record indicated he was the kind of man no politican could control. In spite of this, Redden was appointed and is proving his ability to get along with blacks and is increasing their number in the police department. In 1967, out of a department of 1,175, there were 150 blacks. Now there are 210, and 15 are in high positions. And there are special programs to recruit and upgrade blacks and Puerto Ricans (funded in part by CDA and a grant received through the Police Community Relations staff). Nearly 5,000 applicants were attracted during the latest recruitment campaign.

In recent months the crime index has dropped slightly, and the city is working closely with Essex County in an Organized Crime Task Force and in a city-state-federal narcotics task force. A computer data system is to be established for the courts and city agencies. A full complement of judges and a court administrator are to be added to improve procedures and speed trials.

There are serious problems with fire safety, and the number of fires increased 23 percent from 1970 to 1971 and has continued at this high rate. To offset this situation, a major demolition program has been undertaken, and building inspections were increased more than 120 percent in 1971 over 1970. Gibson also plans a major drive for more black and Puerto Rican firemen.

There are other changes. A citywide Recreation Department has been established. Action Now (complaint) centers received 21,300 complaints and requests in 1971 and serviced 19,700. A Model Cities Consumer Affairs Office has assisted approximately 7,000 people to date. In addition, an ombudsman office has been created so that complaints can be pursued independently and hopefully with greater effectiveness. On the other hand, two of the most troublesome areas have been the city's inability to coordinate effectively and to resolve personal differences among staff.

Model Cities

The success of Model Cities is very much dependent upon its ability to work closely with city departments and motivate personnel into providing better services over the long run. Success is also dependent on its capacity to administer effectively its own program. A review of the characteristics of the Model Neighborhood, program administration, citizen participation, and project effectiveness will shed light on Newark's program.

The Model Neighborhood

The Model Neighborhood is divided into 13 districts. There has always been criticism that boundaries were drawn for political purposes and are poorly defined. The area is composed of 76,087 residents of several ethnic backgrounds, about 77 percent black, 15 percent Spanish-speaking, and 8 percent Italian and other ethnic groups. Approximately 36,000 receive some form of public assistance, and about 17 percent are unemployed.

Health care facilities are inadequate, and all health indices are substantially worse than for the rest of the community. Even figures for the city as a whole are worse than for other areas. The

TABLE 7

Deaths per 1,000 Population for Certain Diseases
1969, Newark

Cause of Death	Number of Deaths (Newark)	Rate in Newark	Rate in N.J.	Rate in U.S.
All causes	4,434	11.0	9.3	9.3
Heart diseases	1,890	470.6	407.9	359.2
Cancer	677	168.6	177.7	156.5
Tuberculosis	34	8.4	2.9	2.9
Diabetes	125	31.1	20.6	18.8
Pneumonia/influenza	154	37.6	29.2	28.2
Cirrhosis of liver	97	24.1	18.1	14.1
Infant mortality (Deaths of infants under age one per 1,000 live births)	312	33.9	20.2	18.4

Source: New Jersey State Department of Health, New Jersey
Health Statistics, 1969, Trenton.

National Commission on Health Services reports that the death rate
for all of Newark is 35 percent above the national standard, after
allowances for variations in population, age, sex, and race.[2] (See
Table 7.) The Hospital and Health Council of Metropolitan New Jersey,
Inc. reports that physicians have left the city in vast numbers; the
doctor population dropped to 469 (1.1 per 1,000 population) in 1968
from 888 (2.1 per 1,000 population) in 1956. And conditions in the
Model Neighborhood are more severe.

The city's crime rate is among the highest in the nation, rising
74 percent between 1960 and 1970, while the total population dropped
5 percent. And crime in the Model Neighborhood is higher than for
the city as a whole.

There are no new or adequate educational facilities here. Ten
of the 14 permanent elementary schools were constructed before 1901;
72 percent of elementary classrooms, 11 elementary schools, one
junior high school, and two special schools need replacing. There is
little environmental incentive to finish high school, and everybody is
aware of the failure of the educational system. In the city as a whole,
elementary schools operate at 112 percent of capacity, with some

having 51 percent more pupils than planned. A May 1969 study by
Research for Better Schools illustrates the negative attitudes of black
Model Neighborhood residents toward the public school system. The
report states, "Both blacks and whites in Newark tend to regard the
public school system as 'only fair to poor'."

Rating	Blacks	Whites
Excellent	4.5	9.1
Good	22.3	34.5
Fair	36.9	29.3
Poor	36.4	26.6

An estimated 85 percent of the housing units in the model area
were built prior to 1940 and 74.3 percent are deficient. Discrimination continues to perpetuate segregation as a living pattern and is as
strong against whites as blacks primarily because of a strong black
nationalist movement. And residents are unable to pay for decent
housing. Over 50 percent of all families earn less than $5,000 a year,
putting the median rent-paying ability at $1,000 per year or $83 per
month (at best)—the low-cost housing range. In the city as a whole,
from 1969 to June 1972, no single family or public housing units were
built, and only 14 two-family and 682 multifamily units were constructed, while close to 10,000 units were demolished.

Traditionally, few agencies have provided multiple social services. Among the most prominent providing services have been the
Community Information and Referral Center, Urban League of Essex
County, and the Boys' Club. New federal funds are acting as a catalyst for new centers. But recreational and cultural facilities are also
inadequate, a problem somewhat alleviated by the creation of a citywide parks and recreation program and funds for cultural activities.
Nevertheless, residents reflect an utter sense of hopelessness and
negativism about services and the quality of life.

Administrative Structure of the Model
Cities Program

These wretched conditions caused city officials to apply to Model
Cities early in the program's history. The city received a $204,000
planning grant from HUD on October 12, 1968, but it was not until
March 17, 1970 that the first action year plan was approved. Subsequently, the second and third years were approved close to schedule,
and fortunately a $7 million Planned Variations Program was approved
as well. With this money, an elaborate administrative staff was developed.

Expanding CDA Functions. The CDA, having been established well
before Model Cities, was eventually charged with developing broad
policies in both physical and human development and coordinating
departments and agencies and encouraging them to meet city goals.
Its early tasks were primarily in the areas of manpower and economic
development, but it gathered strength as it assumed traditional city
planning functions, capital budgeting, and Model Cities.

When Gibson took office in the summer of 1970, CDA was already
empowered to do comprehensive planning but was limited because of
lack of funds. Model Cities became its chief source of money, along
with smaller amounts from criminal justice and health planning services, the New Jersey Department of Community Affairs, HUD physical
planning programs, and the city's existing planning division. The
Model Cities Community Development Agency was looked upon as the
"little CDA" and the city's Community Development Administration,
with citywide mandate, as the "big CDA." It resulted in Model Cities
doing citywide planning because the city lacked a staff of its own.

Reorganizing the CDA. During the planning year and first action year,
Model Cities expenditures were at an all-time low, staff was inadequate,
and there was no training programs to upgrade staff. Programs were
fragmented, small, and ineffective. During these first years there
was criticism that the Addonizio Administration was protecting itself
from "threats represented by possible multi-million dollar funding
and by an organized and demanding community." This inactivity resulted in less than half of the allocated $5.6 million being spent during
the first action year.

When Gibson was elected, he took a new look at Model Cities,
restructured programs, and established new priorities. Model Cities
CDA was to become essentially a comprehensive planning organization, charged with interrelating programs. For example, drug rehabilitation would be correlated with requirements for special housing,
education, health, and legal services; health care centers would involve physical planners for architectual drawings, property approval,
acquisition, and identification of the types of manpower necessary
for construction or renovation. The manpower planner would concern
himself with minority hiring. the health planner and education planner
with programs and training of paraprofessionals, the budget office
with systematic allocation of resources, and so on, and all this would
be integrated in a comprehensive delivery of services to the neighborhood.

Knowing what had to be done, Williams divided the CDA into
five major units: planning, operations, evaluation and information,
community organization, and management services. Under Addonizio,
it was structured along program lines: education, housing, health,

and so on. The new organization allowed fewer professionals and greater expertise to utilize specialized talents in all program areas. Under operations, for example, where contract preparation and compliance is a major part of the work load, technicians now handle contracts for all types of programs, since the nature of the work is the same. Previously, a single coordinator for each program had to plan, negotiate contracts, evaluate, develop citizen participation, and manage finances, purchasing, personnel, training, and public relations. The new arrangement is a considerable improvement.

The first four months of the Gibson Administration were spent recycling existing funds into more meaningful programs, budgeting enough to allow staff to carry out programs adequately, and eliminating duplication. Planners were no longer required to implement programs as part of their function. For the first time, a chief planner was appointed to integrate all plans, and, most importantly, the goal of institutional change was introduced. CDA began looking into city, public, and private agencies to change or improve the way goods and services were delivered to citizens.

Williams wanted plans to be more than empty promises, and he did not want the CDAs, both large and small, encumbered by operational responsibilities. Therefore, in August 1970, the Operation Division was established (now called the Division of Contract Compliance) to see that projects were, in fact, begun and that programs had responsible and capable operators. Where good operators were not found, the CDA had to operate some projects itself.

Although the CDA staff is professional, for the most part it had little prior experience in developing a comprehensive program; therefore, it wisely drew on the expertise of other agencies for help in designing and operating programs. The following is a partial list of these agencies: Association for Retarded Children, College of Medicine and Dentistry of New Jersey at Newark, Housing Development and Rehabilitation Corporation, American Red Cross, Neighborhood Youth Corps, Better Business Bureau, Federal Trade Commission, Newark Housing Council, Princeton University, Essex County Welfare Board, Newark Legal Services, Minority Contractors Association, Essex County Community College, the African Free School, Rutgers University, and Newark College of Engineering.

Administrative Costs. Because of a slow start, administrative costs for the first action year were excessively high: $1,445,000 for $4,209,000 of budgeted projects, or 34 percent. By June 30, 1971, 15 months after the beginning of the first action year, seven projects had incurred no costs and 21 had expenditures of $1,511,707. Administrative costs were $1,573,082 or 104 percent of project costs, due largely to the change in administrations and consequent necessity to reevaluate program priorities and an unusually long planning and action year period. Subsequent action years show a substantial reduction in administrative costs. And when all funds generated and administered annually ($16,562,000), including other than Model Cities money, are compared to administrative costs ($3,073,000), program administration drops to 16 percent. Since the CDA is assuming a large part of the city's planning function, these costs are probably acceptable, based on the responsibilities given to the CDA.

CDA staff is now under an extensive training program. Training is also being provided to other Model Cities personnel and residents involved in the program. Over 31 different training programs are used, all of which are expected to upgrade participants substantially.

Departmental Coordination and Financial Integration

Community Development Administration. Since the creation of the Community Development Administration, its powers have been expanded to include planning and coordination over Model Cities, the Office of Economic Development, Office of Manpower, and Division of City Planning. It has become the principal planning arm of the city and has helped to integrate some planning functions with city services. During these initial stages Williams felt there was little choice but to go around city departments and to serve people in a new way.

The Shadow Government. However, Williams operated independently —like a "second government"—arrogant to department heads and city council. The CDA was never able to develop comprehensive planning capability because it concentrated primarily on Model Cities planning and did only limited city planning and law enforcement and health planning. It has been regarded as little more than the administrative arm of Model Cities and has gotten so closely involved with some projects that it is considered their operator. Some department heads regard it as just another line agency.

Bodine has tried to have traditional city functions transferred to him. In an early meeting with Williams, some rapport was established. They agreed that street lighting contracts should be handled centrally, that there should not be two street cleaning departments, and that certain other functions—code enforcement, street repairs, and capital improvements—should be coordinated by the business administrator. It was also decided that it would be wise to place transportation planning under Bodine because he was in charge of the engineering department, which handled traffic and safety studies. Bodine was also planning a central business district (CBD) study, requiring extensive transportation considerations.

Toward an Integrated Financial System. Almost all federal programs are treated separately from city operations. Federal funds are not included in total city financial statements or budgets, and they are not centrally monitored. The method of funding has encouraged separate bureaucracies and has also created a serious morale problem because employees in federal programs have been able to establish higher salaries for themselves. Separate finance, purchase, and personnel departments were also created. Bodine calls this "reinventing the wheel" and abhors the fact that more money is spent on federal program financing and personnel administration than on the city as a whole. Even outside computers, rather than the city's, are used for federal programs. Bodine believes that at least 12 staff and auxiliary services should be operated centrally for all regular departments and federal-state programing: Finance and Accounting, Computer Data Processing, Engineering, Physical Planning, Legal Counsel, Motor Vehicle Maintenance, Personnel Administration, Purchasing, Office Space Allocation, Central Store, Telephone Communications, and Property Inventory. Fortunately, steps are now being taken to create such an integrated system.

Budget as a Planning Mechanism. In most cities, the budget process is the primary planning mechanism. In an attempt to use the budget to its full advantage, Bodine issued a 52-page operating budget manual in August 1971 that stressed functional performance, productivity, and results. It met with resistance at both the operating and legislative levels. When reports were returned, objectives and productivity standards were missing, most federal programs were excluded, and there was no consistent policy for capital budgeting. Departments were not cognizant of their revenue-producing role, and, in addition, state line-item requirements impaired logical grouping of programs and items. Only slowly are these problems being resolved.

A study prepared by the International City Management Association and the National League of Cities/U.S. Conference of Mayors pointed out that fiscal improvements are made difficult because of an understaffed finance department, inadequate accounting and book-keeping techniques, poor records on project completion, and absence of coordination between planning and budgeting.[3] For example, the city's six-year capital improvement project was planned independently of the Finance Department. And the most vociferous department heads have been getting the largest amount of dollars. One budget staff member summed it up by saying that "city council makes no decisions on a rational basis."

The report goes on to say that full revenues from idle funds are not realized because of failure to invest promptly, and little help is gleaned from accountants appointed to city jobs by the state under

154

patronage contracts. Accountants operate under the State of New Jersey Registered Municipal Accountants (RMA) law but have traditionally been chosen on a favoritism basis.

And as explained earlier, the Budget process is made even more complex because of the independence of the Board of Education budget. City council normally adopts it without the Finance Department getting a look at it, although its staff is too limited to analyze it in detail anyway. Even if the city objects to education expenditures, the Board of Education can appeal to the State Department of Education, which, in the past, has restored all cuts in their entirety. And as noted previously, the Board of School Estimate (a combination of city administration, city council, and school board), city council, and/or city administration can make reductions only to the total education budget, not line items.

The Confused Roles of Chief Executive and Chief Administrator. The roles of the mayor and administrator have also been problems. And key officials visualize them differently. Bodine sees the mayor performing four basic roles: (1) representing the city in a Broad capacity and establishing communication with residents; (2) policy formulation and over-all direction of programs; (3) evaluation of management; and (4) maintaining effective relationships with city council and governments and agencies outside the city. More specifically, he identifies 11 "inescapable activities" under the mayor that cannot be readily reduced in number: legal council; office administration (mayor's office); personal affairs (security, private secretarial); research (Office of Newark Studies); ad hoc intelligence and trouble shooting; projection of image and program; labor policy coordination; local outreach and feedback; program policy formulation and appraisal; program policy relations; and operations management.

Many key personnel prefer to report directly to the mayor as the chief executive officer. Some observers believe that this may not be an impossible task for mayors who are operating under effective and long established organizations with few union or citizen pressures, who do not have to leave the city extensively to lobby for federal and state funds, and, in short, have the experience and time to function as chief administrative officer as well as chief policy-maker. This does not appear to be the case in Newark, where Mayor Gibson has had to busy himself constantly with emergencies and new developments.

Mayor's Staff and Cabinet. The mayor has taken a number of steps to ease his position. He has increased his personal staff so that he may become as informed as possible. He meets with his cabinet—consisting of a flexible group of 15 to 20 department heads and staff aides—every two weeks to discuss general policies and strategy.

155

The business administrator holds weekly staff meetings primarily with department heads to outline programs in greater operating detail. Staff meetings have proved to be a successful management technique. However, they were blighted by the lack of attendance of former CDA Administrator Williams and, at times, other key staff who have complained that little is being accomplished at the meetings. The absence of the city's mayor planning unit from efforts at central coordination has left a serious gap in the effectiveness of Newark's government.

Mayor's Office of Policy and Review. Instead of facing this problem head on, the mayor chose to create the Office of Policy and Review, which he expected would apply some controls, although indirectly, on the CDA. Policy and Review was established as part of the Planned Variations Program and is headed by David Dennison, former deputy director under Williams. It has been assigned the A-95 program review and evaluation process. However, Dennison and Williams were at serious odds with each other on a number of issues, particularly as to how federal programs ought to be handled. Moreover, they operated their departments independently of one another and reported directly to the mayor without the benefit of close liaison with the business administrator. As a result, the necessity to handle voluminous planning and statistical information and day-to-day operational detail was stifled because all related planning and policy functions did not go through one administrative source. Moreover, a number of officials felt that the Office of Policy and Review was headed in the direction of a "fifth wheel" and greater dispersion, rather than to a resolution of the problem. This lack of coordination and integration of departments adversely affected the performance of both the Model Cities and Planned Variations programs.

After many months of frustration and delays, Mayor Gibson finally dismissed Williams in early 1973 and began to take steps to develop a more integrated system of management under more clearly established leadership. But a serious flaw still exists in that major programs remain relatively independent and full planning and coordinating activities have not been delegated to one chief administrative officer; therefore, the responsibility for coordination has fallen on the mayor, an impossible task if he is to perform fully and effectively the major responsibilities of his role.

State and Federal Assistance

Federal and state agencies have been anxious to help Newark. The New Jersey Community Affairs Department, state overseer of Model Cities, has been particularly helpful. It provided $60,000 in initial planning funds and $400,000 for programs in the first action year. A state education specialist was assigned to Newark's program full time. In addition, the city has received technical assistance as well as a planning grant from the State Law Enforcement Planning Agency (SLEPA) and also grants from the Regional Medical Program. New Jersey has also assisted the city by (1) helping to support Martland Hospital; (2) beginning construction of the New Jersey College of Medicine and Dentistry (a project delayed since 1967); (3) doubling untethered urban aid grants; (4) passing legislation to allow the city to impose new taxes of its own; (5) transplanting an entire public health staff to Newark to assist in the construction of a public health system; and (6) picking up much of the local share on projects that it administered itself but that would never have functioned if Newark had to provide the funds.

The city has had unusually good results in grantsmanship because of the great needs and problems of the city and Gibson's sincerity in doing something about them. He has established an Office of Intergovernmental Affairs to seek greater assistance and to keep local officials informed. The city generated $80 million in federal funds and more than 1,000 jobs up to September 1971 (See Table 8). When taking into account federal, state, and private grants, Newark generated over $250 million in 1971, more than the entire city budget.

Citizen Participation

Under both Addonizio and Gibson, before and after reorganization of the CDA, citizen participation remained weak and citizens continued to feel apathetic about the whole program. To date, the Model Neighborhood Council (citizens' board) is not meeting regularly and wields little power. From its inception the council was composed of 52 members who are elected for staggered two-year terms, from 13 districts (four from each district). A brief history of the development of the citizen planning process is important.

The First Elections. As time neared for the first Model Cities election in 1968, a dissident group led by Junius Williams and called the Newark Area Planning Association (NAPA) held its own election outside federal guidelines, in anticipation of gaining control and power. This nearly cost Newark its first year's funding. And HUD was forced to nullify the "election" and call another. It is important to recall that any method of selection short of popular election would have been impossible under the conditions that existed at the time. The second election, conducted with regular city voting machines, drew 6,000 voters and was considered rather successful in terms of numbers and interest. This first council, as well as subsequent ones, retained some Addonizio people and control.

157

TABLE 8

Funds Generated and Expended, Newark, October 1971

Program	Money Allocated[a]	Money Spent[b]	Jobs Generated[c]
Neighborhood improvements and services	$4,077,477	$1,421,656	55
Housing	53,033,400[d]	126,549	9
Health	3,005,966	324,342	84
Social services	2,644, 251	491,128	147
Law enforcement-criminal justice	3,849,972	996,427	403
Education	2,095,968	564,583	225
Manpower and economic development	409,172	94,277	72
Administration (planning, citizen participation, and evaluation)	3,778,710	2,128,816	163
Planned Variations	7,000,000	—	n.a.
Total	$79,894,916[d]	$5,547,778	1,158

[a]Source: CDA Program Report and Comptroller's Office.
[b]Source: Comptroller's Office. Includes HUD, HEW, and N.J. Department of Community Affairs and some SLEPA expenditures only. Does not include expenditures of monies from other sources that are not recorded by CDA comptroller. Thus, this is only a partial listing of expenditures.
[c]Source: CDA Planning Department estimates.
[d]Includes $50,000,000 in Project Rehab loans; however, it distorts the "money spent" column because loans are long-term commitments and are not "spent" by the city.

Early Citizen Involvement. In a review of the historical development of the Model Neighborhood Council,[4] written by Junius Williams, the rise of NAPA is traced from a black community group concerned with urban renewal to the establishment of a task force called Ad Hoc Model Cities Committee, which nominated candidates and arranged the rival election. "The result," says Williams, "was the biggest non-municipal election ever held in Newark at that time, and a defeat for City Hall candidates. Over 500 people voted." But the city called it invalid because it violated HUD guidelines by opening the vote to residents outside the Model Neighborhood. Nevertheless, NAPA insisted that all residents of Newark had the right to vote.

HUD called for new elections. Few residents voted in this second election, in August 1969, because the novelty of the program had worn off and citizens were distrustful. NAPA won three of the four representatives from its district, and, of the 52 total members elected, six were white and six Puerto Rican. But the council reflected severe racial tensions. Anthony Imperiale, a "white vigilante," was elected vice president out of fear, Williams says, by a sizable number of representatives who were backed by city hall. Williams was elected cochairman. Imperiale attended only one Model Cities meeting after his election. It was believed he used his vice-chairmanship only to gain support and get elected to city council.

Shortly after the election, the Addonizio Administration moved decisively to gain control by offering city jobs to Model Neighborhood Council members, Williams states. After attempting to work with the council for some time, Williams resigned because of the inability to work under such a confused power structure and competing chairmen. He notes that the council "represented citizen participation in name only" and that Model Cities "was merely subsidizing 'Uncle Toms'," instead of building leaders. Participation was virtually nonexistent. Many residents considered it "a joke." Outsiders were generally excluded from meetings and had to seek special permission a week in advance in order to attend. Distrust was the predominant feature and disruption the common tactic used to make a point. But if it did not seem to matter because most citizens felt that protest was useless anyway and had achieved nothing but promises.

Business Community and Participation. With this shaky start, the Model Cities Council proceeded to organize. It formed seven task forces that are still used as the basis for citizen input: education, health, housing, social services, law and public safety, manpower and economic development, and neighborhood improvement and services. Model Neighborhood residents, other than elected council members, along with individuals and organizations who represent citywide interests, participated in the task force meetings, which were designed along the lines of "town hall" meetings and were called community assemblies.

Although 127 formal task force meetings were held during the first planning year, very few residents who were not council members participated. Some businesses and organizations participated in a few meetings and provided meeting space and some technical assistance. Some of the participating groups were Prudential Life Insurance Company, Greater Newark Chamber of Commerce, Newark

Hospital and Health Council, New Jersey Pharmaceutical Society, AFL-CIO Industrial Trade Council, Public Service Electric and Gas Company, United Steel Workers, United Community Council, and the Urban League of Essex County. However, involvement for most was shallow and short-lived. As with most Model Cities programs, many agency people and businessmen became discouraged and impatient with the delays and disruption.

Addonizio and Participation. The extent of citizen participation in Newark, over the life of the program, has depended mostly on the intent of the Model Cities director and the administration. The first director, Donald Malafronte, was a former newspaper reporter-editor. Highly capable, he produced quality technical work and was the central figure and architect of the action plan. To make his position more attractive, his $15,000 city salary was supplemented with Model Cities money (as were salaries of some other employees). He worked long hours administering the program, as well as tending to political battles at City Hall. Conversely, Mayor Addonizio was interested in taking political advantage of the program. He saw Malafronte simply as his agent. And it was not long before large numbers of Addonizio supporters were put on the Model Cities payroll as patronage workers. Therefore, the program and citizen participation never got off the ground.

Gibson and Participation. With Gibson it has been a different story. He replaced almost all patronage employees with Model Neighborhood residents, mostly as agreed to by local citizens. And for the most part, he has run a clean, patronage-free ship, in sharp contrast to PEP. Nevertheless, some Model Cities appointments were made as a necessary political expedience, to "keep the peace" and allow the program to run without too much interference.

 With residents as employees, naturally participation increased. And the positive philosophy of both Gibson and Williams helped. For example, Williams believed that citizens should be involved on a block-by-block, house-by-house basis in continuous dialogue and interrelationship. He stated early in 1970 that the Model Neighborhood Council and task forces were enriched by resident input: "As a result of the CDA and Model Neighborhood Council's policy of bringing citizens beyond the Model Neighborhood Council membership—into active participation in all phases of Model Cities work—we have developed in Newark, in less than a year, an official citizens' structure more accountable to citizens as a whole, than any Model Cities area in the nation. . . . Residents of the impacted areas [must become sufficiently] organized to take their destiny into their own hands." Newark's plans have reflected this feeling too. They stress that adequate services, consumer protection, revitalization of the slums, and decreased crime cannot be achieved solely through comprehensive planning—that organized citizen action is needed. All in all, the Gibson Administration has been sincere about citizen participation, yet citizens have never developed any formal strength.

The power of the Model Neighborhood Council has always been limited, even though the council and the CDA share joint veto power over Model Cities programs, as stated in the planning grant and approved by city council: "The Model Neighborhood Council will have the power by majority vote to veto any action program to be funded with Model Cities supplemental grant funds. . . . When an action program has been approved by both the Neighborhood Council and the CDA, it will then be submitted to the local governing body as required by law."

In addition to negative control, the Neighborhood Council has responsibilities of review and approval of all task force program recommendations. Some staff is provided to the task forces on request, and it also has four staff members of its own. However, there is little policy development or decision-making by council members.

The first council was highly inactive and came to a standstill during the mayoral elections. Because of this, it spent most of its time reviewing previous activities and was unable to get the program moving. But council training and educational retreats improved performance. And a successful community conference dispelled some negative community thinking and developed new insights about problems. Since the specialized task forces alone could not reach all constituents, "town hall" meetings and black clubs have been successfully used to involve larger numbers of residents and to help dissipate hostility between the CDA and residents. Resolutions were adopted by each task force through district assemblies. Also, monthly meetings increased contact between Neighborhood Council members and residents, yet none of these have successfully dispelled resident distrust and apathy. The number of citizens involved in programs is low, and people are still waiting for things to happen.

The Neighborhood Council never had much power under Williams because his philosophy of participation was different from that of most Model Cities directors. He believed in "partnership" for the Model Council and the CDA, where each would play a different role. He preferred what he called "teamwork," whereby council members were attached to each division of CDA (personnel, evaluation, and so on) to "guarantee" citizen involvement. There is little question that a close relationship is necessary between council members and staff, but this scheme left little authority in the hands of the citizens' board.

By fall 1972, the council was not having any more success in controlling the program or in its relationships with the CDA and residents. Sally Carroll, chairman of the council and also president of the local NAACP, stated that the CDA overwhelmed the board in a power struggle. Although each was to have veto power, this has not been the case for the Neighborhood Council. Ms. Carroll says that Model Cities decisions are made by city hall and that the Neighborhood Council is only advisory. Model Cities communication with residents is poor, and, in fact, practically nonexistent, she said. The main access to residents is the 13 district assemblies, where "some information is distributed." The community as a whole appears not to be motivated to improving itself, and, citizen enclaves, fighting among themselves, are not helping the situation.

Groups Left out of Participation. In addition to internal struggles, many other groups feel forgotten. Puerto Ricans, particularly, feel left out and are rebelling against the program. And the white minority feels it is on the outside, too. In an August 1972 review of Newark's ethnic problems, David K. Shiplei stated that colleges that "send recruiters to Newark do so in search of blacks, not working-class whites. Federal programs designed to help youngsters get jobs, keep off drugs, provide recreation, and improve schooling are aimed at blacks, staffed by blacks, and located in black neighborhoods."[5]

An umbrella organization, known as the Unified Vailsburg Committee, was created to change this by encompassing many dissident white groups, liberals, John Birchers, and supporters of Alabama's George Wallace. Rev. John R. Sharp, community leader and Presbyterian minister in the mostly white Vailsburg section, believes that the Vailsburg Committee could be more moderate. But one of its members states, "If we did, they'd walk over us, and so what we do is go all the way to the right . . . and we let you guys do all the negotiation." Sharp says, "Now it's a problem of trying to convince the black majority to be humane and just toward the white minority."[6]

Yet there are a number of influential black leaders, among them Baraka, who feel change is not coming fast enough and that as a consequence Gibson is losing credibility. Baraka holds monthly leadership conferences for black elected officials and a few others. He stresses the importance of political awareness, gaining control of city council and the board of education and acquiring economic power. In his view, the system is making Gibson fail.

In the winter of 1972, Baraka's Kawaida Temple set up a corporation that started construction on a 16-story low- and middle-income apartment building that is to include the full "social amenities"—recreation and hobby areas, day care, theater, audiovisual center, compacter for bulk waste, and family counseling. But demonstrators, including two state assemblymen and white militants of the North Ward Citizen Council, temporarily blocked the project. Assemblyman

Anthony Imperiale threatened to chain himself to the gate leading to the project unless construction was halted. And Supreme Court Judge Irwin I. Kimmelman declared a seven-day "cooling off period." Race appears to be the underlying issue.

There is mixed emotion about "black nationalism." Some residents believe it has successfully and legitimately taken hold of certain parts of government. For some blacks and whites alike, it is something sinister and forbidding. It has stirred up turmoil in the government and neighborhoods. Critics say, "It has not improved education, or jobs, or health—it just makes noise." And since the federal programs are where the money and power are, this movement has headed for these programs and gained control of some. Model Cities is still managing to carve its own way, but city council is worried. Nevertheless, in recent months, more and more citizens have begun to look at the movement as a legitimate political and economic system that does not necessarily have to hurt any race. Most observers believe that Gibson has not allowed it to dominate his command of the administration and that he will remain strong enough to lead the city impartially.

Gibson is trying to balance power and treat whites and blacks equitably, in order to retain a mixed community. He has appointed both white and Spanish-speaking persons to key posts. Philosophically, he believes in citizen involvement. But the many dissident groups have not allowed participation to function smoothly. Now, under Planned Variations, he has created an appointive citywide citizen body for more effective central control and in response to city council demands. However, it appears little formal power will be given the new citizens' group. Moreover, in addition to keeping power factions balanced, other problems have crept into the Model Cities Program.

Congressional Hearing on Newark
Model Cities

A hearing on Newark's Model Cities Program conducted by the House Committee on Banking and Currency, September 8, 1972, revealed poor bookkeeping procedures and possible misuse of funds. A review presented by HUD auditors recommended the establishment of an effective monitoring and auditing system for operating agencies, as well as the CDA. The CDA substantially agreed with the findings and attributed faults to insufficient fiscal staff and lack of an effective administrative system to ensure submission of regional statements. The hearing disclosed that

. . . the CDA had not complied with HUD regulations regarding the necessary accounting systems evaluations,

fiscal monitoring and required auditing of the projects
administered by the Operations Agencies (OAs). There
was no systematic collection of data from the various
projects, no effective distribution of this data to the appropriate CDA departments once it had been collected
and, consequently, the CDA had no assurance that the
funds furnished to the OAs were being used effectively
and efficiently to accomplish the purposes for which the
funds were made available.[7]

Audits revealed that in at least six instances local laws were
not followed that require advertising and competitive bids for purchase of items and letting of contracts over $2,500. In one case, a
$10,000 printing press was ordered from Jersey Office Supply Com-
pany in component parts, each costing less than $2,500. And although
$7,500 was paid, no parts were delivered. The order was eventually
canceled. Also, four automobiles were purchased for $2,459 per car.
Allegations from several sources, including an unidentified employee,
contend these and certain other transactions were taken for the purpose of avoiding city bidding requirements. However, Junius Williams
indicated that this was the only way these particular items could be
purchased and that there was no intent to by-pass regulations.
    In regard to expenditures, Curtis A. Prins, chief investigator
of the committee, cited several questionable vouchers, which he said
were among hundreds more. These included a chauffeur for Williams,
purchase of cigarettes, cigars, and alcoholic beverages, and unusually
large dinner and travel expenses. Williams stated "sloppy bookkeeping" measures were to blame for improper charges of cigarettes
and alcohol to HUD accounts, when these should have been charged
to the city, "which allows such expenditures." He also indicated that
in a number of cases liquor bills were paid by personal checks. Unusually large travel expenses were described by Williams as necessi-
ties to meet HUD citizen participation requirements, which at times
obligated the CDA to take large citizen delegations to out-of-town
meetings, so they could become better informed, and also to local
retreats, so they could assist in the timely compilation of plans and
contracts.
    A contract to teach 100 Model Cities children how to ride and
handle horses was questioned by Prins. It was brought out that citizens were not getting the full benefit of Model Cities programs. Prins
stated in this case, expenditures were above the "going rate," lists of
participants were not available, the stables and horses were in deplorable condition, and, in effect, the program was used to give pony
rides to entertain children rather than to teach them. Williams explained this contract not only helped a minority entrepreneur, Wright-

Way, but allowed hundreds of kids to ride, culminating in a citywide Labor Day event featuring riding activities.

An apparent duplication in transportation studies by the city and state was credibly explained by Williams as necessary to convince the state that its plan was unsatisfactory and detrimental to residents. Williams said that the CDA study convinced the state that MacArthur Highway could be upgraded and thus land be spared and that it would be unnecessary to relocate 10,000 to 12,000 residents.[8]

In summary, the hearings revealed that there were some worthy Model Cities programs and that administrative improvements were being made to upgrade the program. However, there was little question that bookkeeping and purchasing procedures have to be drastically improved, operating agencies subjected to much closer surveillance, and questionable expenditures and marginal programs eliminated, if Newark Model Cities is to succeed and provide Model Neighborhood residents with reasonable benefits. The next section examines the effectiveness of some of the Model Cities projects.

Projects

The following is not a detailed description or evaluation of projects but a review of some significant developments in the major program areas during the first two action years. It provides the reader with an understanding—in some cases specific results—of the impact of Model Cities and its potential. Budgets are annual figures for the second action year but in some cases represent funds carried over from the first action year as well. Budgets are presented only to give some idea of the scope of the programs.

Neighborhood Improvements and Services. This program is chiefly concerned with producing a general physical plan for the Model Neighborhood, including design, renewal planning, mass transit, and public facilities. In addition, a $389 million New-Town-in-Town proposal is being developed for 482 acres of land at the eastern end of the MN and renewal areas south of it. The project was allocated $4,077,477, all of which is HUD funds except for $140,000 from the U.S. Department of Transportation, $295,000 from the state of New Jersey, and $225,000 in city money and services. A private consulting firm, Skidmore, Owings and Merrill, helped prepare a general physical plan, which has been published as the basic guide for zoning and new development.

Projects include the following:

1. Construction of 37 bus shelters has been completed.

2. New street lighting and street signs have been installed (2,400 street signs citywide and including alternate street parking signs for better street sweeping).

3. Twenty vest pocket and mini-parks have been built; others are in preparation.

4. A pilot demonstration of urban beautification of two city blocks has been completed (8th and 9th streets between 11th and 12th avenue), including planting of shade trees, tree trimming, and placement of street furniture and trash receptacles. Over 900 trash receptacles have been placed in neighborhoods.

5. A Rodent and Insect Control Program is in operation in over 5,000 units. In the first action year, the State Commissioner of Health halted the program for a time, calling it ineffective; however, it has been considerably improved under the reorganized Health and Welfare Department.

6. About 500 hazardous, abandoned buildings were demolished under a demolition grant and with the aid of PEP workers.

7. An Emergency Repair Service is now in progress to help tenants immediately receive essentials, such as water and heat. Landlords are required to pay the costs of repair. This is part of a Neighborhood Stabilization program to stimulate block associations to improve their environment by providing materials, equipment, and technical assistance to owners and tenants. An individual can receive up to $1,000 of construction materials. CDA operates the Neighborhood Stabilization and Building Improvements project. It has provided fix-up and paintup materials and technical assistance to over 230 owners, tenants, and tenant groups in a 25 block area of the Model Neighborhood. Over 2,700 people have been assisted in a larger area. Low-interest rehabilitation loans and grants are also available for exterior and interior rehabilitation under the Certified Area Program, part of Neighborhood Stabilization. Over 800 families (300 Spanish-speaking) have been assisted in landlord-tenant disputes.

8. Studies are under way for a number of purposes: (1) a transit line along the Springfield boundary of the Model Neighborhood; (2) major renewal activity under HUD's Community Renewal Program (CRP); (3) citywide housing abandonment and litigation involved in tax liens and city ownership of property; and (4) sewage treatment facilities.

Housing. Housing projects total $53,033,400 but include projected rehabilitation loans of $50 million. The remainder is HUD money except for $525,000 from the New Jersey Department of Community Affairs. In April 1970, CDA created the Housing Development and Rehabilitation Corporation (HDRC) as an umbrella agency to coordinate and develop a comprehensive housing program. HDRC sponsors new and rehabilitation projects for low- and moderate income families and acts as prime contractor with public and private developers. Two housing corporations—one for rehabilitation and one for new construction—were

166

combined into HDRC. It administers Newark's Project Rehab, which will eventually insure $50 million in construction loans.

Richard Tager of Skidmore, Owings and Merrill was acting executive director of HDRC until the winter of 1972, when Robert Holmes was appointed full-time director. The corporation secured approval for 300 FHA applications by September 1972 for mortgage guarantees and interest subsidy and is processing 1,000 others. Experienced developers are selected to purchase and rehabilitate property, but some of the local community corporations can also benefit through coalitions with other developers. About 300 units have been rehabilitated and another 240 were under construction at the beginning of 1972. It is estimated about $5 million of development will take place over a two-year period. Tager says this method requires only about six months of processing time as opposed to about two years for normal FHA applications. It is a pilot program with few guidelines, designed to rehabilitate 2,500 units (the remaining 2,000 have been assigned to developers) in Newark over the next two years and will also integrate social services into the plan, including recreation and multipurpose centers, commercial facilities, and health centers.

In conjunction with the program, CDA and its affiliate HDRC operate a $500,000 HUD-funded Relocation Payments Plan, which will assist about 700 Model Neighborhood households displaced by Project Rehab and urban renewal. It is a federal requirement that all families must be provided substitute housing during and after displacement. In a related program, stronger enforcement against blockbusting is taking place because of the transfer of these responsibilities to the city's Human Rights Commission.

HDRC, operating smoothly and efficiently, is one of Model Cities' most successful programs. HUD works closely with it to lessen bureaucratic snags. Tager believes the channels of communication are very good between local and federal agencies, making the program move more rapidly and effectively. In July 1972, James Armstrong, special assistant to Secretary George Romney, called the rehabilitation program "the best in the country." The present strategy is to build a broader role for HDRC as an operating agency for several physical projects (including Neighborhood Stabilization) and also to increase its planning capability. However, some rather difficult organizational and personality problems will have to be overcome first. But the program appears to be headed in the right direction.

Presently, Newark's Housing Authority is responsible for public housing and urban renewal. HDRC is assuming part of the renewal role because of the ineffectiveness of the authority. HUD has charged the Housing Authority with gross incompetence, overstaffing, and lack of effectiveness. In 1971, HUD demanded removal of 47 employees, threatening loss of further funds. But as yet the Housing Authority has not made many changes, although it is under scrutiny for gross mismanagement and bribery. The city has helped it in some reorganization and the selection of a new executive director. The authority has not been able adequately to maintain the 14 public housing projects it supervises, nor has it progressed toward developing the large empty urban renewal sites that deface the city. Many citizens are pinning their hopes on HDRC to do a better job or at least stimulate change. Gibson plans to see that 300 new housing units are under construction during 1973.

Health. Health programs have been allocated $3,005,966, of which the State Health Department will contribute $1,110,000, Newark Health Department $35,000, Medicaid $230,000, State Department of Community Affairs $227,996, HEW $99,768, Regional Medical Program $40,000, City In-Kind $100,000, and New Jersey College of Medicine and Dentistry and Association for Retarded Children over $38,000; almost all of the remainder will be HUD funds.

    1. Provision of Health Services on a Pilot Basis. During the first action year, the Interim Direct Dental Care Project provided care for an estimated 700 adolescents through referrals to private dentists. The plan has been sufficiently successful that dental insurance, despite its risks, is being provided to the 8,000 children in the five Model Schools. The Model Schools Health Program also provides eye and ear testing to these students.

    A Non-Emergency Transportation Service, operated by the Essex County American Red Cross, provides transportation to hospitals and doctors' offices for the elderly and disabled. About 5,000 trips are made each year. It will be expanded to other neighborhoods as well.

    2. Health Education and Referral Services. CDA is responsible for several educational projects. The Lead Poisoning Prevention and Treatment Project initially screened over 2,500 children and inspected over 500 homes but has now been supplemented with an HEW grant to treat the entire city. At least 1,000 children have been treated for lead poisoning. Project Child provides prenatal care to over 1,400 women annually and also makes referrals to private doctors. Also, the Home Management and Training Program, begun in the fall of 1971, teaches parents how to care for handicapped children. Significantly, the Urban League of Essex County has agreed to try to coordinate information on all health services by receiving, processing, and referring any health request.

    3. Coordinated Planning to Increase Health Services, Improve Delivery, and Reduce Health Costs in the Model Neighborhood. Perhaps CDA's most significant accomplishment in the field of health has been implementation of the new Gladys Dickinson Health Station near Columbus Homes in the model area. The center, offering

comprehensive health services to the neighborhood, will provide a
model for a network of 7 to 10 health centers in other Newark locations
(three in the next fiscal year) and is expected to serve 7,500 people.
Expenses are estimated at $800,000 annually, with at least half to be
reimbursed by Medicaid. Residents of the area have formed a central
advisory committee that participates in planning. Intensive recruitment of neighborhood residents to fill jobs in the center is being
conducted.

4. Two Projects Planned to Educate Residents for Health Careers. The Health Services Management Course will encourage employment of community residents in administrative positions in the
health field. The Allied Health Project will provide stipends for 20
Model Neighborhood residents for education leading to employment
in health services, with emphasis on the upgrading of paraprofessionals.

Health Recommendations by Center for Analysis of Public Issues. In
a March 1972 study of the Newark Division of Health by the Center
for Analysis of Public Issues, the ineffectiveness of Newark's health
programs was documented and some indication was given as to how
programs, such as Model Cities, might improve this condition.[9] The
report summarized the city's health as follows:

> Unmet needs span a variety of disease categories.
> Chronic disorders including heart diseases, diabetes, con-
> ditions growing out of alcoholism, and cancer show per-
> sistently high morbidity rates in Newark, in part because
> of failure to mount effective screening and detection pro-
> grams. Infant mortality rates remain among the nation's
> highest in part because one pregnant mother in seven
> fails to receive any pre-natal care, and others receive
> inadequate care. Lead poisoning may have reached epi-
> demic proportions, but inadequate screening efforts have
> missed thousands of afflicted children. And the hundreds
> of lead victims found so far have not received from the
> city adequate legal protection to prevent repoisioning.
> Newark's rate of new tuberculosis cases continues to set
> national records, despite available cures and large ap-
> propriations; the problem is inadequate screening, testing,
> and contact follow-ups. Officials fear venereal disease in
> Newark soon may become almost as widespread as tooth
> decay or the common cold, yet health and sex education
> remain absent from school programs and citywide screen-
> ing has failed to materialize. Dental programs in public
> and parochial schools are moribund, despite a surplus of
> dentists on the city payroll and declining utilization of city

dental clinics. There is evidence that tens of thousands of school children now receive no dental care during their elementary school years. And the health of all Newark citizens is endangered by failure of city and state governments to enforce laws on food sanitation . . . .

. . . Providers of care in Newark collectively have not yet found a suitable substitute for the type of comprehensive care once provided by the now-departed private doctors. The Division of Health is perhaps the best illustration of this failure. The peculiar organization of Division services requires well children to go one place for care, sick children to another; tuberculosis treatment is viewed as entirely separate from venereal disease problems; dispensary services are valuable primarily to those whose illness happens to correspond to a clinic at Martland Hospital. A patient with cardiac problems, diabetes, and alcoholism may well come into contact with several physicians employed by the Division, yet receive neither tests nor treatment for his chronic afflictions. Narrow specialization remains the keystone of the Division's medical services, despite the city's growing need for comprehensive care facilities . . . .

. . . The city's health dollars are not spent wisely. The Division of Health spends large sums to treat declining patient populations at the dispensary and dental clinics, and the Board of Education appropriates $1.4 million each year to provide many of the same services offered by the dispensary and Martland Hospital. The city continues to support a large administrative staff for tuberculosis control programs, although actual operation of the programs passed to county and state control several years ago. And the city needlessly spends $100,000 a year for free pediatric services for children eligible for Medicaid. Only lack of effort on the city's part has stood in the way of reimbursements for the services . . . .

. . . There is lack of coordination among health planning agencies. The Regional Medical Program was organized in 1967 with federal funds to strengthen medical services for heart diseases, cancer, and stroke, in the northern New Jersey region that includes Newark. The State Health Planning Council was organized in the New Jersey Department of Health in 1968 to aid the department in planning health services throughout the state, and the Council has indicated special concern for Newark's problems. The Hospital and Health Council of Metropolitan

170

New Jersey, Inc. is a federal planning unit charged with studying problems of hospital utilization and needs in Region 3 which includes Newark. The Community Development Administration, Newark's Model Cities Agency, is deeply involved in planning the city's role in health services. A similar task has been assigned to the city Director of Health and Welfare. In special cases (including lead poisoning and drug abuse) ad hoc coordinating committees have been formed, to bring together for frequent meetings representatives of various treatment or screening programs.[10]

The study concludes that considerably improved and comprehensive health services could be provided for about an equivalent expenditure of funds if certain programs are eliminated, a new network of neighborhood health centers created to provide complete medical care to whole families, and contracting is effected for dental and pediatric services to the health centers.[11] A summary of the estimated savings and new costs are as follows:

Cutbacks and Savings
Close dispensary	$500,000
Close city dental clinics	270,000
Close public school dental clinic	30,000
Close Child Health Conferences	250,000
Close City Chest Disease Bureau	100,000
Savings	$1,150,000

Recommended New Programs and Costs
Establish new Family Health Center	$500,000
Contract for indigent dental care	270,000
Contract for Child Health Conference services	150,000
Pay health centers to treat sick indigent children	100,000
Pay to Essex County for more TB contact investigators	100,000
	$1,120,000

In addition, the report recommends that the Director of Health and Welfare establish a community health council composed of representatives from the major health providers in Newark, including hospital and neighborhood health centers, city officials, and consumer representatives. The council would coordinate services and standards of the providers so that eventually the providers would operate as a citywide health care network. Specifically, the council should

     a. Set minimum program standards for the health centers. The council should pay particular attention to citywide needs, including screening programs for VD, tuberculosis, and lead poisoning, and expanded prenatal care programs.

     b. Press for authority (and legislation if needed) to control the allocation of state and federal health aid to Newark. The fact that such authority is not now vested in a single agency explains in large part the duplications, waste, and unclear priorities evident in Newark's health care system. We view this step as indispensable to any plan to improve health care in Newark.

     c. Define relationships between neighborhood center and hospitals, to make best use of both types of facilities.

     d. Evaluate performance of the centers, and assess community needs from time to time to ensure that the centers keep pace with changing conditions.[12]

Newark's health problems can best be treated on a citywide basis. Recently the City Department of Health and Welfare requested that its director be given authority over all health grants to the city. With this authority, provided through mayoral CERC (review authority) under Planned Variations and with state and other agency involvement in the community health council, the over-all health care system may begin to function. Almost the entire program can be put into effect without vast new sums of state and federal aid.

The extent of coordination and health planning up to this time has been achieved through the Health Program Development Team, which has taken steps to pull together the College of Medicine and Dentistry and other related institutions, hospitals, and various levels of government. Working agreements were recently reached with all these units for a city-sponsored management unit. The city has also received funding for a comprehensive health planning agency. Much more effective relationships have begun to take place between the CDA and line health departments with a great deal of this credit due to the city's new Health and Welfare director.

Nevertheless, strong backing and mayoral leadership is needed, as well as the effective use of present Model Cities and Planned Variations funds as a catalytic force. Some of the Model Cities programs described above have begun the process toward institutional change in health. They simply need to be more effective and comprehensive.

Social Services. Social Services is funded for $2,644,251 with most money from HUD. Also contributing are HEW ($500,000), State Department of Community Affairs ($216,858), State Division of Mental Retardation ($40,000), and OEO In-Kind ($150,000).

172

1. Some elements of citizen participation are funded from this program. A network of 39 Urban Agents (neighborhood workers), in conjunction with 75 block organizations, work among the residents to organize them, make surveys, and follow up on complaints. There are also four citywide Action Now centers, which receive and process complaints, cutting red tape as much as possible.

2. Grants totaling over $1 million have been received for three multipurpose centers. The first center began operation in the fall of 1971 and houses the following agencies: Newark Public Library; N.J. Commission for the Blind; Project Child; N.J. Rehabilitation Commission; Interim Assistance; Newark Youth Action Council; Boy Scouts; AFL-CIO Human Resources Development Institute; Mt. Carmel Guild; Welfare Rights Organization; Model Cities District Service Office; Neighborhood Stabilization and Building Improvement; and Social Security Administration.

3. Three day-care centers serving 250 children, with classes in homemaking, consumer education, and child care for adults, have been in operation since July 1972.

4. During the first year 200 children were provided craft and recreation programing, and 100 were given a special horseback riding course (described earlier). Some drama classes and projects for the mentally retarded were conducted. A much broader recreation program to make use of existing facilities year round is under development and will be linked with the new City Department of Recreation and Parks.

5. A Consumer Affairs Project, initially operating in one of the public housing projects (Columbus Homes) to provide consumer education and assistance to residents, has been expanded and is considered highly successful.

Effective administration of many of these programs has been lacking. For example, during the 1971 Summer Food Program (funded by the Department of Agriculture for $946,000) thousands of meals were spoiled because of delays. There were sandwiches with stale bread and tainted meat; and thousands of gallons of milk went sour in City Hall because nobody knew where to take it. On the whole, only part of the administrative problems have been solved.

Criminal Justice and Law Enforcement. Criminal Justice receives a total of $3,849,972: HUD $1,061,000; State Law Enforcement Planning Agency (SLEPA) $875,000; HEW $741,000; Department of Justice LEAA $405,000; and local share $571,000. In 1972, the city also received $20 million from the special "Impact City's Program." CDA is the official agency designated to administer LEAA planning funds. Emphasis has been on comprehensive planning, increasing police service and effectiveness, prevention and treatment of narcotics addiction, and services to youth. A number of agencies and persons have praised the Newark program for its comprehensiveness and scope. Eugene Doleschol, director of the Information Center at the National Commission on Crime and Delinquency (NCCD), in June 1972, stated that Newark is one of three cities that stands out above all others, when its Model Cities projects are examined from a city point of view rather than by project. He stated Newark administers the most well-rounded program. It stands out "because of the comprehensiveness of its approach, its planning and coordination, the sophistication of its programs, and its fiscal skill in using Model Cities seed money to attract . . . other funds."[13]

A master project, Comprehensive Law Enforcement and Criminal Justice Planning Project, coordinates subprojects. The Comprehensive Juvenile Delinquency Strategy Program consolidates existing and new juvenile delinquency projects. Youth Service Agency plans, operates, and coordinates community-based youth services that operate from youth centers. The Pilot Project in Pre-Adolescent Services is part of a national strategy of the Youth Development and Delinquency Prevention Administration (YDDPA) in which Newark and 15 other cities have been selected to develop and implement comprehensive demonstration programs and fill gaps. The Narcotics Advisory and Rehabilitation Council consolidates five narcotic prevention and treatment programs. Legal services for residents, three police storefronts, safety lighting, miniature teletype units in patrol cars, walkie-talkies for Police Tactical Squad, and an electronic stenographic system are all part of the program. The following principle projects give an idea of the programs' comprehensiveness.

1. The Public Safety Personnel Project is operated by the Police Department, employing 50 community service officers who patrol the Model Neighborhood four hours each night.

2. The Police Code Project is training 12 persons who entered the program at 18 years of age and will complete three years of training (including several college semesters) in order to enter the regular force at age 21.

3. The Youth Aid and Services Project is operated by the Police Department's Youth Aid Bureau, integrating civilian youth workers with the police juvenile staff. This agreement to employ and house civilian professionals and paraprofessionals in a regular police unit is a significant milestone in police-community relations.

4. Police equipment has been purchased, and studies are under way concerning police policies and work load. Analysis of the police role and functions was completed June 1972. Resource allocation study is under way.

5. A Narcotics Advisory and Rehabilitation Council and an Addiction Planning and Coordinating Agency provide comprehensive

treatment and control of drug abuse, including planning and coordination, narcotics registry, youth residential center for therapeutic treatment of 100 teen-age drug abusers, vocational rehabilitation, and a medical and laboratory center used citywide. CDA has helped establish the Student Congress on the Prevention of Drug Abuse, which has nine prevention units operating in junior and senior high schools so that students can develop their own programs to curb drug abuse. The entire drug program has recently been expanded citywide into a multimodality center with all related agencies for short-term detoxification at a cost of $6 million. There is now a centralized staff for coordination, planning, program development, and evaluation. The Staff is used by the Mayor's Narcotic Advisory Council and also the Council of Executive Directors of Newark Drug Treatment Agencies.

6. A Youth Service Agency has been established as a central planning, coordinating, and operating agency. Three youth centers have been developed. And a citywide youth conference has been held. Vocational and rehabilitation services are also provided. The emphasis is on diverting "delinquent" youth from the police and court process into something with greater chance of rehabilitation. A demonstration program is in operation that uses teen-agers to work with preadolescents.

7. Newarkfields is a nonresidential treatment program, which now has 30 youths, 14 and 15 year olds, referred by the juvenile court.

8. Newark Defendants Employment Project (NDEP) diverts adult defendants into vocational training, counseling, and placement.

9. Municipal Court Management and Improvement Project ($350,000) provides professional administrative staff, new systems and procedures, facility renovations, and pretrial services and management staff. It is linked to the criminal justice information system and NDEP, Bail Project, prosecutors' screening staff, and the public defender. It also includes modified family court procedures, which is particularly relevant to residents of the Model Neighborhood.

10. Criminal Justice Information System ($500,000) is operated within the new city computer system and will eventually include the collection and distribution of all operational and other record information by both the police and courts.

11. Newark Bail Project ($60,000) was developed by a community-based agency but is now funded by CDA and will eventually be absorbed within the Municipal Court program. It screens defendants at arrest for bail or release on recognizance.

12. Juvenile Delinquency Demonstration ($300,000) uses carefully selected professionals to interfuse with existing agencies (police, courts, jails, social services, schools, and so on) dealing with children, in order to achieve institutional change.

Although Newark's program is comprehensive, there appears to be lack of direction. The new impact monies came to the city without formal application or planning, and it was expected that a plan would be developed within three months. But an organization separate from the police and existing coordinating bodies was set up to plan and run it because Washington was looking for immediate impact and no substantial organizational changes. But now the police department is frustrated, believing it will get little of the money and have minimal participation. Chief Redden has complained about the poor work CDA has done in preparing proposals, yet his own Planning and Research Office has been unable to give him much assistance in this regard. CDA has helped the department get funds for a number of SLEPA projects, such as communications, police cadets, information system, public facilities study, police role study, and police resource allocation design. But there appear to be too many "fingers in the soup" and, at least temporarily, coordination and direction have run aground.

Education. Education was allocated $2,095,968, all from HUD except $300,000 from the State Department of Community Affairs and $92,000 from HEW.

1. CDA funded two staff training programs for school personnel. Fifty teachers and 20 aides from Model Neighborhood schools completed the Hilda Taba teaching strategies program designed to promote higher-level thinking skills and more independence in students. Thirty-five aides participated in a career training program conducted by the New Jersey Department of Education, for which they will receive academic credit from Essex County College.

2. A Community Coordinator, funded by Model Cities, held conferences and workshops to increase communication between citizens and the Board of Education. A training manual was prepared to help citizens work with schools more effectively. The Secondary Schools and Community Relations Project provided funds for student-faculty planning for improved relations among high school students. During the second action year and into the summer of 1972, emphasis was on student planning of curriculum models that they feel will meet the needs of Newark's high school students.

3. Two projects operated by CDA are focused on higher education opportuniites for Newark residents. Talent Search counseled 500 students on post-secondary opportunities and placed over 200 in colleges and vocational schools. The Higher Education Assistance Program awarded over $30,000 to 100 students for post-secondary education. It also includes summer jobs counseling and placement.

4. The Classroom Innovation Project involves $30,000 and 21 teachers and 600 students in innovative classroom projects, which will

serve as demonstrations. In the second action year, emphasis will
be on paraprofessionals, parents, and the community, working together
in planning the projects. Money was also granted to the Learning
Center, operated by the Newark Housing Council, for parent and community planning. This group completed educational specifications
for three schools in the Fairmount Urban Renewal Area and submitted
them to the Board of Education for approval.

     5. Experimental Classroom, operated by the African Free
School, will provide 30 students with a supplemental education program, with emphasis on cultural enrichment.

     6. Project LINK is a community-based school for 100 junior
high youths with learning problems, which provides a flexible and
individualized academic program.

     7. In January 1972, CDA created a new project, the Office of
Program and Staff Development (OPSD), which is located within the
Board of Education and responsible to the Superintendent of Schools
and CDA. This office coordinates the Model Schools, health, classroom awards, training, and other CDA education projects. It also
operates the "innovation teams" that assist the Model Neighborhood
in planning and developing new and more responsive school programs
and is expected to stimulate the Board of Education in the direction
of innovation and institutional change. Despite staffing problems,
four technicians were trained, and eye and ear examinations were
given to all pupils in the program. Training workshops were held,
innovation awards presented, and better coordination was established
between the CDA and Board of Education.

     8. The Model Schools project involves five elementary schools,
8,000 students in innovative programs planned by elected joint faculty
community Advisory Committees. Projects include remedial reading
and math, cultural activities, and psychological and guidance services.
Also, each school receives a grant to develop an innovative plan for
institutional change.

     The Advisory Committees interview applicants for Model School
jobs, and the Board of Education appoints persons from among those
recommended. One of the disappointments is the verbal battles between parents and administrators as to who is competent to teach in
specific schools. Much of it is racial. Many teachers have become
alienated, and many have been transferred, even though they are capable.

     In 1972, a Joint Advisory Committee, composed of the five
Model Schools Advisory Committees, was formed and monthly meetings
were held. Ideas were exchanged and better working relationships
developed.

OPSD Evaluation of Model Schools. There are five Model Schools and
five different programs:

1. The Camden Street School project was formed to improve reading and math skills through remedial classes. The Office of Program and Staff Development reports marked improvements for students in their nationwide examinations; although when compared to the national norm, they are in the lowest percentile, when compared to the rest of Newark's students, they are in the upper percentile. From 1971 to 1972 test scores rose in word knowledge from 1.7 to 2.2 and in word discrimination from 1.6 to 2.4

2. Fifteenth Avenue School has three basic goals: providing reading skills, extending and enriching vocabulary, and giving insight on how to adjust and survive in society. Remedial math and reading, plus cultural trips, are part of the program. OPSD reports that the school has become very community conscious, and there is a good deal of parent participation. Teachers do not mind the heavy work load, children are more mature in their presentations, and they could not be compared to the listless group of a few years ago. However, reading and math levels rose only slightly.

3. Franklin School emphasizes Development Reading and Spanish-to-English teaching. There was no significant difference between pretest and posttest scores in reading (perhaps due to a short three-month test period), but Spanish-to-English classes showed considerable improvement. The community is mostly Spanish-speaking. Greater rapport between staff and parents was developed, and staff attitude became very positive.

4. Martin Luther King, Jr. School concentrates on reading and math. Aides visit homes to encourage parental participation, and the community is very active in school affairs. The testing program shows some improvement in skills.

5. McKinley School also emphasizes reading and math skills, focusing on the attention span of students and adjusting the teaching speed to the student. The position of director of community affairs was created. This community is also largely Spanish-speaking. The new community involvement programs have brought staff and citizens much closer. Some improvement is shown in skills.

OPSD concludes that Newark schools cannot be upgraded until the fundamental system is changed; teachers need more than to love, they must possess teaching skills; materials and equipment are secondary to attitude and ability of the teacher; and monthly evaluation of teachers is needed.[14]

Further Evaluation of the Educational Component. Willie Thomas, director of OPSD, states one of the chief assets of the Model Schools Program is that it treats the whole school, not merely a small controlled group, such as federal Title I programs. Everything is given to the teacher that he or she needs, yet the key to success is the ability of the teacher, he says. Some changes have taken place, including institutional changes: Classes have been reduced from 35 to 20 pupils; parents would never have gotten involved without incentives from this program; the Board of Education was encouraged to build more schools as a result of the effort to reduce pupil-teacher ratio; and there has been a significant positive change in students, as seen by the parents and staff. The community attitude was so strong here during the teachers' strike that these five schools remained open and teachers continued to teach.

On the other hand, some local analysts believe this school project is little more than a "Title I project," a block grant program at $100 per pupil, with programs that really have not attacked fundamental problems. Teachers and principals have been receptive to it, but they have also dominated the parental groups, the latter quickly agreeing to staff "thinking" and plans.

In essence, the school system is still the same old structure and bureaucracy. Most believe it should be run differently. And although Model Schools is "conceptually delightful," it has only made minimal progress. The concept needs to be transferred to the whole system, but funds are lacking and Planned Variations will only allow the use of 20 percent of its funds for existing projects. It takes that much simply to include 10 more schools in the Model Schools program.

The Mayor's Task Force on Education will make recommendations on reducing conflict in schools, creating a strong planning arm for the school system, and financing education. The business community is sharing an increased interest in school matters and recently produced an eight-volume Chamber of Commerce study on school management, much of which has been implemented by the Board of Education. The board is finally carefully reviewing executive staff performance and leadership. All these things should help improve the school system.

Manpower and Economic Development. There is $409,172 allocated to this project. All is Model Cities money except for $50,000 from the State Department of Community Affairs. The program consists of training and counseling 35 persons in the Neighborhood Youth Corps, organizing a Newark Minority Contractors Trade Association, studying ways to expand businesses and attract new ones, and training 120 people in the rehabilitation and construction industry.

In addition to Model Cities funds, all other city manpower funds were increased from $18.5 million in 1971 to $30 million in 1972. Summer employment was increased from 4,700 in 1971 to 7,000 in 1972.

Gibson states his 1973 goals are to place 12,000 persons into entry-level jobs and implement affirmative action plans by providing for 50 percent minority apprentices and 30 percent minority journeymen in the construction trades. Newark leaders have estimated that there are only 70 blacks among 11,350 members of the eight major construction trade unions. Recently six airlines and the city, in discussions on airport redevelopment, agreed to the above minority hiring goals; and the airlines consented to financing a $2 million minority basic construction skills training program. The unions have been battling court suits that accuse them of discrimination, and it is still doubtful how far along they will go with the above plan.

Councilmanic Perceptions About Model Cities

At the beginning of the second action year, city councilmen expressed a variety of views about Model Cities and Planned Variations. Some of these ideas are expressed below but may have changed somewhat by the third action year. Not all councilmen could be interviewed.

City Council President Louis M. Turco. Turco is 35, a lawyer and accountant. He was appointed by Addonizio in November 1968 to fill a city council vacancy and was reelected in June 1970 to a full four-year term. He is Democratic Party chairman of the predominantly Italian East Ward and is the first ward councilman to hold the position of Council President. He is active in Democratic politics in Essex County and highly sensitive to public pressure, especially in his own ward. Support for Addonizio is the political test militant blacks use to classify white politicians. Turco is a racist to them. But his philosophy is liberal. He believes militant blacks want to drive all whites out of Newark; and he feels the mayor does not consult often enough with the council.

He understood that Model Cities programs were developed before Junius Williams was hired and therefore was willing to go along with Williams "to a degree" because he wanted to see what kinds of programs he could to develop. "Junius is experiencing the problems that are inherent in the change of an administration," he said at the time.

Turco would prefer federal funds to be handled directly by the city. "If the mayor and council were the overseers of federal funds," he said, "we would not only get progress, but substantial progress. For one thing, there is a great duplication of personnel which could be eliminated."

He believes the Planned Variations Program will have a positive affect. "At least the people in the rest of the city could benefit by all this federal and state money that is being poured into the Model

Neighborhood." He explained that it is difficult to rationalize to constituents the logic of singling out a particular part of the city for federal benefits, while other parts, some just as bad, go unaided.

Councilman Earl Harris. Earl Harris is a councilman-at-large serving his first term and is a former freeholder (county elected official). He ran for Congress in the early 1960s as a Republican; ran for freeholder and was elected as a Democrat; and ran for council as an independent. He was part of the Black-Puerto Rican ticket that also included Mayor Gibson and Councilmen James and Westbrooks. He is generally considered a political pragmatist.

Harris stated, "I have great hopes that positive things will develop out of Model Cities. I haven't seen much to date, however, that excites me. There has been, for far too long, an emphasis on taking care of friends in high positions in the agency." He is concerned that too many people are hired from out of state to fill higher-echelon jobs.

Harris fears that revenue sharing might "only tie up huge amounts of money in politics." And because of the lack of rapport between the council and the mayor's office, Harris feels that untethered grants might not be effective. Yet he prefers revenue sharing to grants to autonomous agencies, "as is done now."

He believes communications between the CDA and the council are improving but was not aware that Model Cities did not use more than $3 million from the first year action plan.

He would concur with expansion of the Model Neighborhood to cover the whole city, principally because it would diffuse what he considers the "segregation" of a special area from the rest of the city. "It would fit into the concept we are trying to push of the 'New Newark'," he said. Whatever the concept, Harris wants "something I can look at and identify as progress."

Councilman Sharpe James. Sharpe James is a black councilman from the South Ward serving his first term. He is a highly articulate, liberal educator who reads everything that comes over his desk. He has significant depth of perception and knowledge of city affairs.

Councilman James is disheartened with the progress of most of these projects. He believes too much time and money is spent on rehashing studies, with no results. Of the proposal to develop a shopping mall with the Greater Newark Chamber of Commerce, he asked, "What does that do for the poor people in Newark? In fact, how do you tell the poor people in Newark that the money that was supposed to be spent to help them not be poor is being spent to help downtown business and suburban shoppers?"

In regards to the mini-park project, James said, "I asked Shapiro [Alfred Shapiro, city planning officer] to show me something—anything —tangible that Model Cities had accomplished. He sent me to see some miniparks." James said that although the parks were only recently installed, they were in virtual ruin. James sees no hope for programs without a great deal of effort given to the education of citizens in creating success and protecting property.

James would like to see Model Cities funds go directly to the city government, where it can really be used to improve Newark, not the "pork barrel bureaucracy for the elite." He believes the entire approach is incorrect and would favor starting at the borders of the city to create stability, encouraging residents to stay before deterioration spreads everywhere. On the other hand, he says, "Model Cities is a pacifier. It says to the poor in the city 'don't riot, there is hope'."

He is extremely upset that people are hired outside the city when qualified residents are available. But he does believe there is a new feeling of accommodation between the city council and Model Cities because if programs do not get approved and advanced, a great deal of federal funds will be lost.

Councilman Anthony Giuliano. Giuliano is a councilman-at-large, former city policeman, and currently serving his first full term. He was elected to a two-year unexpired term in 1968 and reelected in 1970. He is quite conservative but flexible in philosophy.

He says, "Frankly, I do not see any real evidence of progress in the Model Cities program." Jobs have gone to unqualified people. But he believed Junius Williams was serious about doing a good job and should have been given the chance. "Junius assures me, however, that the council will be brought in on plans and proposals and given reports of progress," he had stated earlier.

Giuliano, as does most of the council, prefers that grants go directly to the city and that a "competition bureaucracy," seeking "to set up shop across the street from the council and administration," be eliminated. He believes Planned Variations would be of no significant value if this were perpetuated.

Michael P. Bottone. This is Bottone's first term. He has expressed little political philosophy and at the time of these interviews could express little knowledge about Model Cities programs because of his limited involvement. However, all councilmen approved the Planned Variations projects described in the next section.

Planned Variations

After several refusals by city council to approve Gibson's Planned Variations proposals, first submitted to them in May 1972, council gave approval in September 1972. The delay was mostly due to the desire by council to have greater voice in programs and jobs and generally to improve the process of communication and involvement to all interested parties. Complete satisfaction still does not exist. There continues to be coolness between the executive and legislative branches, but at least the first phase of Planned Variations has been approved.

In the past, Gibson has indicated his priorities for Planned Variations, which include a network of neighborhood health centers, narcotic treatment centers, expanded housing rehabilitation and demo-lition of abandoned buildings, reform of the bail and court system, and effective manpower training projects. The first phase approved by council covers only part of an expanded city program; the second phase will go into all eligible areas of the city.

A citywide citizens council of 27 members—18 appointed by the mayor and 9 by city council (another concession to the legislative branch)—has been appointed. Membership represents a broad spectrum of residents, including persons from each ward and political organiza-tion, business, unions, grass-roots groups, the former Model Neighbor-hood Council, and nationalist and ethnic groups.

The District (or block) Assemblies will continue to function, but the Model Neighborhood Council is now defunct. CDA reports over 250 District Assembly meetings and 7,500 attendees since their inception. An annual Model Neighborhood Conference is also held. The most recent conference held January 14-15, 1972 attracted over 1,000 residents. These methods may continue to be the most active form of citizen participation, since the Model Neighborhood Council has been eliminated and the new citywide council is only advisory. However, some officials believe the citywide council may become influential if it brings mayoral and councilmanic forces together in cooperation and agreement on heretofore difficult issues. It may possibly achieve coordination between conflicting administrative agen-cies as well. It has some money for staff but will mainly rely on David Dennison and his staff as its chief liaison.

Planned Variations projects already approved by city council include the following:

1. Neighborhood Health Centers. Three new centers will be opened by the Department of Health and Welfare, operating in con-junction with four other centers now in existence or under develop-ment. Site locations must be approved by the New Jersey State Depart-ment of Health and proposals granted a Certificate of Need. Funds include $185,000 from Planned Variations and $1,147,000 from HEW, under the Hill-Burton Act.

2. Child Care (day-care) Centers. Five 60-child day-care centers will be developed in each of five wards. Projects must be

approved by the New Jersey Department of Institutions and Agencies, which will also approve funds of $120,000 for each center from Title IV-A of the Social Security Act. The Planned Variations share is $40,000 per center. Nonprofit agencies will operate the centers, which will provide comprehensive educational, social, health and nutritional programs, as well as parental training and participation.

3. Multiservice Centers. The completion of the present center at South 11th Street plus a new center on Camden Street will cost $250,000 in Planned Variations funds and $750,000 in HUD Neighborhood Facility Grants.

4. Office of Program and Staff Development. This program will be operated by the Board of Education and expanded citywide in order to coordinate all education programs and increase innovative programing such as Model Schools, bilingual training, college tuition, and in-service training. The Planned Variations costs are $160,427.

5. Auxiliary Police. This project, designed to utilize 50-70 men, will be operated by the Police Department at a cost of about $216,476 of Planned Variations, SLEPA, and High Impact Program funds; but, as yet, it has not had the approval of the other funding agencies.

6. Neighborhood Improvements. This $150,000 project is designed to provide more street lighting for public safety and alternate street parking signs to facilitate street cleaning and sanitation operations.

7. Relocation. This project is operated by the Housing Authority as the city's central relocation agency and will expend about $967,369 of Model Cities and Planned Variations funds during the third action year to relocate 2,300 households.[15]

Analysis and Recommendations

A Poor Start

Newark's Model Cities Program perhaps had the poorest start in the nation. With very few exceptions, the Addonizio Administration filled it from top to bottom with patronage and incompetence. It took two years to get the first project started. It is still unbelievable that public officials in modern America could get away for so long with the gross misuse of government funds and neglect of its citizens. Nevertheless, it happened. Moreover, most people not only tacitly accepted this corruption and inefficiency but many contributed to it with their votes.

Now although there is not enough to go around anymore, there is still an attitude among some black leaders that the "whites got theirs, now let's get ours." As a consequence, the average Newark citizen has had to make one of several choices: continue to accept corruption and inefficiency, rebel, or leave the city. Some have stayed on passively, and some, like the black nationalists and the North Ward Citizens Council have chosen to fight. But it is obvious, even to the casual onlooker, that leaving the city, if one could afford it, has been the most popular option. In the place of the departing have come the poor, unskilled, unsuspecting blacks from the South, only to find despair and conditions that turn the stomach.

The 1970 mayoral election reinforced faith in the American system, for Gibson's victory was an overwhelming mandate calling for elimination of corruption and improvement of government. But like so many other black mayors who have been elected in this past decade, he was not left much to work with. Deficits, incompetence, deterioration, and poor organization were his inheritance. Yet, for the first time, hope permeated the community and federal funds were available to start rejuvenation. However, it has been necessary for Gibson to spend so much time getting his house in order that he has been unable to devote the attention required of Model Cities and some other federal programs. He has been very successful in obtaining federal and state aid but much less effective administering these resources.

The Need to Reorganize

There was considerable delay in the transition from one administration to the next because of the political, organizational, and administrative restructuring that had to take place. More than a year was consumed in executing the initial steps to discharge patronage employees, hire new staffs, and reorganize city departments—a process that is obviously still going on. If Gibson had stepped into an already effective government and Model Cities Program after a "shakedown" period, it would have most likely meant better programs today. Instead, he had to start over again.

Many things had been done, in the Model Cities Program particularly, that had to be undone. (1) An overabundance of projects had to be trimmed, yet some of low priority had to be kept. Moreover, extensive revision was made impossible because some projects had only recently been implemented and had already generated their own momentum and "turf." (2) Projects had to be redirected because they were not sufficiently related to city line department functions and objectives. (3) Linkages between projects and agencies had to be strengthened and new relationships developed. (4) The CDA had to be reorganized and provided increased staff capacity so it could adequately monitor and evaluate projects and develop an effective financial and budget system. (5) City line departments had to be provided higher-quality staff, and coordination of departments had to be improved. (6) A more effective planning and policy process for the city and CDA had to be developed—a process still under way. (7) Most programs had to have internal changes. The large number of projects, none of which were implemented prior to Gibson, were hastily put into operation under HUD pressure to "move the program," yet project staff needed extensive assistance in internal organization, administration, and training.

Improved Coordination and Integrated Financial System

Administrative and organizational changes have been made by Gibson that have resulted in a considerably improved Model Cities Program. The creation of the Mayor's Policy and Review Office, with its Chief Executive and Review responsibilities, and a more effective CDA, with more extensive planning and fewer operational responsibilities, have improved coordination. Although it took until the winter of 1972, a new Model Cities reporting and monitoring system for planning and program development, which will link into the coordinating mechanisms of the CDA and Policy and Review, has been initiated. And programatically, projects are at last being integrated and consolidated and some transferred to city line departments.

In addition, the new ($600,000) "integrated fiscal accountability system" is perhaps proceeding more expeditiously than other system changes. When completed, it will integrate the budgets and financial management of all city, state, and federal funds under the city's Department of Finance. Accounts payable, revenues, payrolls, and other fiscal components for all projects will function as one unit. Comprehensive and meaningful reports will be disseminated to city council, the mayor, other officials, and the public. Under this process, it will be difficult to conceal expenditures from officials or the public, and it will also more clearly reveal project impact.

Moreover, the CDA has begun to integrate all related grants and local funds within each of its projects. This has involved modification of city budget forms and procedures to accommodate different funding periods and budget formats. The next step, targeted for January 1974, is to make city and Model Cities fiscal years uniform. Indeed, the entire process has been a difficult struggle for Newark, but it represents a significant accomplishment for both the city and Model Cities from what was once an outmoded and impossible system.

Confusion and Disarray Still Present

Nevertheless, in spite of these changes, there is still confusion as to who will have major policy responsibility below the mayor. In one way, tightening the financial network will place more information and greater ability to coordinate in the hands of the business administrator. On the other hand, agency contact and program monitoring will fall primarily to the head of the Office of Policy and Review. Yet the CDA retains major city planning and development responsibilities. (Most cities, for example, combined CDA and CERC responsibilities.) The above triumvirate of mixed authorities cannot but delay progress and the inevitable step of having to place someone in charge.

Yet this game of politics and human manipulation faced by most mayors sometime during their terms must be handled delicately. In this regard, Junius Williams rose to the top of the "bad guy" list in the Gibson Administration, but rather than toss him out on his ear, as any efficient organization might, the strategy was to allow him to "rot on the vine" and hope he would go away. Yet there was no hurry on the part of Williams. In the meantime, Williams and Dennison hardly spoke to each other, and Williams refused to attend Bodine's weekly staff meetings.

Gibson tried to overcome this problem when he proposed a $27,000-a-year executive director for Planned Variations to help pull the pieces together. Ironically, partly because Williams was then out of tune with the mayor, city council refused to go along, which points out the difficulty Gibson has been having with an uncooperative but also uninformed city council. In spite of these delays, Gibson's desire for accomplishment finally prevailed, and he dismissed Williams.

The Role of the Business Administrator

There is still serious question of the appropriate role for the business administrator in the local government hierarchy. Paradoxically, all department heads report to Bodine except the CDA director and Dennison, who pride themselves on a direct mayoral relationship. Under this organization, no one administrative officer has full grasp or understanding of city operations, which weakens both the budget and policy process.

Assuredly, the mayor's role, more than ever, must be closely aligned with that of the administrator because of the vast increase and complexity of services and the necessity for more than one person, more likely a team of individuals, to administer local government. It is readily agreed that no one form of government is best for all cities. Each administration, within the boundaries of law, must devise what is most effective at any particular time. In Newark, there is strong argument for the need of mayoral leadership and for the mayor to have a full grasp of information, despite city council's belief that the mayor's role has become too strong already. Yet, regardless of the degree of mayoral strength, there is no rational organizational reason to split the city's planning and program development responsibilities among several persons without one technical head who has the responsibility for securing knowledge and control of the complete process.

In Newark, the position of business administrator is most closely designed and best suited for this purpose. For the position to operate effectively, the business administrator should have authority delegated from the mayor so that he is able to discipline and participate in the hiring and firing of subordinates. There should be no question that they have an obligation to report to him, attend staff meetings, and together help him develop plans and policies for the mayor and council. If there is question about the qualifications or personal abilities of the administrator, it is up to the mayor to seek out the right man for the job. On the other hand, it is up to the chief administrator to be able to motivate department heads, improve skills, conduct meaningful staff meetings, and improve administration.

The Role of the Mayor

The chief administrator's role is not incompatible with a strong mayor. The business administrator must be responsible to both the mayor and city council. The mayor's staff and the business administrator need to work closely to avoid duplication and confusion. The mayor's chief of staff also needs to be responsive to the chief administrator so that the administrator may be better informed and able to assist in some mayoral functions, as well as utilize the mayor's staff services.

To improve government effectiveness, the distinction between mayoral and administrative responsibilities should be made as clear as possible. Basically, these differences consist of policy formulation, top management evaluation, executive leadership in motivation of the community, and development of better relationships with citizens and other levels of government on the mayor's part, and program operation, technological development, employee motivation, and planning and coordination on the administrative side. Needless to say, there will be overlapping and ambiguity in some areas, part of this generated by what some refer to as the team approach to local government management. The administrative team may consist of the mayor, manager, and a third major element—the consumer advocate (community development director or leading community organizer). Other principals—such as department heads and leaders of coalitions —feed into the team. The skills, personalities, weaknesses, and strengths of individual team members determine, in a practical sense, the part each plays outside traditional lines of authority. For example, the mayor may have to back up weaknesses in an administrator who fails to motivate department heads; the administrator may have to schedule his work load to lobby or develop relationships with other governments based on the mayor's time and ability in this area; and the consumer advocate may have to develop community support in pressuring management for needed changes in departments and agencies.

Sharing and balancing skills are desirable, but the basic organization must be soundly developed from the beginning. In Newark, lines of authority and delegation of responsibility are confusing and weak. In the first instance, no chief administrator can operate effectively without comprehensive planning and operational functions under his thumb. The building of major staff capacity, computerization, and other techniques in the mayor's office, independent of the administrator, forces the latter to use facilities and staff outside his jurisdiction. Under these conditions, the mayor tends to become immersed in technical matters and escapes from the role of responsible political leadership. On the other hand, some mayors are too politically oriented to care about good administrative practices. The delicate balance between these two concepts needs to be found in each circumstance. Some way, the mayor's chosen administrator must be brought in as a leader and unifier of increased, centralized staff capacity. Proper organization needs to be developed and the persons and skills found to fit it—not the other way around. In this case, it will take mayoral leadership and willingness to delegate responsibility in order to resolve this problem.

The Role of City Council

Of equal importance in getting the executive house in order are its relationships with the legislative branch. Certainly, Gibson's attitude of "I am here if you want me" will not create better conditions. And almost as decisively, Bodine has been unable to keep his end of the scale balanced because of his failure to establish effective communications with the council—part of the (written or unwritten) job specification of a chief administrator. Although all department heads in Newark are subject to council confirmation, the head administrator, particularly, must take the responsibility for packaging information, informing councilmen, and receiving and acting on councilmanic requests. Moreover, only part of the business administrator's inability to reach the council can be attributed to lack of control over all department heads and their sources of information. Significantly, however, communication could be greatly improved if the mayor insisted on it.

Indeed, there is a lack of enthusiasm for closer liaison because the city council is suspected of "power grabs" and patronage intentions. Gibson will not sit with council as Addonizio did before him for fear of being co-opted. He has had battles with council over appointments and budget cuts. He has compromised a number of times in order to get programs and budgets approved—for example, allowing the council a quota of patronage employees under PEP and appointments to the citywide Citizens Advisory Council. Confrontations have stymied progress. Only when these two branches of government lay aside animosities and partisan interests will programs like Model Cities and Planned Variations have a chance of success.

Conditions That Hinder Progress

Moreover, the chance of program success would be enhanced if other conditions were favorable. The continual attention that city officials must devote to budget balancing, personnel cuts, high taxes, social conflicts, reorganization, and excessive citizen pressures takes time away from improving service delivery. Ironically, when opportunities arise, they are not used to their best advantage because of this lingering presence of poor government.

Perhaps the classic example is PEP, which most cities effectively managed to use as another form of revenue sharing. (Two excellent examples are St. Louis and Seattle, which hired PEP workers through their regular personnel systems, trained them adequately, and utilized them as regular employees to improve services.) Of course, the program called for priority hiring of certain classes of the unemployed, but the act had every intention of convincing cities to hire able people who would be trained to fill needed slots. Instead, Newark proceeded to hire all patronage employees, rather than using tested personnel procedures, and assigned them to often meaningless jobs. Assuredly, employment was provided, but havoc resulted and the taxpayer got little service for his money. It would have been far better to use some other sources of funds (even by dropping a project) to provide training and supervision and allow these 1,000-plus workers to fill not only the 300 positions dropped since Gibson's inauguration but to augment other services as well. No one questions the need for Congress to improve the act by providing a sense of permanence for PEP employees and orienting the project toward service as much as employment; but the simple fact is that too many local governments failed to perform.

Summary of Management Problems

The influence of Newark's management problems is reflected in Model Cities, Planned Variations, and other programs. Model

Cities started in a corrupt fashion under Addonizio. Gibson cleaned house, appointed MN residents in place of pure patronage people, changed leadership, and improved administrative procedures. However, the basic system has remained substantially unsound because of this necessity to drastically reorganize, the diffusion and overlapping of programs, less than qualified staff, and lack of executive direction. The result has been limited project success.

Gibson has cut programs and redirected others. Model Cities assumed considerable responsibility by beefing up almost any city program that was not delivering. Street cleaning and lighting, extra refuse collection, and a host of other operations were undertaken for the Model Neighborhood. But they were taken almost wholly independently of regular city departments. As a consequence, confusion reigned among city staff, and coordination was practically nonexistent; however, the situation did point up the need for decent services and an increase in city productivity. Eventually, Bodine and Williams worked out the transfer of most operational programs to regular city departments, relegating the CDA to a purely planning agency. Nevertheless, planning has remained ineffective because it is not integrated into the total city planning process and is not under the direction of a single administrator. Moreover, some basic and important planning components, like urban renewal (under the direction of the Housing Authority), are outside the city's jurisdiction. The mayor needs to pull these together.

Model Cities Project Analysis

Most Model Cities projects appear to have improved since their inception, yet some projects need to be eliminated and others improved further. Recent congressional hearings have pointed out some projects that need strengthening or elimination; and the General Accounting Office has disclosed the need to correct program abuses and institute much more effective evaluation and record-keeping procedures. In some cases, there are projects that are marginal but have had to be carried over to the new administration because citizen groups had developed their own "turfs." Nevertheless, ineffective projects should not be carried into the Planned Variations or Community Development Programs.

Neighborhood Improvements and Services. It appears that the Neighborhood Improvements and Services Project is making important headway in improving physical facilities. The citywide recreation department is a major example of an important step forward for the city. Also the combination of private consultant and CDA staff planners have produced excellent physical plans and designs, and the

New-Town-in-Town proposal may have the effect of sparking comprehensive inner city development. Yet, like so many other plans here and elsewhere, beautiful models without financial capability end up on dead-end shelves. What is needed is a coalition of all major community interests to be brought in on the ground floor of planning for this project so that these same resources might be later used to elicit federal state, and private commitments. On the other hand, the ongoing disputes between white and black and the inability to reach compromise in the Kawaida Towers high-rise apartment project may discourage further private and governmental infusion of funds for any other meaningful housing project. A workable, effective coalition of all interest groups is needed to help resolve such conflicts; however, such a coalition appears unlikely under present conditions. The best immediate hope may be the extension of the Housing Development and Rehabilitation Corporation into an impartial, broad-based agency, much like a coalition.

Furthermore, more attention needs to be paid to maintaining physical facilities once constructed. Street signs and bus shelters will disappear or deteriorate without a citywide, ongoing maintenance shop. Some vest pocket parks are already in shameful condition because of lack of maintenance; and, in addition, tree grooming and care needs to be done citywide to be effective. Many of these programs have had poor supervision and lack long-range allocation of resources. The Rodent and Insect Control Program, for example, was halted by the State Commissioner of Health until better supervision and planning could be instituted. Some programs could be assisted in maintenance by a more judicious use of PEP personnel and by giving block organizations greater responsibility and more resources.

Health. Health programs have gotten a shot in the arm with the appointment of a new city director of Health and Welfare. The proposed network of health centers is needed. Again, this, like so many other projects, will depend on the proper selection of staff and the confidence citizens show in the program. It is also a good sign that the mayor has begun to take hold of management and coordination responsibilities. Moreover, the critical analysis of health services by the Princeton Center for Analysis of Public Issues has had a positive influence in instigating change.

Independent, honest evaluation is needed for each of Newark's major services. The Model Cities Agency's own evaluation components have not been able to develop adequate or effective evaluation of projects. Until this can be done, tested, ongoing evaluators ought to be utilized, particularly in the Planned Variations Program. Eventually, this type of evaluation ought to be extended to every city department, and resources for evaluating federal programs should be made more efficient by using them to analyze all of city government.

Social Services. The planned network of multiservice centers is an excellent adjunct to health centers, but some consideration ought to be given to placing social service personnel in health centers (similar to the Boston Comprehensive Health Center Program) to counsel whole families and make referrals to multiservice centers and other agencies. In some cases, both health and social services may be combined into one facility. Furthermore, there is little concern for planning the first multiservice center to achieve coordination of agencies within the facility through a single director who would be delegated responsibility for coordination by order from each participating agency. The normal bureaucratic confusion, overuse of forms, and delay will result without this kind of direction. Families may end up in line to visit each agency rather than being properly channeled through a systematic process designed to speed counseling and resolve several diverse problems at one session. The director needs the authority to (1) hold staff meetings for all participating agencies; (2) develop comprehensive counseling techniques; (3) monitor, evaluate, and improve services; (4) add or subtract agencies; and (5) discipline and transfer personnel. Too many multiservice centers have tended to become merely additional bureaucracies like the agencies they were intended to replace. Not enough preventive steps are being taken in the Newark program to counteract this.

Criminal Justice and Law Enforcement. The Criminal Justice and Law Enforcement Program has received several commendations for its comprehensive nature and sophistication of programs. For too long, the criminal justice system has operated not as a whole system but rather as separate parts, without even sensing the need to fill in gaps. Newark's program attempts to correct some of these problems; however, the police department has lacked sufficient input into this relatively independent body. Traditionally, socially oriented professionals have tended to avoid confrontation and joint planning efforts with police and other law enforcement personnel. Yet the latter are people who need to be involved in the planning and development process if they are ever to understand and perform differently.

In this project, effective coordination has been lacking in its initial planning stages. Some federal officials believe enough social impact funds are being provided to Newark by Model Cities and Planned Variations and a host of other programs and that funds designed for law enforcement purposes ought to be used for that purpose alone. This conflict of interpretation may delay this rather well-constructed local program longer than Newark residents can afford to wait.

Again, it will be necessary for the mayor to negotiate and adjust differences, proving that existing human resources funds can be properly and effectively used. No amount of programing will take away the need for mayoral leadership in healing the community. The recent resignation of Police Director John Redden over policy decisions in the handling of the Kawaida Towers dispute points up the need for a powerful Newark coalition to help resolve conflicts peacefully.

Education. A good deal of innovation in educational programing has been stimulated by Model Cities. The new Office of Program and Staff Development, which is responsible to both the superintendent of schools and the CDA, is an excellent step in the direction of more effective coordination, teacher training, student health, and project innovation. The Model Schools project has been particularly beneficial in encouraging educators to view school practices differently and experiment with concepts that were once merely ideas. Unfortunately, differences between parents and administrators have been heated and have involved destructive racial conflict, as so many other issues in Newark have. Parents still do not have an effective voice in school affairs, although in at least three of the five Model Schools parental involvement has increased. However, it has not increased on the scale necessary to make a substantial difference in the education students receive. Most observers believe that the Model Schools project is essentially an expansion of Title I programs, improved somewhat but still not affecting the fundamental system.

There is agreement that the attitude and ability of teachers are more important than other kinds of changes and that teacher training must be increased substantially and teachers evaluated continually. Conclusions call for more Model Cities funds to be used for teacher motivation awards, increased teacher training, the development of stronger links between city government and the school board, and increased parental involvement in creating a total educational environment in the community—at home and in school.

Manpower and Economic Development. The total of manpower funds —some $30 million—in Newark is impressive, as are Mayor Gibson's goals to employ 12,000 residents and enforce affirmative minority action plans, for example, by requiring 50 percent minority apprentices and 30 percent minority journeymen in the construction trades. The injustice of only 70 blacks among 11,350 construction trade union members will have to be corrected if Newark ever hopes to survive as a viable community. Gibson's victory in gaining minority hiring concessions in airport redevelopment is an excellent beginning toward increasing local job opportunities, but the lack of other major construction projects, needed to continue minority hiring, will hurt long-term employment of minorities.

Only if Newark is able substantially to improve housing, lower crime, resolve racial conflicts peacefully, and mellow differences between the mayor and city council will sizable new industries be interested in the city. State assistance in restructuring the tax base and improving long-range revenue receipts will also be necessary in order to attract large-scale investments. New economic development will largely depend on correcting the above conditions.

Summary

In summary, Model Cities projects have caused some institutional changes, such as the takeover of housing development by the Housing Development and Rehabilitation Corporation, creation of a citywide Recreation Department, parental involvement and a basic change in teacher and student attitudes in the Model Schools, area wide health coordination through city auspices, and a network of health and social service centers. It has improved some services and brought new people into the process of running government. Many residents have learned how to help themselves through block associations and by participating in the development of new plans and in the execution of projects. However, programs are only achieving some of their goals, and the formal citizen participation process leaves much to be desired. Model Cities staff admits that the program is not addressing itself realistically to the immense unemployment problem or to the 20,000 registered drug addicts, for example. It is heartening to see existing institutions perform a little better, yet the philosophy of social change has not really come through, and too many agencies are still acting as they have in the past.

Citizen Participation

Weak Model Neighborhood Council. Citizen participation in Newark Model Cities has always been weak and continues so. Under Addonizio, it was virtually nonexistent and participants were entirely controlled. Gibson changed this by appointing Model Neighborhood residents to jobs and supporting Williams in having residents serve in all aspects of the Model Cities Program. Nevertheless, the Model Neighborhood Council has always been weak, dominated by CDA staff, with few resources of its own and little understanding of the program because the flow of information to it has been haphazard and of poor quality. Without essential facts, the board cannot make reasonable decisions. Furthermore, the understanding that it could exercise veto power provided little strength because disagreements were almost always negotiated away by more informed professionals. The threat of a veto did delay plans on several occasions, such as with the educational component and the entire Model Cities plan at one time. But in the end, the city did what it wanted anyway. And at times Gibson used the veto to sustain arguments against the city council, but its influence was only nominal.

The substitution of resident employment in place of strong board leadership has left a serious void in citizen participation and has not had the effect of developing new grass-roots leadership. The District Assembly meetings, of which there have been over 250, have been Newark's most effective means of citizen participation. These, and block association meetings, have forced the city to be more responsive, yet these mass meetings have mainly been used to inform and engender discussion, not to transfer any authority. It is understood that government today cannot be run effectively or expeditiously by means of town hall meetings.

Citywide Citizens Council. In spite of some bitterness, it was easy for the mayor and council to eliminate the weak, 52-member Model Neighborhood Council in favor of an appointed 27-member citywide advisory council. Since the new council has not been given any substantial powers, it appears that citizen participation will continue to take a back seat. Moreover, HUD has been agreeable to an appointive, relatively weak council. In addition, Gibson may feel this is the only way to expedite and save projects, for much catching up needs to be done. With both the mayor and council now participating in the appointment of members, the citywide council may act as a catalyst to bring these two antagonistic forces together for the benefit of the city. Also, agreements on salary ranges for new employees and city council participation in the creation of any new positions should help relationships.

Democratic Selection of Members Necessary. Although the advisory council is composed of a good cross-section of community people, it does not represent the free choice of neighborhood residents and groups. This citizens' council, as is the case in almost any Model Cities or Planned Variations program, ought to be composed of at least 50 percent residents freely chosen in their neighborhoods in order to give it some independence and a continual source of new blood, and to diminish dominance by established figures. The mayor and city council may share in the appointment of the remaining members. As the program progresses, Gibson ought to consider letting neighborhoods participate in the choosing of citizen council members.

Substantial Authority Necessary. Gibson ought also to give the citywide council meaningful powers, so that its decisions would have to be seriously considered by the mayor and council. To overturn decisions, a two-thirds city council vote and more stringent executive procedures (arbitration, for example) should be required. Advisory councils and coalitions without substantive authority tend to lose the interest of their members, and effectiveness disintegrates or the councils linger on as meaningless "rubber stanps," as experience has demonstrated in city after city.

Citywide Orientation an Improvement

Planned Variations has provided the Gibson Administration with the opportunity to improve upon the Model Cities concept. The administration is doing this by proceeding with citywide projects and coordination, yet concentrating funds in the most disadvantaged areas. The Chief Executive Review and Comment Process has strengthened the mayor's position to deal with other agencies and governments in concentrating on Newark's priorities and making programs more effective. Increasing local government's staff capacity may also eventually mean better services. But more fundamental issues must be resolved: development of a unified, single administrative command; cooperative relations with city council; authoritative coalition of businessmen, union members, educators, and white and black citizens; and a sincere attempt to confront the most sensitive and pressing issues regarding personnel and programs. Although Gibson has committed himself to hiring the best man for each job, the best have not been hired in enough cases. Also, the basic issues that influence city development, such as tax restructuring, control of population shifts, effective mass transportation, and more equitable income distribution, are largely out of his hands. Furthermore, Gibson himself admits that "there has been no reduction in community needs and no diminution in the forces that cause the needs."

The feeling of new birth in Newark has been somewhat dashed because progress has been slow. Still, Mayor Gibson has a mandate from Newark residents to push ahead. He appears to have the executive ability to do it. Hopefully, he will further demonstrate that ability and exercise the necessary leadership to go with it.

Notes

1. "City Government," Organization and Operations Review, December 1970, Touche Ross and Company, Newark, pp. 5-13.
2. National Commission on Health Services, Newark Area Community Health Services Study, Report no. 1, June 1969, pp. 33-34.

3. International City Management Association, National League of Cities/U.S. Conference of Mayors, Newark Field Visit Study, Washington, D.C., January 1972.

4. Junius W. Williams, The Impact of Citizen Participation, Newark Housing Council, May 1970, p. 4.

5. David K. Shiplei, "The White Niggers of Newark," Harpers Magazine, August 1972, pp. 77-83.

6. Ibid.

7. U.S. Congress, Model Cities Program, Newark, New Jersey, Hearings Before the Subcommittee on Housing, Committee on Banking and Currency, House of Representatives, September 8, 1972, pp. 14-16.

8. Ibid., pp. 31-39 and 77-109.

9. Center for Analysis of Public Issues, The Doctor Is Out, A Report on the Newark, New Jersey Division of Health, Princeton, N.J., March 1972.

10. Ibid., pp. 84, 86.

11. Ibid., p. 90.

12. Ibid., pp. 90-91.

13. Eugene Doleschol, "Criminal Justice Programs In Model Cities," Crime and Delinquency Literature 4, 2 (June 1972): 318-321.

14. Office of Program and Staff Development, An Evaluation of the Model Schools Program, Newark, September 1972, pp. 1-48.

15. Community Development Administration, Model Cities-Planned Variations Expansion Projects, Newark, September 12, 1972.

9

A NEW BEGINNING FOR SAVANNAH

The City

Savannah, "Mother City of Georgia," was founded by James Edward Oglethorpe in 1733. The distinctive grid plan with its many green squares was conceived in England and applied here that same year, making it one of the first planned cities in North America. It is the second largest city in Georgia, located on the Savannah River, 24 miles from the Atlantic Ocean, and its history is that of a proud southern port city. But Savannah will not be another Atlanta. Neither its geography nor its citizens will let it happen. While Savannah residents encourage tourists, they do not aspire to the hustle and bustle of big city life. Although major highways pass through and nearby the city, Savannah remains quaint and quiet. Its population actually declined from 1960 (149,000) because some blacks migrated north, various other segments of the population also sought opportunities elsewhere, and several areas were deannexed. Also, many of the young, white and black, who go away to college, stay where the opportunities are. Others have moved to the outer counties so they would not have to pay both county and city taxes, a burden that exists for people living within the city. Savannah is 21.2 square miles, and the 1970 population was 118,000, with 43 percent black. It is the seat of Chatham county, whose population was 187,000 in 1970 and whose land area is 441 square miles.

Union Camp Corporation, one of the world's largest paper manufacturing plants, is the major employer in Savannah and Chatham county. It employs approximately 5,000 workers, but it is also a major source of air and water pollution and a major political force. As the Democratic Party goes in the county, so goes Union Camp, although many of its corporate leaders are Republican in orientation. The

only time in recent years that a Union Camp employee was not on the
city council was during Mayor J. Curtis Lewis's Republican administration from 1966 to 1970, largely because of the company's disagreement with the populist philosophy of the administration. With this
exception, almost every county commission has had a Union Camp
employee.

Downtown Savannah is mostly business and commercial coupled
with a large belt of historic residential areas; surrounding that is a
larger belt of poor, black neighborhoods, now the Model Neighborhood,
ringed by a huge, fairly old, middle-class and higher-income residential area; and on the far southside are the newly booming suburbs
with their accompanying shopping centers and strip commercial development.

The city's budget in 1970 was $14,426,352, and its assessed
valuation was $232,691,000. The local tax rate was $6.785 per $100
of assessed valuation in 1970. Property is assessed at 40 percent of
market value, recently lowered from 55 percent. There is a state
income tax and sales tax; however, none of this revenue is specifically
reserved for cities. The state does make general purpose grants to
municipalities, of which Savannah receives $600,000 annually. The
state gasoline tax is of some assistance. Only a small proportion of
the revenues from the water and sewer utilities is transferred to the
city's General Fund; the balance remains in the Water and Sewer
Utility Fund. A 50 cent per month per household charge helps defray
refuse collection costs.

Two factors have been responsible for holding down Savannah's
property tax: (1) an unwillingness to face up to the revenues needed
to maintain services at the levels required and (2) the fruitful situation
of a rather dramatic increase in state grants. This condition changed
in 1972. For the first time in more than 20 years, the City of Savannah
increased its property tax. The rate increased from $2.60 to $3 per
$100 of assessed valuation (26 mills to 30 mills). This increase plus
other revenue changes have totaled $3.5 million annually. Without
these increases, the city would have found itself in a serious deficit
position.

Savannah's unemployment rate remained about 3.4 percent during
early 1972. Employment is usually better than prevailing national
conditions because of a fairly stable commercial and industrial base
and good employee-management relations.

Government

Structure and Politics

Savannah has been governed under the council-manager system
since 1953. The present mayor is John P. Rousakis, who spends a

great deal of his time on the job, although the position is part time. Traditionally, the city has had strong mayors and weak city councils. Only one black alderman sits on the six-member city council under this at-large system, though it would appear the 43 percent black population could elect two or three aldermen. But elections are held by party slates, and the black power structure probably feels it can get better "deals" by supporting the entire Democratic slate.

Savannah had a genuine "kingmaker" in Johnny Bouhan, a local Democratic attorney whose firm represents Union Camp. The Bouhan machine functioned until 1954, at which time the council-manager form of government went into effect. Thereafter, the machine held power only in the county and only until 1960. The election of Republicans in 1966 heralded the genesis of the two-party system, not only in Savannah and Chatham county but also in the rest of Georgia. It also represented a reaction to Savannah's efforts to bring about peaceful integration of public accommodations, permit blacks a greater role in community affairs, and establish equal opportunity employment in city government.

The black vote, traditionally controlled by the local NAACP, elects people in Savannah, and blacks are realizing their political clout. For example, the slate that was defeated in 1970 received only 800 black votes out of 13,000. However, the NAACP has moved very slowly and has settled for small favors, like one black alderman and an appointment to a city court judgeship. But young blacks are working for more meaningful representation, although to get it they may have to move outside the conservative NAACP. Present NAACP leadership is doing nothing to hold them back and in fact has encouraged black community groups to work together to press for their goals, such as better housing and living conditions.

The city manager appoints all department heads, prepares the budget, and is generally responsible for management of the city. Arthur A. Mendonsa, the present city manager, is serving a second term in that position. During his first term, he found it difficult to develop an acceptable council-manager relationship with the administration elected in 1966, because some members of city council refused to comply with the City Charter's council-manager requirements. Mendonsa felt it to be in the best interest of the city to resign in May 1967; he was reappointed again by a new administration in 1971.

One of his principal accomplishments was the development of the city's current management system. He established a Planning, Programing, Budgeting System (PPBS) and other systems analysis techniques within a Department of Management and Engineering Services responsible for research and budget, civil engineering, internal audit, and data processing. (See Chart 3.) During this period there was little accomplished in the area of human resources; however,

CHART 3

Functional Organization of the City of Savannah

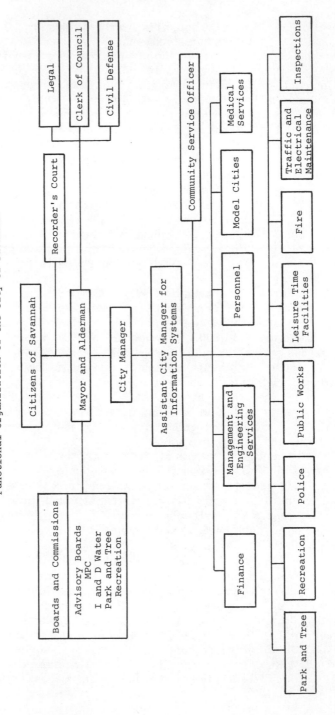

Source: Savannah, City Manager's Office, 1971.

Mendonsa instituted a Police-Community Relations Program and intended to move into other human services programs eventually. Now, under more preferable circumstances, he has the opportunity to pursue programs begun under the manager who succeeded him in 1967.

Picot B. Floyd was appointed manager in 1967. A professionally oriented person, he led city officials into a significant involvement in human resources and in the Model Cities Program. Floyd began his Savannah career under a highly conservative Republican mayor and council, described by many community leaders as a "populist government with racist overtones." It was primarily Floyd—former OEO Atlanta Regional Coordinator of the Community Action Program, for Alabama and Mississippi; member of American Civil Liberties Union; and contributor to the Democratic Study Group—who was instrumental in getting Model Cities for Savannah. In the fall of 1967, Floyd began the arduous process of applying as a second-round city. At that time there was no clamor or interest from disadvantaged areas. Some interested agencies participated in the planning, but, in general, citizen groups, business, and unions have shown little interest during planning or execution stages of the program. HUD made it easier on Savannah by requiring a smaller document (some 75 pages compared to 700-800 for other plans) and eliminating the need to develop a first-year proposal. One or two members of the city council pushed for "all the federal money the city could get." However, Floyd had to sell the program to a mostly reluctant council on the basis that it would be sound economics, and they bought it. Savannah already had three major urban renewal projects totaling $21 million, so Model Cities was viewed as a "new industry" that would bring in more federal dollars.

There had to be consensus on a moderate director for this program, one who would not fight the city council yet would get along with both blacks and whites in the neighborhoods. This was retired Lt. Col. Thomas Sears, who was very military, had no history of civil rights militancy, but was personally committed to equality. He had been brought to Savannah by the U.S. Army to encourage realtors and community leaders to support "open housing": as a requirement for reopening former Hunter Air Force Base as an army helicopter training base. In this capacity, he performed tactfully and successfully in getting over 90 percent to sign fair housing declarations.

Floyd stayed with the city until May 1971, when he accepted the position of vice president with Public Technology, Inc. (associated with the International City Management Association), Washington, D.C. Sears was employed until August 1971, when it was mutually agreed by him and the city commission that he should leave his post. There were questions of sloppy bookkeeping and poor financial and administrative controls. The main problem, however, was the inability

203

of Sears to administer the programs effectively. The present director, Edward Badgett, was hired January 3, 1972, coming on the job with an extensive background in local Model Cities programs elsewhere.

City Service Effectiveness

Perhaps city government's performance can best be understood by reference to a report that reviews services in the Model Neighborhood and whose findings generally hold true for most low-income areas in Savannah. Midwest Research Institute (Kansas City, Missouri) released a study in October 1969 exploring this subject. It reviewed five city services (garbage collection, housing code inspection, police, fire, and recreation services) and found four below the "level and quality" of service in the rest of the city. Only fire protection was "quite high in comparison with coverage throughout the city." It found that garbage was left uncollected in the Model Neighborhood and trash collections were unequal and not properly scheduled. As a result, Model Cities sought and received HEW funds for a piece of refuse collection equipment called the "shark," which was used in the Model Neighborhood for awhile but later discontinued from this service and put into general city use.

Midwest found a "lack of decision-making continuity" between the city and the county in building code enforcement programs, so that when the County Health Department recommended building demolition in its enforcement of the codes within city limits, city government seldom had the funds to do anything about it anyway. Although the responsibility to demolish a structure is the property owner's, if he fails to act, the city is obliged to demolish and assess the cost to the property owner. (Some officials believe that, rather than a lack of funds, the major problem in code enforcement is the lack of reinspection. Once a building has been inspected, there is simply no follow-up.)

Midwest also found that based on the number of crimes committed in the Model Neighborhood, insufficient police manpower was assigned to it. And it found recreation space grossly inadequate in the Model Neighborhood, noting that the city had "never purchased any land for the express purpose of recreation" in this area. Model Cities is now trying to fill this vacuum through mini-parks.

These findings of conditions in the Model Neighborhood are not unusual compared to the experiences of other cities. Most Model Cities communities have experienced lower levels of service in their Model Neighborhoods in comparison to higher-income areas. In Savannah's case, although these conditions were found to exist, there is some question whether the Model Cities Program satisfactorily addressed itself to them. Many of the problems still exist. However,

Savannah's present mayor and city council are cognizant of the problems and appear to be anxious to solve them. When Floyd was manager, he felt the mayor and council were "completely committed to Model Cities" and that considerable progress had been made. In a show of support, the new city council held its first official meeting in the Model Cities headquarters to sign contracts for the program. In a progressive spirit, Mendonsa has continued to encourage the support of the city council. He has also documented problems and their causes more precisely and is designing programs to deal effectively with them.

Model Cities

History of Model Cities

For a clearer understanding of Savannah's Model Cities Program, a review of its history is important.

The First Year. The mayor and aldermen authorized the city manager to proceed with a formal application for a Model Cities planning grant on March 8, 1968. The application was completed with assistance of the Research Group, Inc., and Eric Hill Associates, consultants. A week later, a letter of intent was sent to HUD indicating the city's desire to participate. Preparation of the application was subsequently completed, largely through efforts of the city manager, assistant city manager for administrative services, budgeting and engineering department, Metropolitan Planning Commission, 10 problem area discussion committees, an interagency coordinating group, and the city's consultants.

A significant number of participants were black. Some 25 black leaders and other groups of grass-roots persons were involved in the process. However, only when the whole package was approved and on paper did the program reveal itself to be predominantly for blacks. It is speculated that this role was downplayed so as not to upset a conservative mayor and city council. The council approved the application April 8, 1968.

Although the NAACP was active in helping to plan the Model Cities application, its field director, Sherman Roberson, a civil rights moderate, asked HUD to postpone indefinitely approval of the planning grant for the Model Cities Program because of exclusion of black people from participation in city government, in general. Roberson was later named executive administrator of the Neighborhood Council, the citizen participation component, but eventually resigned to run for a seat in the state legislature, which he did not win. In the opinion of many Model Cities staff members, he was not able to lead the council effectively.

During this same period, the executive committee of the Savannah NAACP sent a telegram, signed by chapter president W. W. Law, to HUD endorsing Savannah's application for the planning grant. This endorsement was viewed as expediency on Law's part. One local observer said that Law "when in doubt, will always take the easy way out."

In spite of efforts to postpone approval, Savannah's application to HUD for a grant to plan a comprehensive Model Cities Program was submitted and Savannah was designated, in September 1968, as one of 33 cities to receive "second round" Model Cities planning grants.

Another problem arose at this time. The city manager received a letter from Earl H. Metzgar, assistant regional administrator for Model Cities of HUD in Atlanta, stating that funds for Model Cities planning would be withheld until the Savannah Housing Authority complied with tenant assignment guidelines. This problem was later solved, and since then the Housing Authority has become fairly responsive to the Model Cities program. Although it is not aggressively offering assistance, it is at least adequately performing its basic functions and responsibilities.

On December 2, 1968 City Manager Floyd appointed Sears executive director of Model Cities. At this stage Floyd received a "letter to proceed" from the regional administrator of HUD. This letter permitted hiring of core staff and use of supporting funds prior to the execution of a planning grant contract. This placed the CDA in what is called the "preplanning" phase of the program.

The Model Cities director was given permission by the Public School Board to set up temporary offices in the Spencer Elementary School. Prior to this the director was working out of the city manager's office. E. Graham Martin was appointed physical planning coordinator, and Otis Johnson was appointed social planning coordinator of the Model Cities Program.

On January 30, 1969 the first Model Cities residents meeting was held at the Hellenic Community Center with 300 persons in attendance. Three subneighborhood groups were established.

In April, the Neighborhood Council held its second mass convention, attracting some 800 people. A middle-ground, largely cooperative level of participation was developed between the Neighborhood Council and the city. (This cooperative system has continued throughout the program, with most Model Neighborhood citizens— normally apathetic—apparently feeling it represents their views.) On April 24 the Model Cities Executive Committee met for the first time and approved selection of City Demonstration Agency (CDA) staff and locations for six mini-parks in the target area.

A community survey was conducted in July 1969 under the direction of Otis Johnson. A total of 800 interviews in the Model

Neighborhood were made to assess attitudes toward nine task force areas. The results of the survey showed residents' priorities as education, health, employment and economic development, housing, social services and income maintenance, recreation and cultural activities, crime and juvenile delinquency prevention, neighborhood design and physical improvements, and transportation, respectively. The priorities were approved by the Technical Advisory Committee. The executive committee, however, moved crime and juvenile delinquency prevention to third on the list.

In this same month, the Neighborhood Council received word that OEO had granted it $67,000 for training and technical assistance in low-income areas of the Model Neighborhood. Also city department heads were briefed on Model Cities in an effort to increase "in-kind" services needed to make up the 20 percent of the city's share of the Model Cities planning grant. (The city still has difficulty in getting "in-kind" services but always manages to do it. Most city departments and agencies outside city government are not enthusiastic about assisting the program but do what they have to do.)

On October 15, 1969 Savannah Model Cities submitted the "mid-planning statement" to the Region III office of HUD in Atlanta.

Sherman Roberson resigned on December 5, 1969. Otis Johnson was selected by the Neighborhood Council to replace him. On December 15, representatives from the regional office of the Small Business Administration and the Economic Development Administration visited the economic development task force to give technical assistance in establishing a nonprofit, resident economic development corporation.

On January 12, 1970, the Neighborhood Council began monthly joint staff meetings with the Economic Opportunity Authority (EOA-Community Action Agency) to bring about a closer working relationship between the two organizations operating in the same neighborhoods. EOA relies on the city and Model Cities for its needed 25 percent matching funds. (Floyd described the EOA "as better than most but one which plays it safe." It has a relatively limited number of functions and is considered nonmilitant.)

Legal work of incorporating the Savannah Neighborhood Council began on February 4, 1970. On February 18 the Neighborhood Council voted to send a delegation to Washington to seek a commitment from HUD on urban renewal money for the Model Neighborhood. Residents requested a larger appropriation than the proposed $5 million grant indicated by John Edmunds of the HUD Region II (now Region IV) office. It was estimated that it would take $18-20 million to redevelop the entire Model Neighborhood.

The Neighborhood Council and a city delegation attended a conference March 4-6, 1970 with Assistant Secretary Floyd Hyde and HUD urban renewal officials to discuss Savannah's Model Cities plans in regard to the need for $18-20 million in urban renewal funds. Attending the conference were Alderman Joseph Myatt, CDA Director Thomas Sears, eight neighborhood residents, and city consultant Eric Hill. No commitment was received, but Savannah residents assumed the urban renewal grant was going to be $5 million. The Neighborhood Council worked to approve a proposed urban renewal site in the northeast section of the Model Neighborhood, and a proposed land use design plan was presented to the Neighborhood Council by the Metropolitan Planning Commission and local architects.

On April 17, 1970, city council authorized sending applications to HUD for a $2.6 million Model Cities first action year, a $5 million urban renewal program, and a $360,000 neighborhood facilities grant. On April 22 Otis Johnson resigned as Neighborhood Council executive administrator and was appointed CDA deputy director for Operations and Continuing Planning. Robert Vaughn was appointed executive administrator in June 1970 but resigned in March 1971 because he felt the Neighborhood Council failed to involve residents in the program sufficiently. Concerning the council, he said, "We have not followed the processes necessary to become the strong resident group we need to be."

HUD approved $5,826,000 for the Model Cities urban renewal project in the northeast section of the Model Neighborhood on June 18, 1970, and, shortly thereafter, the Housing Authority of Savannah approved a contract with HUD to receive $481,000 to plan for urban renewal in the Model Cities area.

On September 1, CDA received a "letter of credit" for the Model Cities Program for $2,092,126. The remainder of the $2.6 million grant was reserved until revisions could be made on such projects as a manpower center, a housing corporation, and juvenile delinquency prevention. In this same month, the Housing Authority awarded Eric Hill Associates of Atlanta $84,350 to plan the Model Cities urban renewal area.

On October 9, 1970 the mayor and aldermen signed 10 contracts with nine agencies for a total of $1,050,752 in Model Cities funds during a ceremony at Model Cities headquarters. All contracts were eventually signed on time. In this same month, CDA began work on a Planned Variations proposal to HUD; however, Savannah was not chosen as one of the nation's 20 cities under this program. It was picked by HUD as one of four cities to develop a model social service delivery coordination system. As a result, three Washington-based firms were chosen to work with the city in developing the system: Volt Information Sciences, Inc.; Transcentury Corp.; and Hammer, Green, Siler Associates. When the plan was finally unveiled in early 1972, city and agency officials felt it was impractical and "yielded almost nothing." In the words of one prominent official concerning the end product,

"never has so much been spent for so little." Soon thereafter, City
Manager Mendonsa drafted a new proposal for coordinating agencies.
It is to use the resources of HEW and HUD and the Model Cities process
as a model for demonstrating a system of coordination and cooperation.

On January 5, 1971 the Board of Education agreed to allow Model
Cities to use a portion of Paulsen Playground to construct a neighborhood facility. (The elected school board is considerably more liberal
than past boards and works closely with Model Cities.)

The first action year ended September 1, 1971. The program
stressed education. All projects were placed under contract on time
and progressed at a satisfactory pace.

Second action year program priorities were changed to emphasize
employment, economic development, and implementation of urban renewal projects in order to create greater visibility. In the development of the third action year, the number of Model Cities projects
were reduced from 29 to 17, placing greater emphasis on programs
that dealt specifically with Model Neighborhood problems. Mendonsa,
at the beginning of his second term as city manager, noted that many
of the problems originally outlined by Model Cities still existed; therefore, he intended to redirect many of the programs.

The Model Neighborhood

General. The target area of Savannah's Model Neighborhood contains
an extremely heavy concentration of the usual urban problems: poverty,
lack of education, absence of job skills, racism, poor health, crowded
and dilapidated housing, broken homes, crime and delinquency, and
loss of hope and motivation. The area is all too typical of many other
depressed areas in the city. The Model Neighborhood population is
approximately 21,500, an estimated 70 percent black.

Employment. Unemployment in the Model Neighborhood in early 1972
was 6.2 percent, compared with 3.4 percent for the city. The unemployment rate on a 12-month average was somewhat lower: 3.3 percent, Savannah; 4.7 percent, Model Neighborhood. For women, the
rate was higher: 7.1 percent, target area; 5 percent, Savannah. Black
females are especially hard hit, suffering intense employment discrimination because of both race and sex. And underemployment is
a serious problem. Over 54 percent of the families make less than
$3,000 a year, and 71 percent of employed persons have unskilled
jobs. Twenty-six percent of the city's unemployed males over 14
reside in the target area.

Education. One of the main causes for the low economic level in the
Model Neighborhood is lack of education. Fifty-three percent of adults

209

over 25 have less than an eighth grade education. And 10 of the 11 schools in the target area have mental maturity, reading, and arithmetic norms one and two grades below the national average. Most students do not go beyond high school, and the drop-out rate is 16 percent, compared to 9 percent for the school system as a whole.

Housing. The Model Neighborhood is one of the oldest areas in the city. More than 60 percent of its housing units were constructed prior to 1930, and very little construction has taken place since 1940. At present, there is no public or federally subsidized housing in the model area. Substandard housing totals 6,211 units, and only 4 percent of the housing in the Model Neighborhood is considered "standard." Existence of outside toilets attests to the primitive conditions in the area.

Overcrowding and Health. Overcrowding is characteristic. Since 1960, the population has increased while the number of housing units has decreased. Physical appearance of the general area is poor, with incompatible land use, little open space, and no recreational areas for children. Only three supervised playgrounds with a combined area of 2.6 acres are in the Model Neighborhood. This represents only 5.9 percent of the total supervised playground area of the city available to 15 percent of the population—a low ratio. There are eight miles of unpaved streets and sidewalks in the area, and the paved streets are poorly maintained. The area stands in sharp contrast to "historic Savannah," with its beautiful old buildings and well-kept parks and gardens.

In such an environment, poor health conditions are no surprise. Infant mortality rates per 100,000 (1968) were 42.5 in the county and 60 in the Model Neighborhood. Tuberculosis rates per 100,000 were 42 in the county, 105 in the target area. Infectious syphilis rates per 100,000 in the county were 27.6; in the Model Cities area 115. Narcotics are readily available in both the city and the target area. Good public health facilities to help alleviate some of the extreme problems are lacking.

Crime. Life in the target area is further threatened by a high incidence of crime. Thirty-three percent of the homicides and rapes, and 27 percent of the felonious assults committed in Savannah occur in the Model Neighborhood. Juvenile delinquency is also high—the arrest rate of persons under 18 years of age in the target area is 48.2 per thousand, compared to 33.8 for the whole city.

Welfare. There is heavy dependence on public welfare. Out of 6,000 families, 2,000 were on public assistance; yet only 823 received food stamps in 1967. Few social service agencies are located within the Model Neighborhood, and fewer have outreach services to the target area. Residents also complain of inadequate coordination of public and private agencies providing social services. The federally funded demonstration to coordinate the social service delivery system apparently is not making much of a difference.

City Services. Considerable resident dissatisfaction is aimed at the city for failure to provide adequate municipal services. For example, lack of recreational facilities can be attributed to lack of sufficient funding. City per capita expenditure for public recreation is $2.85. The national norm is $6, and the city as a whole would need almost three times more recreational space to meet Department of Interior standards of 1.5 acres of supervised playground per 1,000 persons. Housing inspection and police protection are inadequate. Almost all physical problems, such as unpaved streets, lack of sidewalks, inadequate lighting, and inferior and inadequate garbage collection, storm drainage systems, animal control, and traffic control could be remedied by improvement in city service delivery assisted with Model Cities funds.

No description of the Model Neighborhood is complete without considering what the Savannah Model Cities Program identifies as "attitude." Attitude surveys indicate that there is a general feeling of hopelessness, apathy, and frustration in the target area, and residents have come to accept as inevitable the poverty, crime, and disease that blight their daily lives.

Administrative Structure and Coordination

State and County Coordination. The Savannah Model Cities first action year plan states that "overall coordination between local, state, and federal governmental agencies and between residents and other Savannah citizens has been significantly enhanced due to the development of planning under the Model Cities program." In the early stages, federal regional officials worked closely with city staff. They continue to do so. This has created better coordination because it has attracted state officials, such as the Office of the Governor, State Highway Department, and State Health Department. However, Picot Floyd's impression was that the state was typically unresponsive to the needs of the city and the Model Cities program in particular. But he pointed to two recent developments that could improve this.

The first is enactment by the General Assembly of Georgia Act 1066, which carries the idea of A-95 (local review and comment on specific federal programs) one step further and requires all applications for federal or foundation grants to be reviewed by state, regional, and metropolitan planning bureaus. This provides a multi-county, areawide review that should improve coordination of projects as well as relationships between state and local jurisdictions. Coordination is not a serious problem here because with only eight communities there are not as many programs as are usually encountered in other metropolitan areas, and there are few "grantsmanship" disputes.

Secondly, Georgia's governor, Jimmy Carter, is committed to areawide planning and community action. It appears the state will increase funding and technical assistance to local Model Cities programs. Savannah is now using technical assistance provided by HEW's regional office to open doors to the state health and education departments.

Internal Coordination. Although Model Cities has always been considered a city department, it has not functioned like other departments. Sears saw himself "outside City Hall," and regular department heads saw Model Cities as a separate federal project, not a city operation. City purchasing and budget personnel have said that Model Cities considered itself above city regulations. Sears ran into difficulty in late 1971, when it was discovered that many of the projects were operating without financial controls or records. Although Sears was outstanding in mobilizing residents and neighborhood resources, he was ill-equipped to administer the Model Cities Program. As a result, steps were taken by Floyd to integrate the Model Cities operations into the city's computerized financial management system and to consolidate the Model Cities and regular city budgets. Mendonsa completed the integration shortly after his arrival. Eventually Sears was relieved of his position, and a new director was appointed by Mendonsa.

Model Cities Organization. The Model Cities City Demonstration Agency is, in effect, the Model Cities Department, which, in addition to its regular staff, is assisted by city staff. CDA works in conjunction with a Model Cities Neighborhood Council, Executive Committee, and Technical Advisory Committee. (See Chart 4.)

The 43 members on the Model Neighborhood Council, Inc. were initially chosen by a mass convention, organized with the help of the local community action agency. Members are now elected from voluntary organizations, which operate in the three subneighborhoods. Nonresidents may also participate as associate (nonvoting) members. Officers are elected annually from council members selected by a nominating committee. The council has a staff of five, including an executive administrator who coordinates plans closely with the CDA staff under a "parallel planning agreement," which attempts to have avoided duplication and misinformation. This parallel planning consists

212

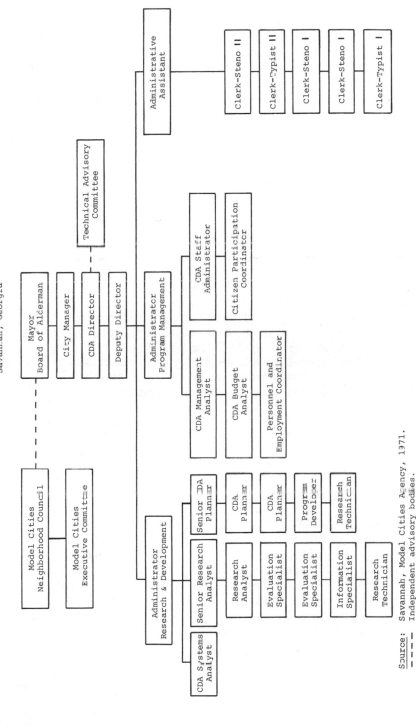

CHART 4

City Demonstration Agency Organizational Chart
Savannah, Georgia

Model Cities Neighborhood Council

Model Cities Executive Committee

Mayor
Board of Alderman

City Manager

CDA Director

Deputy Director

Technical Advisory Committee

Administrative Assistant

Clerk-Steno II

Clerk-Typist II

Clerk-Steno I

Clerk-Steno I

Clerk-Typist I

Administrator Research & Development

Administrator Program Management

CDA Systems Analyst

Senior Research Analyst

Senior CDA Planner

Research Analyst

CDA Planner

Evaluation Specialist

CDA Planner

Evaluation Specialist

Program Developer

Information Specialist

Research Technician

Research Technician

CDA Management Analyst

CDA Budget Analyst

Personnel and Employment Coordinator

CDA Staff Administrator

Citizen Participation Coordinator

Source: Savannah, Model Cities Agency, 1971.
- - - - Independent advisory bodies.

of bimonthly, combined staff meetings, inclusion of representatives
of both staffs in all significant meetings, and the use of common office
space. The council is an advisory citizen participation structure.
The plan says it is a semiautonomous group that functions in partnership with the city in planning, execution, and evaluation of the program.
However, this "partnership" does not have nearly the strength of the
partnership arrangements in Dayton and Boston, for example. Its
impact is minimal in getting approval for the programs it wants.
This is primarily true because public and private agencies exert a
strong controlling influence on ideas and programs, and the Neighborhood Council tends to go along with them.

The Executive Committee is advisory also and consists of the
mayor, the chairman of the county commissioners, the president of
the school board, the chairman of the Neighborhood Council, two
representatives from the Neighborhood Council (elected by the members
of the council), and a citizen at large. It meets infrequently, and there
is question as to whether it ought to continue at all. The real decision-
making authority rests with the mayor, aldermen, and city manager.
The Technical Advisory Committee, composed of principal officers
of public and private agencies, simply advises the council, Executive
Committee, and city staff. In time and efficiency, this structure has
worked well—one of the best examples is that all contracts were under
way within 90 days of approval by HUD.

The principal administrative staff consists of a deputy director,
administrative assistant in charge of the clerical staff, administrator
for research and development, and an administrator for program
management. The CDA staff budget for the first action year was
$376,408. Approximately $100,000 went to the Neighborhood Council
staff. The staff is young, is hired locally, and had to develop its competence on the job. Under the present administration, considerable
upgrading of staff has taken place.

Citizen Participation

Little History of Involvement. There is little history of citizen involvement in the Model Neighborhood prior to the Model Cities and Community Action Programs; therefore, one of the main problems was
to convince residents to be actors, not audience. Most residents had
never belonged to a club, group, or organization Apathy and alienation
were the rule, and residents felt their ideas would be of little value
and probably not be considered anyway—attitudes reflecting years of
unfulfilled government promises and the usual bewildering bureaucratic
maze.

Task Forces and Subneighborhoods. It was not surprising that there
was no clamor from residents to bring Model Cities to Savannah.

214

City Manager Floyd initiated planning; and Economic Opportunity Authority outreach workers encouraged citizens to come to meetings. An initial community convention was held (mass conventions had drawn as many as 1,000 persons) where the residents grouped themselves into three subneighborhoods and nine subcommittees for each neighborhood, paralleling the plan's priorities as outlined by the staff. Officers of the subcommittees elected a Model Neighborhood chairman, vice chairman, secretary, and two other representatives to the Executive Committee, and participation began. The basic planning unit turned out to be nine task forces (later dropped to three), which included residents from the corresponding neighborhood subcommittees (one of whom was elected chairman for each function) and representatives from public and private agencies. Task force members were crowded into the same offices as city planners, but this close proximity led to more effective exchange of information. Membership on task forces was never restrictive, and meetings were always open, but progress was slow until members became familiar with HUD guidelines. Each task force was assigned a coordinator from the CDA staff, and eventually professionals and residents learned to work together.

During planning stages, primary responsibility for coordination was assigned to the social and physical planning coordinators. An economic coordinator was added for the execution phase. Task force meetings are now held at least twice a month. A three-day workshop and 10 general training sessions for residents were conducted by Savannah State College and the University of Georgia. Also a two-day first-phase planning training exercise was held, and technical help from Volt Information Sciences consultants for a $67,000 training grant from OEO was approved by the Neighborhood Council. The council was also authorized auxiliary planning aides and clerical help.

Citizen Involvement Matures. This participation process, compared to most other local forms of citizen participation, has led to fairly active involvement by once passive residents. Floyd was highly impressed with the success of this mobilization and considers the active development of the Neighborhood Council the most significant accomplishment of the Savannah program. It was his belief that the organizational "know-how" and political maturity would continue, regardless of the fate of Model Cities. On the other hand, the mayor and city council have been less inclined toward strong citizen involvement.

Sears and Otis Johnson believed effective citizen participation was necessary to ensure long-lasting program success and that it was also essential for citizens to understand program limitations to avoid disenchantment. So far, residents appear to be satisfied with the level of participation and feel the process is representative.

Sears said proof of Neighborhood Council influence is that "100 percent of their proposals have been accepted by the city." Nevertheless, there seem to be strong arguments in favor of the position that agencies strongly influence the decisions of the council.

Factions Disrupt the Neighborhood Council. Despite the maturity of citizen participation, its development has been no smoother or easier than in other cities. For example, from its beginning, the Neighborhood Council has been split into two roughly equally influential factions, a situation that has rendered it virtually ineffective a good deal of the time. Board members have not always encouraged resident participation, and some have been more concerned with getting their friends hired than in developing effective programs. One critic defined the council as "ignorant and petty, too large to get anything done, and everybody with their own ideas of what they should be doing." Criticism by the "in" faction of the Neighborhood Council over the health clinic project caused the resignation of the health director, Dr. Theisen Ray. His staff was accused of discriminating against hiring Model Neighborhood residents. Many felt this criticism unfair because the director needed reliable professionals who were not available in the target area. They also felt that jeopardizing the entire program over this issue was not constructive and would hurt other programs as well.

The "out" faction of the council—about half its members—did not take part in council meetings or training sessions during this crisis period. A new executive director for the board, Lu James Groover, hired in April 1971, replaced the entire council staff with new personnel "to put the operation on a businesslike basis." City Manager Floyd did not want to get directly involved because he felt these internal conflicts would have to be resolved by the members themselves, in their own way, if they were to be acceptable to the neighborhood. Most officials felt that conflicts were inevitable until the board learned the objectives and limitations of the program. Meanwhile, Groover was fired for mismanagement and unethical practices. As a consequence, the city placed stronger controls on the council's operations. Eventually, these problems were corrected and the program moved forward.

Task Forces as an Educational Process. In contrast, the task forces have had little conflict because their sessions are primarily informational as opposed to being devoted to making decisions. Most members have little knowledge of program planning; therefore, planners largely mold their thinking. Agency representation on the task forces varies from 6 (on the Neighborhood Design and Physical Improvement Task Force) to 15 persons (on the Health Task Force). These professionals have displayed diplomacy and sensitivity in this process,

216

which in the long run should help to develop more independent resident thinking. This has certainly occurred in the more action-oriented EOA, where strong community groups have been spawned. EOA's six years of experience and the program's strong citizen participation mandate have encouraged this, however. Before Model Cities, the EOA-funded Eastside Neighborhood Action Center, located on the outside perimeter of the Model Neighborhood, was the only organized citizen group in the area designed to involve residents.

Clients Grow. In spite of conflicts and a weak history of citizen organization, the number of program participants continues to grow. Most programs are expected to be operating at capacity by the end of the second action year, and CDA is considering an advertising campaign to sell participation and a better understanding of the program. As projects with greater visibility take effect, natural community interest should be generated. Sears believed that a "sense of community" had already developed in the neighborhood because of the program's presence. Moreover, at this juncture, residents appear to have developed reliance on these increased services.

Citizens Plan Continued Involvement. With the fear that at some point the program might lose federal funds in favor of revenue sharing, and the $5 million already spent would have been used in vain, CDA (in spring 1971) proposed that the city expand its concern to all poverty pockets of the city, promote citywide citizen participation, and appoint a director and staff to maintain a new program. The Metropolitan Planning Commission originally identified 11 poverty areas outside the Model Neighborhood. CDA proposed that one representative be elected from each 1,000 residents of the poverty areas—a total of 40 members—to a Community Advisory Council and be paid for attending meetings and workshops. Areas would be dropped as they advanced beyond the substandard category. However, city council postponed this decision until more could be learned about the status of federal funding.

The City's Planned Variations Proposal. While Savannah was still being considered for the Planned Variations Program, the city made proposals somewhat similar to those of the CDA: Neighborhood groups would be formed (using the assistance of EOA) in each of the target areas; the Neighborhood Council would be expanded to include elected representatives from each of these areas; Neighborhood Council officers would be recognized citywide leaders (as some are now) to encourage further citizen participation and cooperation; the city's PPB system would be strengthened within the Department of Management and Engineering Services; attempts would be made to institutionalize the coordinating efforts of the Technical Advisory Committee on

217

a citywide basis; other agencies would be encouraged to work with Model Cities citywide, as is now being done with the Cooperative Area Manpower Planning System (CAMPS) and the Urban Corps (SPUR—Student Participation in Urban Revitalization). By 1973, the city planned to put some of these into effect.

Aldermanic Viewpoints. Aldermanic reactions to proposals for city-wide use of revenue-sharing funds vary considerably. Alderman Leo Center favors continuation of Model Cities concepts even under revenue sharing but realizes that pressures from other areas in the city would necessarily force the cutback of services in the Model Neighborhood. He believes it would be a "waste," however, to drop Model Cities after such a short experimental period.

On the other hand, Alderman Frank Rossiter feels there would not be overpowering pressure to reduce commitments to the Model Neighborhood if general revenue sharing were in effect because "the black vote is so powerful." But Rossiter has been dissatisfied with the local administration of the program and believes "the city could fashion something as well as the federal government for the Model Neighborhood." In regards to revenue sharing, he said, "It would be no great loss to the neighborhood if Model Cities fell."

The first black alderman in Savannah's post-reconstruction history, Bowles C. Ford, believes that "enough work has been done here so that a similar program would be continued" and that the level of services and long-range plans would be maintained. He is not satisfied with progress, however, and feels that greater emphasis should be placed on hardware, such as streets and housing.

Programs

General. Citizen involvement is a significant contribution of Savannah's Model Cities Program, but so is the recognition of the need to improve services. It is safe to assume that new services and the extension of old ones would not have taken place if agencies had to reduce services elsewhere and focus on traditionally neglected areas. Financial and political pressures would not have allowed it. To some extent, Model Cities made it possible for agencies and city departments to break out of this mold.

However, the battle for improved services still rages. For example, Model Cities stimulated the Health Department to request three additional inspectors to improve housing code enforcement, but the city did not approve the budget request. The Police Department admits no wrong. The Housing Authority acts only as fast as it has to. And the Department of Public Works maintains that garbage and trash collections are equal in all parts of the city, despite CDA contentions to the contrary. And the conservative county commission has refused to continue providing matching funds for a health program.

The projects described here show how Model Cities is trying to change attitudes and improve services. City agencies are now aware of the program, and many, for the first time, are aware of the severity of target area problems. The mayor and aldermen have shown a definite commitment to Model Cities objectives; however, they perhaps depend too much on these funds to solve all Model Neighborhood problems. Over all, the money has probably relieved more pressures for elected officials than it has created. There is some comfort for them in the knowledge that a large chunk of federal money is earmarked for a specific substandard area and that local pressures cannot divert it to less needy areas. In the past, city programs merely maintained existing conditions in the Model Neighborhood.

Setting Priorities. Setting program priorities has not been a critical problem. The first priority was placed on education, partially because of its noncontroversial nature. But for the second action year residents switched their priorities to economics and quick implementation of the urban renewal package. Priorities were resolved rather easily, but NAACP President Law expressed dissatisfaction with too many frill programs and indicated that program stress should be on social change, motivation, jobs, and training. Some CDA staff believed there were too many programs and it would be better to concentrate on a few successes. As a result, the number of programs were reduced and less important ones deemphasized.

In a few cases, results are already apparent. Educational programs have considerably improved communications between Model Neighborhood residents and the school board by demonstrating successful programs and helping the board acquire grants. Model Cities has contracted with EOA to operate three day-care centers, which has facilitated coordination between the day-care program and EOA's Head Start activity. Almost all projects planned for the first and second action years have gotten under way satisfactorily. The principal programs in the first action year are described below.

Education

1. In-service Teacher Training ($10,304). Thirty Model Neighborhood teachers were taught new methods of instructing poverty children and are now used as lead teachers in their respective schools to provide ongoing in-service training.

2. Expanded Free Lunch Program ($107,800). Free or reduced-price balanced lunches were provided to 3,393 poverty pupils per day in 11 Model Neighborhood schools.

219

3. Career Opportunity Programs ($122,000). Seventy-two persons received college training at Savannah State College as teacher aides and were given stipends for work in the classroom. Over 300 persons have applied for these positions, most of whom never had considered college.

4. Curriculum Evaluation Study Design Project ($30,000). The Peabody College division of surveys and research conducted a comprehensive study of the entire Savannah/Chatham County School System. The report was accepted by the Board of Education and was highly commended.

5. Training and Absenteeism Reduction Program ($60,325). About 856 cases were handled, apparently with little success. The project was not continued for the second action year because children were being bused out of the Model Neighborhood and were spread throughout the total county school system, defeating the purpose of improving Model Cities schools.

6. Community School Program ($110,000). Two community schools extending regular school hours were opened to all students in the Model Neighborhood, and 400 persons were enrolled for educational and prevocational courses.

Employment and Economic Development

1. Manpower Center ($39,827). In the first four months, 200 residents were interviewed, 30 tested, 70 referred to jobs, and 15 placed. Vocational rehabilitation and vocational training are just getting under way. The center operates from Model Cities headquarters and has been instrumental in bringing together under one roof the services of the Georgia Department of Labor, State Office of Rehabilitation Services, and Savannah/Chatham Board of Education.

2. Housing Code Updating. The city adopted the latest Southeastern Region Housing Code, which will meet FHA standards for the Model Neighborhood urban renewal area.

3. Equal Housing. This program was adopted to ensure compliance with the 1968 National Housing Legislation, but the mayor and city council have taken no action.

4. Urban Renewal Survey and Planning Application. The planning year is completed for this $5 million project in the northeast area. Execution was expected to start early in 1972. The Northwest area is now in the planning stage for a Neighborhood Development Program (NDP).

Urban renewal really started in Savannah through Model Cities. At first, city officials felt they could concentrate on the rest of the city while federal funds took care of the Model Neighborhood. But Mayor Rousakis realized the active role the city would have to play in the urban renewal effort. He took several tours of the area and was visibly impressed at the lack of code enforcement and water and sewer facilities. His concern has helped better enforcement and speeded progress.

5. Housing Center ($300,000). The center idea was dropped in favor of Savannah Housing and Development Corporation (SHADCO), set up to provide seed money and technical assistance to nonprofit housing sponsors and to establish a land bank.

Health

1. Comprehensive Health Center ($199,376). This clinic is for medical indigents, not those on welfare or Medicaid. It has doubled its work load from 8 to 16 persons per day and is expected to be operating at full capacity in several months. At first it had difficulty in hiring a full-time physician and two dentists, but these initial problems have been overcome.

2. Family Planning Project ($99,829). Model Cities did not participate in this county health project the first year but will absorb 25 percent of the budget the second year. About 35 percent of the case load is Model Neighborhood residents.

Crime and Juvenile Delinquency Prevention

1. Police Training Project ($60,000). Over 236 Model Neighborhood residents and 190 police officers (Savannah's total force is 200) received 32 hours of joint classroom training. All participants were asked to rate the course, which received a combined average of 4.2 on a five-point scale. The classroom experience was successful. However, whether it will be applied outside by either group has yet to be determined.

2. Police-Community Relations ($57,957). Three teen recreation centers, each staffed with a manager and a community relations police officer, were established, and monthly attendance was over 1,000 persons for each center. Both Model Cities and the Police Department believe there has been a significant reduction in crime in these areas.

Resident Programs

1. Unwed Mothers Comprehensive Services ($78,800). A total of 75 unwed mothers, babies, boyfriends, parents, and siblings were involved in the first action year.

2. Senior Citizen Services ($119,467). More than 3,000 elderly shut-ins were served the first year in five service categories: meals on wheels, homemaking, prescription delivery, transportation, and

community service order. Model Cities reports that "this project has accomplished far more than anticipated for the first action year, and services rendered to these elderly citizens has been lauded by many community groups and organizations." Many local officials believe it may be Model Cities' most successful program.

3. Consumer Education ($4,926). This program reached 125 persons per month in its first five months, and a survey showed 85 percent of the participants felt they had saved money as a result. The budget will be increased to $11,000 the second year.

4. Day Care ($191,705). Two centers served 100 children and their families the first year. Five more are scheduled for the second year to reach 300 additional children and their families for year-round care.

5. Neighborhood Council, Inc. ($128,145). Minimum accomplishments were realized the first year due to inexperience in operating an agency of this nature. It strove to involve 25 percent of Model Neighborhood residents in the program but only achieved about 60 percent of this objective. Seven residents were hired as staff.

Recreation and Cultural Activities

1. Recreation Leaders ($36,549). All city parks are fully staffed through this project. Average participation level for all recreational activities is 11,704 per month.

2. Mobile Recreation Program ($71,315). Three mobile vans are operating six days per week, and streets are blocked off for recreation purposes. It served 57,648 persons in the first year.

3. All Day Golden Age Center ($25,976). The unavailability of a building large enough to accommodate 100 elderly residents limited the Golden Age Center to 35-40 participants in the first year. Negotiations are currently under way to acquire larger quarters for the second action year.

4. Cultural Center ($83,991). More than 300 participants have enrolled in the center, and 4,000 persons witnessed performances and exhibits.

5. Store-Front Libraries ($60,000). This did not operate the first year.

6. Recreation Equipment for Forsyth Park. No new equipment was purchased in the first year.

7. Tot Lots. Two parks were completed in the first action year. In addition, several Savannah banks have cooperated with the city to develop four mini-playgrounds in the Model Neighborhood.

8. Playgrounds. No new playgrounds were developed.

Municipal Services

1. Changes in Garbage and Refuse Collection. The city's capability for garbage pickup with its present number of trucks and personnel remains inadequate for the Model Neighborhood. City Manager
Mendonsa has instituted a study of the total refuse collection system
and is taking steps to correct inadequacies.

2. Special Trash Removal ($40,000). The inadequate cyclical
pickup system used by the city and the lack of an administrative procedure to confirm trash pickup continue to pose a problem in the Model
Neighborhood. The "shark" vehicle has not been as effective as anticipated. Other measures are now being tried.

3. Loose Animal Sweep. This stray animal program was not
implemented during the first action year.

4. Traffic Control Update ($200,000). This is designed to control
traffic flow based on demand, but unfortunately most improvements
under this program have occurred in commercial areas and traffic
arterials rather than where the Model Neighborhood residents desired
them.

5. Upgrading Street Lighting. The city is planning to install
74 new lights and replace 62 old ones.

6. Storm Drainage Plan. No action was taken by the city.

7. Operation Junk Car Removal. This would encourage private
enterprise to remove old junk automobiles, but as yet no action has
been taken.

Analysis

Accomplishments

Savannah Model Cities has been a catalyst for several major
accomplishments. It has alerted local elected officials to the problems
of the city's poor, and it has brought them to the target areas to in-
spect conditions firsthand and propose solutions. It has aroused
apathetic and alienated residents into believing that their voices can
be heard and some of their needs and desires fulfilled. And it has
provided much-needed funds for a long-forgotten area of the city,
significantly improving services there.

City Commitment Strengthened. Model Cities has made an important
start in Savannah by arousing official concern for the poor, although
it still is far short of its goals. It is unlikely that another source of
funds such as general revenue sharing (designed to supplement cities'
general funds) would have made these same gains. Some of Savannah's

elected officials admit it would have been difficult to funnel large chunks of general purpose money into predominantly poor areas, particularly black neighborhoods. These same officials feel relieved that they do not have to justify to the rest of the community why Model Cities funds are going where they are. In this respect, Congress has taken them off the hook, although they feel new money (such as under Planned Variations) could be acceptably distributed citywide as long as emphasis remained in areas of greatest need. If any significant development occurs in Savannah's disadvantaged areas, it will be through block grants designated for that purpose. The disadvantaged have still not gained sufficient strength to guide funds to their areas.

Fearing the eventual loss of funds, Model Cities participants have designed many of their programs with long-term effects in mind and with permanence and objectives that might encourage city officials to continue them. Most programs would not have come into existence without federal earmaking of funds, and only a few are strong enough to be continued without special funding. On the other hand, Model Cities has forced local officials to take a look at the worst of the city's problems, and it will not be easy for officials to discontinue projects that address themselves to these problems.

Hope Created. Besides arousing official interest in the target area, Model Cities has been successful in convincing poor residents that they can be heard and in creating hope for minorities. The lethargic environment in which many of Savannah's citizens grew up was broken by Model Cities. Local institutions failed to wrest citizens from this historic stagnancy, and only federal intervention made the difference, spurred by local government acceptance.

Many local citizens believe that Savannah's Model Cities Program will in itself train and qualify more blacks for local government service than could have been developed in a generation without it. Picot Floyd, former city manager, felt the program's "most significant accomplishment was the active development of the Neighborhood Council" and its creation of new spirit and leadership in the community.

Although the Neighborhood Council's power is weak compared to most other Model Cities boards, residents are participating in decision-making and helping to decide the course of their lives and neighborhood. They have not previously experienced this kind of authority. It should result in new leadership. The Neighborhood Council's inexperience and disputes among its several factions have not helped its growth, but if one realizes that most of this nation's legislative bodies experience similar factional struggles, one can understand why these occur. Further time and maturing are necessary if Savannah is to witness a responsible and effective citizens' council.

Timely and Efficient Programs. In addition to inducing official reaction and developing local leadership, Model Cities has selected its
programs wisely. The projects were selected primarily to improve
those services that had been traditionally neglected in the target area.
The city has had a long history of fiscal inertia, an unwillingness to
raise property taxes and improve services. Department heads knew
it was useless to request budget increases based on real needs. Model
Cities broke this mold.

Most of these new projects have reached a reasonable level of
success, and almost all have been put into operation on time. Programs
are perhaps still spread too thinly. Lately, however, weaker programs
are being weeded out, and the city manager and CDA staff are in the
process of documenting in more precise terms exact problems and
causes and designing programs to deal with them. Although the program has run into difficulty because of poor record-keeping and fiscal
control, this can be easily alleviated by integrating the system into
the city's central operation. Stronger direction is evident from the
city manager's office and from an upgraded Model Cities staff.

As to the future, the most important change may take place in
the role the city is able to take in coordinating other public and private
agencies. Although Savannah's Model Cities programs are not particularly innovative—having merely extended existing programs—they
have made agencies more effective, increased communication between
residents and the agencies, and encouraged apathetic agencies to seek
federal grants they otherwise would not have. The comprehensive
social services delivery system proposal proved to be impractical,
and once again officials are looking to Model Cities as a way to coordinate agencies that have heretofore been unwilling to give up any part
of their individual planning and delivery systems. It may be necessary
that a coordinating commission be appointed by the governor and mayor
to achieve this goal, with a mandate for agency and department cooperation. In any case, the city administration is now developing a new
proposal for coordination.

Coalition of Interests Needed

For the first time in its long history, Savannah is honestly facing
up to what has been one of its most carefully hidden problems—the
city's poor black and white. It is unfortunate that as yet business,
unions, and civic groups are not also actively pursuing this problem,
whose resolution could very well upgrade the entire city. The mayor
and Model Cities ought to take the initiative to involve them effectively
in this process by providing staff and assistance to develop a coalition
body. Already a sense of community has developed among the Model
Neighborhood residents. Now private resources and a well-conceived
coalition of all other interests are needed to achieve long-term results.

10

CHICAGO DEMONSTRATES
EFFICIENCY

The City

General

Chicago is the nation's second largest city and the most important Great Lakes port, the world's largest railroad terminal and busiest
airport, and a leading producer of steel, telephone equipment, appli-
ances, electrical machinery, plastic products, and diesel engines.

Chicago is also one major U.S. city that delivers most city
services well. It has had few of the breakdowns in essential services
that have plagued other cities. It can boast an integrated bus and rail
transportation system, clean and well-illuminated streets and alleys,
police and fire departments considered highly effective, a decreasing
crime rate (decreasing 2.6 percent in major crimes over the two-year
period 1969-71), liberal zoning laws and flexible tax policies that have
kept giant industrial firms within the city limits, substantial private
investment in the central business district (about $5 billion in the last
decade), 45,000 low-income housing units in the near north, west and
south side ghettos, no city budget deficit in 17 years, and municipal
bonds with the highest rating awarded by Standard and Poor.

But Chicago has far from escaped the urban crisis. It has generated more than its share of highways, parking lots, and commercial
complexes, but it has lost 149 downtown ground-level businesses since
1968 and gained only 24. Businessmen are worried about the intense
development of office space and sparse housing construction. Many
believe that the central city lacks a heart, a culture, and sufficient
people who live in or near it. But more importantly, Chicago has been
unable to make a significant dent in solving the problems of the poor
and disadvantaged. Neither have most other cities, but in Chicago
human resource problems stand out more, particularly in contrast

to better physical planning and service programs. The city's infant-mortality rate is the highest in the United States; 51 of Chicago's 57 high schools are below national norms in IQ scores; and beginning in October 1971, the United States District Court held up some $70 million in Urban Renewal and Model Cities funds because the city failed to provide an adequate, new housing integration plan.

In March 1972, a higher court overruled the District Court, stating that the suit had no relationship to Model Cities and the $26 million held in penalty. Funds were not immediately released by HUD because it claimed that indeed a relationship did exist through relocation payments that Model Cities pays to displacees. However, this last court challenge was dismissed, freeing the $26 million to Chicago Model Cities. In the meantime, the suspension of funds had hurt the program. The details of the Model Cities Program are discussed below.

Fiscal Accountability

Of the city's total 1971 budget of $899 million, $83 million or 9.2 percent went for debt services. Personnel expenditures accounted for $537.2 million or 59.7 percent, broken down into salaries ($480 million, 53.4 percent), medical contributions ($6.6 million, 0.7 percent), and pensions ($50.6 million, 5.6 percent). Capital expenditures were $29 million, or 3.2 percent of the total budget. Over the five years from 1973 to 1978 they are projected at $5.2 billion, including $2.2 billion for city agencies and $3.2 billion for other public agencies. The remainder of the operating budget is primarily for equipment, supplies, and services.

State aid, along with several sharp real estate tax increases in the past few years have been major factors in keeping the city's budget balanced. State aid has jumped from $68.6 million in 1968 to $137 million in 1972. A principal factor in this increase is the state income tax, added in 1970, which delivered $26.5 million to Chicago in 1972. The state motor fuel tax has increased from $26.9 million in 1968 to $35 million in 1972; the sales tax from $41.7 million in 1968 to $75.5 million in 1972. In spite of these increases, Mayor Richard Daley is able to point out that the state collects $1 billion in income taxes annually—half of which is paid by Chicago residents and businessmen—and returns only 2.6 percent to the city (the same argument espoused by most big-city mayors).

Chicago's 1972 tax rate was $7.85 per $100 of valuation based on 35 percent assessment (property is assessed at 23 percent of market value but equalized to match other Illinois jurisdictions by a factor of 1.59, resulting in the higher rate). It has risen nearly 500 percent since the late 1950s yet is still lower than 40 out of 50 suburbs.

Chicago's water rates are also lower than most suburbs, and the city has no refuse and sewer charge. The 1968 assessed valuation was $11.4 billion and was estimated at $13.1 billion in 1971. The downtown construction boom and inflation have increased Chicago's tax base, but the rapidly deteriorating residential areas have held growth back.

Neighborhood stagnation and decay have, in fact, been hastened by overemphasis on the business district and an expressway construction program that has given little consideration to historic neighborhood boundaries. The three major expressways built since the 1960s displaced great numbers of families and destroyed once vibrant communities. Plans for the Crosstown Expressway connecting O'Hare and Midway airports and intersecting with the Dan Ryan Expressway, propose that the expressway be depressed, follow neighborhood boundaries whenever possible, and provide a median strip for public transportation. Air rights are proposed for schools, shopping centers, and other public buildings. But there are many groups opposed to its construction, contending that it will destroy a significant amount of housing and commercial projects and that relocation will be a serious problem. Governor Richard Ogilvie requested that further public hearings be held, which effectively postponed—if not killed—the Crosstown construction.

Population and Race

From 1960 to 1970, Chicago's center city population declined 5 percent, from 3,768,588 to 3,580,404, while the suburban population jumped 45 percent The Chicago metropolitan population, excluding Indiana, increased 12 percent from 6,221,000 to 6,979,000 and represents 63 percent of Illinois's 11,114,000 people. But Chicago now has 48 percent of the metropolitan population, compared to 57 percent in 1960. It lost 505,000 whites and gained 327,000 nonwhites, as 24 percent of the 1960 white population moved out. Chicago blacks number 34 percent, while blacks in the suburbs have remained stable at 3 percent.

"Chicago is the nation's most racially segregated large city," reports Pierre DeVise, director of the Chicago Regional Hospital Study. Ranking behind Chicago, according to his study, in order are Indianapolis, Milwaukee, Dallas, St. Louis, Cleveland, Detroit, Baltimore, Houston, and Philadelphia. Washington, New York, and Los Angeles follow. DeVise's measurements for segregation are based on four criteria: (1) tendency to confine blacks to the central city; (2) rapidity of racial transition of neighborhoods; (3) percent of blacks in all-black neighborhoods (90 percent or more); and (4) uneven geographic distribution of blacks in the metropolitan area. He notes that about 70 percent of Chicago's blacks live in contiguous neighborhoods that are at least 90 percent black. Another 28 percent live in neighbor-hoods that are becoming black and only 2 percent live in stable, pre-dominantly white neighborhoods.[1]

DeVise says this "relegation of a million of our citizens to black reservations" has forced people to live in communities they cannot afford, overcrowded the housing and schools, and caused a breakdown of community life and the takeover by street gangs. Some demographers report that blacks are spreading into white neighborhoods at a rate of five blacks per week; others believe this figure is much higher. Ten-sions inevitably run high, and arson against the first house on a block bought by a black family is so commonplace that it often goes unre-ported in the press, though the more unusual cases are reported.

Chicagoans, like most U.S. citizens, think more in terms of their neighborhoods and in ethnic, religious, racial, social, and economic terms than of broader city objectives. Moreover, the feelings of the majority of the Catholic population must be taken seriously in making any major decision in Chicago. Still clinging to their neighborhoods are the strong ethnic enclaves of Irish, Bohemians, Lithuanians, Greeks, Germans, Italians, Jews, and Poles. The melting pot is not melting easily here, but neither is it elsewhere in urban America.

Philip M. Hauser, University of Chicago sociologist, predicts that Chicago will be 75 percent nonwhite by 1985. With 1.1 million blacks, an estimated 400,000 Latins, and unknown numbers of Indians and other brown people, the city already is about 50 percent nonwhite.

Mayor Daley, recognizing the statistics, has refused to yield to federal pressures to construct low-income housing in white areas for fear of further hostility, a greater exodus of whites, and an influx of poor. Pressure from various ethnic groups has also been strong against low-income housing.

Employment

Total Jobs. Despite the large number of poor in Chicago,* the city weathers recessions relatively well, largely because of its extremely diversified industry. Unemployment for the first five months of 1972 averaged 4.4 percent (among black males as high as 11 percent and in some areas for black male and female household heads 35 to 40 percent). According to the Bureau of Labor Statistics, while the total number of jobs in the eight-county Standard Consolidated Area jumped

---

*Poor neighborhoods are prevalent in Chicago. The Chicago Committee on Urban Opportunity (CCUO—Community Action Agency) divides the city into 75 "community areas" and defines 24 of them as poor, containing 42 percent of the city's population.

45 percent between 1960 and 1969, Chicago jobs increased only 8 percent. Chicago Urban League statistics, expressed in different terms, point to the same sort of imbalance. The vast bulk of new jobs have been created in the suburbs.* The Urban League cited transportation as the major problem preventing more city dwellers from taking suburban jobs. Urban mass transit lines do not go to the suburban industrial areas, and for some it takes as long as an hour and 20 minutes to get to work.

Industrial Development. Industrial development in the city totaled $762.2 million from 1957 to 1969; however, in the rest of Cook County it reached $1.169 billion, and in the remaining five counties in the SMSA, $964.5 million. As to the future, Illinois State Employment Service figures project that suburban plants (excluding those in Indiana) will pass Chicago in manufacturing employment by 1974.

The city is also losing construction jobs. From 1960 through 1969, they dropped from 70,000 to 69,000, while construction jobs in the suburbs increased one-third, from 60,000 to 81,000.

Chicago Plan for Equal Opportunity. The building that has gone on in the city has generally been without benefit of black help. A building trades integration plan, the Chicago Plan for Equal Opportunity, Inc., was finally drafted in January 1970 in the mayor's office after negotiations between the Building Trades Council (19 unions), the Coalition for United Community Action (a black umbrella organization), and the city's contractors, who were seeking to end the prolonged picketing by blacks on construction sites, which on one occasion erupted in gunfire. Almost daily, for months, construction workers abandoned sites and marched angrily to the central business district. The mayor was under immense pressure to find a solution.

Although the Chicago Plan called for 4,000 jobs and apprenticeship slots within a year for blacks and other minorities, the unions, deeply entrenched politically, were left to decide how and when the plan would be implemented. The plan was praised universally by local editorial writers as the answer to the problem of integrating the building trades. But most observers see it somewhat differently: as an expedient to get people off the streets, cool off a dangerous situation, and retain the political loyalty of the unions.

---

*Chicago Urban League reports that nearly 80 percent of all new employment in this six-county Chicago SMSA is located outside the city: 437,000 new jobs from 1960 to 1970, as compared to Chicago's 134,000.

By April 1971 the director of the Chicago Plan, Fred Hubbard, a black city alderman, could report only 855 persons placed. Labor Department officials, who authorized $833,000 to support the program, were calling it unsuccessful and announced plans to impose quotas, similar to those set in the Philadelphia Plan. Meanwhile, Hubbard disappeared on May 1, along with the remaining $100,000 in Chicago Plan funds, which he allegedly obtained by forging cosignatures on checks. He has since been indicted in absentia twice by county grand juries and once by a federal grand jury. This first Chicago Plan made little further progress, although racial quotas were carefully maintained on all federally funded construction jobs.

In July 1972, a new Chicago Plan, developed by the Department of Labor, Chicago Building Trades Council, Building Constructors Employers Association, Chicago Urban League, and several community groups, pledged enrollment in the building trade unions of 10,000 blacks and other minority groups at the rate of 6 percent of union membership in Cook County through 1975. Most unions have committed themselves to specific goals of membership; the Urban League has been given surveying powers to refer minority workers directly to employers as journeymen or advanced apprentices. Records will be inspected by the Urban League and Department of Labor. A referral committee of the Urban League includes representatives of labor and management and will classify minority persons in respect to skills, abilities, qualifications, and experience. Opposition to the plan includes several unions that have refused to accept its conditions and some minority groups that feel they should have a strong voice along with the Urban League. But it appears progress is being made.

Government Jobs. Government is a large employer in Chicago. It is estimated that Daley has more than 40,000 patronage jobs (including 12,000 state jobs) at his disposal as head of the Cook County Democratic Central Committee.

Technically, the city pays only "prevailing wages" found in private industry. However, its actual rates are kept higher in several ways: (1) by paying "construction rates" to full-time employees, calculated by private industry to include the seasonality of work; (2) by overclassifying less skilled employees; and (3) by giving fringe benefits of sick leave, vacation, and pensions that are considerably more liberal than those in private industry. A man who washes trucks, for example, is paid the drivers' rate. A driver in the city is paid Teamster over-the-road wages. Not much labor negotiation is needed between the mayor and unions because the city scale is automatically geared to increases won by private trade unions in their bargaining sessions with private industry. It is an easier but more costly way to run government. Although there are some variances in wages within a position based on skill and length of service, the lowest paid gets outside construction rates. There is no such thing as the maintenance rates to which most cities adhere. The guarantee of 12 months' work annually is also an enticing government inducement.

Board of Education

Education is one of Chicago's more serious problems. The Board of Education projects a 1972 deficit of $68 million, largely the result of expected state funds that never materialized.

Excluding 11 experimental schools in Chicago with higher-than-normal costs, per pupil expenditures range from $335 to $599. Differences are accounted for largely by salaries of teachers and administrators. White schools tend to be highest in per pupil expenditure; all-black schools are in the middle; and schools in unstable, transitional areas are the lowest. Experienced teachers who earn more also have more seniority, which entitles them to pick their assignments—usually outside the ghetto.

As in most urban schools in large cities, average eighth-graders in Chicago are more than a year behind national norms in reading and arithmetic, and in some ghetto schools the lag is three years. In the public high schools, two students drop out for every three who graduate, and any educational experimentation has been limited because of costs. In the past five years, teachers' raises have eaten up most funds the board could have used for this purpose. A large, conservative bureaucracy tends to inhibit experimentation, although the Model Cities Program has made some inroads.

The mayor appoints the Board of Education (a June 8, 1971 referendum turned down a proposal for an elected board), and although he tries to maintain an image of noninvolvement in education, he has gone to extremes on occasion to make certain his loyalists remain in control of the few reformers he occasionally appoints. Meetings have been held up, once by turning the clock back, while the city council convened in special session three blocks away to approve mayoral appointments to school board vacancies just in time for key votes.

Most observers point to three principal areas of concern that keep Mayor Daley involved in board policy:

1. Labor negotiations, which guarantee top wages not only for teachers but also for clerical and maintenance employees.

2. Real estate, important because the board holds substantial Loop (central city) property leased long term at lower-than-market rates to companies that supply blue-ribbon members of reelection committees and public boards and money for campaigns. Midway Airport is also located on Board of Education property and leased to the city at a bargain rate (an arrangement that is now being challenged in court).

3. Race, an explosive political issue in Chicago. Integration has not been attempted in the schools in any serious way.

The school system reflects residential patterns. At least 90 percent of black elementary pupils attend all-black schools. HEW, in a 1970 survey, found Chicago the most segregated school system in any major northern city. Negotiations have been under way for two years on a federally ordered teacher desegregation plan, which has moved slowly. The Board of Education again failed in 1972 to meet a deadline to integrate teachers.

City Housing

Public Housing. There is no central housing agency in Chicago. City departments of Development and Planning, Urban Renewal, and Buildings all have some responsibilities, as do the Chicago Housing Authority (CHA), the independent public housing agency with members appointed by the mayor, and the Chicago Dwellings Association, also mayorally appointed, a quasipublic corporation authorized to build and manage moderate-income housing. CHA manages 36,623 units with 160,000 tenants; 18 percent of the units are for the elderly. A study by Social Planning Associates shows 57 percent of CHA units are in the larger Model Cities study areas and 20 percent are concentrated within the smaller target areas. Turnover is only 10 percent in CHA housing, compared with a citywide average of 25 percent, which reflects limited housing opportunity for the black families who occupy more than 90 percent of CHA units. About 25 percent of the heads of CHA families have grown up in public housing developments.

The housing authority has not built any new family units since July 1969, when U.S. District Judge Richard B. Austin issued a desegregation order requiring the next 700 units and three-fourths of all subsequent units to be built in white neighborhoods. City council, which must pass on all sites, historically has screened out public housing in white neighborhoods, since each alderman has an actual veto of public housing projects in his ward. And although 60 percent of the city's 1.3 million dwelling units were built before 1920, a HUD reservation for 1,500 units, representing approximately $30 million, has gone unused for more than two years.

Although abandonment of structurally sound buildings in ghetto communities has reached astounding rates in Chicago, the city Buildings Department has no effective system of annual inspections to catch deterioration before it gets out of hand. Property owners, finding it unprofitable to maintain buildings in poverty areas, prefer to "walk away from them." Early code enforcement could prevent much of this.

Woodlawn, one of the four Model Cities areas, best illustrates this neglect. Nearly 400 buildings have been abandoned, burned, or demolished in the four years it has been a Model Cities target area because of increasing deterioration and lowered property values. Population has decreased from 65,000 to 35,000 since 1967. Although arson is suspected in the 200 larger fires, no one has been caught, and may blame the real estate dealers for starting the fires themselves or paying to have others do so to collect insurance. And the $9 million Woodlawn Gardens project started six years ago, as the pride of Woodlawn, is now in default on its mortgage. Leon Finney, executive director of the Woodlawn Organization, says the "people are demoralized" and even the notorious Black Stone Rangers have lost interest in the area. U.S. Representative Abner J. Mikva called Woodlawn "an indictment of our government and its housing policies—local, state and federal."

In Lawndale, another Model Cities area, the $2 million, 116-unit Kedvale Square project is also in default. Completed three years ago by the Community Renewal Society, it won a design award from the American Institute of Architects.

Urban Renewal. Urban renewal, with expenditures of $353,316,223 since its inception in Chicago, has demolished over 30,000 dwelling units while replacing only 11,000. Those removed housed low-income black and Latin families; those built under urban renewal generally have not. The Chicago strategy has been to fill in shrinking ghettos with middle-income private developments, made attractive through land cost write-downs, creating a buffer around the central business district. This has worked well where a strong client institution existed with a vested interest in preserving and redeveloping the surrounding community as an attraction for middle-class whites, but not elsewhere.

A successful example is Chicago's near south side, scene of vast redevelopment over a 20-year period. Once the heart of the city's black belt and repository for its oldest, worst housing, it now boasts gleaming high-rises and carefully designed, costly town houses adjacent to the Michael Reese Hospital complex and the Illinois Institute of Technology. The same general pattern has prevailed in Hyde Park, home of the University of Chicago, where the only truly integrated neighborhood in the city has been retrieved from the incipient slums of the late 1950s.

Another example is the near west side, where an old, stable but poor Mexican and Italian community was obliterated for the 23-acre University of Illinois's Chicago Circle Campus. Now, a stunning architectural collection of campus buildings is surrounded by the remains of the old neighborhood, as well as a development of new and expensive town houses (most of which go begging and are sold at reduced prices) for university faculty and medical professionals attached to the sprawling complex to the west composed of the University's

medical school, Cook County Hospital, and Presbyterian-St. Luke's
hospital.

The urban renewal department's haste to arrest blight in a neighborhood by clearing the worst housing—usually occupied by minority
group families—has caused land to lie fallow in urban renewal areas
for up to 10 years. The destruction of housing for the poor finally
caught up with Chicago's Department of Urban Renewal in the spring
of 1969 when HUD temporarily withheld the city's application for $17
million in annual Neighborhood Development Program (NDP) funds
pending a resolution of a critical relocation problem. caused in part
by city demolition.

HUD's scrutiny of the city's Workable Program for the period
ending in June 1971 found public demolition for the two-year span
wiping out 6,100 more low-income units than were added to the housing
stock from all sources.

In addition to the problems of urban renewal, the city's obdurate
refusal to take the politically dangerous course of building public
housing in white neighborhoods adds to the difficulty of getting the
Crosstown Expressway project approved. Relocation housing for the
4,000 families that would be displaced is not likely to be available.

Welfare

The welfare case load in Chicago, as in other northern cities,
is rising. Total costs rose 36 percent between 1969 and 1970, and by
December 1970, there were 429,941 persons in Chicago receiving
some form of aid, up 26.6 percent over the previous year. About one
in eight Chicagoans are on welfare, roughly the same rate as in Los
Angles and slightly lower than in New York. But despite rising costs
and case loads, an estimated 32 percent of those in Chicago below the
$3,000 per year income level have not applied for aid.

Assistance costs in Chicago, as is true in most cities except
New York, are borne virtually in toto by the federal government and
the state. Cook County contributes about $14 million annually to wel-
fare. The city itself has no welfare program, which eliminates a large
burden from its budget. However, rising costs have put stress on the
over-all system. Case workers handle as many as 150 cases a piece,
not uncommon in large cities but well above the HEW maximum of
60. They have filed suit to reduce the work load, but it remains at
the same level.

Republican Governor Richard B. Ogilvie budgeted $1.12 billion
for welfare in 1971, admittedly below need, on the gamble that the
Family Assistance Program would pass Congress in time to balance
the 1971 budget. It did not, forcing the governor to engage in a losing
battle with Cook County Democrats to cut the county's "general

assistance" case load (90 percent state funds, 10 percent county) by eliminating approximately 20,000 single "employable" males. He did convince them to ease the state's burden by shifting many of the "general assistance" clients to categorical classifications, whereby the federal government pays from 50 to 75 percent of the costs.

It is difficult to find jobs for welfare recipients. In the month of February 1971, for example, the Cook County Welfare Rehabilitation Service processed 7,000 recipients (mainly handicapped) for job training and placement. Only 513 could be placed. Of the half-million persons on welfare in Chicago, only about 9.4 percent are potentially employable. The rest are children (61.8 percent), parents needed in the home (13 percent), blind, disabled, or aged (10.6 percent), and those already employed or being trained (5.2 percent).

City Health

Health care delivery is another in the mounting roster of "most critical problems." While New York City spent an average of $110 per person on health care in 1969, Chicago spent $5.49, and the infant mortality rate for the city is 27.7 per 1,000, compared with a national average of 21.8.

In theory, Chicago's poor can be treated at any of Chicago's many fine private hospitals. Welfare recipients and the medically needy are issued special "green cards" to facilitate their access. In practice, for many reasons, most end up at Cook County Hospital, the single public hospital in the county (more than 95 percent of Cook County Hospital's patients are black). A look at the major reasons illustrates the plight of Chicago's indigent sick: (1) the poor have limited access to the private physicians, who make referrals to private hospitals; (2) of the 80 hospitals in Chicago, 73 do not accept welfare patients, although several of these, containing 50 percent of all hospital beds in the city, are located in or near Model Cities target areas;* and (3) of the hospitals that do treat indigents, several—having experienced lengthy delays in being reimbursed by the Welfare Department—provide emergency treatment only and ship patients in ambulances or police paddy wagons to Cook County for more extensive care.

Critics of Chicago's health care include, according to Pierre DeVise, even such "establishment" leaders as the president of the Chicago Board of Health and the head of the Chicago Medical Society. Says DeVise:

---

*Of 19,476 beds in the city, 1,701 are in target areas and another 9,400 are within eight blocks of the areas.

These critics point to local infant death rates higher than
any state in the Union and higher than any advanced nation.
They point to the use of Cook County Hospital as an emergency dumping ground for 700,000 Negroes who live an
average of eight miles away and wait an average of two
hours to be seen. They point to 78 physicians (out of
6,000) dishing out cafeteria-style medicine to 170,000
welfare recipients, at a cost to the taxpayer of $50,000
per physician. They compare Chicago's puny $12 million
Board of Health budget to New York City's $900 million
health budget! They deplore Chicago's loss of 2,000 physicians in the last 40 years. They ask for new systems
and new leaders to replace 19th century public health
systems and 19th century leaders.[2]

Dr. Murray Brown, the city health commissioner, is fond of
reminding critics that the function of the Board of Health, appointed
by the mayor, is to be "a watchdog, not to provide care." And so, only
gradually and reluctantly, has the board, which spent $18 million in
1971, moved to provide a few, limited health services, such as prenatal
clinics and infant welfare stations (seldom in the same location) and
immunization programs. Model Cities has encouraged decentralization
and more services in health clinics in the target areas. Improved
staffing and direction of the city's health program is beginning to take
shape. These are first steps toward improving general health care,
but the integration of public and private facilities and other improvements are progressing slowly.

The Mayor and City Council

Structurally, Chicago's government is a weak-mayor form, with
final control over budgets and appointments legally vested in the city
council. In 1955 the legislature strengthened the power of the executive
branch by transferring the power to plan, create, and administer the
budget to the mayor. The mayor can only vote in case of a tie, but he
has veto power over ordinances and appropriation bills. In practice,
during Richard Daley's 17 years as mayor (he is now in his fifth term),
the mayor has controlled at least 37 Democratic members of the 50-
member, ward-elected city council by virtue of his position as head
of the Cook County Democratic Party. Of the 13 black aldermen, 11
are selected by the regular Democratic organization (two are independent). It has been difficult for opposition blacks and others to get
out a countervote as long as their people are getting some of the action.
Republicans represent about 10 percent of the electorate and independents a somewhat smaller percentage. Council members and the mayor

are elected for four-year terms. Aldermanic candidates are not permitted to run under party banners, but both parties slate candidates and send precinct captains out to elect their men. By law, council elections are supposed to be nonpartisan, while mayoral elections are partisan, but campaign posters and material contain tell-tale lines such as "Endorsed by the Democratic Central Committee." A primary is held in February of the election year (same date as mayoral primary), and the candidate receiving a majority of the votes at that time becomes alderman. If no one receives a majority, the top two vote-getters appear in a runoff in April, during the mayoral election. Only four or five wards had such runoffs in 1971.

The city's 50 wards have recently been redrawn under a federal court order to meet one-man, one-vote requirements. The average ward contains 67,347 voters, the court order allowing a 0.5 percent variation. A recent survey by the Chicago Better Government Association (BGA—a private, nonprofit investigating group) showed the new wards ranging in size from 56,000 to 75,000, with ethnic blocs split up.

Daley's strong ally on council, Tom Keane, redrew ward boundaries to break up bloc voting where it has or could hurt the Democratic Party. The passage of Keane's ward map through the city council is an example of the mayor's ability to get his program's approved. Ten or more aldermen voting against the map could have stopped it. However, Keane made a deal with about five of the dissidents, and in return for their votes drew ward lines to ensure their continued election.

In return for their rubber stamp, Daley allows loyalists to alter projects to their liking in their wards and receive priority treatment. The 37 faithful (some independents are actually true Democrats) Democratic aldermen and the ward committeemen of the other 13 wards are overseers of the Democratic Party machine. (These committeemen are also strong because they get the patronage in their wards, rather than the elected Republican or independent alderman.) Their vote totals provide their main source of employment as well as the clout they dispense to others in exchange for support. At one time in Chicago history, before Daley, the council actually ran the city.

The strength of the Democratic Party comes in some measure from Illinois Election laws, which make it almost impossible for an independent to become a candidate. He needs 5 percent of the previous total vote on his petition, or about 60,000 to 70,000 signatures of persons legally defined as independents who did not vote in the last partisan primaries. (Only about 7,500 signatures are needed in New York, and only about 500 in Los Angeles.)

Mayor Daley prefers a clean looking machine and is regarded as indisputably honest himself. But critics say that he overlooks corruption by others, unless it is brought to public attention or threatens the party, for preservation of the party is most important, and if some corruption is needed to keep it going, so be it.

Patronage

How it Works. Patronage is the heart of Daley's control. Below the committeemen are precinct captains, the normal "tickets" for getting the city jobs that, though billed as "temporary civil service," are usually permanent. Temporary status permits circumvention of the civil service list and requires only simple reappointment every 90 days. It also makes removal easier, if a precinct should go Republican or independent. A worker is much more likely to be fired for bad political performance than he is for poor job performance. If a job holder does well in his precinct but gets caught loafing or cheating, he will likely be moved to another payroll further from public scrutiny.

The mayor does not hide patronage policies. City Hall has two clearly marked offices, one for patronage and one for civil service applicants. Of the 48,000 city employees, patronage accounts for about 9,000 jobs. (Except police and firemen who are practically all civil service, this accounts for 35 percent of the work force. An effective committeeman may be allocated 500 to 700 patronage jobs for his ward.)[3] The other 25,000 to 30,000 patronage spots come from the county board and virtually all other elected offices and special governmental districts. Since Democratic governors depend on Daley to get them elected, a great deal of state patronage comes back to Chicago. This may substantially change under newly elected Democratic Governor Daniel Walker.

The patronage system has been challenged in Chicago. In April 1971, the Supreme Court refused to disturb a lower court ruling that the city's patronage system denied non-Democratic candidates and voters an equal voice in government. The suit was filed by Michael L. Shakman, an unsuccessful candidate for delegate to the Illinois Constitutional Convention, who charged that patronage abuses hamper, if not prevent, the election of other candidates. As a result of the Shakman vs. Daley consent decree, Democratic and Republican party leaders agreed out of court to limit certain controls over patronage, most notably the power to fire workers for failure to perform political duties. Of course, since many other reasons can be found for terminating an employee, it still remains uncertain how the traditional patronage system will be affected.

Patronage to Legislators. Patronage also functions as an informal subsidy for and control of state legislators, although at $17,500 they are among the highest paid in the nation. At least 34 Cook County

239

legislators are on the payroll of the city, county, or park district, 32 Democrats and two nominal Republicans. They receive no pay on days when they are working in the legislature in Springfield, but pension benefits are arranged so they continue as though on the payroll full-time. Many of their second jobs pay well, above $20,000 annually in five cases. The highest paid, at $26,724, is state Senator Edward A. Nihill, superintendent of water collections in Chicago. In the 1971 legislative session, a bill to prevent holding two government jobs was easily defeated in the State Senate's executive committee, eight to four.

Power Structure

Blue Ribbon Committees. Power may come in the form of committees. One of the mayor's administrative styles is to appoint blue-ribbon committees to oversee a great variety of problems. These committees always include influential businessmen, labor leaders, and a few persons knowledgable about a particular issue. Most observers point out that group recommendations usually parallel Daley's known feelings on the subject; however, his decision is final anyway. An example is a decision made by the city in 1971 to build a behemoth sports stadium. About a dozen men were named to a study group, including several industrialists and financiers who live in the suburbs, several labor leaders, and the owners of the major sports teams. Their task was to select a site for the new edifice. The city had its eye on razing Soldier Field, on the lakefront, and replacing it with a new domed structure. Three alternative sites were also considered, each with better access to transportation than the lakefront location. Selection was narrowed to two places—Soldier Field and railroad air rights about a quarter-mile west of it—both on the lakefront, and both complementing the McCormick Place Convention Center. In either location, the stadium would represent a fitting monument to the brick and mortar principles of the Daley administration. The decision was finally made to renovate Soldier Field rather than build a totally new structure.

The News Media. Newspapers wield power in Chicago, more so than in most communities. The Chicago Tribune, which strongly pressured to get McCormick Place built and then rebuilt (after a fire), influenced the decision for a lakefront stadium location. At times, Daley will withstand massive opposition and criticism from the media and not budge; other times he will bend. Ironically, all four Chicago papers backed him editorially in the race against Richard Friedman, his 1971 opponent. However, a large portion of the newspapers staffs took out paid advertisements of their own voicing opposition to this endorsement.

Labor. Daley is a strong supporter of labor, and most of labor's principal leaders are his boyhood friends, which makes negotiation a little easier. His close friendship with both business and labor leaders is one of his strongest assets. There are traditional positions for labor on all appointed boards and commissions, such as the school board, park district, and housing authority. Daley frequently settles troublesome strikes by bringing both sides of a dispute into his office for last-minute negotiations. But organized labor is highly influential and seldom loses. Mayor Daley's personal friendships and control extend beyond labor and business leaders. He has influence over a variety of positions and exerts control over the selection of judgeships, the Cook County attorney's office, and other important positions by utilizing the Democratic organization's power to almost guarantee election of anyone it endorses.

Business. Unions are the most powerful influence in the city power structure, followed closely by the Catholic Archdiocese of Chicago, and then, in order, business, civic groups, and citizens. Daley works hard at keeping businessmen happy and has mounted campaigns to keep their taxable property in Chicago. Businessmen forget their traditional GOP ties when Daley is running for office and liberally donate money and time to him. In return, Daley has put tremendous emphasis on building up the downtown business area.

Civil Groups and Citizens. Civic groups and citizens must have a powerful backlog of facts in their favor before they can gain much footing in City Hall. Community corporations, war-on-poverty groups, and Model Cities have not developed substantial influence because memberships are largely controlled by the city administration and local politicians. However, the mayor is very astute about bringing in leaders and groups of wide-ranging philosophies before reaching decisions on crucial matters. He appears to be more adept at this than most other political leaders. But he treats most suggestions from groups like the BGA, Civic Federation (private tax watchdog group), and Independent Voters of Illinois with silence and disdain. However, to Daley's credit he usually orders that corrections be made, although in his own way and at his own pace. If a group suggests an improvement that appeals to Daley or some of his aides, it may be brought forward at a later date as an official city program.

City Service

Complaint Handling. The Mayor's Office of Inquiry and Information receives 300,000 to 500,000 referrals (matters for other departments and agencies) and information requests annually, as well as 40,000 to 50,000 complaints which it follows up more closely. Each complaint is answered and the appropriate alderman's help sought where political clout is needed to get something done. This is quite often the case because, for the most part, one gets things done in Chicago if he knows someone. It is a fact of life here, that to get a tree cut down or have a sidewalk fixed, one goes to the precinct captain, alderman, or ward committeeman. He, in turn, will call the responsible agency if he deems the request important.

The Office of Inquiry and Information and a similar complaint office in the Department of Streets and Sanitation (which itself handles about 300,000 complaints annually) systematically and as professionally as possible handle requests but appear to be overshadowed by the political process. Citizens are left with the impression that to get anything done involving government "you have to know someone."

Department Effectiveness

Traditional city services are delivered well in Chicago but generally at high cost. Each of 600 garbage trucks has a four-man crew, while most cities operate with two- or three-man crews. Garbage pickup is considered good, but $3 million went for overtime in 1970, largely because city crews had so many "private pay" customers serviced on city time that they could not get their required work done, resulting in a high percentage of refuse that did not get picked up. As indicated previously, an unskilled refuse collector and laborer receives the equivalent of private construction wages (drivers $5.05 per hour and loaders $5.09 per hour in 1972).

Personnel merit principles have slipped in some departments. A portion of the police force has reverted to some of the slipshod practices of pre-Orlando Wilson days, and some local black leaders, in particular, are demanding a civilian police review board with substantial power and other changes to improve the department. (Wilson was employed, due to public demand for a better police department, during the late 1950s because of the Summerdale Scandal, when some policemen were found to be part of burglary ring.)

In the main, however, city employees operate under merit principles in a fairly effective civil service system. The National Civil Service League praises Chicago's civil service system as one of the best. It pursues advanced and widespread training methods, administers a very active recruitment and examination program, utilizes effective related-to-work tests, and has a good classification structure. The chief criticism is that promotion policies are too rigid, keeping some of the best talent from jobs that best suit them. There are also complaints that some civil service employees engage in active politicking and fund raising. Mayor Daley has partial control over the system through appointment of the Civil Service Commission and through his power to influence changes in a direction favorable to him.

242

Compared to most large cities, Chicago appears to be more effective in street cleaning, alley lighting, snow removal, fire services, mass transportation, budget control, and the employment of competent professionals to head most city services. Although patronage and inefficiencies exist in a number of departments, Mayor Daley follows the axiom that "good government is good politics" and delivers well on the basic services expected by all citizens. Even independent Alderman Leon Despres, one of Daley's stanchest critics, says the city delivers these services with reasonable effectiveness in all wards (although some wards get faster treatment and extra attention) because not to do so "would be political suicide." But Daley falls short on human resources, poverty, race, housing, health, and education—problems plaguing every major urban area but suffering unusual neglect in Chicago. A look at the Chicago Model Cities Program (in the following section) indicates how such a comprehensive attack on human problems has fared in this setting.

Model Cities

Model Cities Administration

In October 1971, after federal funds for Model Cities were suspended, steps were taken to integrate Chicago's Model Cities Program with the Chicago Committee on Urban Opportunity (CCUO—Community Action Program). This was a good opportunity to merge two agencies that overlapped in citizen participation jurisdictions and some operating programs. Since CCUO staff was involved primarily in planning, monitoring, and evaluation, merger was made easier. Through consolidation, Model Cities staff and programs were enabled to be continued on a limited basis with funds from an ongoing program, supplemented by city and state agency money. However, CCUO and local resources were not able to support Model Cities very long. The main reasons for integration were to gain the greatest economy possible from limited resources and to create a more effective program. Both programs cover about 80 percent of the disadvantaged minority.

Erwin France, Model Cities director and administrative assistant to the mayor, was appointed director of both programs, replacing Murrell Syler, former director of CCUO. Mrs. Syler now heads the city's day-care program and reports directly to Daley, by-passing the city's separate Department of Human Resources (DHR), headed by Dr. Deton Brooks, who reports directly to the mayor. France also reports directly to the mayor; and the Model Cities-Community Action structure is simply treated as another city department. Moreover, although integration of DHR with Model Cities and CCUO appears to make sense and to be in the best interests of human resource programs, the mayor apparently favors a more independent operation because of Brooks's strong and loyal political support for him.

Model Cities always has been the "mayor's program," and Daley has made it his personal responsibility. All final plans are approved by him. If an alderman disagrees with a particular part of the program, his ultimate clout will rest with Daley, for it is difficult to short-circuit a Model Cities project at a lower rung even if you are a politician. At present, both programs are even more a direct concern of the mayor, although the Community Action Program has always been operated by the city.

In consolidating Model Cities and CCUO, France has made it clear to the staffs that they are employees of one agency and henceforth, should think in those terms. However, there are difficulties in combining the citizen participation structures. At least one council, the Uptown Model Area Council, for example, is opposed to the merger because it was not fully consulted. It objects to the proposal that half of the 40 new neighborhood council members be elected "at-large" from anywhere in the city (20 members would be appointed by the mayor). Currently, Model Cities Councils are comprised of 32 members from the target area and eight from a broader "study area"; anyone living outside the community is automatically barred from serving. The Uptown Council has complained that elections from anywhere in the city would deprive the neighborhood of any real representation in its own affairs.

In addition, the proposal that neighborhood councils would have to report to the central, citywide (Committee on Urban Opportunity is unsatisfactory to local members because this might serve as another barrier between the people and government agencies. Some local council members call the proposals a scheme to stack the councils with "yes men" who must remain docile to a central council. Because of strong city control, however, it appears these differences will be submerged.

While consolidation remains an issue, it is important to understand the circumstances that led to the suspension of Model Cities funds.

Housing Discrimination and Model Cities Funds. In 1966, the Illinois Division of the American Civil Liberties Union (ACLU) filed suit in U.S. District Court in Chicago. The plaintiffs were black public housing residents and applicants; the defendants were the Chicago Housing Authority and the Department of Housing and Urban Development. The charge, subsequently proved with an overwhelming preponderance of evidence, was that the CHA had discriminated against blacks and denied them equal access to decent housing, and, further, that those few projects built in white neighborhoods were reserved for whites, although

CHA's waiting list was overwhelmingly black. The judge severed the two defendants and decided to take evidence against the housing authority first. HUD was named because it condoned the alleged discriminatory practices by continuing to fund CHA construction.

By early 1969, judge Richard B. Austin found CHA guilty of the charges and in July of that year drafted a strict order designed to correct the historic racial imbalance in public housing in Chicago. Key elements of the order required CHA to build its first 700 units in white neighborhoods and to make up for the number already under construction or being planned in black areas at the time the order was issued. After that, three-fourths of subsequent units were to be built in areas defined as white. High-rise construction was forbidden. Further, provisions hold that no more than 15 percent of the dwelling units in any census tract may be public housing and 50 percent of each project must be reserved for residents of the immediate neighborhood. The housing authority did not appeal the finding or the order. By July 1970, however, no sites had been submitted to city council for approval, a move required by Illinois law for Chicago but for no other city.

Judge Austin, growing impatient, ordered the housing authority immediately to submit sites to the council. With fall election campaigns in progress, the city administration had the housing authority appeal that order. The appeal dragged on until the eve of the April 6, 1971 mayoral election, but finally the CHA was forced to make public a list of 275 sites, most in white neighborhoods. The expected adverse impact on Daley's election campaign did not materialize because he came out strongly against the public housing proposals before the election, while his opponent, Friedman, hedged. Daley won a fifth term with 70 percent of the vote. After the election, he moved away from his strong preelection opposition.

Making the sites public, however, turned out to be a long way from getting council approval. Under pressure from HUD, still holding back Model Cities and urban renewal funds, the council finally reluctantly approved a few sites in white neighborhoods, all of them in north and near-northwest side wards, where resistance was light or nonexistent.

While under pressure from the court on one side to act, the city was simultaneously under pressure from HUD to make up a deficit of 4,300 low-income housing units for the current two-year Workable Program period, ending in June 1971. HUD could not require public housing to make up the deficit, but because that is the only fiscally realistic way of providing low-income housing, the city found itself squeezed between HUD, demanding low-income housing in exchange for the release of millions in funds, and the court, which decreed that public housing had to be in white areas. There would have been no problem if both sets of pressure had not been applied at once. Without the court, public housing in the ghetto could be built to satisfy HUD's demand for more low-income housing. Without HUD's demand for low-income housing, the city could just stop building public housing, altogether. But segregated housing patterns would remain the same.

The Model Cities Program got dragged directly into court action when ACLU revived its case against HUD and Judge Austin dismissed it. In fall 1971, the Court of Appeals found HUD guilty of discrimination and passed the case back to Judge Austin for a remedy.

ACLU, on the theory that only the threatened loss of the whole Model Cities Program was a sufficiently big stick to move the city administration to desegregate public housing, demanded that the court order HUD to withhold funds until public housing was built. The judge agreed and on October 1, 1971 froze all second-year funds not committed ($26 million), although as recently as June 1971 HUD Regional Administrator George Vavoulis had released funds for "the good of the poor people of Chicago."

Chicago's first action year program began August 6, 1969, and was scheduled to run to October 31, 1970. The second action year was scheduled to begin then but was delayed two months by HUD. HUD later authorized second-year spending to begin January 1, 1971 but withheld a guarantee of reimbursement if the city failed to solve the relocation housing problems.

Of the first-year supplemental funds of $38 million, $8 million had to be reprogramed in June 1970 because of start-up delays. The bulk of the $8 million went into quick-spending summer employment and youth programs and into an immunization program operated by the Board of Health. The CDA staff was eager to establish a record of being able to spend the annual supplemental funds for fear the money would be reduced if it could not use the funds.

For almost a year, CDA and sponsoring agencies were substantially without federal funding for the Model Cities projects, except for $12 million CDA managed to commit between mid-June and October 1, 1971. According to CDA staff members, the 4,000 or so employees on the payroll were paid with city funds and Model Cities "salvage," left over from first-year programs from October 31, 1970 to June 16, 1971. After January 1972, the program ran entirely on city funds until federal money was finally released some months later.

Federal, State, and Local Views of the Program

On the positive side, Chicago Model Cities has always been well-organized and has had competent staff. Relations with the federal government have been good, except for an initial rift over the degree and structure of Model Neighborhood councils, which Mayor Daley agreed to amend more to HUD's liking, though still not to the satisfaction of residents. HUD's Assistant Secretary for Community

Development, Floyd Hyde, called Chicago Model Cities "the best in the country," during its first year. Regional HUD officials and Chicago Model Cities staff realized Daley's strength had enabled the program to get off the ground smoothly. Model Cities staff said that "Daley was able to get anything he wanted done in Chicago and if he wanted Model Cities to be a success, it would be." Several aspects of the program were moving in that direction before funds were cut off.

There have been some interesting adverse revelations too. Information put together early in 1972, after four months of investigation by two Chicago Tribune reporters, Cornelia Honchar and Peter Negronida, revealed that 17 of 160 Model Cities Council members illegally held jobs in the program; more than approved numbers of Model Cities Council members attended local workshops in hotels and wasted funds; the director had a $250 per month phone in his car; over 50 percent of the budget ($30 million) during the two and one-half years of the program was spent on administrative and project staff salaries; $65,000 was spent on telephones in this interval; $170,000 was spent on furniture and office equipment during this time; rent ran $8,000 per month; $30,000 was slated for travel expenses; there was a public relations staff of nine; two policemen were used as drivers for the director; patronage was abundant; favoritism influenced contract awards; and citizens were controlled by the administration—among other items.[4] Some of these abuses have been corrected, but many still exist.

In February 1972, Alderman Dick Simpson introduced a resolution in city council, referred to committee, calling on the federal government to make changes in the program and charging Model Cities with many of the abuses cited above: (1) citizen councils "controlled entirely" by Daley; (2) patronage running rampant over civil service procedures; (3) favoritism in letting contracts; (4) misexpenditures; (5) certain employees employed at the urging of government and party officials; and (6) some Model Cities Council members illegally holding jobs in the program.[5]

At the same time, J. Terrence Brunner, executive director of the Better Government Association, said, "A much more subtle way of controlling poor people—buying their loyalty by letting them spend public money wastefully" is taking place in the Model Cities Program.

"Most jobs in the Lawndale area go to relatives and friends of Council members, precinct captains and others connected with the Democratic Organization, says Gibbs Clay, an elected member of the Lawndale Model Cities Area Council. He flatly states that a letter from the ward committeeman as sponsor is required before anyone can get a job and that Model Cities sanitation workers were told they would lose their jobs if they did not "work a precinct." A worker is graded, he believes, more on his political work than his job performance; and some bona-fide community leaders have been given Model

Cities jobs with the understanding that they withdraw from their opposition organizations.

Fred Peavy, 27th Ward Republican committeeman, tells of numerous cases of precinct captains being fired from city jobs because of Democratic losses in the 1968 general election and then given a chance to redeem themselves through employment as Model Cities community representatives and in non-Model Cities jobs as community relations aides and building inspectors—positions in which it would be possible to regain support. Prior to the 1971 mayoral election, many of these building inspectors issued code violation tickets to homeowners who then were told to take them to their ward committeemen—a procedure similar to "getting the ticket fixed" and chilling many possible opposition votes.

Relationships with the state have been minimal. For the most part, Governor Ogilvie kept his distance from Chicago, and Mayor Daley wants no interference from state personnel. However, two Model Cities programs—Day Care and Police Community Service Aides—receive state funds on a three-to-one matching basis. The police project gets three-fourths of its $2 million-plus budget from the Illinois Law Enforcement Commission (funded by the Justice Department); Day Care similarly relies on the Illinois Department of Children and Family Services. Some $19 million was made available for 1972 by the state to Model Cities neighborhoods and public housing projects throughout the state. Chicago will receive most of this; the federal government reimburses the state up to 85 percent of the cost. Without state aid, several of the Model Cities programs could not continue.

In short, Chicago Model Cities started off smoothly and had good relations with the federal government because it was believed to be an effective program. It has had minimal relations with the state, and disputes about citizen participation and housing discrimination have hurt its relations with HUD. There is no doubt the program was severely crippled because of federal funding delays; yet, somehow, it has managed to limp along and possibly—over the long run—may actually be strengthened by the need to impose greater efficiency and effectiveness. Alderman William Singer says that despite the large patronage army, some Model Cities programs are among the most effective projects in the city, particularly those dealing with model schools, day care, and health facilities. The program has both faults and virtues. The rest of this report will attempt to assess these, particularly with regard to citizen participation and key projects, beginning with an examination of the neighborhoods Model Cities has sought to rehabilitate.

Demography of the Four Model Neighborhoods

Of the four Model Neighborhoods, three are black: Woodlawn ("mid-south," 60,030 persons), Grand Boulevard-North Kenwood ("near south," 115,877), and Lawndale ("west side," 96,916). Uptown ("north side," 54,000) is populated predominantly with poor Appalachian whites (about 15,000), along with sizable settlements of American Indians, blacks, and Orientals (about 5,000 of each) and lesser numbers of Puerto Ricans and other ethnic groups. Model Cities boundaries leave out any single large grouping of Latins.

The 1970 census showed 259,092 persons in the four areas, 8 percent of the city total. Estimates based on the 1960 census placed the population at 327,000. Decay and abandonment of residential buildings, combined with urban renewal displacement, probably account for the loss of population.

In 1969, the net income of target area families averaged $5,000 — 46 percent of the city average of $10,775. Twenty-four percent of target area residents had incomes under $2,500.

Fifty percent of residents were under 20 years old, only 5.5 percent were 65 or older, compared with a citywide average of 11 percent (for over 55). However, Uptown, where a major share of the city's retirement and shelter-care homes are concentrated, has 10 percent over 65. The following unemployment rates for the model areas are based on 1969 statistics and have probably increased because of the worsened economy:

	Percent Unemployed: Male Household Heads	Percent Unemployed: Female Household Heads	Total
Target Areas	11	66	37
Grand Boulevard	10	65	41
Lawndale	7	75	35
Uptown	12	51	28
Woodlawn	15	71	41

In 1968, infant mortality rates for the four areas were 40 per 1,000 live births, about 25 percent more than the city and almost twice that of the nation. Target area mortality rate (per 1,000 population) was 14.52, compared with the city's 11.69, and even more dramatic in light of the unusually young population. The expected rate for the target areas, based upon the 1960 U.S. Life Table, would be 6.12.

No one questions the fact that the Model Neighborhoods are decrepit, although there are some equally bad areas on both the south and west sides. High density, high crime rates, poor education, and badly deteriorated housing abound. This tends to deepen the despair of the nursing home residents and mental patients in halfway houses in the north area and also breeds potentially explosive violence within the two sets of public housing high-rises in the near south side. In Woodlawn, located near the University of Chicago, the deplorable conditions have also spurred power struggles among the more aggresive community groups of the area.

Citizen Participation

Citizen participation in Chicago Model Cities is advisory only, taking place at the neighborhood level. There are four Model Area Councils, formally empowered to approve or reject plans for projects in their areas; but projects may be put into operation without their consent (in most cases, however, CDA does consider their requests). The councils are not tied into a central participation mechanism able to strengthen citizen input at higher decision-making levels, nor do they have technical staffs to allow them to develop polished plans of their own. (Under the merger plan with the Community Action Program, a central council is planned.) The administration can place economic sanctions against many council members, so the membership is generally regarded as "city-controlled." Yet, according to former Chicago HUD Regional Model Cities Coordinator, Ted Robinson, "Citizens have a bigger piece of the action now than they had in the past." The Model Cities planning document lists citizen participation as Chicago's key strategy for institutional change.

Initial Stages. The first Model Area Councils in Chicago were 25-member organizations, appointed by the mayor from a hand-picked group of target area and "study area"* residents. "Town Hall" meetings were announced and publicized in each model area, and residents drew up lists of priority services. These lists were then reviewed by city planners (from the Department of Development and Planning) and passed on to appropriate public agencies, which incorporated requests into program proposals. The proposals matched, in most cases, what the agencies themselves wanted but were unable to provide because of lack of funds.

These proposals were returned to city planners for further refinement and passed on to Model Area Councils, which usually suggested only minor revisions. Again, they went back to planners for final drafting and then back, at last, to the councils for final action. The whole process was tedious and time-consuming, with over six months' work put in by the Department of Development and Planning

---

*Study areas are larger areas surrounding the target areas.

before HUD planning funds were made available (HUD released $200,000 in planning money to Chicago in 1968). And it did not take long before even the "hand-picked appointees" complained about the process—for example, that they received the final drafts (bulky, 2,500 page documents) only at the last possible moment, accompanied by warnings that unless they were immediately approved, HUD's deadline for submission of the application would pass. In some cases, councils had only 24 or 48 hours to pass on the documents, which typically contained projects they had never before studied.

The first action year program was approved in this fashion, with appointed councils. But HUD, too, was displeased with the level of citizen participation. Early criticism came from as high up as the Justice Department's Community Relations Service which took Chicago's program to task in an April 17, 1969 memorandum to the HUD Regional director: "A look at citizen participation reveals that it is under control of the city, it has no accountability to the neighborhoods and if the plan is accepted as presently written, residents participating in the program gain no control. True partnership is nonexistent." The memorandum, however, made no specific recommendations.

At first Mayor Daley insisted that no one, not even the federal government was going to tell him how to run his city and that there would be no electing of neighborhood councils; however, after similar criticism came from both his own blue-ribbon Community Improvement Advisory Committee* and public hearings held by the city council, he agreed that councils would be 50 percent elected and 50 percent appointed, as long as he could make all the appointments.

The strongest independent community organization in the areas had wanted to appoint at least half the council members themselves, knowing they were no match for the Democratic machine in an election. The Woodlawn Organization (TWO), a community council representing some 85 groups ranging from block clubs to businessmen and the University of Chicago, went so far as to write its own Model Cities plan, but city council rejected it. Five large umbrella groups representing all four model areas tried to stop the plan, charging that, in effect, it constituted only "citizen notification" after the fact. But having already been accepted by the Chicago Planning Commission, the plan stood up to all challenges.

The next phase involved preparing for Model Area Council elections. In April 1969, the interim councils appointed an ad hoc committee to devise an election code. Lengthy struggles to obtain approval

---

*The Community Improvement Advisory Committee was formed in 1954 and later was used as the Workable Program Advisory Committee.

from city council and the Board of Election Commissioners delayed registration until a year later, when the planning process for the second year was already under way. Again, the citizens and the city locked horns. Although the ad hoc committee recommended election by precincts, the administration supported at-large elections, which would improve its chances of electing a full Democratic organizational slate. As usual, the administration won.

Open to all model area residents age 19 or older, the April 14 election received the highest percentage turnout of any Model Cities election in the nation—about 30 percent of those registered actually voted (24,059 residents). But the election, run by the Chicago Board of Election Commissioners, cost $186,000, or about $6 per vote, and in almost all areas, as feared, Democratic-machine-backed slates easily won nearly all seats. In Uptown, for instance, 19 out of 20 seats went to candidates picked by State Senator Robert Cherry. Only in Woodlawn, where TWO waged an extensive door-to-door campaign, did 13 nonmachine candidates get in (still leaving seven seats for the organization Democrats). In each of the other two areas, only one non-organization candidate won.

Daley's appointments, made immediately following the election, demonstrated his political astuteness, his instinct for not overplaying his hand. With control of each council secured in the election process, he attempted, through Model Cities Director Erwin France, to select a balanced cross-section of appointees, representing grass-roots residents. Too strong political control and too many political figures would have destroyed the program completely and would have invited crime syndicate influence in at least one of the areas. Thus, partial elections resulted in greater legitimacy to the program and more citizen involvement than probably would have come about in a fully elected council.

As a matter of fact, the election is still being contested. Upon reports of poll-watchers from the Independent Precinct Organization (an effective liberal campaign organization), the Community Legal Council and Legal Aid lawyers filed a contest petition immediately after the election, charging violations of regular and special Model Cities election laws, vote buying, and voting by people who did not exist. Stanley Kusper, Board of Election commissioner, threw out the petition on a technicality, as did the circuit judge But the case is now before the 1st District Illinois Appellate Court, with briefs filed by Legal Aid—but not the Board of Election Commissioners, due to "the press of duties caused by recent elections."

Structure and Function. As they currently exist, each of the four Model Area Councils consists of 20 members appointed by the mayor and 20 elected (40 in all). Eight of the appointees come from the target area and 12 from the "study area." Members serve two-year terms, the first term ending April 30 (1972), and vacancies are filled by the councils themselves. Members are not paid for attending meetings, and the attrition rate in some areas is high. For example, Uptown had a turnover of 15 members in 13 months. But most council members are loyal and take pride in their role, and pay does not appear to be a major factor in their active participation. They do get reimbursed for expenses such as baby-sitting and transportation. Council chairmen each have a secretary, but no other paid staff.

Erwin France retains a strong voice in selection of council members, and, more often than not, Daley will accept his recommendations over others. However, some appointments originate with aldermen, congressmen, pressure groups, civic groups, private agencies, and block clubs. Both city staff and critics maintain that the interim councils, in operation before the elections, were more effective and hard-working. They generally rate appointees higher in quality and representativeness than elected members.

Each council has a mix of income groups but in direct contrast to their proportions in the neighborhoods; the middle class is vastly overrepresented, the poor and uneducated vastly underrepresented, indicative of the usual prejudice against a strong voice from the latter group. Professionals have some posts—for example, the council chairman in Uptown is an assistant city corporation counsel, and certain other members are under the employ of agencies. All four council chairmen have become known for their strong leadership and, on occasion, have challenged city policies. The chairmen meet periodically with subcommittee chairmen and the CDA area administrator to keep better informed.

During the first action year, each Model Area Council was divided into 10 subcommittees (called task forces), one for each program component. Most observers, including city staff, admit the task forces were fragmented and not very effective; some members floated from one group to another without becoming knowledgeable about any function, project staff often did not participate, and task force attendance ran 50 percent or less. Task forces were not utilized properly and were not given enough information on which to act.

In the second action year, two umbrella coordinating committees were created for each council to oversee the task forces. One, the Human Development Committee, encompasses subcommittees on Education, Health, Law and Order, Justice and Corrections, Child and Family Services, Leisure Time, and Manpower task forces. The other, the Environmental Development Committee, encompasses Housing and Relocation, Economic Development, Environment, and Transportation task forces. In addition to the umbrella groups, each council has subcommittees on public information, by-laws, and operations.

Each task force has about six members and meets monthly, in addition to workshop meetings. But despite the reorganization, there is still not much evidence of substantive accomplishment.

The prime function of the Model Area Councils, as explained in the second action year plan, is to monitor and review all Model Cities proposals. Although the councils are authorized, among other things, to "initiate proposals for public and private action," it seems clear from the wording of the plan that the initiation and the substantive work of planning proposals is expected to emanate from elsewhere—that is, from the CDA. For instance, the councils are empowered "to prepare a budget of an amount agreed upon with the City Demonstration Agency."

Technical assistance to the councils was provided by CDA staff during the first year; during the second, although the plan states the councils are empowered "to hire their own Professional Technical Assistance," to be paid for out of the individual council budget, the CDA still retained the right to review prior to the actual hiring of consultants. In fact, there never was enough money for councils to hire consultants.

For the second year, CDA allocated $250,000 for Model Area Council activities to be distributed on a per capita basis as follows:

Area	Population	Percent	Amount
Near South	115,877	35.4	$87,500
West	96,916	29.6	75,000
Mid-South	60,030	18.4	45,000
North	54,185	16.6	42,500
Total	325,008	100.0	$250,000

Priscilla Dombek, the only nonorganization elected member of the Uptown Council, feels that allocations for councils have been inadequate all along and that council members have been denied free access to vital information, such as facts on available jobs, salaries, and names and addresses of people holding them. She was elected chairman of her council on March 15, 1972.

Although the plan speaks of "a more active role in project planning and evaluation" for the councils in the second action year and refers to establishment of a Planning and Evaluation Committee of Council Members, it states clearly that "certain agreed upon parameters for citizen participation will be observed." There is no indication that the council role has been expanded. Councils still depend on the central agencies for advice and assistance.

Degree of Authority. No one, not even the mayor himself, claims that Chicago's citizen participation structure gives citizens any degree of

real control over Model Cities. Alderman Despres says that there is
"nothing genuine about citizen participation" in Chicago. Citizens are
advisers, not decision-makers, and they are well aware of their role.
For this reason, community leaders, such as those of TWO, have
historically lined up against the program. Although some black leaders
on the west side, at first militant, have been hired into the program
as paid staff, many more still share the sentiments of TWO director
Leon Finney, who feels it is of little use to elect people to the Model
Cities Council because (1) they are outvoted, and (2) they have no real
power to influence decisions anyway. (See Table 9 for a listing of
Model Area Council functions and responsibilities, most of which have
never been put into effect.)

Chronic complaints from the beginning have centered on the
absence of independent technical assistance and enforced dependence
on CDA planners, superficial problem analysis, and the city's decision
to contract out virtually every major Model Cities project to existing
agencies.

DeWitt Gilpin, an official of the United Auto Workers and member
of the Uptown Area Council, described the planning process in a tone
of disturbed resignation:

> Control and direction remained under the professional
> staff of the city. The money was allocated to sustain the
> status quo of existing agencies. It seemed to me that what
> was developed was not necessarily innovative, but followed
> existing programs.
>
> The staff came out with a project for a given com-
> munity and the Council got it on a take it or leave it basis.
>
> I never served with the illusion that in Chicago the
> Councils would be allowed to function as autonomous
> entities. If there wasn't such a paralyzing fear of a little
> democracy, of letting the people have a little say, this
> could be worked out. But you know the monolithic char-
> acter of politics in Chicago.

Earlier as well, the Justice Department complained about problem
analysis and lack of innovation:

> The problem analysis consistently fails to challenge the
> specific policies and procedures now in operation in
> major public institutions.
>
> Most of the programs using federal supplemental
> funds go to city agencies that have historically and con-
> sistently carried out policies of overt discrimination and
> racism.

TABLE 9

Functions and Responsibilities of
Model Area Councils

Each program which has been proposed in the City's application will be assigned to a subcommittee for continued monitoring, review and comment to the full Model Area Council, and through that body to the CDA. To ensure that the residents have access to and influence on the program, the following authority is vested in each Model Area Council:

1. To prepare a budget of an amount agreed upon with the City Demonstration Agency.
2. To administer and be accountable for the expenditure of Model Cities funds allocated for support of Model Area Councils. Checks will be disbursed by the Office of the Comptroller of the City of Chicago and audited in the usual manner of other funded programs.
3. To initiate proposals for public and private action.
4. To review and comment on proposals for the expenditure of public funds.
5. The CDA will not advance to the City Council any proposed program in the areas of Health, Housing, Education, Law, Order, Justice and Corrections, Child and Family Services, Economic Development, Environment, Leisure Time, Manpower, and Transportation, without the approval of the Councils.
6. To appoint sub-committee members and to develop specific by-laws for the operation of the Council and its sub-committees as long as such by-laws are not in contradiction to the guidelines set forth above, and as long as they are not in violation of the contract between the City and the Department of Housing and Urban Development.
7. To convene monthly city-wide forums, including members of all Councils, with the assistance of the CDA Citizen Participation Specialist.
8. To conduct training programs for neighborhood residents.
9. To designate delegates to sit on the Personnel Committee of the CDA.
10. To name delegates of their choice to Model Cities related meetings and conferences within the framework of the Council's budget allocation where funds are required.
11. To recruit, interview, screen and recommend the employment of staff for those positions that are a part of the Model Area Council budgets.

12. To participate in ongoing planning, evaluation and program imple-
    mentation.
13. To participate in training of staff and residents involved in Model
    Cities Programs and projects.
14. To hire its own Professional Technical Assistance.

Source: Chicago Model Cities Handbook, 1969.

*   *   *

We cannot expect [the Model Cities Program] to do
more than add another layer of bureaucratic programs to
existing layers—layers already demonstrated to be ineffective over the years.[6]

Pierre DeVise, general dissenter, has asked, "What kind of
credentials do these agencies have? They are the very agencies that
have made such programs necessary. We're talking about functions
in which the city has failed miserably and yet the city wants to do it
on its own. The only innovation is in language."
Warren Hill, Community Legal Council (CLC) lawyer, pointed
out that almost all civic groups, churches, and even the Indians, numerous in Uptown, were ultimately shunted away from any real programs.
According to the official view, however, sacrifices in innovation
were compensated for by gains in start-up time. Erwin France, in an
interview in 1970, stated, "Our ability to get funds in the future depends
on a certain extent on our ability to spend funds." It is this type of
rigid management control that eventually led HUD officials to praise
Chicago's Model Cities Program for efficiency in spending, in sharp
contrast, for example, to New York Model Cities, which was unable
to spend its funds or effectively manage its program, particularly
during the first two years
The city staff also takes the view that Model Area Councils
have played a large role in decision-making, citing their help in defining problems before the program was written. From the standpoint
of some community spokesmen, however, this is past history, and they
feel that in the second year the councils had no real voice in planning
or overseeing existing projects. Other council members disagree,
maintaining that the CDA responds to any valid criticism and has even
made itself unpopular with the city administration in a number of cases
because of its strong advocacy of programs for the poor. In general,
council participation involves little initial planning input but calls for
a more active role in project revision. Although a council veto can
theoretically stop a program, lawyers for the OEO-funded Community
Legal Counsel say that several Model Cities projects have met with

Model Area Council disapproval and have still been passed by the city council. Three cases can be cited. One, in which two 236 housing developments planned for the Uptown area, were vetoed by the Model Area Council and then passed by city council, calling the Model Area Council vetoes "merely advisory."

A second, in which a community group in Uptown completely planned and received federal backing for the Edgewater Mental Health Association clinics (with Community Legal Counsel help), but city council approved the program over a Model Area Council veto. Part of the reason for the Model Area Council veto initially resulted because CDA gave its approval before the Model Area Council had ever been consulted. Community people say this underscores what they feel to be the real impotency of the Model Area Councils.

In still a third case, the city started a program for the Urbanization of Appalachian whites without Model Area Council clearance. When Community Legal Counsel lawyers challenged, the city dropped the project and called it a "study."

Conversely, when several Model Area Councils objected to city hiring policies for various Model Cities positions, they were given the right to screen prospects and submit their own recommendations (still only "advisory," however).

Though the decision-making authority of Chicago's Model Area Councils is limited in terms of federal program goals, it comes off better when compared with that of Chicago's only other citizen participation program—CCUO. Model Cities seems to have a much higher level of participation on boards, at meetings, and at other functions. CCUO has no elections, and its Urban Progress Center Boards are hand-picked by the center director, largely through political recommendations.

Model Cities in Chicago also enjoys more enthusiastic support from its employees and others associated with its projects. In joint training sessions held in 1971 for Model Area Council and CCUO council members, the city staff reported that Model Cities people were more numerous and more attentive. At the graduation ceremonies marking the end of training, they were clearly in the majority, even though CCUO has 11 councils.

The Woodlawn Organization Experience

Because the Woodlawn Organization community involvement experience is unique, a brief history of its development and eventual confrontation with Model Cities is important. The Woodlawn Organization was founded in 1960 and has spent much of its time battling governmental and private special interest groups, through Saul Alinsky-type methods. By the summer of 1968, the University of Chicago joined the battle and loaned staff and resources to develop a plan of neighborhood rehabilitation. Monthly workshops organized by the University's Center for Urban Studies enabled TWO to respond quickly to the Model Cities Program

When TWO was unable to carve out a role for itself with the city in helping to plan Model Cities, it decided to offer its own plan as a viable alternative.

The document emerged from six months of planning, hundreds of meetings, even public hearings, and town meetings that drew as many as 2,000 persons. It detailed six main issues of community interest:

1. Delivery of Services—attempts to alter the way services are controlled by the professions.

2. Evaluation as a Management Instrument—being selective rather than comprehensive about modifying programs.

3. Ordering Goals—testing each function against the goals.

4. Environment—physical changes will be considered only after the community is able to deal with the social and economic effects.

5. Government—attempts to achieve functional centralization among agencies at the community level.

6. New Techniques—achieving goals outside the traditional institutional practices.

A 100-member board (all residents of Woodlawn) would oversee specific proposed programs in health, social services, financial assistance, legal services, environmental planning, education, and manpower and economic development, whose total cost was estimated at $146 million for a five-year period, and $19 million for the first action year.

But the city was putting its own plan together at the same time, which, although initially turned back by HUD, was eventually accepted. The city rejected TWO's proposed independent role and proceeded with its own version of Model Cities, laying to rest TWO's attempts to change the ongoing system and killing from the start any meaningful citizen participation. To this day, TWO is still trying to implement certain elements of its plan with available Model Cities and private funds, but Leon Finney says that residents are demoralized, community groups are in disarray, and it is the city's strategy to see any real local strength fall apart.[7]

Programs

Goals. For many, the effectiveness of Model Cities projects is more important than who decides which programs are implemented. The second action year plan emphasizes revitalized communities and strengthening of sense of community by encouraging participation in community activities—"the idea of living in a place where one's own efforts and ideas are important." Six objectives are identified: raising resident income; improving housing and environment; strengthening family life; enhancing community responsibility; enlarging human opportunities; and improving city capability.

Priority Allocations. In the first action year, 64 Model Cities projects were operated by 33 different public and private agencies. They were organized around 10 typical Model Cities categories to ensure comprehensiveness. Although Chicago had many different projects, it wisely chose to concentrate most of its funds in a few projects to create maximum impact, something most cities did not do. In the second action year, after a reevaluation of priorities by the Model Area Councils, housing was to receive stronger emphasis, along with health, social services, and education. Although the councils placed housing first, CDA ranked it lower, and when the city announced a $21.3 million plan for five "little city halls" (multiservice centers), a black businessman's group asked that the money go for housing instead; but the centers won priority.

The number of separate projects was reduced to 56 (42 were proposed in the third action year), and resources were to be allocated as follows:

31 percent educational
14 percent housing construction, conservation, relocation
12 percent environmental protection and development (housing)
10 percent crime and delinquency
9 percent health services
7 percent social services
5 percent manpower and job development
3 percent recreation and culture, economic and business development
9 percent citizen participation, evaluation and information, program administration

This allocation was based on a total budget of $52 million, $38 million of HUD supplemental funds, and $14 million in federal, state, and local resources. However, because federal money was withheld from the city, not all programs were implemented. In February 1972, less than $400,000 was left in second action year funds to finance the programs. Three projects—Co-Plus (Cooperatively Planned Urban Schools), health centers, and police aides—have accounted for well over half of Model Cities funds and indicate the city's thrust to place services where it has been weakest, particularly in education and health. When residents are asked to list successful programs, these usually are the only three mentioned. Paul McCloskey, special assistant to Erwin France, considers these and day care most significant—all creating some degree of institutional change. The operating agencies of these programs appear to have good administrative staffs, competent in fiscal management, and generally aggressive and innovative. Over-all, Chicago's programs seem to have been well-operated. Progress of some of the principal programs is indicated in the following pages.

Education: Co-Plus Program. With a budget of over $8 million in HUD money, Co-Plus has come to be regarded as one of the most important and successful Model Cities programs. It is operated by the Board of Education and was designed to establish concentrated supplementary programs for children and adults in seven model area schools and to individualize instruction through smaller classes. Medical and nutritional programs, a preschool program, expanded use of audiovisual equipment, free formal education (including college-level courses), in-service training for teachers, classroom aides, and other school personnel are all included. School buildings remain open an extra six hours per day, seven days a week (if needed).

A component of Co-Plus is Schome (an amalgam of "school" and "home"), a preschool educational program costing $1.2 million and designed to ease the transition of about 840 three- and four-year-olds from home to school. Plans called for new prefabricated structures (costing approximately $30,000 each) to be built to house the Schomes as an adjunct to the seven community schools. Eventually, permanent structures would be built costing $2.5 million. They would be designed so that preschoolers could attend half-day classes while their mothers were in the same building attending homemaking classes. Medical and nutritional services were to be included, and the manpower component called for training 550 model area residents as classroom aides and numerous others as janitors and school firemen. At its peak, about 2,000 area residents were hired to work in some phase of the Model Cities education program, but with a shortage of funds the number was cut to 1,500. About 69 percent of the positions were held by model area residents. Many school aides, especially those middle-aged and older, were content just to have a job and were not interested in upgrading themselves into a more competitive milieu as classroom teachers. Nevertheless, the city has indicated it will refuse to rehire those who do not fulfill upgrading requirements.

In February 1971, Educational Testing Service (ETS) reported that citywide achievement test scores of Co-Plus pupils "give rise to the hope that the steady downward trend in academic achievement has been halted." But they also indicated difficulties by the Board of Education in winning widespread community support and high parent turnout.

ETS felt the health and Schome components might turn out to be the most successful projects and also recommended that the Co-Plus school concept be expanded to include more schools.[8]

The Uptown Model Area Council reported in June 1971 that Co-Plus had successfully addressed the majority of problems stated in the 1968 Model Cities Problem Statement with the execption of over-crowding and truancy. They made further recommendations for re-habilitation of all existing schools, more playgrounds, a comprehensive dropout program, smaller classes, and special education for the re-tarded.[9]

In May 1971, Blaine DeNye, project coordinator of the Chicago School Board Model Cities projects, stated that three Schomes were built and in use, a fourth would open shortly, and land for two others had been acquired. The seventh was still in the planning stage. Co-Plus programs were operating in six schools in four areas: Lawndale, Uptown, Mid-South, and Near South.

Parent-team planning—one of the strong concepts of Co-Plus, envisioning parents working in the classroom—"did not work very well," admitted Nye. He blamed lack of parent participation on the fact that it was the same parents on the planning team who were in-volved in other phases of Model Cities activity and that their efforts were being spread too thin. (Other reports indicated participation in adult education and recreation had fallen off.) While Nye also praised the program, "The concentrated expenditure of $1,600 per pupil has brought attitude changes and improved language skills," he said current financial difficulties have stripped the Board of Education of much of the staff needed to operate its projects. Approximately 500 of its 2,000 Model Cities personnel have left the program, and no money exists for replacement. One project cut reduced in-service training for Co-Plus staff from 72 hours in the first action year to 40 in the second. But even with this temporary setback, the Board of Education believes Co-Plus is successful and wants it expanded to as many schools as possible, using Model Cities supplemental funds and cate-gorical grants. Erwin France describes this program as an excellent example of "buying into the system" and creating institutional change. This seven-school pilot project could lead to changes in hundreds of Chicago schools.

Health. Erwin France outlined the goals of the health program and the residents' perceptions of problems to the American Medical As-sociation Resources Conference on Improving the Quality of Life in November 1970:

Goals
1. Develop a comprehensive system of health serv-ices for each of the four Model Neighborhoods.

262

2. Strengthen the role of the Chicago Board of Health as the agency of principal responsibility for health services at the municipal level.

3. Begin to rationalize the health system and generate coordination of health services in the Model Neighborhoods.

4. Generate greater public and private cooperation in the health delivery systems of each Model Neighborhood.

5. Bridge the gap between the black medical and dental practitioners in the Model Neighborhoods and the larger health establishment.

6. Build a greater voice for neighborhood residents in development of health services in their neighborhoods. This does not mean community control, but cooperative efforts between residents and agencies.

7. Get better use of existing facilities and build or create new facilities for health delivery.

Residents' feelings, obtained through the initial Model Cities neighborhood meetings and workshops held during the planning process, are summarized below:

Residents' Perceptions

1. Lack of adequate, easily accessible health facilities.

2. Overcrowding at Cook County Hospital.

3. Lack of evening clinics (one of the many reasons many Model Area residents said they had to do without health services almost entirely).

4. Exodus of private physicians for more profitable communities; and reluctance of new medical graduates to locate in the inner city.

5. Reluctance of local hospitals in predominantly black communities to fill openings with qualified local residents.

6. An impersonalized clinical process preventing confidential, trusting, one-to-one doctor-patient relationships.

7. High costs.

8. Lack of preventive health care and education, particularly in the areas of prenatal and child care, family planning, and personal hygiene.

Community health centers have begun to eradicate some of these ills; however, they have not yet realized their original goals of providing complete ambulatory out-patient care on the premises (under direction of the Chicago Board of Health) and backup care from nearby private hospitals. During the first action year, according to Model Cities staff, basic health services have been provided in temporary quarters in all four areas, and temporary services were contracted with some hospitals: Marine (near north), Providence and University of Chicago (near south), and Mt. Sinai (west). Ultimately, plans call for each area to receive "permanent health centers" housed in "free standing facilities." The second action year was to be a time for expanding temporary services (mental health and ambulance services specifically) and planning the permanent ones. The original second year budget of $6.7 million, one of the largest chunks of the total Model Cities budget, included paramedical training for approximately 200 Model Neighborhood residents.

By 1971, remodeling of the Epstein Clinic at Providence Hospital, to serve near-south residents, was completed. The Model Cities Target (newspaper of the Chicago Model Cities Program) announced imminent groundbreaking for a health center in Uptown, designed to handle 25,000 persons a year, and stated contracts had been let for two more centers in the mid-south area to handle 11,000 persons each. A center for Lawndale has been held up because of lack of funds.

Pierre DeVise questions the health programs' success. While Model Cities officials were talking about comprehensive health care in neighborhood centers for entire target area populations, DeVise flatly predicted that the Model Cities centers will be able to handle only 7-10 percent of the local residents, and the rest will continue to be shipped to County Hospital. So far the program has neither proved nor disproved DeVise's prediction, as it passes from one funding crisis to another. The four health centers planned for three of the target areas (excluding Lawndale) would serve a total enrollment of 47,000 persons—18 percent of the total target area population, 25 percent of the population of the three areas where they are to be located—with something less than comprehensive care. But actual enrollees, more than two years after Model Cities began, were well below DeVise's 7 percent projection. Two of the centers are completed and ready to open soon, but Model Cities is having a difficult time putting together funds from other programs to pay doctors' salaries. Dr. Edward Avery, a consultant at the Uptown Center, reports that people are dropping out because of lack of funds to deliver services.

Some benefits are evident, however. Donald B. Smith, Model Cities deputy director, believes that the health program has created institutional change in two ways—acceptance by medical professionals, and citizen involvement. Citizen advisory boards are planned for all centers. One has been appointed by the commissioner of the Board of Health, consisting of 20 target area residents selected from lists provided by community groups. While it would appear that citizens will now have an increased opportunity to help create policies, the Uptown Model Area Council believes the advisory boards are not representative enough of the community. This council, however, does feel that its own interim health center has had some impact on health problems, that the Board of Health has had considerable impact on child health care, and that ambulance service has been very effective.* (The innovative ambulance project has been serving over 7,000 patients annually in all four model areas with 10 ambulances.) It felt, however, that special health care programs for senior citizens and unwed mothers and a 24-hour emergency service were still unmet needs.[10]

Uptown's former health center director, Norman Webb, attributes the center's problems to the diminishing role of community groups as well as a lack of funds. The partnership of 14 north-side hospitals that were to guide the center, along with a citizen's advisory board, lost most of its power to the Board of Health, Webb said. And the Board of Health made it clear it would deal only with fiscally proven operators. The North Side Health Planning Commission (hospital group operators) wanted strong community participation to prevent sit-ins and delays. Dr. Murray Brown, director of the Board of Health, still feels the advisory board will have an important voice.[11]

Critics complain that Model Cities funds are being used simply to further consolidate city control over Board of Health clinics and the County Hospital, which will, in turn, further isolate these institutions from the private health sector. Many believe that the teaching hospitals and the medical societies should have been involved in the planning and operation of the Model Cities health program to bring them into the mainstream of assistance programs and help eliminate the double standard of health care in Chicago. Model Cities may simply serve to perpetuate the dual system unless it can encourage private participation. The best use of Model Cities funds may be to integrate the systems.

Housing. Chicago's Model Cities housing program had good intentions: "to provide equal housing opportunities throughout the city and metropolitan area for Model Area residents," states the Model Cities plan. But putting them into practice has been difficult. Among the six projects listed in the second action year plan (land acquisition, technical assistance to developers, information and assistance to residents wishing to move, upgrading existing housing, establishment of a mortgage assistance fund for loans to low-income residents, and housing construction), not one was designed to take residents out of the target

---

*Although drug abuse and veneral disease, the Uptown Council stated, were worse problems in 1971 than in 1968.

area. The Model Cities Housing Construction Project, sponsored by the Chicago Dwellings Association (a not-for-profit corporation) had as its objective the construction of 1,000 to 1,500 dwelling units "in the target area and fringes (one-half mile radius of target area)," which meant in essence that black target areas would remain black and white neighborhoods would remain white. And even at that, only 25 homes have actually been built (in Lawndale and Woodlawn), a poor record that Model Cities officials charge to unwillingness by the FHA to make more than 25 loan commitments. (The 85 parcels of land for which Model Cities paid $217,000 to the Chicago Housing Authority remain unused—"too small and too scattered" to be workable, according to Model Cities official Theron O'Toole.)

The efforts are growing even weaker. In 1969, after the successful housing discrimination suit by the American Civil Liberties Union, the Chicago Housing Authority (sponsor of most of the public housing projects) was ordered to build 700 units of public housing in white areas. When the CHA took no action, HUD was ordered to withhold Model Cities and Urban Renewal funds to force compliance. But so far, compliance has not been forthcoming.

Day Care. Perhaps the smallest gap between intent and accomplishment is to be found in Chicago's day-care program. Twelve centers were planned, and 12 are operating, along with 91 private homes licensed to provide day care for target area children. Though all children are from low-income families, not all receive free care—families who can do so pay a sliding-scale fee. Staff consists of approximately 150 persons, about 60 from the target area, who have been trained and employed by the program. Program costs per child average $125 per month. There is now space for 1,000 children (in centers and homes), and capacity was expected to reach 4,000 when the expansion program was completed at the end of 1972. Most expansion money has come from the Illinois Department of Children and Family Services, which is providing $3 for every $1 from Model Cities. This undoubtedly is why the program appears financially healthier than the rest.

Even this program has shortcomings. In 1971, Ebony Management Associates reported 40 percent of the centers had no mode of transportation; 50 percent had station wagons too small to do the job; there was lack of educational and operational equipment and supplies in 70 percent of the centers; only 20 percent of the centers had clear definitions of purposes and objectives for parent councils; there were minimal efforts to involve males; there were varying titles of parent groups which caused confusion; serious performance problems existed among untrained staff of Neighborhood Youth Corps (NYC), Concentrated Employment Program (CEP), and Project Venus girls; and a number of other administrative and operational difficulties existed.

In general, it found the basic purposes of the program—early education for children and employment and training opportunities for parents—not being met.[12]

Many of the same faults were cited by the Uptown Model Area Council later in the year. Its report also mentioned no programs for girls similar to those offered by the Boys' Club, no day-care services for older children of working mothers, and no overnight (or 24 hour) emergency care.[13]

Probably the first to point to the program's failings were officials of the Illinois Department of Public Aid (IDPA), a state agency, who criticized its lack of after-school care, family care, and lunch programs. Despite indications of improvement in some areas (centers are now open from 7 a.m. to 6 p.m. weekdays, and each child may receive breakfast, a hot lunch, and two snacks daily, as well as medical and dental examinations upon enrollment), IDPA still feels that the program does not provide proper training and job development for adults. IDPA says too many mothers spend their time shopping, visiting, or going to the movies while their children attend free centers.

Perhaps its most serious criticism of the program is in the area of coordination. IDPA charges little coordination of day-care programs between the two agencies, a poor understanding of social philosophy on the part of Model Cities, and an unwillingness for staffs to meet regularly. They feel Model Cities has been too independent of the state program. It appears, however, that the failure to cooperate and take initiative to meet lies equally with both staffs.

The job of coordinating the day-care program in Chicago is an enormous one. Administered by the Chicago Department of Human Resources, the Chicago Housing Authority, and Marillac House (a Catholic settlement house), the program has involved some 15 separate agencies, three previously engaged in day care, the others new to the field. Keeping the quality of all programs uniformly high has admittedly been difficult and coordination a major problem. Yet the program has managed to serve 4,000 target area children out of 28,000 estimated to need day care, certainly a respectable start. (Total need in Chicago is estimated to be for 100,000 children.) And the program has at least as many fans as critics. One of them, Sylvia Sutton of the Day Care Crisis Council, calls the Model Cities day-care project the brightest light—truly creative and innovative.

Crime and Delinquency. The purpose of the crime and delinquency project is to develop better understanding between police and residents, improve police services, and generate innovative projects for juvenile parolees and misdemeanants. Six police-community centers are in operation, as well as two correctional service centers, where about 1,000 youths annually are counseled. As an alternative to jail, 85 young misdemeanants have been provided with housing, counseling, training, and education, and 43 have received jobs since the program began. Also four youth service homes are in the process of being developed.

The Criminal Justice Educational Foundation, which studied the project in 1971, saw great potential in the program for misdemeanants. But difficulties are encountered in the failure of courts to refer an adequate number of enrollees and in the enrollees themselves. Of 69 juveniles enrolled since the beginning, 23 left the program without permission or were discharged for violating rules. More professional help and more in-service training of staff are needed.

According to Lawndale residents and some staff members, at least part of the problem is lack of counseling at the time of arrest. Community representatives, who are supposed to provide counsel on rights and bail, have been stuck in the back of police stations shuffling papers. This, they say, reflects police antipathy toward the type of community representative selected—usually chosen politically rather than for the ability to do the job.

Police Community Aide. The Police Community Aide project is perhaps the most impressive component of the crime and delinquency program. The Criminal Justice Educational Foundation, together with Ernst and Ernst consultants, found, through detailed interviews of aides and police, that the most important goals of the program were (1) upgrading the community (97 percent of the police and 94 percent of the aides believed this); (2) improvement of police-community relations (68 percent of the police and 26 percent of the aides); (3) reduction of crime (8 percent of the police and 3 percent of the aides). The consultants felt the over-all administration and management of the project had been good and most preliminary objectives met; however, they cited lack of clear-cut policy direction and insufficient contact with district police. They recommended a Project Policy Coordinating Council, career development ladder, increased contacts with district police, more in-service training, and longer hours at the six Community Service Centers, among other improvements.[14]

The Uptown Council felt the program had definitely made some impact on improving police-community relations but that there was lack of communication between various groups and police and inadequate patrol of schools and playgrounds.[15]

In its manpower aspect, the program has created 486 positions for residents and rich opportunities for advancement and training. Among the aides, 124 are enrolled in basic education, 106 in GED courses, and 151 in colleges. Three aides, so far, have risen to a full patrolman's rank. But police say that while it has created jobs for residents, the project has neither helped significantly to reduce crime nor freed police for more important assignments. Residents seem pleased with the program but do not know whether it has reduced crime. Moreover, no statistics are available. TWO director Finney says the aides spend too much time walking around, chatting, and playing cards. "It is simply a way of putting people on the payroll," he says. However, the general feeling is that the program has been beneficial, and even its critics say good things about it.

Equal Opportunity. High among the objectives of the Chicago Model Cities Program are the elimination of discrimination against model area residents in employment, in law enforcement, and in provision of other public services, and concomitantly, the eradication of block-busting and panic peddling in housing, which in Chicago have been re-fined to a high art. A Mayor's Office of Inquiry and Information and a Registrar of Citizen Complaints were established in each Model Neighborhood to assume some of this work, and at least one multi-service center is planned for each model area. According to the CDA, these offices processed 1,825 complaints the first year. In other com-ponents, 172 investigations were made among firms to assure fair employment policies; 23 complaints against the police were resolved; 1,362 jobs were analyzed to determine if experience and educational qualifications for Model Cities positions are reasonable and appropriate; an agreement was made between the Board of Education and the glaziers' union to allow Model Cities residents to become union apprentices; and agreements with other agencies were made to allow Model Cities resi-dents to be hired as trainees in the fire fighting, janitorial, and engi-neering fields.

Besides the complaint centers mentioned above, the Police Com-munity Service Centers, Consumer Code Enforcement, and CCUO out-reach centers all handle citizen requests in the target areas. But in many cases, the centers overlap and some, CCUO in particular, handle few complaints of limited types. Some of the staffs could be readily integrated. The consolidation of Model Cities and CCUO may accom-plish a great deal in this regard. CCUO neighborhood workers could easily be trained to handle a variety of complaints representing differ-ent functional areas, thus freeing other staff members for other serv-ices.

Manpower. Emphasis was placed upon hiring residents in Model pro-grams. Of course, even area residents in some cases had to have political connections to get jobs. In the first year, 3,511 persons were hired in Model Cities projects; 2,837 (81 percent) were model area residents. Erwin France and other city officials view this as an in-stitutional change in itself.

In addition to the above employment, CDA reported that during the first year, 1,284 residents received job orientation and counseling; 538 persons received job training; 1,190 persons received support services (transportation and medical examinations); 321 youths were paid stipends for job training; 300 children of participants received free day care; and 283 residents were placed in jobs.

Noting that the program has made some impact on the community, the Uptown Model Area council has recommended demonstration on-the-job training programs in private industry, removal of citizenship requirements, better transportation, aid to first pay day as needed, and removal of nonessential job requirements.[16]

Environmental Services. In first-year accomplishments for this project, the CDA reported 487 jobs created for residents; 28,000 tons refuse and 29,000 cubic yards bulky trash removed; 3,743 miles curbs swept; 920 tons of salt spread over 697 miles of streets; 240 miles of streets snow-plowed; 283 vacant lots cleaned; 10,000 abandoned autos towed; 100,000 lineal feet of cement repair work on curbs, gutters, and sidewalks; 750 trees planted; and an education and motivation program established for residents to upgrade the physical appearance of their own communities.

Residents generally seemed pleased with the program. The Uptown Model Area Council said that alleys were "much cleaner," trash pickup "adequate," the curb and gutter program "very successful," summer beautification had improved neighborhood appearance a "great deal," and the program had "developed a sense of responsibility" among the neighborhood people "working with the program." It suggested improvements to include more frequent street cleanups and removal of abandoned vehicles, provision for better parking facilities, and a " "good strong educational program for residents" to develop a sense of responsibility. However, as in most of the nation's Model Cities programs, even where cleanup programs have been effective, the original, severely blighted conditions remain. The general impression one gets is still that of an acute slum environment.

Booz Allen and Hamilton, private consultants, stated that the first-year program "should be judged a successful one." All components were performing their functions on schedule. They also reported, however, that innovation was almost completely lacking. They noted, "This reflects the lack of a planning or research capability within the Department of Streets and Sanitation," which operated the project, "as well as a lack of pressure from the Model Cities agency," and recommended that a portion of Model Cities funds be used to provide a planning capability within the sanitation department and that new methods of operation and innovation techniques at the department and ward levels be instituted. Booz Allen felt, too, that an expanded effort

270

to actively involve residents was needed and that job security and career development should be provided to Model Cities employees in the program.[17]

Leisure Time. This component concentrated on providing educational, recreational, and cultural activities. For first-year accomplishments, the CDA reported the following: (1) letting of 54 subcontracts for Model Cities neighborhood programs in which 146 facilities and 584 activities were developed, with 67,641 residents participating; (2) a summer services program that gave employment to 172 persons and bused residents to leisure-time activities on 812 separate occasions. Nearly 120,000 participated in the program; and (3) establishment of four leisure-time councils, one in each neighborhood, where more than 100 residents participated in the assessment of existing and potential programs to determine which should be implemented with Model Cities funds.

The Uptown Council was particularly concerned that gang activities had discouraged participation in these programs and stressed the need for better transportation, and extensive year-round program (not just summer), and more programs for families and senior citizens.[18]

Employment and Economic Development. It is questionable whether economic development of the target areas is actually working. Latest reports are that the Chicago Financial Development Corporation (CFDC), which was to furnish initial loans to new target area businesses so they could then borrow larger sums from the Small Business Administration, has itself suffered funding delays that have made its operation minimal. So far, this organization has only made three loans, totaling $86,000 to expand three Model Area businesses. From the beginning, it had trouble working out procedures with the city comptroller's office so that the normal waiting period for release of funds could be considerably reduced.

CFDC has increased its area of operation outside the Model Cities area and has received $312,000 in other federal funds. With fewer restrictions and a larger area, it has been able to make eight loans for a total of $214,000.[19] Also, its companion organization, Chicago Economic Development Corporation (CEDC), which had contracted with Model Cities to provide technical assistance to new or expanding businesses in the target areas, eventually severed its connection with the program completely. Federal red tape, delays in getting funds approved, and the need to work with citizens' advisory councils were cited as reasons for severance by Garland Guice, CEDC director.

According to Guice:

It is impossible to have a business development program
in a vacuum. . . . Those communities [target areas] are
deteriorating because there is no new housing. And so
they're losing people. . . . The primary reason we pulled
out of the Model Cities program was a lack of progress in
the whole program. It was difficult to work within the program's framework because of all the rules and regulations,
the slowness of getting approval for funds, and working with
the citizen's advisory councils. Then there was the paper
work—it was driving us crazy—cost control reports,
monthly reports. There is a limit to how much paper
stuffing and how much work you can do.[20]

CEDC is now financed by a $500,000 grant from the Department
of Commerce. During the two years, 1970-71, that it worked with
Model Cities, it gave technical advice to 45 groups, which were able
to acquire over $1.5 million in loans for new or expanded businesses.
Outside the target area, CEDC helped new businesses get more than
$6 million in loans, but inside, it was never able to really make a
significant impact.[21]

Institutional Change

In principle, there is no equivocation about Chicago's belief in
the need for institutional change through Model Cities. Year One, an
evaluation of the first action year, prepared by the Chicago Model
Cities office, states:

Basic to the philosophy of the Model Cities program is a
commitment to bringing about institutional change. . . .
The money that Model Cities spends in the target areas
must be spent in such a way that it will first of all change
the institutions and, proceeding from this, generate additional community resources and improve the quality of
resident's lives. . . . Responding to the voiced concern
of residents over discrimination in the model areas,
changes have been accomplished in those agencies of
city government especially concerned with ensuring
equal opportunity for all. These changes, which are a
part of the Model Cities Program, contain innovations
which will decentralize these agencies and bring their
services right into the target area. Without changes such
as these, and changes in the philosophy and practices of

institutions, private agencies, businesses and other organizations, Model Cities would be yet one more program increasing community dependency on outside aid.

Yet equivocation does enter the picture when the discussion turns to the specifics of "change" and whether those changes brought about by Model Cities will, in fact, decrease target area dependence on outside aid.

Some of the main examples of "institutional change" as stated by Chicago officials are the following: (1) employment and training of Model Neighborhood residents, not only to provide immediate jobs within the program but also to "raise the career potential of the employed residents so that they can earn more money to bolster the economy of their neighborhood"; providing opportunities for teachers' aides to earn college degrees, making "arrangements" with unions to allow Model Neighborhood residents to be hired as janitorial staff for Co-Plus schools during extended hours, and police aid training are cited specifically; (2) economic development of the Model Neighborhoods, by making low-interest equity loans available to residents who want to start their own businesses, thereby bringing more money into the areas and making them self-sufficient; (3) creating models of decentralized, comprehensive health facilities in each target area; and (4) developing model schools and parental involvement, which has received Board of Education endorsement.

The basic assumptions for career development have yet to be borne out. Few residents have actually completed training and Model Cities still exists as the prime employer. Skepticism over the quality of training and its usefulness in long-range career goals has in fact been voiced by residents themselves.[22] Economic development is minimal, but the health centers and model schools have forced important institutional changes.

Critique and Analysis

Mayor Adopts Model Cities

To the envy of most large U.S. cities, the combination of strong political control and able professional management has created a system in Chicago that successfully delivers traditional city services. Effective street cleaning and garbage pickup, street and alley lighting, police and fire protection, and mass transportation (as well as business stability and fiscal responsibility) are trademarks of the Daley Administration. These services are expensive and not always equally distributed, but at least the great majority of Chicagoans are convinced they are better here than elsewhere.

It was only natural that this same system, superimposed on
Model Cities, would make Model Cities one of the smoothest-running
programs in the nation. In effect, the mayor adopted the program, an
ingredient for success that many cities have lacked. Some federal
officials even called it "the best" because there were few "hangups,"
there was good planning, money was spent on time, most funds were
concentrated on four or five basic priorities to create impact (over
half the proposals submitted to the CDA by local groups were rejected),
comprehensiveness existed, and most programs met their objectives.
It has continued to function, however, with such notable defects as lack
of genuine citizen involvement, excessive patronage, discouragement
of substantive state participation, little innovation, and, most importantly, the temporary cutoff of federal funds because of the city's refusal to build public housing units in all areas of the city.

Strengths

Institutional Change. While most cities have spread their Model Cities
funds to thinly, Chicago held the number of projects to 62 (later reduced
to 42) and focused over 50 percent of its $38 million of funds on Co-
Plus schools, day care, police aides, and health centers. These four
projects, in addition to over-all resident employment, are held up by
Director France as the main evidence of Model Cities accomplishment
and institutional change. It appears that some important institutional
changes have occurred and that much more could be done, given more
time.

Resident Employment. It is true that the hiring of thousands of residents (3,500 from model areas) and the training of paraprofessionals
represent the beginning of institutional change. However, permanence
will result only if their employment is continued through meaningful
projects and career ladder development. While the training, career
ladder development, and tuition-free Model Cities programs are among
the best of their kind in the country, there is considerable room for
improvement. Furthermore, there is real question whether the jobs
for which residents are being trained would exist without Model Cities.
    The widespread use of patronage in employment undermines the
goals of the program. The whole idea of hiring people because they
are friends, relatives, or vote-getters works at cross-purposes to a
program that purports to be developing marketable skills and attitudes.
It is degrading to those hired and unfair to the majority of citizens,
who are not even considered because they lack the right connections.*

---

    *Recent relevations in the Lerner Community newspaper and
television broadcasts showed widespread violations of the Hatch Act

Model Cities might best demonstrate its ability at innovation and institutional change in the area of personnel administration by instituting impartial hiring practices, in addition to providing effective services.

Co-Plus Schools. Co-Plus is probably the most significant of Chicago's programs. From its beginning in only seven schools, its impact has been felt throughout the school system. If adopted citywide, Co-Plus elements could help in raising achievement levels in the school system generally. The Board of Education has seen the value of resident aides (some 2,000 trained through New Careers), teacher training, advisory boards, adult education (bilingual classes alone have enrolled 200 people), better learning environment for 10,000 children, free meals for 20,000, and parental involvement. Recent financial problems almost caused the closing of summer Co-Plus; however, this was avoided and it is now possible that the school board might institutionalize Co-Plus as money permits so that not only the present schools continue the program but the entire system is eventually included.

Health Centers. Though far from realizing their potential, the health centers have been instrumental in effecting change. They have brought many new health care services to families who need them most and never before had them; they have drawn additional physicians and medical technicians into the area; and the program has helped to convince Mayor Daley that new leadership was needed in city health administration, resulting in the appointment of a new health director and other improvements. The criticism is still valid, as it is in most urban areas, that the system is not adequately integrated with private health care and the best care is still not available to poor citizens. Board of Health leadership still appears docile. It has relegated the citizen advisory board to a meaningless role, and technical help is still in short supply; however, a giant health step has been taken in Chicago's ghettos toward providing residents with what may eventually be the complete package of quality care envisioned by the planners.

Police Aides. The police aide program appears to be psychologically good for community people, and many aides have received excellent training. Still, there are problems. One of the program's main objectives—to free regular policemen from routine duties to concentrate on serious crimes—has not worked, according to the police, who also feel the program has not had much effect on reducing crime. It has been difficult to get males involved (there are 236 females and 132

---

and caused Erwin France to issue a memorandum insisting on strict compliance by his staff with federal law.

male aides), and apparently a substantial number of aides have not taken the work seriously. As mentioned previously, few have managed to carry out the counseling aspects of their jobs, either through their own lack of ability or through deliberate efforts by the police to keep then out of sight, relegated to paper shuffling. The concepts of the program—police aides, community relations, and citizen support—are vital to the operation of Chicago's police department. Yet it is entirely premature to claim that institutional change has already occurred. Active acceptance and cooperation on the part of the police are still missing—necessary ingredients before the concept can actually be integrated into regular police work. Aide jobs must become regularized positions with more than "make-work" responsibilities. The mayor ought to formalize this.

Day-Care Centers. Quantitatively, day care has met its objectives, with 11 centers serving 4,000 model area residents. Although 28,000 children need the service in the target areas, the program has made a good start in numbers and physical locations. Qualitatively, the picture is not as bright. Rather than achieving the educational and cultural training for children originally envisioned, the centers are providing little more than custodial care. Parents, instead of seeking education or employment, are inclined to use the centers merely to shop and visit with friends. The centers must provide preschool education for children, and parents must use their time more productively if the program is to be of value; otherwise, parents may just as well take care of their children at home. And although Model Cities has provided a link between the many day-care programs operating in Chicago, still greater coordination and cooperation are needed, primarily with state agencies.

Weaknesses

Other programs have not achieved an equal degree of success. They were of lesser priority in the first place, and suffered considerable cutbacks when federal funds were withheld. At least two of the Model Cities Councils admit that their sanitation service is no better than previously and that building code enforcement has actually declined. Charges of patronage, contract favoritism, mismanagement, and misuse of funds have not helped the program's image, and on the whole, the program has declined from its peak of success. It could begin to ascend as full funding resumes and more effective management is instituted so that ridiculous and extravagant expenditures are eliminated. The program faces three other problems, as well: lack of innovation, poor coordination, and superficial citizen involvement.

Little Innovation. From the beginning the program was criticized for lack of innovation. Almost all projects were to be operated by the established agencies with past records of ineffectiveness and lack of regard for the poor. In general, their performance is the same under Model Cities. There are exceptions. There are agencies where some innovation has taken place, and where Model Cities has benefited from being operated by an existing institution. But where the agency is unresponsive, it is necessary to seek new contractors, despite the fact that the administration prefers to work with a known system. The program should not remain saddled with one approach. Competitive operations are desirable to speed the process and go beyond minimal improvements.

Poor Coordination. Unwillingness to deal with state administration officials hurts Model Cities in two ways—it means fewer state funds for Chicago and turns attempts at coordination into city-state power struggles. Mayor Daley wants no outside interference in "his city"; yet the state can be of real assistance. Steps should be taken to establish coordinating commissions or corporations in each major functional area—health, employment, day care, and so on—to unify scattered programs. Creating a city Department of Human Resources was a first step in bringing together like functions, but the department has not done enough to integrate state functions into its operation. Now Model Cities has an excellent opportunity to demonstrate that it and CCUO can operate as one, avoid duplication, conserve staff, and produce more effective programs. This desirable step should not exclude the coordination of state and private agency programs of a similar nature, and it should take another giant leap by integrating the Department of Human Resources, Model Cities, CCUO, and day care. The programs of these departments involve human resource planning, coordination, and implementation that can best be accomplished by an integrated, unitary staff. Though politics may now dictate against this unification, efforts should be made to achieve the goal.

Superficial Citizen Involvement. Though citizens have more voice in Model Cities than in any previous program, including Community Action (where both control and administration lie with the city), it is difficult to find anyone who does not believe all decisions are made at the top. Model Cities Council elections are largely controlled by the Democratic organization, and appointments are controlled by Daley. Real opposition has no chance of forming.

No responsible person advocates that militants or opportunists take over boards or that spokesmen dominate them to the disadvantage of the poor. However, if true neighborhood leadership is to be developed, selection of council membership must be fair. In the beginning, the city turned down the services of the American Arbitration Association to administer Model Cities elections; yet the association would have been far more able than the machine-controlled Election Board to provide some degree of consensus and free choice.

It may be fruitless to suggest that the administration loosen its control over the program, but that is precisely what is needed. To help save Chicago's neighborhoods and increase respect for its government, there is a need for community councils elected under impartial supervision in all areas of the city where residents petition for a council; for each council to be responsible for coordinating and integrating all services connected with neighborhood community development, human resource, and certain other city programs; and for councils to be given substantial authority for local decisions under guidelines of mediation and arbitration (as suggested in the over-all analysis of this study). Importantly, residents of each council area should make up the majority membership of local policy boards. If a central, citywide body is used for coordinating neighborhood councils and formulating citywide community development policy, the majority membership should come from the elected members of the neighborhood councils; the mayor should appoint a minority member. The central council should act on issues of a citywide nature and allocate funds to neighborhood councils on an equitable basis of population and need. Within a citywide formula, neighborhood councils should be able to make independent decisions that cannot be overturned by the central council. It should preferably take a three-fourths majority of city council to overturn local decisions

Strengthening Administration and Councils. In addition to the questions of authority and selection, councils ought to be budgeted sufficient staff to develop their own ideas. Councils should be able to pay members for expenses and time loss for attending meetings, in order to encourage greater participation and to compensate the members more equitably.

The CDA area administrator should be given greater responsibility for overseeing programs in his area, coordinating project directors, and bringing these directors officially before the Model Area Council and task force sessions. The responsibility of keeping the councils informed should be laid squarely on the shoulders of area administrators. As it is now, the area administrators are ineffective and the councils uninformed.

Moreover, area administrators could assume the responsibility for calling mini-cabinet meetings (as is done in New York and Boston, for example, by convening district superintendents in monthly meetings to assess neighborhood problems and become more familiar with local needs) and directing department and agency priorities toward achieving community goals. In this sense, neighborhood residents would have more to say about how local services ought to be run.

The Need for a New Commitment

A broader question now faces Chicago. Can its neighborhoods survive? In the beginning, the Woodlawn Organization developed its own Model Cities plan, which the city promptly ignored. After several years and $15 million pumped in, the area has steadily declined, with more and more homes abandoned by a receding population, and the life blood of the community—its people and organization—draining away. What advantage is this to the city?

When Model Area Councils asked for more housing, the administration pushed their requests further down the priority scale, largely because of integration problems. Now, third-year emphasis has shifted to less controversial service areas in order to be able to show tangible results; yet it is in housing and other human resources where the need is greatest. Better refuse collection and alley lights are necessary but not sufficient to keep a neighborhood alive. As downtown was made viable and the business establishment secure, so now must each neighborhood be made strong, much like new towns—with health and community facilities, new and rehabilitated housing, Co-Plus schools and day care, police aides, parks, and independent citizen groups that play a strong role in creating and maintaining their own communities. The city's Department of Development and Planning's 1966 Comprehensive Plan calls for 16 cohesive, identifiable development areas or urban towns (citywide and composed of from 150,000 to 250,000 persons each) and the annual expenditure of hundreds of millions of dollars to rebuild these areas. This kind of total approach is necessary with realistic and meaningful community boundaries that can be accepted and citizen councils with limited but important powers in each of these development areas. Model Cities has not been able to develop the ability to save neighborhoods, but it has improved services and demonstrated some models for action. If anyone has the power to create a successful model, it is Mayor Daley.

Model Cities was never properly funded to achieve its comprehensive objectives. With only enough money for temporary expedients, much of its resources have been wasted because it has been stopped short. Local revenue sources have not been able to guarantee high-quality basic services in all neighborhoods, so it is unrealistic to espect new general revenue sharing funds to be able to support expensive, nontraditional services. Therefore, an adequate outlay of federal, state, and city funds must be committed for comprehensive community development purposes. Inaction by all levels of government over too long a time has brought us to the point where only a total plan, fully funded, involving maximum cooperation from all sectors, has any hope of revitalizing our cities.

Survival of the cities is too important for the politics of exclusion; survival will take the cooperation and resources of all factions. It is now a matter of committing substantial funds and developing a plan for the help of a dedicated coalition of interests from all levels of government and walks of life. In discussing national priorities, Mayor Daley recently pledged to Chicagoans that he would strive to the best of his power to handle all well. Now is the time for him to bring the coalition of forces together to act on a comprehensive proposal to build new viable inner cities. Chicago already has committed substantial funds to capital improvements. Tying city and state funds to community development (including Model Cities) and general revenue sharing funds in a comprehensive and coordinated plan is necessary.

Notes

1. Pierre DeVise, "Chicago's Widening Color Gap: 1971 Status Report," paper presented May 1970 to the South Side Planning Board.

2. Pierre DeVise, "Chicago Hospitals: A Disaster," Focus/Midwest 8, 51 (1971): 18.

3. Milton Rakove, Great Cities of the World: Chicago (Beverly Hills, Cal.: Sage Publications, 1972), vol. I, pp. 349-350.

4. Cornelia Honchar and Peter Negronida, "Model Cities Program," Chicago Tribune, February 22-25 and 27, 1972.

5. Model Cities Program, Resolution Introduced by Alderman Richard Simpson, Chicago Council, February 1972.

6. Model Cities Memorandum, U.S. Justice Department, Community Relations Service, April 1969.

7. Most of this information was obtained from two documents called TWO's Model Cities Plan, one prepared by the U.S. Commission on Civil Rights in December 1969 and the other by the Woodlawn Organization in 1970.

8. Educational Testing Service, An Evaluation of Selected Projects, Cooperatively Planned Urban Schools, Barton-Aschman Associates, Inc., February 1971, pp. 25-27.

9. Uptown Model Area Council, Highlights of 1971 Community Statement, June 1971, p. 4.

10. Ibid., p. 2.

11. Chicago Tribune, February 27, 1972, p. 7.

12. Ebony Management Associates, An Evaluation of Selected Projects, Day Care Services, Barton-Aschman Associates, Inc., February 1971, pp. 39-47.

13. Uptown Model Area Council, op. cit.

14. Criminal Justice Educational Foundation and Ernst and Ernst, Police Community Aides, Barton-Aschman Associates, Inc., February 1971, pp. 32-35.

15. Uptown, op. cit., p. 5.

16. Ibid., pp. 11-12.

17. Booz Allen and Hamilton, Environmental Services, Barton-Aschman Associates, Inc., February 1971, pp. 51-56.

18. Uptown, op. cit., p. 10.

19. Chicago Tribune, February 25, 1972.

20. Ibid.

21. Ibid.

22. Findings of a study done on selected Model Cities programs in Chicago by Barton-Aschman Associates, Inc., released February 1971, p. 61.

11

COMPETENCE
IS BOSTON'S HALLMARK

The City

Boston Model Cities has been inevitably glued to city politics, bureaucracy, and the official kingdom. These elements need to be reviewed in the context of Model Cities discussion, for it is this system and its institutions that Boston Model Cities has been trying to change.

Boston's political power—the power to resolve conflicts of interests, allocate scarce resources, and respond to urgent demands and needs—is shifting, elusive, and fragmented. It is not, as many people think, in the hands of a small group of men in a smoke-filled room or a 30th-floor corporate office. Rather, the capacity to deliver, respond, or resolve conflict is something that must be pieced and pulled together as each issue and problem arises. Though city hall has been dominated by the Irish since the early 1900s and Boston has had an Irish mayor for 58 of the past 70 years, state government and those peculiarly apolitical "independent authorities" such as the Port Authority still are under Yankee control. Indeed, the present governor, Francis Sargent, his lieutenant, Donald Dwight, and key appointees like George Sears Lodge (head of the Massachusetts Bay Transit Authority) and John Sears (head of the Metropolitan District Commission) show that the traditional patterns of Yankee influence still have a hold.

Power, when so fragmented, is difficult to delegate to any new institution or any person. The United States Constitution gives no legal powers to cities, which exist and act through grants of power from state legislatures. Cities have little home rule. Boston's condition is even more critical in many respects than most because of a combination of historical and institutional factors, such as the size and structure of the core city in relation to the metropolitan area and the history of immigration that has bred such a diversified population.

Boston makes up a smaller part of the metropolitan area than other major central cities. The metropolitan area, which includes

76 cities and towns, has a population of over 2.9 million (1970). The city, with an area of 47.8 square miles, has only 23 percent of this population. Because the surrounding communities hold three-fourths of the metropolitan population and a vast voting advantage on Beacon Hill, the city has never been able to get more in taxes and revenue than the "potentates of the periphery" permitted.

A strong neighborhood identification is present in most sections of Boston, reflecting the history of annexation, as well as strong ethnic and social ties. Irish and then Italian immigration threatened Yankee control of the central city, which is and was the home of the key cultural, educational, and health-related institutions of New England. Its small size is one of its many constraints.

Demography

Boston's population composition is unique. Irish make up 22 percent of Bostonians, Italians 11 percent, blacks 18 percent, white Protestants (from Western and Northern Europe) 13 percent, and Jews 6 percent. While the population has fallen from over 800,000 in 1950 to 641,071 in 1970, nonwhites have increased from 43,000 to more than 105,000 during the same period. The Spanish-speaking, principally Puerto Rican, have rapidly increased to an estimated 25,000 in 1970.

Italians are prevalent in the city's North End and East Boston and in large numbers in sections of Hyde Park, Jamaica Plain, West Roxbury, and Roslindale. Blacks are predominately concentrated in Washington Park, North Dorchester, and Lower Roxbury (part of the South End and Campus High School renewal projects) and are moving into Mattapan and sections of Jamaica Plain.

As in most other northern cities, blacks do not have the option to rent or buy dwellings in large areas of the city or in many suburban areas. "Snob" zoning and subdivision controls in the suburbs surrounding Boston have the effect of excluding blacks and lower-income whites. For blacks, who have even fewer options than lower-income whites, the lack of choice in housing means that they pay higher rents for generally poorer housing.

Economics and Taxes

On the fiscal side, Boston has benefited from large-scale increases in productivity, production of goods and services, and growth in total number of jobs since 1963; nevertheless, tax revenues are its "Achillies heel," regressive and inelastic. More than 60 percent of city revenue comes from the property tax, yet 50 percent of its land mass is tax exempt and its per capita taxable property is only 62 percent of the metropolitan area average. A major problem is the continuing exodus of manufacturing jobs, especially those that employ the least skilled.

"The Expanding City of Boston's Economy," an analysis by Alexander Ganz,[1] notes that despite steady economic growth since World War II, there has been very little improvement in Boston's unemployment rate and wage scale. In 1971 the Division of Employment Security for the Commonwealth of Massachusetts reported the unemployment rate for the metropolitan area as 6.2 percent and for the city as 9.1 percent. In the Model Cities area, unemployment has averaged above 14 percent. And approximately one in every five city residents receives some form of public assistance. Instead of more employment, Ganz reports, gains have come in production of goods and services, which rose from $5.6 billion in 1947 to an estimated $9.6 billion in 1970, and output per worker, which is higher in the center city than either the metropolitan area or the United States as a whole. Underlying growth in productivity were "outstanding" increases in manufacturing output per worker and a fundamental relative shift of jobs from manufacturing to the services sector.

Boston Redevelopment Authority (BRA) estimates that in the 1970s the city of Boston has the potential to grow by 100,000 jobs and to increase production of goods and services by 50 percent or $5 billion. City officials anticipate a small gain in manufacturing jobs in the 1970s if the Economic Development and Industrial Commission (EDC), which would have land assembly powers and ability to sell bonds, receives state legislative approval. Employment should rise in governmental and educational areas as well. As a cultural center, Boston has attracted museums and universities, and as the state capital and federal regional headquarters city, it has many governmental institutions.

Boston is experiencing a fiscal squeeze, despite productivity gains and a larger tax effort than its suburbs. The city's property tax from all sources was $156.80 per $1,000 valuation in 1970, assessed at 30 percent of market value; assessed valuation was $1.72 billion. Property taxes raise two-thirds of the city's total revenue—a painful and uniquely high percentage. The property tax is "a wholly inadequate and irrational revenue source, yet the only one available to the mayor to meet the spiralling costs of city government" (a situation common to most American cities), says Barney Frank, former executive assistant to the present mayor, Kevin White.

Boston has no alternate source of tax revenue and generally receives less state aid than most other cities. It ranked 12th in state aid in 1968. In 1967, per capita state aid (excluding welfare) in Massachusetts was lower than the national average.

Boston's fiscal problems have become more serious. Yet its debt is still within the limits set by the state. The inequities of the property tax that are hurting most cities affect Boston even more. Property taxes are scheduled to go up again, and there appears to be no tax relief from the state, in spite of the efforts by Mayor White's coalition of city and town officials to press for major tax reform. Problems continue to mount because Boston is an old city where it is not uncommon to dig up wooden water and sewer pipes, and it has a higher percentage of persons requiring high levels of service. Its history shows long neglect of public facilities: parks, schools, hospitals, streets, lights, and most public works. Encouragingly, in the past decade considerable progress has been made to improve these facilities, especially through urban renewal programs.

Capital Improvements

Capital public improvements averaged $18 million between 1950 and 1966. Expenditures were increased threefold between 1966 and 1970 to the national average of $54 million in 1970. The city spends $60 per capita, which must be maintained during the 1970s or its economic growth may be severely inhibited. For example, the city purchases water from the Metropolitan District Commission, but its public works department distributes and meters it. Amazingly, 45 percent of the purchased water is lost because of aged facilities. A substantial capital investment will have to be made to replace a large part of this system.

A citizen's group called the Filene Committee successfully secured capital improvements in the first two decades of the century. And earlier, Frederick Law Olmsted designed for Boston what many planners believe is the finest network of parks in the nation. But since the Depression, such expenditures have been astonishingly low. The result is financially and visually painful.

It is being helped by the extremely ambitious urban renewal program, which encompasses 20 percent of the population and one-sixth of the land area. More than $90 million in federal funds have been received and another $100 million committed. The local share will be $100 million. This multipurpose renewal combines residential, institutional, and commercial expansion and efforts to upgrade public facilities.

Urban renewal inspired development of the Prudential Center, a 52-acre government complex with a new $30 million City Hall completed in 1969, the start of a massive conversion of the waterfront and rehabilitation of the Faneweil Hall area, and substantial activity in the Washington Park, Charlestown, and North Howard areas.

The West End renewal project is one of the most traumatic and frequently written about in the country. It wiped out an entire neighborhood and replaced it with high-rent buildings of dubious architectural quality. Despite recent efforts such as the massive, 604-acre South End project (70 percent rehabilitation), the West End remains the image of what renewal is. As a result, the Boston Redevelopment Authority is viewed with suspicion. This imposes a constraint on many of its efforts, even in nonrenewal areas. In addition, urban renewal is still severely hampered by federal regulations and the inadequacy of housing subsidy programs. Nevertheless, city officials view renewal as a valuable tool in improving public facilities and housing. In 1972, Mayor White cited 3,500 units of new housing under construction or recently completed, with another 5,000 in the planning stage and 5,000 more proposed.

Boston Model Cities has established slightly different priorities for urban renewal. It stresses rehabilitation rather than new construction and was influenced by the Washington Park and West End renewal plans. Many perceived Washington Park as an attempt to create a black middle-class neighborhood by uprooting lower-income blacks and relocating them in the Model Cities area. Because of this, Model Cities is placing high priority on proper relocation.

The Government and the Power Structure

The State and Independent Agencies

The state retains control not only over the city's sources of revenue, but also over its recruitment and job categories. Boston's civil service procedures and rules for municipal departments can be changed only through negotiation with the state, sometimes requiring legislative approval.

In addition to state control over important functions, independent metropolitan authorities shape major parts of the city's physical frame and are subject to little or no direction from city officials. These authorities control extensive domains: water, sewer, and major park facilities (the Metropolitan District Commission); the transit system (Massachusetts Bay Transit Authority, MBTA); airport and harbor development and administration (Port Authority); and major roadways (Massachusetts Turnpike Authority). (Construction of other major roadways, including the inner Belt and Southwest Expressway, currently halted because of city opposition, is carried out by the State Department of Public Works.)

Even authorities closely identified with city government are not always amenable to the mayor's control. The redevelopment and housing authorities are both governed by five-man boards, a majority of whom cannot be mayoral appointees until the mayor has been in office for three years.

Public education, a critically important city function, is carried out through a school system controlled by an independently elected five-man School Committee. Several department heads, including the police and fire commissioners, are appointed to terms not coterminous with the mayor's. A governor-controlled but city-financed investigating body, the Finance Commission, and a governor-appointed alcoholic beverage licensing board are further examples of this fragmentation of power.

In 1968, Mayor White appointed a Home Rule Commission of citizens and public officials to study these problems and to recommend changes. Their report characterizes Boston as "an example of municipal government structured on a premise of basic distrust of the people who govern the city."[2]

The commission says this dilution of authority results in lessened quality of administration as well as a confusion in the voter's mind about who is accountable for decisions. The major recommendations all aim at strengthening the mayor and city council to increase responsibility and accountability of local government.

A summary of the Home Rule Commission's six key recommendations is as follows:

Strengthen the role of the mayor; abolish the School Committee, putting the school department directly under the mayor; change the makeup of the city council, with some councilmen elected at-large, others from districts; abolish several agencies including BRA, BHA,* the Public Facilities Department and the Finance Commission; decentralize various government services and the school system; modernize the city's budget system.

In a section on its "basic position," the commission reports:

Boston has long been an example of a municipal government structured on a premise of basic distrust of the people who govern the city. The hallmarks of this attitude are the Finance Commission, established as a permanent governor-controlled and city-financed investigating body in 1907; the Licensing Board, which from 1906 has overseen alcoholic beverage licensing from the perspective of the governor of the Commonwealth who appoints its members; and the State Civil Service Commission, which sets qualifications and procedures for hiring of city employees.[3]

---

*Boston Housing Authority.

Boston's first government was a mayor-council form, in which the legislative branch of 12 aldermen and 75 members of a common council shared powers with a mayor. As a growing population demanded more efficient government and more extensive municipal services, this sharing of powers came to be inadequate. With new departments needed to administer and deliver new services, a change in form was necessary.

To bring about a succession of reforms, residents pressured the state to approve charter amendments and, later, charter revisions. Between 1900 and 1960, the city charter was substantially revised three times with final approval by referenda.

The present strong-mayor/weak-council form of government was fully defined in a 1949 charter revision. The mayor has the power to appoint most city department heads except police commissioner, corporation counsel, building commissioner, fire commissioner, and penal institutions commissioner. He also appoints members of boards and commissions, with a few exceptions being those appointed by the governor. He also draws up the city budget and thereby sets annual city priorities. The budget must be approved by city council, which can reduce but not increase or redistribute the funds. The mayor cannot override the council's veto (See Chart 5).

Several analyses of city government point to the need to strengthen ties between budgeting and planning; the Home Rule Commission recommends a budgeting-planning-management unit directly responsible to the mayor. Presently, capital budgeting is in the hands of a Public Facilities Commission, and planning is carried out with minimal coordination by the Planning Commission, part of the Redevelopment Authority. Program budgeting has recently been introduced by the operating budget, which is prepared by the Administrative Services Department.

The Mayor

While the mayor's control over the budget—on paper—appears considerable, Mayor White has frequently pointed out that less than 50 percent of the budget is controllable expenditures and that such areas as the MBTA debt payments, the school budget's annual allowable increases, and debt service charges cannot be reduced by him.

The mayor signs all city contracts over $2,000, which gives him a considerable amount of leverage over city business, much of which is done by private contracting (including sanitation, snowplowing, towing).

He also oversees about 1,000 patronage (provisional) jobs, primarily within the Department of Health and Hospitals. Jobs within his own newly created offices, such as the Office of Public Service

CHART 5

Organization of Boston's City Government

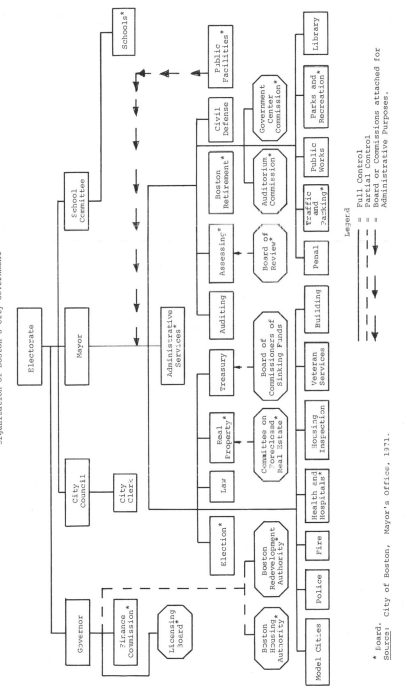

Legend

—————— = Full Control
– – – – = Partial Control
⟶ = Board or Commissions attached for
          Administrative Purposes.

* Board.

Source: City of Boston, Mayor's Office, 1971.

(OPS, which includes Little City Halls programs), the Commission on the Affairs of the Elderly, and Summerthing, add about 250 more under his direct control. Also about 250 non-civil service employees work in the Model Cities Program. However, most of these employees are selected by a legitimate personnel process that attempts to screen people for their job qualifications.

Although patronage control is a relatively small percentage of the total city employment of 25,000, it has had significant impact. The Mayor's Office has not publicly denied that its employees worked on behalf of White's gubernational and mayoral campaigns. Eric A. Nordlinger, in a Boston Urban Observatory Study of Little City Halls, states that at least one-third of the OPS staff worked on the campaign for White's gubernatorial candidacy and that a "significant number of employees who did not make such [campaign] efforts were given low ratings by the mayor's patronage secretary and were subsequently fired. The OPS director did manage, however, to limit these firings to those staff persons who were not thought to be performing well on other, more legitimate criteria."

Nordlinger adds, "Many more OPS staff worked on the mayoral campaign. At least three-quarters did so; and to a far greater extent than in the gubernatorial campaign the work was on the city's time." He says that OPS's contributions to the mayor's candidacies can be defined as a case of "good politics" making for "good government." Nordlinger concludes, "the staff's campaign work indirectly contributed to the fulfillment of OPS' purpose by making it somewhat likely that the organization will survive beyond 1971 when White's first term ran out." He says two of White's opponents in the mayoral elections would have eliminated or emasculated the program. [4]

The Office of Public Service and the Little City Halls Program have been Mayor White's main innovations. OPS is the central monitoring and coordinating body, and Little City Halls are designed to improve communications between residents and the city, answer citizen complaints, and improve services. The program has been an important instrument in stimulating the bureaucracy. [5] Nordlinger characterizes the program as a success. However, he states that OPS, which manages the Little City Halls Program, has failed as a monitoring agency, has been unable to follow up complaints adequately, and has been ineffective in setting up Local Advisory Councils in the Little City Halls areas. He suggests that the citizen advisory councils have not been influential, have been "rubber stamps" for city policies, and that neither the mayor or OPS has evidenced a strong and enduring commitment to them. On the other hand, he points out that OPS and Little City Halls are very much a bargain because the quantity of city services has been increased significantly and that they are effective change agents because alternative channels for improving services are not useful.

Finally, he states, contrary to criticisms of OPS as the mayor's private political resource, political involvements of Little City Halls managers and OPS central staff are severely circumscribed, and that over-all OPS electoral efforts on White's behalf have indirectly contributed to the fulfillment of OPS's own functions and purposes.[6]

The Office of the Mayor has been strengthened, under Kevin White, since 1968. Acting on the widespread sense that previous mayors had focused on downtown development and responded to business interests, he has made a considerable attempt to provide greater access for and response to residents' concerns. Little City Halls; Summerthing, a neighborhood-controlled arts festival; the Office of Human Rights, focusing on equal employment and other opportunities; a Board of Rent Appeals; air pollution and drug programs, these have all reached into the neighborhoods. In early 1972, White greatly expanded his direct planning staff in order to increase the effectiveness of OPS, develop the capacity to integrate Model Cities with city departments, and expand Model Cities citywide. The renewed commitment may have the effect of stimulating a stagnant bureaucracy.

City Council

The nine-member Boston City Council is elected at large for two-year terms, in nonpartisan elections held in odd-numbered years. Terms are not staggered. Each member, formally at least, is responsible to all the voters in the city, rather than to residents of any particular section; however, each tends to have a "voter base" in particular neighborhoods.

Each January, the council chooses one member as its president. The president chairs all council meetings and acts as mayor when the mayor is out of town of if he should leave office before his term is completed. He also appoints committee chairmen and members to each of the 15 standing committees and to special committees.

Each councillor has a staff of two, and the council as a whole is responsible for the choice of city clerk, messenger, librarian, and research director. Each councillor is paid $10,000 per year, and the president receives an additional $2,000.

In addition to approving the budget, council approves or rejects federal loans and grants for programs in which the city pays a share, votes on several mayoral appointments, and authorizes loans and land sales. It also acts in an advisory and investigatory role. It has the power to subpoena witnesses to aid in its investigations, within the limits of its jurisdiction, which are very narrow. Council issues ordinances (sometimes as a result of hearings), making changes in the laws on matters over which it has authority. Such ordinances must be approved by the mayor, and his veto can be overruled by a vote of two-thirds of those present.

More frequently, council issues resolutions that do not require mayoral approval, such as those authorizing memorial days or dedicating squares and parks. Council can also issue orders or directives requesting information from the mayor or from a department head through the mayor.

Without substantial legislative power, council will on occasion try to focus attention on matters that concern citizens. Councillors, despite their at-large constituencies, do a large volume of client work, such as helping citizens to find jobs and get veterans' benefits. Commenting on the Little City Halls Program budget, one councillor recently said, "Why, I run a Little City Hall right in my office. People need that kind of help."

Council as a legislative body is highly disorganized. Reports from committees have little impact on actions of the whole council. Most councillors hold another job, with five of the current incumbents having their own law practices. They tend to do little detailed staff work and have failed to fill the position of research director, for which they allocated funds. Personnel from the Mayor's Office frequently cite examples of votes of councillors that have been obtained because of promises of patronage or other favors to the councillors by department heads. In other words, council does not seem to function as the policy-making body acting on citywide concerns that earlier reformers had envisioned.

Limits on budgetary power of council have significant consequences. The Home Rule Commission report states that the

> present distribution of budgetary powers . . . can lead to irresponsibility on the part of the council. Because councillors have no power to initiate a new program or increase existing programs, they are free to advocate the establishment of various programs, no matter how extravagant. In this way, the councillors can gain the allegiance of various interest groups and can place pressure on the Mayor to initiate perhaps unwise programs. Yet it is the Mayor who, if such a program is initiated, must bear the responsibility for the cost and effectiveness of any new program.[7]

Councillors can favor anything without risking the blame of a costly program or one that does not work.

The Home Rule Commission Report lists several additional reasons why the current council lacks effectiveness. First, name recognition is a critical factor in electing a councillor because of the large number of candidates running at large. This, the commission felt, tends to lessen the importance of a particular candidate's programs, policies, or positions.

Secondly, the cost for a campaign is exceedingly high; former Councillor John Saltonstall claimed to have spent $40,000 in the last election. The high cost tends to put elections out of reach of many new and younger would-be councillors. Third, the constant competition to gain attention in citywide media, the incessant competition with every other member of the council, tends to constrain the close working relationships possible in other legislatures. Fourth, and perhaps most significantly, the at-large system limits the representativeness of the council. "An analysis of the results of the last ten city council elections reveals that Dorchester, South Boston and West Roxbury have elected 63 percent of the councillors and that many substantial areas such as Mattapan and Charlestown have elected none." And a high proportion of incumbent or former councillors are returned to office.

The ethnic composition of the council has tended toward Irish and Italian. One Protestant and one black have been elected since the council structure was changed in 1949. As the Home Rule Commission says, "an at large election is probably not the best system for insuring that the population's actual diversity of viewpoints is accurately reflected in the make-up of the council."

Certain other factors tend to limit council effectiveness. It is extremely difficult, with an at-large constituency and limited powers of initiation, for a councillor to establish a clear "image" on the council. It is difficult for a young politician to use this body as a stepping stone. From the mid-1950s until Louise Day Hicks was elected to Congress in 1970, no councillor was elected to higher office.

These factors hamper the recruitment process and reinforce the structural weaknesses of the council. Dispassionate discussion of policy options is seldom if ever heard, and name-calling and displays of temper have led local press observers to comment about the "theatre of the absurd" that the legislative sessions sometimes become.

The Home Rule Commission has recommended that council be restructured so that some members are elected from districts and some at-large. And in order to correct what it calls the irresponsibility of council with money matters, it recommends that the fiscal power of council be increased. Council would have authority to initiate budget requests and increase budget items initiated by the mayor. The mayor would retain veto power over such council actions.

Civil Service

One out of 12 workers in Boston is a government employee, and civil service is an important part of the city's employment market. Boston is the state capital and home of federal regional offices, and its Government Center is a symbol not only of urban renewal but also of the presence of several levels of government. The number of city employees is high compared to total city population.

But absolute numbers and percentages do not adequately describe the importance of civil service in Boston. "Nowhere in America has civil service's limited opportunities, its structure and its pace so dominated the general outlook," wrote Peter Schrage in Village School Downtown.[8] The civil service bureaucracy has been the main ladder of mobility and source of security for Irish and later Italian immigrants.

All of Boston's operating and administrative departments, under control of the mayor or School Committee, operate under state civil service regulations. The only exceptions are the Public Facilities Department, created in 1966, which has relatively flexible hiring and promotional policies, and the Model Cities agency, which, though employing a substantial number of people, has a program goal of job preference for local residents. Too, some agencies not directly under control of elected officials, notably the Boston Redevelopment Authority and the Boston Housing Authority, are regulated by civil service. One of the major goals of Model Cities has been to find ways to transfer its employees to regular city departments under civil service.

Political Power

Boston's politics is strongly personalized. Though the vote is overwhelmingly Democratic in national elections, its local political patterns do not reflect party orientation to the same degree. Strong personal organizations rather than party shape local political careers and fortunes.

The word "tribal" may suggest the spirit as well as the form of Boston's political contests. The city's political style has been much celebrated for its vigor, color, and excitement. Hale Champion commented: "It has its charms, but they are not sufficient to justify its belligerence, its hostility, its pettiness, or its nearly paranoidal suspicions. Trust . . . a willingness to believe in other than totally selfish and personal motivation on the part of others . . . is the scarest commodity on the local political scene."[9]

The term "machine" has been misapplied to Boston politics. The city has never had an effective party-dominated city network. Rather, it has had several strong personal organizations (such as that of James Michael Curley) built on alliances with strong ward bosses or local political leaders like Martin Lomasney (West End), the Norton brothers (Dorchester), (more recently) John Powers (South Boston), John Craven (Jamaica Plain), and Michael Paul Feeney (Hyde Park). Though some newer personal organizations still dominate some sections, the older power bases have eroded or become factionalized and most local leaders' ability to deliver votes is severely limited.

Absence of party organization means that patronage and contracts are directly in the hands of the mayor and their benefits accrue to his organization. Conversely, he, or any political leader, has little to say about new political entrants or the promotion and retirement of the experienced. Ward committees for both parties are inactive between elections and have a limited capacity to deliver votes or to recruit and nominate candidates.

Business Power

The belief that business and financial interests have a shaping influence on Boston affairs, that they are a local power elite, is an exaggeration of fact. Despite remants of Yankee aristocracy in Boston's financial and commercial circles, the city's business leaders have a limited influence on city government. While there has been a strong tradition of support for philanthropies and for the city's cultural and educational institutions, there is comparative indifference to city government, perhaps because of the taint of politics.

Certainly it is fair to say that Boston has never felt the concentrated effect of the combined efforts of business interests in the way other major cities have. The business community is quite fragmented and somewhat indifferent and acts as one of many elements that may be active or passive and that must be bargained with when there are issues perceived as affecting their interests.

Boston's Model Cities

History

In February 1967, Mayor John F. Collins announced plans to seek Model Cities funds. By April 1967, the Boston Redevelopment Authority and Action for Boston Community Development, Inc. (ABCD)— Community Action Program—had prepared the planning grant application requesting $240,000 in federal funds. At the same time, representatives of organizations in the Model Neighborhood held a resident forum to determine the extent of citizen control in the program and the form elections would take. These suggestions were adopted at the community meeting and later by city council. They provided for an elected citizens board and a professional staff. On April 28, 1967, Collins signed the application, which outlined two major thrusts: first, to implement a striking improvement in the quality of services delivered to the community and, second, to develop new measures to make an even larger portion of the Model Neighborhood population self-supporting.

On August 1, 1967, 12 percent of the Model Neighborhood elector-ate chose 18 members for the board, and Daniel Richardson of Dor-chester was selected as acting chairman. Mayor Collins appointed Daniel Finn administrator of the program. Mayor White, elected in December 1967, named a new administrator, Paul Parks, who has remained in this post. After a year of staff and community study, the first year plan was approved by city council on November 25, 1968. It was not until June of 1969 that HUD Secretary George Romney an-nounced the award of $7,718,000, to be granted annually for five years. The third year plan was given federal approval June 25, 1971; the fourth year plan was approved the following spring. Total expenditures from all sources through the third action year were $32 million, in-cluding $10 million from sources other than HUD.

Structure and Demography

Two structures were created: Model Cities Administration (CDA), designed to help coordinate city departments and agencies and focus their attention on problems of the Model Neighborhood, and the Model Neighborhood Board (MNB) or citizen planning and policy arm. The CDA at first was part of the Mayor's Office, then was designated a "regular" city department. A Community Development Corporation (CDA), designed to enable residents to sponsor nonprofit housing development and improvement centers and to contract for programs with city agencies, was also created. The intention has been to have CDA carry on Model Cities programs after the discontinuance of Model Cities funding.

The original plan focused on crime prevention, legal services, citizen education and rehabilitation, and police/community relations. The first and second action years dealt with these issues; some pro-jects, which proved unsuccessful, were abandoned.

One of these was police/community relations, which was dropped from the third action year because of funding problems and difficulty in structuring a program acceptable to both Model Cities and the Police Department. Part of the reason for the failure stems from the uneasy relationship between the mayor and the Police Department emanating from an earlier feud. One of Mayor White's first actions upon assuming office in 1968 was an unsuccessful attempt to fire Police Commissioner Edmund McNamara, which created a difficult working relationship with the Police Department.

From the beginning, Model Cities has been concerned about the small percentage of blacks employed by the Police Department, so small that the NAACP has filed suits to force additional employment. Of the 300 police hired in 1969 and 1970, two were black. At first, Model Cities actively engaged in recruiting residents for the force but eventually discontinued these efforts because few were hired.

Under jobs and income, Model Cities prepared a pilot program to supplement family income, which was promptly eliminated by city council.

The 1,900-acre model area is doughnut-shaped, with the Washington Park urban renewal area "in the hole." The Model Neighborhood's population is 57,000: black 67.8 percent, white 19.3 percent, Spanish-speaking 11.3 percent, and Indian and Asian 1.6 percent. This area was chosen because urban renewal programs adjacent to it had generated substantial public and private development, creating a major physical disparity. The mayor (then John F. Collins) felt that,

> an area with substantial Negro population should be chosen because the entire syndrome of poverty is compounded by a history of racial prejudice. At the same time, he decided that it would be unwise to define a racial ghetto by drawing a cordon around an exclusively Negro area.
>
> In the area finally chosen not only is there a combination of white and non-white families, but in many sections such families live side-by-side. The area was chosen because there is the opportunity for real racial harmony on the one hand and, on the other, the chance that without a strong effort to improve conditions, the area will deteriorate so badly that interracial tension could conceivably result.[10]

While not suffering major riots like Detroit and Los Angeles, Boston experienced severe racial disturbances in the summer of 1967 in the Grove Hall section of Roxbury. The planners state:

> The real tragedy of the area selected was that we could not take the program into Mattapan. . . . There was a change to save Mattapan, but we couldn't take the program down that far.*
>
> . . . Boston welcomes the opportunity to take what advantage it can of the Model Neighborhood program; however, we are concerned that a program which has aroused so many expectations must begin by cutting out more than half of the area in the city which should be included.
>
> We are concerned too with the uncertainty of the Model Neighborhood money that will be available to us

---

*Mattapan is now an area of considerable tension between blacks, Jews, and Irish Catholics. It was until recently primarily Jewish with a large number of lower-middle-income Irish Catholics. But whites are leaving in large numbers, and blacks are moving in.

for the execution phase and with the uncertainty about the matter of appropriations.[11]

Stability of the Model Neighborhood has been a problem because of mostly white migration out of the area. U.S. Census data show the following population drop in the model area:

Year	Population
1950	80,000
1960	62,877
1970	57,004

R. L. Polk Company (which does an annual enumeration for commercial purposes) showed a net loss of 832 households, or 7.1 percent decrease, in the area between 1969 and 1970.

Organization of Model Cities Administration

The administrator of the Model Cities Administration (CDA) is appointed by and serves at the discretion of the mayor. Administrator Paul Parks, a graduate engineer who formerly was a partner in an architectual firm, reports directly to the mayor and serves in his cabinet, which meets weekly. From this vantage point, he is able to negotiate directly with city department heads, as well as work closely with the mayor.

The Model Cities administrator must submit all proposals to the Model Neighborhood Board for review and approval. In case of dispute, arbitration procedures are available (described later in this report) but have never yet been utilized. Parks meets with the board every two weeks to discuss issues and maintain communication. All plans and programs must be approved by the mayor and city council before submission to HUD (See Chart 6). With the exception of more cumbersome procedures caused by the MNB structure, there have been few difficulties between the MNB and city officials. Parks has gotten along well with the mayor, city council, and the MNB. In brief, the administrator and his staff hold the balance of professional expertise and skill in relationship to the MNB. This is reinforced by HUD guidelines designed to allow the CDA to frame programs and define alternatives, while the board and its staff are designated responsibilities to interpret, evaluate, and approve or reject programs. Lately, the mayor has been integrating the skills of his staff with the CDA's to create a more effective and efficient administration.

CHART 6

Organization Chart,
Boston Model City Administration

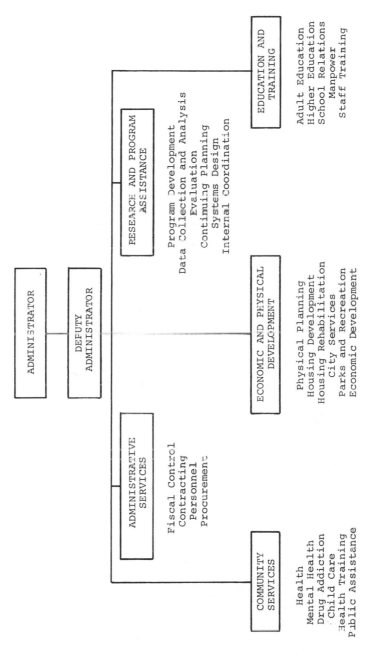

Source: Model Cities Administration, City of Boston, 1971.

CDA Staff

Of the 265 CDA employees operating in the third action year, 185 come from the Model Neighborhood. Also about 300 Model Cities residents are employed by neighborhood organizations or agencies that contract with Model Cities. Boston Model Cities says 81 percent of its money is spent in the community, mostly on salaries.

Staff turnover is very low and members are well-qualified, reports Deputy Administrator Samuel Thompson, who received a Ph.D from Harvard and formerly worked with BRA as project director of Washington Park Urban Renewal. Frederick Paulsen, assistant administrator for Physical Planning and Economic Development, also worked for BRA and received a law degree from Harvard Law School. Former director of Housing, Langley Keyes, received a PhD from MIT. The other assistant administrators are Charles Beard, a graduate of Harvard and Harvard Law School, and Barbara Jackson, in charge of the Division of Education and Training with a doctorate from Harvard Graduate School of Education. Salaries are competitive with the private employment market in Boston and generally better than those in municipal agencies in the area. Of the seven top administrators, five are black and two are women.

Federal Government and Model Cities

Boston has had good relationships with the federal government, helped, for example, by the understanding of former HEW Secretary Elliot Richardson, who had been lieutenant governor and attorney general of Massachusetts and took an interest in Boston's Model Cities. Paul Parks has the uncanny ability to converse personally with a number of important figures, which has helped diminish the deadening layers of bureaucratic red tape.

However, Boston's Model Cities Division of Research and Program Assistance assailed the red tape and lack of federal support in comments made in a 1971 report:

> Although support has been produced from certain areas
> of HEW and is beginning to come from HUD's physical
> development sections, Federal support overall has failed.
> HUD has not been able to break into the protected pro-
> grammatic pipe line from Federal sources to established
> state and local agencies. CDA, on the local level, has not
> been able to disturb the symbolic relationship between
> Federal agencies and their state and local counterparts.
> Consideration of the type of Federal support gained by
> CDA reveals that CDA applications are most often success-
> ful when (1) either the actual applicant is an established

"client" agency of the Feds (e.g. BRA, Boston State Hospital), or (2) there is no established counterpart agency (Talent Search, special projects, educational grants, and, most recently, juvenile delinquency program funds).[12]

While some local government officials feel that much more success should be demonstrated with the amount of funds made available, some also feel the principal problem of the program is its underfunded mandate, taken with breathless, almost adolescent passion, to solve all city problems and in a five-year period:

> . . . to plan, develop, and carry out locally prepared and scheduled comprehensive city demonstration programs containing new and imaginative proposals to rebuild or revitalize large slum and blighted areas; to expand housing, job, and income opportunities; to reduce dependence on welfare payments; to improve educational facilities and programs; to combat disease and ill health; to reduce the incidence of crime and delinquency; to enhance recreational and cultural opportunities; to establish better access between homes and jobs; and generally to improve living conditions for the people who live in such acreas, and to accomplish these objectives through the most effective and economical concentration and coordination of Federal, State, and local public and private efforts to improve the quality of urban life.[13]

State Government and Model Cities

The state of Massachusetts's involvement in Model Cities has been very limited. It has not directly funded Model Cities but has readily passed grants to Boston, particularly HEW money. It has passed special legislation exempting Boston Model Cities employees from the civil service laws, permitting freer choice of neighborhood residents; however, most state contact is based on professional personal ties rather than any formalized institutional arrangements. Paul Parks is particularly competent at negotiating tradeoffs with state officials, but this is made more difficult because there is no single point to bargain with the state. Boston's Model Cities evaluation report states:

> . . . Because of the separation of executive, legislative, and open line operational power, there is no single effective point at which CDA can approach the state. The state coordinating unit, the Department of Community Affairs

[DCA], has been able to offer little more than peripheral technical assistance, a commodity needed far less than funds. Most effective relationships have been formed with state agencies already committed to decentralization. Other than Welfare, state agency funding has been either formal (pass through of federal funds) or strategic (to avoid turning back federal money). State operational participation (i.e., Boston State) has been based on the leverage provided by Supplemental funds.

The Model Neighborhood Board in its meeting with the Governor has defined for itself an important advocacy and lobbying role. At the state operational and technical assistance level, the support to be expected of the Department of Community Affairs is minimal; the HUD proposal for formula grant demonstration which would give DCA some leverage on a range of state agencies is bogged down by HUD-HEW rivalry. The emerging interest of the Office of Planning and Program Coordination in Model Cities may provide some leverage for mounting coordinated pressure on state agencies' the planned placement of OPPC within Administration and Finance is an indication the office maybe able to develop significant interagency coordinating capability.[14]

Local Relationships

For the third year the program calls for strengthening relationships with the Boston Redevelopment Authority. The present Memorandum of Understanding is a major innovation in how the city operates in the Model Neighborhood. Planning is carried out by the community; and BRA will not submit developers to its five-member board without approval by the Model Neighborhood Board and the CDA.

The Model Cities staff believes similarly strong relationships exist with the Department of Parks and Recreation, Department of Health and Hospitals, and the Youth Activities Commission. They are trying to develop more effective relationships with the Boston School Department, Housing Inspection Department, and Public Works Department.

Business (with a few exceptions), the church, and civic groups have not had a major impact on the program. Unions and civil service have not been influential and have failed in efforts to bring Model Cities under civil service regulations.

Parks contends that from its inception Boston Model Cities was "billed as a laboratory for citywide changes, not as help for a particular section." But the mayor's staff has been largely responsible for the citywide approach to problems. Parks believes that the changing of institutions can be best accomplished by working with them and in bargaining with officials. Since most institutions operate citywide, he feels the broader approach is justified. "We can't go citywide with the dollars, but we can go citywide with the effectiveness," he says. This means institutional change and "buying into" other agencies with supplemental funds. But he's afraid the city's financial dire needs and special revenue sharing proposals may shift Model Cities attention from institutional change to support of existing programs. The evaluation report explores these attitudes:

> A range of causes are modifying the Model Cities Program's relation to Boston. The change in national program focus, the New Federalism and revenue sharing may well produce some rethinking of the way the model cities program can be used to serve a variety of purposes and needs. The City's fiscal condition will increase the pressure for quickening absorption of CDA programs into the city structure and for the conversion of institutional change oriented activities into service provision. Past CDA practice (re: Summerthing) has already led to the identification in the City Council of Model Cities funds as a ready source for funding "nonessential" programs. Similarly, within the Model Neighborhood community, the effects of First Year reprogramming have reinforced the incorrect perception that CDA is (1) a direct service provider, (2) a broker or grant agency.[15]

Evaluation is a step to institutional change, and this is perhaps why Robert Weinberg, White's former general counsel, believed Model Cities ought to build its evaluative capability much like the Office of Public Service—the city's prime analysis section. Approximately $200,000 of Model Cities funds has been granted to OPS to support this role. The Mayor's Office feels Model Cities should be used more and more as a catalyst to improve ongoing services, as distinct from innovation. Recently, the mayor's staff has been greatly expanded to promote this philosophy.

Citizen Participation

It is difficult to view the effectiveness of citizen participation as something apart from over-all program success and failures. In Boston, the program's ability to deliver services may "give confidence to the people" in ways that conferences and committee meetings cannot. But frustration, rather than any discernible life in morale or increased belief in society's willingness to be equitable, has marked a good deal of the history of the Model Cities Board's efforts.

Development. Groundwork for citizen participation was laid in the poverty program and in earlier renewal planning in Washington Park. Within the Model Cities area are parts of four Community Action Programs or ABCD target areas, each with an elected local Area Planning Action Council (APAC). The APAC administers programs for manpower training, neighborhood youth corps, and Headstart, among others. Initially, APAC acted to recruit for Model Neighborhood participation and planning. Many black community leaders were residents of Washington Park and had been through the citizen participation traumas of urban renewal. Though not Model Neighborhood residents, many took an active interest in shaping the program.

After a summer of planning, a communitywide election was held, with three representatives from each of six subareas chosen to serve two-year terms. This elected board was to be the principal agent for citizen participation in planning and program design. It would work with an extensive network of subarea-level groups. It was widely agreed, however, that a community development corporation would be a necessary part of this participation effort and eventually would supercede the board to operate as a quasi-legal-political agency after Model Cities termination in five years.

Model Neighborhood Board Staff. For its first year, the board received Model Cities funds of $267,000 from HUD and $115,917 from OEO for advocacy planning. The OEO grant helped create a Model Neighborhood Board staff "completely independent of the CDA" to represent the interests of the board and residents. Goals were to create a communication network to make residents of the area aware of Model Cities programs and plans, give technical assistance so plans included resident priorities, and maintain and further develop the policy-making role of the board. (See Chart 7.)

The ordinance gives the board legal authority to review, approve, or reject in whole or in part all Model Cities plans and contracts. It can recommend programs for the area, initiate proposals, and review performance of the Model Cities administrator. If the mayor rejects the board's recommendations for administrator appointee, he must do so publicly, in writing. Disputes are settled through binding arbitration.

A memorandum of understanding between the Redevelopment Authority and the Model Cities Administration also establishes board authority to review all development proposals in the Model Cities area before they go to the BRA board.

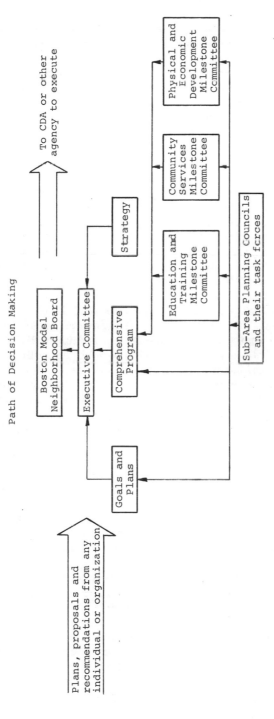

CHART 7

Boston Model Neighborhood Board—Structure-Staff

Path of Decision Making

Plans, proposals and recommendations from any individual or organization

Goals and Plans

Boston Model Neighborhood Board

Executive Committee

Strategy

Comprehensive Program

To CDA or other agency to execute

Education and Training Milestone Committee

Community Services Milestone Committee

Physical and Economic Development Milestone Committee

Sub-Area Planning Councils and their task forces

Note: The Executive Committee receives and logs all plans, proposals or recommendations from whatever source—individuals or organizations. It determines the path of review and decision-making through the Citizen Participation structure. Whatever the starting point of the review, proposals flow only in the direction of the arrows.

Source: Model Cities Administration, City of Boston, 1971.

305

In practice, the board reviews all contracts in the area made by the Model Cities agency (though not by all other city departments), including areas of (1) scope of services, (2) contractor selection, (3) budget, (4) time table, and (5) role of the MNB in monitoring and evaluating plans and programs and the contract. To avoid delays, the board must take action within 21 days after the receipt of each contract or the contract is considered approved. The majority of the board makes confirmed recommendations to the administrator, who either follows them or submits the issue to binding arbitration before three arbitrators, one chosen by the board, one by the administrator, and one by agreement between the board and administrator. A Kirschner Associates report suggests that this "hand on the faucet" role, the power to review all grants in the area using Model Cities funds, is extremely important in establishing the board's primacy among local resident groups.[16]

The board receives funds from the Model Cities Administration and is the operating agent for three programs: (1) Citizen Education, (2) Citizen Evaluation, and (3) School-Community Communications.

1. The Citizen Education Program provides basic staffing for the board. Funded at $667,765 for the third action year, it includes 51 people, the subarea workers and staff for Model Neighborhood Board committees. Interviews with staff members suggest that their role has been a changing one, ranging from handling individual problems to getting out the vote at a board election to lobbying with the city council and state legislature on matters of concern to the board. Citizen education resulted in extensive citizen input into Family Life Center planning and reevaluation of the Police-Community Relations project. This last project was terminated when the board judged that the city's Office of Justice Administration could better handle police-community relations.

2. The Citizen Evaluation Program was funded for $106,000 in the third year. Its staff of six is working closely with the CDA Research and Program Assistance Division to complete a citizen response and opinion survey of the over-all impact of the Model Cities Program, and it will also monitor Model Neighborhood Board programs and subcontracts. Distinct from the board's evaluation program, the CDA Projects Evaluation, Data Collection and Information Systems Program, budgeted in excess of $500,000 annually, is in the process of evaluating the 27 Model Cities programs and developing a real-time information system so that the status of projects can be known at any given time.

3. The School Community Communication program was funded at $153,067 for the third year and had a staff of 14. According to the third action year plan, its goal is "to produce a measurable improvement in the communication between the parents and school personnel in the Model Neighborhood." The plan continues, "Initial difficulties in coordinating program activities through the Boston School

Department forced the program to focus most of its early efforts on establishing good working relationships with the school administration."

Eventually, the program will attempt to form or strengthen parent advisory councils for each of the 12 schools in the Model Neighborhood. Six of these councils are operating now.

Board Membership. Board composition fairly accurately reflects the ethnic makeup of the area, with a little over one-third white membership. In the 1971 election, 10 of the original 18 members were reelected; in the 1972 election more whites and women and fewer original board members were elected. Several former board members who now have jobs with the CDA or board staff resigned because they perceived a conflict of interest in continuing on the board. Jobs held by former board members include director of a family life center, head of the board's evaluation staff, and a principal coordinator in the Community Development Corporation.

Compensation for board members caused a dispute during the first year. Some CDA officials apparently felt that the integrity of independent citizen participation would be compromised by compensation. The dispute was resolved so that board members receive compensation for travel and other expenses like baby-sitting. Most staff now feel that such support for long hours of hard work is essential to sustain the board's effectiveness.

The board has gained sophistication during the past three years. But it has also become increasingly frustrated with delay, bureaucratic red tape, and cumbersome mechanisms of participation itself. However, the quality of the board membership and the sincerity of their effort are seldom, if ever, questioned. "I have never seen more dedication and hard work" comments a community organizer for the board, who has worked with community groups for 20 years. "It is incredible that they have the stamina" she says, commenting on members who come to meetings directly from overtime work or after feeding a large family of small children and bringing their own sandwich supper in a brown paper bag.

The board is described by nearly all observers as a "conservative body," no place for radicals and even those close to the center. "They have to be sold on radical ideas," says a CDA staff member, who feels that this conservative impact is a useful check on CDA proposals. The board rhetoric is careful; it seldom criticizes city government or the CDA directly or publicly. The most frequent outbursts—in print—have been against the federal government and, quite specifically, the Nixon Administration for its southern (and nonurban) strategy, emphasis on the state role in funding, and "cynical lack of support" for the Model Cities effort and other programs aiding the inner city.

It seems that board members do not see themselves as innovators, but as watchdogs, making sure that programs incorporate features crucial to the community. Perhaps more important, they see themselves as a lobby group for funding and as a builder of political strength for the area. During the 1972 election year, for example, members participated actively in a voter registration drive and sponsored a well-attended candidates' night for residents. They have organized energetic letter-writing campaigns and personal visits to elected representatives—Senators Edward Brooke and Edward Kennedy and Representative John McCormack. Board members took Governor Francis Sargent on a guided tour of the area's housing, open space, and traffic problems, showing him where state funds could be used.

Resident Employment. Along with its other functions, the board sees itself as a granter of jobs for community residents. It frequently equates citizen participation with "green power" and employment for residents. "Community participation means neighborhood youth getting summer jobs," says a board editorial.

Resident training and employment programs have been a focal point of board and CDA concern, reinforced from HUD regulations (CDA letter 11) emphasizing the importance of these issues. However, the greatest potential for employment may still be the "Boston Plan," negotiated with construction unions in 1969 to place 2,000 minority workers in the construction trades over a five-year period. Although it has favored the Boston Plan, Model Cities' role appears to be minimal. Those involved in the administration of the plan are unable to give any specific examples of Model Cities participation nor are they certain of Paul Parks's position in its implementation. The Mayor's Office contract compliance officer points out that the plan has recently been rejected in the black community and that the apparent ambivalence of the CDA is a response to community pressure for a more sweeping approach to the problems of black employment.

Other Model Cities area manpower efforts seem more successful. Summer employment opportunities for teen-agers have been substantial, with earlier programs such as Neighborhood Youth Corps being integrated with funds from the Federal Interim Assistance Program. Close to 1,000 local young people were part of the 1970 and 1971 summer work program.

Resident employment with the CDA, directly or on a contract basis, is substantial. Dr. Samuel Thompson, deputy administrator, estimates that nearly 500 residents are employed directly or indirectly through Model Cities. Recruitment in the area has been stressed for Model Cities staff as well as programs under contract. The Blue Hill Christian Center and NICE, Inc. have contracted with Model Cities to operate child care centers and will also operate—in cooperation with the Welfare Department—an early childhood development center. Resident training as day-care staff is a goal for all three centers.

Similar training and employment programs are part of nearly all Model Cities programs, though the number of residents involved has been small. Three programs attempt to open employment opportunities with city agencies. Residents have been employed as rehabilitation finance specialists and as community planners and planning aides through a grant for two programs from the Department of Community Affairs. Twelve residents were trained as city service inspectors and transferred to the Housing Inspection Department.

With initiation of the Family Life Center Program, 20 residents were trained as family health workers, paraprofessional positions. While this promises to be an important source of training, the delay in getting all of the centers started has held back original plans to train 20 such aides each year.

Stress on resident employment has meant that even programs not specifically designed to include training have been sources of employment. The 43 resident interviewers for an extensive service delivery study received "good training in social science interview techniques," says the program director, Mary Davidson. She reported that after their work on her project, many were employed by local consulting firms like ABT, OSTI, and Trans-century as interviewers.

Within the CDA, staff development and skill upgrading are emphasized. Again, numbers involved are fairly small. Of 16 clerical employees enrolled, 11 successfully completed a secreterial course that "raised their skill levels substantially," reports the CDA evaluation department. Approximately 100 CDA staff have used tuition reimbursement programs to take courses at 20 local educational institutions. Most observers see Model Cities as effective in providing job skills.

A program to train eight urban planners (course and field work on urban development agency) under contract with Boston University will help meet the shortage of trained planners from the local community.

Employment After Model Cities. A Community Development Corporation (CDC), a private, nonprofit corporation responsive to Model Cities residents, is envisioned by Model Cities planners as a key part of overall program effort and essential to continuation of program goals at the end of the five-year demonstration period. Despite the fact that planning for the CDC began in the first program year, the contract for funds was not signed until September 16, 1970. The third action year plan comments, "After two years of negotiating, the fact of program operation is in itself an achievement."

The CDC is viewed by the board as a way of sustaining resident participation in the Model Cities area and has been supported in several issues of its newspaper. The board linked the delay in funding to the

Nixon Administration's "hypocritical rhetoric" about community economic self-determination, describing its own view of the CDC:

> Recently, the Boston Model Neighborhood Board took a
> significant step toward establishing a community run eco-
> nomic base in this area by organizing a CDC to serve as
> the focus for housing and business development in the
> Boston Model Cities. Potentially, the CDC is the most
> important activity in the entire catalogue of Model Cities
> programs. When Model Cities is officially phased out
> after five years, it is envisioned that the CDC will remain
> to carry out business development, employment and hous-
> ing construction programs . . . the areas where concrete
> results are most visible.
>   Once the CDC is funded, it will begin operations. It
> will initiate and operate its own programs, act as a prime
> contractor working with community organizations, coor-
> dinate with existing programs. Profits generated in these
> three areas will be used for expansion of the functions of
> the CDC, eventually to the point where the CDC is com-
> pletely self-supporting and no longer dependent on federal
> funds.
>   Within this context, the CDC will operate programs
> of business investment and brokerage, industrial and
> franchise developer, site acquisition, leasing and mainte-
> nance, manpower development and training and insurance
> underwriting. These programs will be financing, legal
> services, public relations and providing community organi-
> zation specialists in Model Cities Neighborhoods to coor-
> dinate CDC programs with other community needs.
>   The issues of community control with respect to the
> CDC is highlighted by the Model Neighborhood Board's
> decision to appoint four of its own members to the CDC
> Board. This decision . . . throws the issues of community
> control squarely into the laps of Federal officials.

HUD delayed approval of the CDC plan because of a dispute
centering on the appointment of four Model Neighborhood Board members as CDC directors. HUD felt that this overlap was a potential
conflict of interest, despite the mayor's support for this plan. To his
local constituency, Paul Parks said that a "subtle review in Washington
of the Model Cities program had resulted in a reversal of policy on
the local control of Model Cities projects" (December 1969).
      The CDC that emerged in autumn of the following year (1970)
named neighborhood residents other than board members to serve as
directors.

The board's goals for the CDC, as reflected in the editorial, are extremely ambitious—and 1973's program is modest in comparison. The CDC will focus on developing small locally based companies in sanitation and transportation, to concentrate employment services and cash flow in the community. The CDC has been granted $700,000 for the two-year period.

Evaluation of the CDC is difficult because of its short period of operation. It got off to a very slow start and, as it involved one of the most protracted funding disputes with Washington, was clearly a source of disappointment and frustration to the board and CDA.

Effectiveness of the Board. Real competition for a seat on the Model Neighborhood Board is rare, and few incumbents have been ousted. Turnout for the 1971 election was slightly lower than in previous years, with greater participation in those subareas where there were several candidates for board seats. Staff effort to get out the vote accounts for some of the variation.

In only one instance has a group attempted to win control of the board. A black activist organization, RAP, attempted to win board seats in subarea 2 in 1969. "They lost," says a CDA staff member, "because they scared everyone . . . older blacks, most whites, and especially the hippies, who voted 85 to 0 against them." Although, as a group they lost, one of its members won a seat.

Relations with the poverty program have been good from the start. Contradictory program guidelines (for example, for income eligibility) have caused some confusion. There is considerable over-lap in committee membership, and program coordination is weak; however, the Model Neighborhood Board supports Area Planning Action Council programs and lends assistance where possible.

Most of the area's more militant groups see the board as part of the "establishment" and give it little attention. Paradoxically, CDA staff has given help to groups like the Black Panthers and the National Welfare Rights Organization by such activities as printing literature and lobbying for their interests. Most community leaders not on the board or involved with Model Cities are "doing their own thing," frequently with Model Cities funds. "Model Cities is the Permanent Charities for this area," said one CDA staff member. "We have funded nearly every visible organization—Center for Inner City Change, etc." He stressed that this was not a strategy to buy off opposition or co-opt groups, but rather, that funding a few groups seemed to create good results and so it was continued. He says the feeling among those groups was "don't jump aboard," just stay out there and use the resources as they are given out.

Langely Keyes, former director of housing for Model Cities and the author of a book about citizen participation in Boston's urban

311

renewal projects, comments, "The remarkable thing is that Board decisions have an aura of sanctity. The legitimacy of the decisions is never questioned. For example, the board strongly supported the Infill housing program, a scattered site program for large, low-income families, and that stand was accepted as community sentiment." Keyes believes the electoral process is important in that it legitimizes the board and its decisions—but so has a city ordinance, adopted by the city council, giving the board substantial powers.

The board has an impact on the planning and operation of Model Cities programs. "This is a Greek democracy," said one CDA staff member, "and we don't budge without going to the Board." He says he frequently holds back plans and proposals if he knows the lack provisions to meet consistent board concerns. He comments that the review process means a planner must do his homework, know his program and test its assumptions. Another CDA staff member says the conservative tenor of the board is useful in keeping proposals realistic.

A housing developer made a similar comment, pointing out that the board and its subarea committees are good at pointing to the real needs of the area. For example, in a proposal made for a $3 million housing complex, the board response was to ask that space be set aside for a day care center. The developer said that if the board could get a group to run the center, the plan could include the space. "A developer must meet their challenges," he says.

The board introduces many community concerns to housing programs, insisting, for example, that a "developer's working agreement" for all contracts requires a relocation plan guaranteeing that present tenants of housing to be rehabilitated will be treated well and that local workers will be used. Several developers say prior approval by a subarea committee is a "good community check."

There is frustration by the cumbersome structure. "Sometimes you have to go through five committees," a developer says, but adds that the structure "is good, responsive to the needs of the community. I hate to deal with them, but I know that they are doing a service."

Most persons close to the program agree on the importance of the board's role as a check, a guarantee that community concerns are incorporated into proposals. The board has made sure that many governmental programs in the Model Cities area (like Urban Beautification and Interim Assistance program) are being implemented according to board desires. The board has had a say in the location of facilities and in certain contract provisions.

Despite agreement that the board is active, there is considerable disagreement about its over-all effectiveness. This disagreement is in part a result of the variety of definitions and range of goals that people have for "effective citizen participation."

The Kirschner Associates report relates, "The Board has not played a significant role in securing changes in the original goals and substance of the Model Cities program policies."17 Moreover, it has had little real effect on program priorities. The board has consistently chosen housing and economic development as its key concerns, yet over-all program stress has been on the Family Life Centers and health care. "These are someone else's priorities," says a board staff member who believes Paul Parks's personal interest is in health care delivery systems. But the Family Life Centers have turned out to be the most effective and well-groomed program. Housing and economic development are still major priorities but have been caught in unusual local and federal delays.

Model Cities Programs

The budgets and client figures for the programs listed below are for the second action year, except when otherwise indicated.

Community Services

Several important and interesting programs are operated under the Division of Community Services.

1. Family Life Center. Most people believe this is the single most successful program of all Model Cities projects. It is a program where considerable time and money has been concentrated and is always the first item mentioned in local Model Cities literature.

The Family Life Center budget was $1,052,239, excluding $30,000 for mental health services, $133,068 for speech and hearing clinical facilities, and $211,385 for "Information and Evaluation," which provides social service counseling, referral, outreach and evaluation of social services. About one-third of the total Model Cities budget is spent here.

"The Family Life Centers were established so that any Model Neighborhood resident could get many different kinds of service under one roof," a Model Cities brochure informs readers. "Each Center is designed to meet family health needs and to help solve other kinds of difficulties such as finding a good job or better housing. All services are free to area residents."

Assistant Administrator for Community Services Charles Beard, says, "The Centers put medical care in its proper relationship to total family needs. This is one place where you can deal with a headache and the anxiety that causes the headache and the employment problem that causes the anxiety in a simple, coordinated fashion. We expect that in the long run we will be able to provide a higher quality care and keep the population much healthier than other models because we are able to deal with the total spectrum of problems."

Two Family Life Centers have been opened, and a third is about to open. Center One began in a group of large mobile trailers in a church parking lot and now operates from the basement of the Lady of Lourdes Church. It provides adult medicine, pediatrics, obstetrics, gynecology, social service assistance, mental health, speech and hearing treatment, and drug counseling. Its budget was $439,442, including a $71,080 contract for in-patient and speciality care for patients without insurance. A $998,000 HUD Neighborhood Facilities Grant has been awarded to build a permanent structure.

In its first two years of operation, the center, which opened in May 1970, had a case load of 100 patients a week and 30 registered families. It services an area of 10,000 persons. Medical backup service is provided by Beth Israel Hospital, but a contract had not been signed by the third action year because of debate over third-party payments. The hospital was reluctant to make a complete commitment and to be financially responsible for all patients seen at a Family Life Center; however, hospital administrators have tried to treat patients to the best of their ability and resources.

Family Life Center Two, the Mary E. Mahoney Center, opened in February 1971 in a remodeled building near a major commercial center in Roxbury. The weekly case load is 75 to 100 patients, with a registration of 472 families. The area served is 10,000 persons. Its budget was $519,042, including a $16,000 contract for pharmacy support services.

A contract has been signed with the Peter Bent Brigham Hospital for back-up facilities. The hospital holds the clinic license and collects whatever third-party payments it can at both the center and the hospital. Model Cities has agreed to cover uncollectable accounts on a year-to-year basis.

A third Family Life Center is expected to be opened with Boston City Hospital providing back-up services. A CDA-submitted $131,000 National Institute of Mental Health (NIMH) staffing grant has been awarded to Boston State Hospital to help staff the mental health component of this center. The other three Model Cities subareas are now serviced by the Roxbury Comprehensive Community Health Center (funded by OEO) with Boston University providing back-up services.

Central administrative and planning staff for the Family Life Centers consists of five professionals and two clerical positions. Center operating staff consists of 51 medical, paramedical, and allied health personnel—specifically, 2 medical directors, 11 physicians, with pediatric, gynecological, and internal medicine specializations. There are also eight nurses, two nurse practitioners, 11 family health workers, a corpsman, four medical records specialists, two medical secretaries, a medical assistant, two lab technicians, two dentists, two dental hygienists, two dental secretaries, and two dental assistants.

In addition there is a consultant contract for $8,920 with the Havard Medical School laboratory of community psychiatry to provide "coordination and evaluation of mental health services at the Family Life Centers."

Beard believes that Family Life Centers have been most successful in meeting a defined need and in creating a model both of cooperation between public and private sectors and of training and creative use of community people. "Willingness of institutions to cooperate" is a prime reason for the success, Beard suggests.

> They've all been supportive. We had use of physicians during the planning stage to work out design problems, equipment problems. We had several young doctors in this program in leadership positions.
>
> Their attitude has been much more progressive than traditional ones. The result is an eagerness to get feedback about the quality and style of health care. They're interested in how to coordinate medical care with other kinds of care. . . . Everybody has bent a little really. The social service team has been willing to work closely with physicians and physicians I think have new perspectives. They're seeing the sociological symptoms of illness as well as the physical.

Federal officials have praised the health centers and the advances made in the delivery of health care. "I was tremendously impressed with the efficient and dedicated service being rendered at these institutions," the regional director of HEW stated in January 1971 about health delivery in the Roxbury area.

Paul Parks believes the new class of trained Model Cities professionals is making a positive impact on the medical profession. But he also states that there are still philosophical differences between social service teams and physicians, making relationships less than smooth. And although quality and comprehensiveness of service are high, attendance is low. Only one-third the anticipated number were registered by the end of the second action year, and even less used the facilities regularly. The Model Cities staff as well as the mayor's staff have been frustrated by their inability to encourage more residents to use this high-quality, free service. However, by the end of the third action year, clients increased considerably, and it appeared the program was on a path to success.

2. Another interesting program under Community Services is the Council of Elders, Inc., which operates five Senior Action Centers

throughout the Model Neighborhood, to provide services for the elderly. Among these are 20 "Home Aides" to "do housekeeping, shop, run errands, and provide company." There is a Nutrition Project that prepares and delivers hot metals to homes and a "program to train elderly residents as geriatric aides." The budget was $319,886, and it served about 600 residents. Its former director, Jack Leff, was appointed to a new state cabinet post, secretary for Elderly, by Governor Sargent in 1972.

    3. Also under Community Services is the Blue Hill Christian Center, which runs a day-care center for 92 Model Cities children from ages three to five. An Early Childhood Demonstration Center and day-care center with a budget of $147,603 to be run by NICE was still in development stage. Citywide interagency cooperation resulted in a procedure manual for day-care center start-up and operation, a local Coordinated Community Day Care Association, and development of a communitywide Inner City Day Care Council. Coordination, as a result of Model Cities efforts, has reached an above-average level of success in day care.

Housing. A major priority of the Model Neighborhood Board is housing. Several programs were in progress in the second action year:

    1. About 719 units of housing rehabilitation are "in the pipeline." Liberal use has been made of leased housing and rent supplements, the only programs that can bring rental levels down to a price people in the Model Cities area can afford. However, tax shelters have been the primary lure for large developers.

    2. Housing Innovations, Inc., a black-owned firm, is building 94 infill wood frame housing units of two, three, four, five, and six bedrooms on vacant city-owned land. DCA Development Corporation is building another 56 units of infill, using prefabricated concrete with brick veneer.

    3. Brunswick Gardens is a 129-unit development using the FHA 236 program. Originally a 221(d) (3) development that had faltered, as had many other 221(d) (3) projects because of high construction costs in Boston's sandy soil, it was given an injection of $10,000 in Model Cities money for engineering costs, and the city also picked up part of the cost of site improvements. With this public assistance, the development was resurrected, and construction was to be completed in late 1972.

    4. In the Campus High School Urban Renewal Area, 400 units of housing will be built by Lower Roxbury Community Corporation. The Boston Redevelopment Authority has given the neighborhood sponsoring group approval, and there is a preliminary FHA 236 allocation. Construction is expected to begin in the fall of 1972.

5. In 1970, the Boston Model Cities area became eligible for granting 312 loans and 115 grants, which cover the rehabilitation of homes. About 10 applications per month are being made but comparatively few processed. No federal funds have been made available yet. For this program Model Cities trained nine area residents to work as rehabilitation specialists.

6. Two Survey and Planning grants for small urban renewal projects totaling 250 units have been approved by HUD. A $100,000 absentee homeownership rehabilitation grant will be initiated to supplement repair costs.

7. In addition, Model Cities provides a wide range of homeownership counseling for low- and moderate-income families as well as tenant counseling and organizing, and there is also a referral service for renters.

At least two major constraints severely circumscribe any large-scale housing programs. First, "effective demand," the ability of large numbers of Model Cities residents to pay for housing, is considerably lower than in Boston as a whole. More people have low incomes. In a report written for the Model Cities Agency by Justin Gray Associates,[18] it is pointed out that 35 percent of the households in the Model Neighborhood have incomes under $3,000 a year; 39 percent range from $3,000 to $6,000; 19 percent $6,000 to $10,000; and 6 percent more than $10,000. "A clear and critical need exists in the Model Cities area for housing at very low costs—under $65 monthly rent," the report says. Among current needs for housing in this price bracket, it lists at least 2,000 one-bedroom units, half for elderly households, and at least 1,750 new two-or three-bedroom units.

Secondly, as the property tax increases, the incentive to maintain rental housing in good condition decreases because investment income is lower. Also a fear of reassessment among property owners makes them reluctant to put money into improving their properties.

The Justin Gray report says that

the amount of rental income produced by property [in Model Cities] simply is not sufficient to provide adequate maintenance—incomes are too low and housing costs are too high. The problem is aggravated as property changes hands since the seller tries to make a profit and new-mortgages are more expensive so that even more of an already limited rental income is drawn off into debt retirement, and less, if any, is left for repairs.

The Boston Model Cities area includes some 350 city blocks and 17,302 dwelling units. The housing stock is primarily two- and three-family frame buildings with "the majority . . . badly dilapidated."

Because of lack of resident income, lack of incentives to developers and private owners, limited amount of city revenue, and constraints of federal subsidies, it would seem unlikely that there can, in the foreseeable future, be a comprehensive upgrading in the housing stock in the Model Neighborhood area. New federal initiatives and resources are needed.

City Services. City services fall under the Physical Planning and Economic Development Division. Programs for the second action year included the following:

1. Training was completed and employment found for 12 neighborhood residents as city housing inspectors.

2. A rodent control survey was made over a 147-square-block area. Some 13,000 copies of a rodent control handbook were distributed, 5,000 in Spanish.

3. A pilot program to test plastic bags was begun. Some 100,000 plastic garbage bags were provided to 2,000 families to see if there was improvement in garbage collection and rodent control.

4. A parks and recreation program for all ages was conducted with several local community agencies. Long-range plans include implementation of a master plan for recreation and park maintenance. A first step has been the development of a plan to decentralize the city's Park and Recreation Department.

5. An Economic Planning and Development project, conducted through the independent Community Development Corporation, will establish community-based sanitation companies and a local busing service. A program to establish a revolving loan account to assist local contractors in obtaining bonds and equity money is also under development.

The goal of city services is to increase the level of services and use local people as much as possible. One constraint has been that most city departments do not have a planning capacity to receive Model Cities input intelligently or plan and implement new projects.

"They don't really look at how their departments service neighborhoods in terms of dollars and men," a Model Cities official says. "Therefore, it is difficult to get your hands on how to improve the service. Aside from that, most departments have poor equipment that breaks down and they don't have money for repairs."

The Model Cities agency has recently hired a graduate civil engineer who will work in the city's Public Works Department as engineering planner for the Model Neighborhood area. This engineer should help the department's planning capacity.

Education and Training: 1. Under Education and Training, the most visibly effective program has been "Talent Search" or Educational

318

Counseling. Four counselors provide assistance for high school students on procedures for filing college applications and obtaining financial aid. Over three years, more than 1,000 students have been enrolled in colleges who most likely would not have gone without this assistance. Model Cities prepared and received the $102,000 grant from the Office of Education.

2. A $358,543 (third action year) Higher Education program offers college level courses to about 300 neighborhood residents in mathematics, science, social sciences, and communications. There are no entrance requirements and no charges for books or registration. The only requirement is "motivation and ability to learn." Sixty-five of these students have transferred to Boston-area colleges under the auspices of this program in two and one-half years.

3. Adult Education, under a contract with the New Urban League, provides courses in basic literacy for adults who want high school diplomas or for Spanish-speaking residents who want to learn English. Also special-interest courses such as karate, typing, and sewing classes are provided under this contract. Model Cities cost for adult education is $216,606, with an additional $70,000 from HEW for special projects involving tutoring and Spanish courses for mothers.

4. There is also a program aimed at "children with learning problems." Some $31,000 was used to evaluate "the quality of special education in the public school system" and the referral of Model Neighborhood residents to agencies dealing with retarded children.

5. The $451,946 Youth Development program, in cooperation with several agencies, provided 200 summer jobs for Model Neighborhood teen-agers, developed a summer camp, "Youth in Summer Motion," for 1,000 youth on Cape Cod (Otis Air Force Base), and established "teen centers" used by 150 teen-agers.

Also a successful Youth-Tutoring-Youth program is operated in cooperation with the Boston School Department. And a grant from HEW's Juvenile Delinquency Administration will fund a Street Academy to provide educational services to youth.

Dr. Barbara Jackson, assistant administrator for education and training, believes that programs for adults have been the most visibly successful. They have been catalytic in building concern about urban problems in a consortium of colleges that have started adults in college courses, changed curricula, made credit-granting policies more flexible, and united for the first time in providing unusual service to the community. Dr. Jackson says, "Success of this program is an important inroad for institutional change."

The Start of Citywide Decentralization

Although Boston is not one of the 20 cities chosen by HUD in the Planned Variations Program, it is proceeding on its own to implement some of the program's principles.

A major component of Planned Variations is its citywide approach. Early in his first term, Mayor White created 14 Little City Halls in all areas of the city to receive citizen requests and improve the delivery of services. He was perhaps the first in the nation to decentralize a number of city services on a communitywide basis, in spite of considerable criticism from some city council members and citizens about the program's costs.

In 1970, Mayor White requested Little City Hall managers to help create community councils in all sections of the city. However, development has been slow, and not much authority has been given the councils. Six are now functioning in a limited fashion; others are being developed. Methods for selection of members vary, and their powers are still being debated, but it appears they will have a voice in local planning decisions and elements of the city budget affecting their areas.

The Home Rule Commission strongly recommended steps toward major city government administrative and political decentralization as an essential prerequisite to responsive delivery of city services. It recommended establishment of districts citywide and the election of district councils. The councils would set local priorities and be involved in the annual executive budget-making process. The commission felt this was only an initial stage in what may be a long process of developing community self-government in Boston. The proposals are still under discussion. And both the state legislature and city council must approve such recommendations for them to take effect.

Along with decentralization, the commission also recommended greater centralization of power in the mayor's office, to tighten control over independent agencies. The A-95 coordinating and review process of federal grants, together with Annual Arrangements—designed to match more realistically the availability of federal funds to local priorities—should strengthen the mayor's office. The mayor has also, after some discharges and upgrading of staff, reinforced the professional capacity of his office in order to increase the effectiveness of departments and agencies, to integrate Model Cities with city functions, and to improve the city's Management Information and Systems process. In addition, a citywide model for a computerized information, program funding, and coordination system was under development in 1972, designed to go beyond the life of the CDA.

Analysis and Recommendations

To understand more clearly the role of Model Cities in relationship to city government, we have had to look at Boston's politics and bureaucracy. The principal objectives of Boston Model Cities—to improve the quality of services delivered to the entire community and to develop measures to make a larger portion of the Model Neighborhood population self-supporting—are very much related to local government responsiveness. To a large extent, local politics and a reluctant bureaucracy have slowed progress in this program. Model Cities has put together a competent staff and a number of effective programs in an attempt to crack the bureaucracy. In spite of this, the newness of programs combined with general staff inexperience and low client participation have cut into efficiency— not unlike many other Model Cities communities. But progress has been made, and the future looks bright. There is evidence of institutional change and more self-supporting residents. In addition, the Model Cities process has generated new concepts and has improved coordination among agencies.

The Government

On the other hand, since Boston has limited local powers, a regressive and inelastic tax structure, and little influence areawide, a broader approach may be necessary to solve its problems. Its population is only 23 percent of the metropolitan area; it relies heavily on the property tax for city financing, yet 50 percent of its land is tax exempt; and the state government retains control not only over the city's sources of revenue but also over job categories and recruitment of its personnel.

State revenue sharing for municipalities based on need and a more equitable distribution of metropolitan taxes (much like the St. Paul-Minneapolis distribution to local communities of 40 percent of the metropolitan area's property taxes from new commercial and industrial development) are needed to improve Boston's economic base and make its tax structure more attractive to businesses. Granting the city other revenue sources— such as a local income tax—would alleviate further pressures on the property tax. Despite belief by some political theorists that local governments can raise sufficient revenues, federal revenue sharing is needed in larger percentages in this wicked jungle of special tax districts and deteriorating neighborhoods. In addition, metropolitan solutions to housing and school integration are necessary for long-term neighborhood stabilization and community confidence. Housing must be made available to all income groups on a regional basis, and educational integration must be achieved without destroying viable neighborhoods.

The city's inability to make any significant inroads into developing merit procedures in the civil service system has resulted primarily from both regressive state civil service laws and a poorly administered civil service commission. Improved work rules, deemphasis on seniority and veterans' preference, progressive merit pay and bonuses, and improved recruitment and promotional methods are all necessary. It is essential that local officials be given the authority to determine municipal salaries, but it is equally important that elected officials be unafraid to impress upon employees the demands of citizens for high service and productivity. Neighborhood councils, the League of Women Voters, Chamber of Commerce, Model Cities, Community Action, and other groups should be just as insistent about achieving quality government. The mayor and city council need to inspire better employee performance, something organizational structure and procedures cannot do alone. Moreover, they will have to do this regardless of political repercussions, or it may never get done.

Model Cities

Civil Service and Model Cities. Model Cities has made some progress in improving service quality. It has dented the civil service bureaucracy by convincing the state civil service to grant employment preference to Model Neighborhood residents by liberalizing the civil service rules. However, such preferential treatment has largely been inspired by federal regulation, which helped to convince the state commission to modify its law. On the other hand, Model Cities has not been as successful in convincing the Police Department and School Committee to change their hiring policies, but neither has it sufficiently emphasized these changes.

There has been some attempt to use Model Cities funds to supplement city salaries and provide work incentives. However, it appears clear that there should be more extensive use of Model Cities funds for this purpose and also some funds used as a catalyst in city departments for the initiation of performance rating, increased productivity, and progressive hiring practices. In addition (using examples of the Model Personnel Ordinance of the National Civil Service League and other progressive personnel systems), Boston Model Cities might sponsor citywide personnel educational forums and help draft a local model personnel ordinance for consideration by the state legislature.

Health Care. The program that has elicited the most praise and attention and perhaps has had the greatest effect on local institutions is the health delivery system. This health center concept of relating individual medical problems to total social needs of the family is commendable. The Mary E. Mahoney Family Life Center, for example, is located conveniently for residents, well maintained, and fully staffed with employment, social, and family counselors as well as health specialists. Facilities and staff reception are excellent. Attendance for the first year of operation was only one-third of that anticipated; however, it has been progressively climbing. Attendance for all centers increased from 18,000 in 1971 to 68,000 in 1972. Greater commitment from hospitals and physicians would add to the program's prestige and would very likely increase attendance.

In addition, elected officials need to show greater concern about health care delivery. White has demonstrated innovation and citywide concern through his Little City Halls Program, and he has shifted service emphasis from business interests to the disadvantaged; yet, in the past, he did not devote enough attention to the Model Cities Program and health care, for example. Possibly, elected officials, in general, would participate more fully in Model Cities if programs stressed citywide involvement. In Boston's case, White could very well stress Model Neighborhood institutional innovation in health care delivery on a citywide basis, particularly since some of these innovations are now being used in other health centers in the city. It takes an in-depth involvement on the part of the mayor to effect coordination and innovation in health care delivery, as well as other human resource programs. We have reached the point where city officials need to feel that health care is as important as street maintenance or garbage collection. The mayor, for example, might initiate a legally supported, citywide health care committee with representation from the Model Neighborhood Board, other residents, hospitals, medical and nursing groups, and other appropriate bodies, in order to coordinate activities and find a common ground for agreement and solution. In 1972, the mayor began to play an increasingly stronger role in these programs.

Education for Adults. The second most successful set of programs is in adult education. These programs have made inroads in institutional change, particularly by arousing interest from a consortium of colleges in urban problems. The consortium has enrolled adults in college courses, changed curriculums, eased credit-granting policies, and, for the first time, united together to solve problems. In 1972, nearly 100 adults were placed in college, taking college-level courses, or received high school diplomas.

Other Projects. Other successful projects involve centers for senior citizens, day care, and youth. New and rehabilitated housing has been provided, housing inspectors have been trained, pilot programs in refuse collection and rodent control have been initiated, and planning assistance has been provided for some city departments. Thousands of residents use Model Cities centers and play areas. Model Neighborhood Board members have received extensive education in government processes, and Model Neighborhood residents have reached a higher level of understanding of community problems and solutions. The School Community Communication program has established greater parental involvement in school affairs and better working relationships with the school administration. Moreover, when one considers Model Cities as a manpower program in itself and that over 500 residents are employed directly or indirectly by it, it can be called an important source of new leadership and economic well-being.

Not as successful is the partnership school concept, which was developed as a pilot project to achieve racial balance but has not been accepted by the School Committee. Perhaps even less successful is the Boston job plan, which has placed few minority members in construction trades. From the beginning, Model Cities decided to tread lightly in the construction jobs arena because it did not want to disturb progress in other areas. Over-all, Boston's Model Cities Program has only dented the vast bureaucracy.

Citizen Participation. The most significant institutional change has occurred in involvement of citizens in the decision-making process and enlightenment of residents about city problems and solutions. The Boston Partnership Arrangement certainly is one of the strongest Model Cities components in the nation. (Comparable in strength is Dayton's Equal Partnership concept, but it is perhaps less enduring because it has largely functioned outside existing institutions, a situation making permanent change difficult.) Paul Parks attributes its strength to the fact that Model Cities operates within the system. White has sanctioned its efforts by taking steps to integrate Model Cities staff and regular city staff to work together for institutional change. Moreover, Boston's plan is legally backed by city ordinance, declaring that whenever a majority of the board makes a confirmed recommendation, the administrator must follow that recommendation or submit the issue to binding arbitration. So far, it has been unnecessary to use arbitration. Furthermore, the mayor and city council have not turned back any substantive board recommendations.

This combination of genuine and responsible citizen participation has created a feeling in the Model Neighborhood that democratic principles exist and that residents have an important voice, not only over their own lives and neighborhood but over citywide issues, too. The board has received substantial legitimacy in the Model Neighborhood and has found new leadership and courage in neighborhood people, as well as creating an improved image of the system. On the other hand, citizens in certain other neighborhoods have been outspokenly concerned about the attention and money focused in the Model Neighborhood. White's citywide Little City Halls Program and its limited resources have not been enough to satisfy all residents. Indeed, there is the realization that changes will be limited without wider participation and even greater concern about communitywide involvement.

Target Area vs. Citywide Concern. The Model Cities target area approach appears not to have had much success in creating institutional changes. Any lasting effects will mostly likely come about by mobilizing the entire city.

This is true of citizen participation. Consideration should be given to the strengthening of other citizen boards much like the Model Neighborhood Board; otherwise, confrontations may continue. For example, much of the $1 million budgeted for staffing the Model Neighborhood Board and for citizen education could more effectively serve the objectives of better service delivery and institutional change by developing citizen participation structures citywide. Under revenue sharing, the city would be encouraged to go in this direction anyway. Moreover, the existing citywide Little City Halls Program could be used as a basis for expansion. Limited staffing of an additional 13 community boards (plus the existing Little City Halls staffs of four or five each), paying expenses of members to attend monthly meetings, and absorbing miscellaneous costs could be accomplished with about $600,000 of present Model Cities or Community Development funds. Parenthetically, such a reallocation of funds and change in objectives would bring the city much closer to the decentralization proposals of the Home Rule Commission.

A citywide program would not have to be imposed at the expense of the Model Neighborhood. With few exceptions, present Model Cities funds could still be used in the target area. However, if Model Cities wishes to achieve its institutional goals, it should take a lead in citywide decentralization by sharing some of its funds. Sharing decision-making with citizens on use of revenue sharing funds and present city monies could be the beginning of a program for the new councils. But much stronger commitment from the mayor and city council is needed. An ordinance establishing the rights of citywide councils should be adopted.

In short, Model Cities in Boston has created an appreciation for quality service and a feeling that such service can be achieved. It has recognized that meaningful and lasting institutional changes cannot be made without the help of the mayor and city council; and the mayor realizes that citizen support is necessary to effect change. The elements of this teamwork are about ripe. With the addition of city council to the team, it can work.

Comprehensiveness. Program comprehensiveness should be pursued; at the same time, a much broader client impact needs to be made. Although significant numbers of residents are affected in health care, housing, rodent control, and recreation, most citizens do not feel program impact because projects touch only a small number of people— 600 senior citizens, 92 day-care children, about 300-400 in adult education, and so on. Model Cities is comprehensive in scope but not in numbers served, so the desires of the great bulk of residents go unfulfilled. The problem primarily is the need for additional resources.

This failure to make an impressive impact, this tendency toward smallness, has been a principal fault of Model Cities all over the country. The fault lies primarily with the original federal mandate, which set an impossible objective: to solve all problems and to create a Model Neighborhood with limited funds. The actual projects fall far short of the model; therefore, citizens have become disenchanted. And yet, in another sense, this mandate to solve all problems has been a strength, for it has forced officials to look at all agencies and achieve some degree of coordination and stimulation. With these initial first years in the background, it is appropriate to continue comprehensive planning, coordination of agencies, and experimentation with pilot projects. At the same time, the bulk of funds needs to be placed in several major projects to effect meaningful impact in at least a few areas.

For example, one drug center serving 25 people and a limited drug-abuse education program cannot create sufficient target area impact. Hopefully, such a demonstration would lead to larger resources and a more comprehensive program. But since funds are limited, the community has to be more selective in choosing priorities—even though some projects might suffer. On the other hand, the whole of Model Cities may suffer if service impact is not felt and communitywide effects are not achieved.

Boston Model Cities has had some important achievements. More than ever, Mayor White is involved in the program. Paul Parks has developed a competent staff. The mayor and Model Neighborhood Board have achieved an enviable record of cooperation and successful citizen participation. In fact, Boston may be a proving ground in this respect. And if Model Cities spreads its influence citywide, continues to pursue institutional change, and increases the city's management capacity to deal with human resource and Model Cities principles, it need not fear revenue sharing. Local officials, for example, now realize that CDC, the Community Development Corporation, cannot develop the capacity to carry on Model Cities objectives without significant federal or state funding. Block grants may be necessary to sustain it. In the meantime, with its limited resources, Boston must choose to deal with several problems more comprehensively rather than too many superficially. Only a national, fully funded urban strategy will allow it to confront all problems.

Notes

1. Alexander Ganz, "The Expanding City of Boston's Economy," Boston Redevelopment Authority, July 1970.

2. Home Rule Commission, Boston Home Rule Commission Report, 1972.

3. Ibid.

4. Eric A. Nordlinger, Decentralizing the City: A Study of Boston's Little City Halls (Boston Urban Observatory, April 1972), pp. 296-298.

5. George J. Washnis, Municipal Decentralization and Neighborhood Resources (New York: Praeger Publishers, September 1972).

6. Nordlinger, op. cit., p. 298.

7. Home Rule Commission, op. cit., p. 40. Subsequent quotations, unless otherwise indicated, are also from various sections of this report.

8. Peter Schrage, Village School Downtown (Boston: Beacon Press, 1967).

9. Home Rule Commission, op. cit.

10. Model Cities Planning Grant Application, Boston Model Cities Program, 1967.

11. Ibid.

12. Division of Research and Program Assistance, Boston Model Cities, Technical Support to Management in the Boston Model Cities Program, Boston, 1971.

13. Model Cities Planning Grant Application, op. cit.

14. Division of Research and Program Assistance, Boston Model Cities, Evaluation Report, Boston, 1971.

15. Ibid.

16. Kirschner Associates, "A Description and Evaluation of Advocacy Planning Programs," January 1971, OEO Contract B89-4558.

17. Ibid., p. 141.

18. Justin Gray Associates, Model Cities Housing Report, Boston Model Cities Program, 1970.

12

The City

The National Center

With all its problems, New York manifests great strength. However, the average person appears to be more familiar with its negative aspects—crime, corruption, neighborhood deterioration, power breakdowns, subway failures, poor city services, strikes, and fiscal problems. The Planning Commission points out that the air is polluted, rivers are fouled, and streets and subways are dirty, noisy, and jammed. Also, there is a severe housing shortage, and the municipal plant needs vast capital improvements. Budget deficits appear each year. Furthermore, the city is paying part of its past operating costs with $640 million in bonds every year—a discrediting fiscal practice. Perhaps the greatest problem is the slums, where the Model Cities Program has focused. Crime and poor health here are double the city averages. And while the city's unemployment reached 5.7 percent in June 1972, unemployment in the ghettos is more than twice the city average and welfare rolls are growing at an alarming rate. As usual a great deal more people are out of work but not counted because they have temporarily given up looking.

This bustling city of 7,894,862 persons (1.9 million Jewish, 1.3 million black, and 969,700 Puerto Rican in 1970) has much that is good. It is in a metropolitan area of over 19 million people—the national center for finance, communications, advertising, publishing, the arts, theater, fashion, and a large share of major corporations. Since the early 1950s, twice as much new office space has been built in Manhattan than in the next nine largest U.S. cities combined; and presently 25 percent of all office space under construction in the country is being built in New York City (although there is a pressing

problem of filling the vacant office space in postwar skyscrapers).
The city hums with life, and there are more possibilities of "the unexpected than anywhere else."

Bruce Kivner illustrated some of this excitement in New York
Magazine.[1] Examples tell about day-care centers doubling to 270,
with another 243 to be open by 1974; six new major hospital facilities,
ranging in size from 200 to 950 beds each, a new 25-story $138 million
Bellevue Hospital with 1,274 beds to be finished in 1973, and citywide
drug clinics; 14 sewage treatment plants being upgraded for completion
by 1976 at a cost of $1.9 billion, to make the city the first on the Hud-
son with fully treated sewage; a third tunnel for drinking water to be
completed by 1977 at a cost of $1 billion; a new brightly lit pedestrian
tunnel with eight porcelain murals now serving Bryant Park at 42d
Street; 8,000 trees planted each year, twice the figure of five years
ago; Greenwich Street Plan construction in lower Manhattan, which
will include enclosed shopping malls, a park, and underground walks;
additional historic preservation districts and numerous elegant little
parks; new tourist attractions; 42 off-track betting parlors and 60
more planned; the start of Waterside, with terraces overlooking the
East River and shops, restaurants, and 1,460 apartments; the $325
million community on Welfare Island, which will include housing,
schools, offices, recreational facilities, and shops; downtown Brooklyn
developments that include a six-story Con Edison (the city's utilities
company) building, an 18-story office tower, a six-story diagnostic
center, 1,500 middle- and low-income housing units, and $55 million
of other projects in a 19-block area; and the Second Avenue Subway,
a link to Welfare Island, and extensions of the BMT and Sixth Avenue
lines that are under construction or in advanced planning and will
include modern, quieter cars. Certainly an impressive list of accomplishments.

Fiscal Crisis

Of its problems, keeping solvent is perhaps New York's most
pressing. New grants, such as Model Cities, have not been able to
help very much because they are a small part of the city's massive
budget. They have also had little effect where it has been necessary
to cut back personnel and services because of revenue shortages. In
the long run, federal and state programs will not have much impact
if the city has to wrestle continually with fiscal crises, for it is difficult to solve new problems or even plan solutions if old headaches
persist.

It is not unusual for New York to face annual financial chaos.
Commenting on the prospect for the city's immediate future, C. Lowell
Harriss, professor of economics at Columbia University, stated in

February 1972 that "apparently unescapable increases in expenditures will exceed the growth of revenue from existing sources by two or three to one." During the 1960s, spending unbelievably quintupled (the operating budget jumped from $2 billion in 1958 to almost $10 billion in the 1973 fiscal year, and if the same rate of expenditures continues, former city Comptroller Abraham Beame, who was elected mayor in 1973, predicts the budget will jump to $18 billion by 1977), per capita expenditures went from $320 to $1,000, city taxes more than doubled, and state and federal aid in 1972 is five times what it was in 1962. The increase in aid in five years—$2.2 billion—can be compared with a rise in city tax collections of $1.8 billion. State-federal aid rose from 25 to 45 percent of total revenues.[2]

Harriss also notes that state and local taxes in New York are the heaviest in the country per dollar of personal income. The Bureau of the Census found that, among 38 selected metropolitan areas, New York City per capita taxes of $359 in 1968-69 were the highest in the nation except for Washington, D.C. and San Francisco. Harriss says New York is "the heaviest taxer and the largest spender." The combined city and state sales taxes of 7 percent are the highest in the country. Furthermore, he believes that the city's taxes on business earnings hamper the process of income creation and that large businesses continually assess shifting their headquarters outside New York, whereas few others consider moving in.[3]

Assuredly, money is not the single answer to New York's problems. One need only to look at the miraculously high budget and public dissatisfaction with services. Political scientist David Bernstein of the Citizens Budget Commission (private citizen's watchdog group) stated in early 1969:

> There are some who seem to believe that merely money would solve most, if not all, of the city's other problems. The experience of the past decade . . . one in which the amount spent by the New York City government has tripled, while virtually all of its problems have intensified rather than abated . . . would seem to belie that belief. While money is required to solve many of these problems, money alone will solve few, if any of them, however essential it may be.[4]

Undoubtedly, part of the financial problem will have to be solved by streamlining government and by introducing innovations. A great many New York citizens believe the city is capable of running by itself anyway and the less government, the better. It will take a considerably improved government to win these citizens over.

From the beginning, Model Cities was conceived as one vehicle to more effective government. In this regard, the following sections

330

review the program in its relationship to general government, city officials, the bureaucracy, the administration of Model Cities, resident support, and the effectiveness of Model Cities projects.

Government

There are five bodies and individuals elected to represent New York City—the mayor, city council, president of the city council, five borough presidents, and a comptroller. There are, of course, congressmen, state senators, and state assemblymen elected from these districts, also. The geography includes five counties within the city's borders, known also as boroughs (Manhattan, 1,960,101; the Bronx, 1,424,815; Brooklyn, 2,627,319; Queens, 1,809,578; Staten Island, 221,991—four of them bigger than the populations of many of our states.)

Under New York City's unusually complex governmental system, the mayor operates in a strong-mayor/council form of government, with 38 city councilmen paid to spend most of their time attending to city business (annual salaries $20,000, plus $5,000 contingency expenses). Twenty-seven are elected from single-member districts and two at-large from each of five boroughs; the council president is elected at-large. City council's responsibilities are limited. Its chief activities relate to the budget, "home rule messages" to the state legislature, and program review. It seldom originates action and seldom prevents or modifies actions by others. And it has been severely criticized by citizen groups for failure to perform even these functions.

In addition to the mayor and council, there are five elected borough presidents (annual salaries, $35,000), who along with the mayor, comptroller, and president of city council make up the Board of Estimate. Borough presidents have two votes each, and the other three members four votes each, a total of 22. The Board of Estimate must approve all substantial capital projects, as well as decisions such as street closings, sale of city-owned land, and leases of city property. The board is a full-time participant with the mayor in governing the city, a role city council does not have. Almost everything the mayor proposes needs board approval. In addition, some engineering and planning functions are operated from borough halls, giving borough presidents some administrative responsibilities; nevertheless, they are political officers, not administrators.

In a recent analysis, Wallace Sayre, a political scientist who has studied the city extensively, called the five boroughs and their five coterminous counties "government shells (without legislative organs)." Each county has a district attorney (county prosecutor) elected county-wide and an appointed staff. Most judges are elected by the counties; the grand and petit juries are county agencies. And there are no governmental links between boroughs and counties.[5]

Even with charter changes made in 1961, which officially give more authority to city council, the council has not taken advantage of this legalized strength, and Board of Estimate members have shown resilience and persistence in preserving theirs. But the charter also strengthened the position of mayor, giving him a clear leadership role in budget and power to reorganize administrative agencies. The comptroller was left essentially untouched, remaining the most potent opponent of the mayor because of his citywide election and autonomous fiscal powers. Much of the time, the borough presidents rally around the comptroller for a better bargaining position.

Until his 1973 election as mayor, Abraham Beame held the comptroller's reins. He used his power frequently to halt payment on questionable city expenditures and has been one of those cited by Model Cities as a foe. On the other hand, certain Model Cities officials admit they prefer to have his close surveillance of funds than chance the misuse of money.

The continued ineffectiveness of city council was emphasized in a 1972 report by the Citizens Union (a private citizen organization), which questioned its $2.5 million annual expenditure (and an additional $500,000 in the council president's office) as a waste because the council "is a burnt-out case and perhaps should be abolished or it and the Board of Estimate replaced by a single well-staffed body that might get something done." The report cited too many committees, too many assignments to councilmen, unclear jurisdictions, and incorrect bill referrals to committees. "The Finance Committee rarely investigates anything," it stated. "The parity pay [between police and firemen] mistake by the city administration cost over $25 million—but the committee never investigated who in the Budget Bureau, Personnel Department or Office of Labor Relations approved the mistake."

A recent New York Times editorial commented, "The mayor's proposal of an expense budget up by roughly $1.4 billion from last year's can hardly be considered responsible.... But the Council's failure even to examine such a massive budget is much worse."[6] Lately, certain councilmen have become more active, have pursued budget issues, and even conducted some investigations of their own including looking at the Model Cities Program. But most observers feel the council has a long way to go before it becomes an effective unit. Although the Citizens Union admits some councilmen do good work, it concluded in the above report that drastic reforms are necessary to improve the council's ability to develop and screen legislation, to analyze critically budgets, and to investigate agencies.[7]

Power Structure

Political Power

Of the major city government powers, by far the most strength is with the mayor. He initiates programs, appoints all department heads, and is in charge of day-to-day city operations. The others exert their power more in terms of a veto on his actions. But Lindsay's ability to exercise his power turned out to be largely ephemeral because of fragmented political parties and interest groups, which prevent even a reform mayor from implementing his programs.

There is no citywide party organization. Next in line above the borough (or county) level is the state committee. New York politics primarily focuses on the individual boroughs, and there is strong independence below this level from assembly district leaders, a situation that makes party organization internally competitive and denies the mayor a strong party leadership role.

Politically, city council has grown relatively weaker because it has lost influence and leadership. When Democrat Robert Wagner was mayor from 1953 to 1965, the Democrats held every council seat but one, as well as all other elective city offices. This is no longer true, even though they hold a majority. Lindsay's election by Republican, Liberal, and independent voters in 1965 as a "fusion" mayor took away some power from Thomas Cuite, regular Democratic majority leader, and reduced his ability to control the council. On the other hand, with the majority of city council of the opposition party, Lindsay, until he switched to the Democratic Party in 1971, had difficulty in getting his policies across.

There are several factors that weakened Lindsay's leadership. Unlike Wagner, who played the role of mediator, Lindsay assumed the role of activist-reformer. Commenting on this, David Rogers says that Lindsay's political ethic was based on good, nonpartisan government and that he believed strongly in efficiency, fairness, planning, and strong executive-type government with a lot of professional urbanists, chosen regardless of their party affiliation. But Rogers says that Lindsay's emotions and arrogance sometimes hurt him, and "his comments about bureaucratic power brokers" reinforced negative images of himself by the city's civil servants. "In addition," he comments, "Lindsay is regarded by some of the private agencies as a bad manager, a dilettante at city government, and inept at negotiations."[8] It was difficult for Lindsay to dispel this image, but since early 1972 he stayed home, pressing for reform, insisting on better service and productivity, and trying desperately to pull the administrative machinery together.

Second to mayoral power is that of the Board of Estimate. Although the 1961 charter was supposed to weaken the board, former Mayor Wagner did not press hard to maximize the new powers of the mayor at that time or put the board in a clearly subordinate position; therefore, the board's strength has endured. For example, the Lindsay Administration complained about delays in approving contracts and bills, noting the board met only every other week with an average agenda of over 300 items. And the board complained about receiving proposals, such as Model Cities plans, too late to be reviewed to meet HUD deadlines. A case in point: the city council president submitted a disclaimer on the second action year plans, noting that he had only a few days to review thousands of pages of documents. Some officials infer Lindsay purposely did this to retain tighter control of the use of Model Cities funds (a practice not uncommon in several cities). Disputes are common, and Lindsay received only mixed cooperation from the borough presidents. Furthermore, a common desire for more power appeared to run through the declarations of all five borough presidents.

City Planning Commission

Besides locally elected power, there are other strong influences on policy. One of the most important is the City Planning Commission, whose members are appointed by the mayor (the chairman's tenure is subject to the pleasure of the mayor, and the chairman is, in effect, the planning director) for eight-year terms and which continues to play an independent role, primarily because of its political isolation. It is considered as having been ineffective because of lack of accomplishment generally and particularly for its failure to develop a master plan until only recently. It wields power because it officially reviews and makes recommendations to the mayor and Board of Estimate on all major development plans. Capital budgeting was taken away from it in the charter of 1961, but it still is charged with developing a comprehensive budget package. In practice, both the mayor and Board of Estimate use this budgeting process as their own instrument of policy. Any mayoral vetoes may be overridden by separate votes of the city council and Board of Estimate.

The State

A further influence on city government is the power of the state legislature, which has veto power over every city budget expenditure. In 1972 legislative session, ending in late spring, the city received a serious blow to its budget, with funds cut for many programs in poor neighborhoods, such as those for health and education.

Consequently, the importance of Model Cities money in the city was strongly enhanced as a means for filling in where appropriations were reduced. Although the mayor issued disclaimers that such would be the case, few believed his statements, as a considerable portion of Model Cities funds were used simply to maintain ongoing programs.

As a result of the state's large role in determining city budget priorities, state legislators from the city play a big part in personally influencing city hall decisions. A strong concentration of black and Puerto Rican state representatives frequently combine their strength with congressmen: Shirley Chisholm of Bedford-Stuyvesant, Charles Rangel of Harlem, and Herman Badillo of the tri-part district, which essentially consists of the Bronx. There are only two blacks and no Puerto Ricans on the city council, and generally councilmen are not as well-known as assemblymen and state senators; therefore, city-elected minority members as a group are not very effective. A proposed state bill to add additional councilmen from minority areas would still leave minority communities underrepresented in proportion to their numbers because of gerrymandered districts and the demographic character of the city.

Business

There are two major business communities. First, because of the national importance of the city, there is a large concentration of Wall Street financial firms and national corporate headquarters. Their influence is strong because they provide hundreds of thousands of jobs. And their prevailing interest seems to be in maintaining good transportation and housing for their workers, many of whom commute. For many, New York is really just downtown and midtown Manhattan. The rest of the city is not seen and not very important to them.

The second business community is made up of local merchants and real estate owners whose main interest centers on keeping property taxes from rising, maintaining police security (particularly against robberies), and receiving good city services (especially sanitation).

New York City's businessmen are probably less involved in civic activity and more fragmented than in other large cities. "The fact that there is no New York City equivalent to the Greater Philadelphia Movement, the Allegheny Conference in Pittsburgh, the Central Area Committee of Chicago, Civic Progress in St. Louis, or the Civic Conference in Boston is one indication of the fragmentation of New York's business elite," states David Rogers.[9] There is, however, a promising beginning of business involvement in programs between city hall and the Economic Development Council, the Urban Coalition, and other development ventures. But there are no signs of a grand coalition truly dedicated to the transformation of the city.

Unions

Municipal Unions. Unions are extremely powerful in the city. Chief among them are the municipal unions. Two major ones have been politically against Lindsay—the Patrolman's Benevolent Association (PBA) and the Firefighters, both of which endorsed Nelson Rockefeller, while Lindsay was backing Arthur Goldberg in the 1970 gubernatorial race. Other major municipal unions are the Transit Workers, whose leadership is primarily Italian and Irish while about 70 percent of the membership is black and Puerto Rican. This is a pattern throughout the city's union structure, minority persons being frozen out of leadership and frequently membership.

Two municipal unions are slightly more liberal—the United Federation of Teachers (UFT) and the AFL-CIO State, County and Municipal Employees Union, District Council 37. The UFT, led by Albert Shanker, however, took a conservative turn following the disastrous teachers strike of 1968 in which strong friction between blacks and Jews emerged.

Two other municipal unions do not quite fit the above pattern. The Sanitationman's Union, led by John DeLurie, is in many ways conservative. However, DeLurie supported Lindsay in the 1969 election, perhaps because of the generous salary and pension increases his union had won in prior settlements. The Council of Supervisors and Administrators (CSA) is fairly conservative compared with the UFT. It represents the city's school principals and supervisors, many of whom feel threatened by pressure from blacks and Puerto Ricans, who are extremely underrepresented in administrative posts. Recently the CSA was dealt a strong blow when a federal judge threw out the discriminatory "eligibility list" from which principals were selected in the city. The list is prepared by the Board of Examiners.

Civil Service. Selfishness and protectionism are just as prevalent in the civil service system. Some civil service groups have become centers of ethnic power, despite the so-called merit system—the Irish dominate the Police and Fire Departments; the Italians, the Department of Sanitation; the Jews, the school system and welfare agencies; the blacks,and Puerto Ricans, Model Cities. Each has taken a domain and has successfully resisted major reform. Lindsay privately blames them for much of the city's inefficiency, and, because of such special interests, Model Cities has had a particularly difficult time breaking into other jurisdictions and influencing agencies. In addition, outmoded testing procedures, unfair job qualifications, and time-consuming recruitment methods have also hurt good personnel practices and delayed Model Cities programs. However, recently civil service has been cooperating with Model Cities and has made some concessions.

Nonmunicipal Unions. A nonmunicipal union that has had a strong negative influence on the city is the Building and Construction Trades Council, which has played an effective role in freezing blacks and Puerto Ricans from construction jobs by not allowing them to gain union membership. The council was run by Peter Brennan until he became U.S. secretary of Labor; Brennan gained notoriety through his leadership in the hardhat demonstrations at City Hall, which included the beating of students, and his subsequent presentation of a hardhat to Nixon. The council is so strong that Lindsay backed down on the extent of minority hiring during the development of the New York Plan. Prior to the plan, the city had ostensibly insisted on one minority trainee for every four journeymen employed on city construction projects. As finally conceived, however, only 800 trainees were to be employed throughout the city, and with no guarantee of union membership. Moreover, despite the leniency of this plan, some unions (notably the steam fitters and sheet metal workers) have resisted cooperation. As of June 30, 1972, the unions reported 466 trainees in jobs during the plan's first six months, or more than half the goal of 800 set for the first year. But city council hearings revealed that the plan had only produced a total of 297 training positions in the multibillion-dollar construction industry, that 79 trained had dropped out, and that only 22 persons had been permitted to join unions.[10] Minority organizations called for 50 percent of government-assisted construction jobs in ghetto areas and threatened continued demonstrations.

Another powerful representative of unions is the Central Labor Council, led by Harry Van Arsdale, who has exerted subtle pressure to aid municipal unions in gaining salary and pension increases.

Administering the Bureaucracy

With its diffused political organization and complex legislative structure, the executive branch of New York's government is massive and cumbersome. Any government trying to regulate 300,000 employees and some 70 or 80 major divisions and boards is bound to show signs of wrinkled lines of authority, too broad a span of control, poor communication, high administrative costs, unresponsive operations, inequitable levels of service, and some frustration. At the same time, many effective services exist, and some rewarding changes have taken place.

As explained previously, the charter changes of 1961 particularly have strengthened the mayor's ability to administer the city, even though political diffusion has had the opposite effect. Mayor Lindsay has used the tools at hand, in some ways like his predecessors and in other ways quite differently.

Deputy Mayors

Lindsay has utilized deputy mayors much like his predecessors, as trouble-shooters without stable assignments. The Office of City Administrator has been used as an expendable resource (recently held by the unsuccessful candidate of the Liberal Party for council president) by placing it at the margin rather than the center of administration and influence. The office began to lose its importance as a managerial arm during the 12 years of the Wagner Administration and has continued to decline. Its management analysis units, about 15 staff members of its 200-employee office, were logically integrated in early 1972 with other qualitative components and the central computerization of the Bureau of the Budget (BOB). The office under the direction of a new deputy mayor (there are two deputy mayors), Edward A. Morrison, engages more in long-range studies and has the responsibilities of liaison with city council, contract compliance, project innovation, Urban Fellowship Program, Program for the Aged, Urban Corps, Volunteers Program, Civil Defense, Collective Bargaining, Civic Assembly, and a number of programs that do not seem to fit anywhere else. (See Chart 8.) The Civic Assembly, which has just recently been reactivated, has 15 committees (some 30-40 members each) assigned to each major area of concern. As a group of over 100 private citizens and representatives of organizations, it recommends policy, supports bond issues, and so on. In addition, the mayor appoints ad hoc citywide task forces for special, more pressing problem areas.

On the other hand, the deputy mayor of the executive office, Edward K. Hamilton, is in effect the city administrator. A team of analysts has been placed under the direction of Hamilton and assigned to keep tabs on each of the city's administrations and major departments. Formally, administrators and department heads report directly to the mayor, but in practice they are short-stopped by the deputy mayor and his staff of experts. Lindsay passes orders through Hamilton (who had previously gained invaluable experience as budget director), in whom he has the greatest confidence, boasting of his ability and the fact that New York City should have had this caliber of man long ago. Morrison, in reality, too, reports through Hamilton and perhaps even more directly through David Grossman, budget director. The strength of the position of city administrator here,

CHART 8

The Government of the City of New York

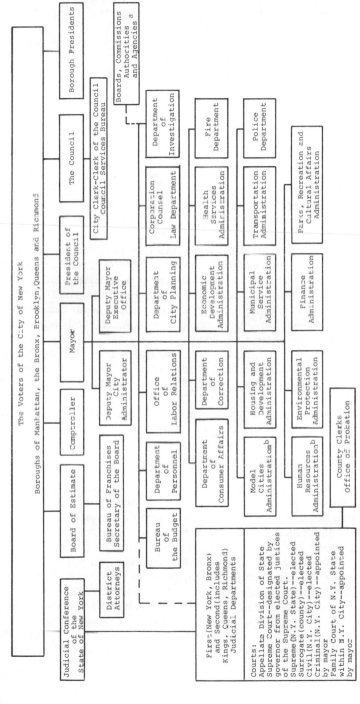

The Voters of the City of New York

Boroughs of Manhattan, the Bronx, Brooklyn, Queens and Richmond

Courts:
First—(New York, Bronx)
and Second(includes
Kings, Queens, Richmond)
Judicial Departments

Appellate Division of State
Supreme Court—designated by
governor from elected justices
of the Supreme Court.
Supreme(N.Y. State)—elected
Surrogate(county)—elected
Civil(N.Y. City)—elected
Criminal(N.Y. City)—appointed
by mayor
Family Court of N.Y. State
within N.Y. City—appointed
by mayor

--Independent bodies.
 a Appointed by mayor.
 b Legislation not yet adopted by city council.
 Source: Office of the mayor, office of administration, January 1971.

339

as in many other cities, has been dependent on the capabilities of the person assigned to the job and how much authority the mayor has wanted to delegate. Top-priority projects, emergencies, short-term policy development, the latest productivity goals project, and other elements designed to improve services are mostly directed from here.

Superagencies

When he took office in 1966, Lindsay was first confronted with reshaping the bureaucracy. He proceeded to create nine superagencies by grouping approximately 62 departments and agencies into what was intended to become an integrated administrative system. These nine administrations are Health Services Administration (HSA); Environmental Protection Administration (EPA); Housing and Development Administration (HDA); Human Resources Administration (HRA); Municipal Services Administration (MSA); Transportation Administration; Finance Administration; Economic Development Administration (EDA); and Parks Recreation and Cultural Affairs Administration. In 1970, Model Cities was also made into an administration organizationally but as yet has not been formally approved as such by city council. HRA, established by executive order in 1968, has also never been officially approved by council as an administration. Police, Fire, Corrections, and the Consumer Affairs Departments remain separate, as do a number of commissions, boards, and agencies (chief among them are the Board of Education and the Board of Higher Education, which are beyond the effective reach of the mayor). Also, the several staff units under the mayor are finally being made into a unified system that can best serve him.

Model Cities as a Superagency

The superagencies appear to have advantages over a separate department system, although some observers believe services were performed better under more independent departments. But the concept has helped Model Cities. To begin with, it was made into an administration in order to give central officials authority to take full control of the program, to get projects moving, and to give Model Cities influence comparable to that of other superagencies. More effective leadership and direction of the program has resulted. Prior to 1970, Model Cities was under the authority of a Model Cities Committee of high city officials appointed by the mayor from the following agencies: Human Resources Administration, Council Against Poverty (CAP), Bureau of the Budget, Housing and Development Administration, and the New York City Housing Authority. In spite of the high caliber of officials, the central committee exerted little control over the program and was unable to devote sufficient time to Model Cities. Subordinates were sent to meetings, neighborhood directors by-passed the committee and its executive secretary, Eugenia M. Flatow, for the mayor whenever they felt it was to their advantage, and committee members ended up feeling their whole assignment was a "joke." The committee was replaced by a reorganized Model Cities (advisory) Board consisting of representatives from the neighborhood, as well as special interest groups and officials. New elections were ordered for the three powerful Model Cities Neighborhood Policy Committees, and their authority was drastically reduced. The central board was given little power, but the program's administrator was legally handed all the powers held by the former central committee—that is, administration, hiring, budget, operation, resource allocation, and review and initiation of plans. The strategy was to gain central control and replace the weak liaison role played by the executive secretary of the first committee. The new administrator was placed in the mayor's cabinet and made an equal to the other nine administrators.

Even in its role as a superagency, Model Cities depends on several overhead service agencies for processing administrative details and authorizing certain actions. Three of these agencies are the Department of Law (Corporation Counsel), Personnel, and Investigations, outside the superagency structure. Two others, which are closely related to Model Cities, are Purchase and Real Estate, part of the Municipal Services Administration. Together with the Bureau of the Budget, they have considerable impact on the efficiency and effectiveness of Model Cities.

Model Cities and Service Agencies

Of the service agencies, the Corporation Counsel has been particularly helpful to Model Cities, ruling in favor of liberalizing civil service rules to give preference to the employment of Model Neighborhood residents and to change certain discriminatory examination procedures.

On the other hand, the Department of Personnel has been an obstacle in the path of these changes, with a long history of irrelevant employee testing, promotion by seniority rather than merit, inadequate training programs, and little concern for more productive employees. Recently, Personnel has begun to cooperate by designing tests more relevant to Model Cities, eliminating high school requirements where not necessary, adding more Spanish-language tests, and giving preferential treatment to Model Neighborhood (MN) residents, as outlined by federal guidelines. But it has been unable to get Model Cities personnel certified as permanent civil service workers, a goal largely beyond its reach because of union opposition and several pending court suits.

The most critical complaint by Model Cities is against the Division of Investigations because of delay, as much as two or three months, in performing background checks on prospective employees—many of whom find other jobs in the meantime. Model Cities has been able to overcome this by persuading Investigations to conduct inquiries after persons are hired for key jobs. It has also been connected with Investigations because of a most embarrassing scandal involving some Model Cities employees in the Municipal Loan Program, which is designed to give low-interest loans for housing rehabilitation in poor neighborhoods. The division's head, Commissioner Robert Roslan, was criticized by Councilman Robert Postel for failure to move rapidly in the corruption investigation, which is now, however, well under way after having implicated a former loan program head as being involved in fraud with two of the largest loan recipients. This and the scandal-ridden Emergency Repair Program (designed to make immediate repairs to dangerous buildings) have tarnished Model Cities' image.

The Bureau of the Budget has been particularly concerned about reducing red tape and making agencies more responsive yet has itself stymied Model Cities progress. When Frederick Hayes, a former federal official, was BOB director in 1971, he expressed special concern about the inability of top management to take hold of the bureaucracies under them. He said that "agencies resembled an Indian village pattern—fragmented bureaucratic world of governmental tribes with tremendous power, insulated from policy-makers and citizens, yet incapable of performing well."11 Hayes made wide use of consultants and new systems and stringent standards in evaluating expenditures, but the bureaucracy did not seem to move very much.

Model Cities has been trapped in this procedural web. Since its funds are considered city money, all anticipated expenditures must be cleared by BOB, and after expenditures, payment must be cleared by the comptroller. The bottleneck has been in Budget, where it has taken 30 days to receive approvals for budget modifications. However, through the prodding of Model Cities officials, this time has been cut to 10 days..

Edward Hamilton was budget director after Hayes, followed by David Grossman in the winter of 1971, when Hamilton, as deputy mayor, began to assume much of the mayor's role while Lindsay campaigned for the presidency. All three directors made substantial improvements in the operation of BOB and city government in general, which have helped to expedite Model Cities projects. In this respect, BOB was instrumental in putting into operation the management office, designed to cut through red tape and assure the rapid completion of projects by using consultants and special staff teams for certain programs. Model Cities is now getting some of this priority treatment.

Model Cities and Superagencies

In regards to Model Cities' relationships to the other superagencies, the Real Estate Division of the Municipal Services Administration has been pointed to as one of the program's major obstacles. Numerous Model Cities programs have been delayed for months, some six months or longer, because of failure to obtain approval for space rental and building and land purchase. The Emergency Repair Program was held up for several months, and certain open space programs were delayed even longer. Much of the delay is due to overabundant bureaucratic red tape and the necessity to obtain Board of Estimate approval of almost every transaction.

Most of the superagencies are involved with Model Cities in some fashion. The Economic Development; Parks, Recreation and Cultural Affairs; Health Services; and Environmental Protection administrations are all operating some programs for Model Cities. This has permitted quicker implementation of projects that were difficult to get started and has substantially aided the maintenance of some existing city services as well as adding some new ones. Also, the success or failure of Model Cities manpower programs is very much dependent on the ability of EDA to develop jobs; Model Cities citywide recreation is dependent on the effectiveness of Recreation and Cultural Affairs, which runs the program; and better health coordination will come about only partially through use of Model Cities funds and mostly through the efforts of HSA and its resources. The quality of the Model Cities sanitation program depends on EPA's skills in motivating its work force and making the best use of Model Cities personnel and equipment. Implementation of the Model Cities transportation study is contingent upon how much the Transportation Administration believes in it. To a large extent, the success of Model Cities is dependent on the other superagencies. A critique of the program, thus, must be a look at New York City government itself.

Two other agencies substantiate this point of view—Housing Department and Human Resources. For example, alone it is extremely difficult for Model Cities to construct or rehabilitate housing. HDA has the primary responsibility in this area and has been working closely with Model Cities. However, HDA's lack of success has severely damaged Model Cities' image. HDA successfully expended $80 million in HUD money to demolish buildings but failed to put up housing and implement the Vest Pocket Housing Program started in 1968, which the public has always associated with Model Cities. This relationship has increased resident skepticism about Model Cities.

HRA operates some Model Cities projects but is in a sense a competitor because many of its programs are similar, and its new project funds are diminishing in comparison to Model Cities. Its departments include Community Development Agency, Manpower and Career Development Agency, Department of Social Services, Youth Services Agency, Addiction Services Agency, and the Child Development Agency. The Community Development Agency (CDA) helps to coordinate 25 Community Corporations and acts as staff for the Council Against Poverty (the community action board), which is composed of 51 members from poverty areas, agencies, and citywide civic groups. CDA has frequently complained about its lack of access to Model Cities funds and the inability of Model Cities to spend money; however, federal guidelines have prohibited the direct use of Model Cities funds for OEO program support. Nevertheless, HRA is operating some programs with Model Cities funds that it would be otherwise operating with OEO funds, if they were available, such as Early Childhood Day Care, Camping, Project Children, and others.

There are also a number of other city agencies and departments—such as Corrections, Police and Fire, Housing Authority, Board of Education—that operate Model Cities projects. They are discussed below in the section entitled "Model Cities Projects."

Decentralization

Urban Action Task Forces and Neighborhood Government. Along with the goal of improving government's capacity to do its job, the Model Cities concept involves decentralization of services to the neighborhood level. This experiment has met with limited success. However, for a long time, the city administration has been interested in decentralization. The school system was decentralized into 31 local boards in 1969 with mixed success. And beginning in 1966, Mayor Lindsay experimented with Little City Halls and Urban Action Task Forces (the latter are citizen bodies, chaired by principal city officials to expedite services), which reached a peak of 50 task forces and 25 local offices in 1970. However, city council was never enthusiastic about the idea and refused to appropriate money for this purpose, fearing Little City Halls would be more political storefronts than service centers. Private contributions of about $600,000 annually kept most of the centers operating, until a much broader concept of neighborhood government was presented by Mayor Lindsay. This concept proposed changing the appointment by borough presidents of the city's 62 Community (Planning) Boards to election by residents and the combining of budgets of several decentralized functions into an Office of Neighborhood Government with increased powers.

Neighborhood Action Councils and Command Decentralization. While
this plan remained under discussion and virtual inactivity, the city
administration began experimenting with a much more modest plan
involving five Neighborhood Action Councils. The city council and
Board of Estimate approved $5 million in capital improvement funds
for these areas and permitted part of it to be used as support of the
pilot neighborhood councils. This, plus $305,000 from the federal
government, got the neighborhood plan started. Their authority lies
mostly in the area of making local decisions about the use of capital
funds but involves some general planning decisions and neighborhood
service problems, as well. The arrangements are informal in order
to avoid conflicts with unions, in particular, and with other groups
that feel some of their power may be taken away by a local council.

Further steps were taken in December 1971 to decentralize the
administration of services in six neighborhoods (now eight) by integrating the services of eight agencies into coterminous districts,
appointing district managers to supervise field supervisors, and
developing district service cabinets of the field supervisors. Neighborhood Action Councils operate in two of these districts in order
to determine what affect the combination of political and functional
decentralization might have.

Other Proposals. In addition to the above proposals and to the extent
that decentralization already exists, Bronx President Robert Abrams,
the Bar Association of the City of New York, and others have presented
ideas on decentralization for different purposes: power, coordination,
and effectiveness. Possibly the most significant proposal politically
came from the State Study Commission for New York City, appointed
by former Governor Nelson Rockefeller to review and make recommendations on improving New York City government. This plan
presented a concept of dividing the city into 30 to 35 districts, each
with an elected council and an elected or appointed chief executive
officer, who would hire personnel and operate such local services as
refuse collection, street maintenance, social services, and parks.
Central government would still operate many citywide services, but
superagencies would be abolished, and the Board of Estimate would
be reconstituted as a more powerful City Policy Board, having the
effect of weakening the mayor and strengthening borough government.
Since release of this proposal, in October 1972, a City Charter Review
Commission was appointed and is reviewing city government structure
in anticipation of possible charter amendments in 1973.

Steps to Productivity. And while the discussion of and experiments
with decentralization continue, Mayor Lindsay has taken some prag-
matic steps to improve government efficiency, without changing

structure. Sensitive to criticism of poor management and high costs of government, he has let attrition reduce employees in most departments and instituted productivity measures that include increasing the tons of refuse collected, doubling potholes to be filled per manday, deploying police more effectively, increasing the number of sanitary inspections, expanding community service officers and housing construction and rehabilitation in Model Cities areas, and other measures for almost every unit of government. This has been an impressive innovation and has added a new spark to local government. Yet there is serious question about its ability to endure.

By November 1972, Lindsay began to back away from his "microscopic" balance of attrition versus productivity, indicating that the city had reached the "crises-cross" where "attrition losses exceed productivity gains." In his drive to make the "city safer and healthier," Lindsay ended the job freeze on uniformed services and ordered the hiring of 3,150 policemen, 800 firemen, and 780 sanitationmen by June 1974. This increase in employment, however, will have little effect on jobs for Model Neighborhood residents and minorities because existing civil service lists, which tend to favor middle-class education and background, must be used.*

The Role of Model Cities. Model Cities, too, was conceived as increasing productivity, the effectiveness of local government, and meaningful involvement of residents in the government process by various means, including methods of decentralization. Following is a review of the development of New York's Model Cities Program, its administration, degree of citizen involvement, and program effectiveness. One should be aware that the successes and failures of Model Cities must be viewed in light of the total effectiveness of the city's bureaucratic machinery, institutions, and politics.

Model Cities

The New York Model Cities Program is divided into three areas with populations totaling about 1 million residents located in three different boroughs—the Bronx, Manhattan, and Brooklyn. In all three areas, unemployment is almost twice the national average (Puerto Rican unemployment is considerably higher than black unemployment),

----

*In October 1972, blacks made up about 6 percent and Spanish-speaking persons 1.9 percent of the approximately 30,000-member police force. There are approximately 600 blacks in the 13,500-member fire force.

and the average age of residents is 19 (four years younger than the
city average) so that manpower programs are concentrated on the
young. Students are more than two academic years behind the national
average in both reading and mathematics by the end of the eighth year
of learning. Crime is increasing, yet one-third of city arrests take
place now in the Model Neighborhoods, which contain 20 percent of
the city's population (about $30 million is lost annually through crim-
inal acts in the MN). Drug addiction is approximately five times
greater than for the city as a whole. Over half of the crimes are drug-
related, and 8,378 arrests were made in 1971 for the use, possession,
or sale of dangerous drugs. Model Neighborhood residents have
shorter life expectancies, and nearly 8 percent of all deaths are of
infants under one year old, compared to 3 percent for the rest of the
city. Alcoholism is estimated at four times the city rate. Almost
any problem that one chooses to analyze turns out to be more severe
than for the city as a whole; however, there are 25 designated poverty
areas in the city with statistics almost as alarming. And lately poor
Puerto Ricans, Jews, Italians, Irish, and other ethnics have been
clamoring for special treatment. It seems the poor everywhere need
help and Model Cities is caught in the dilemma of concentrating its
resources, or spreading at least some of them, citywide.

Demography

The characteristics of each MN are described below.

South Bronx. There are approximately 260,000 people in South Bronx
Model Neighborhood. In 1940, 96 percent were white. In 1965, 9
percent were white, 31 percent were black, and 60 percent were
Puerto Rican. By 1972, the white population had declined even further.
Of the area's 1,500 acres, only 3 percent are parks. About 80 percent
of the housing is moderately to completely dilapidated. The total
population is declining slightly, and much of it is segregated. Morris-
ania is mostly black, the South Bronx is mostly Puerto Rican, and
Hunts Point is evenly divided. The percentage of persons on public
assistance here is three times that of the city as a whole. Recorded
unemployment is over 12 percent, and the average income is below
$4,000.

Harlem-East Harlem. This Model Neighborhood is divided into two
parts—mostly black Central Harlem and mostly Puerto Rican East
Harlem with a large Italian community. Only 21 percent of the area's
housing is sound, as compared to 64 percent citywide. About 92 percent of the area's housing is deteriorating. Apartments are overcrowded. Twelve percent of the apartments have more than 1.5

persons per room as compared with only 3.9 percent for the entire city. Some 60,000 people in the area are on welfare. And over half the families have incomes under $4,000. Sixty-four percent of the employed males of the area have unskilled or service jobs as compared to 38 percent citywide. And one person of every five is unemployed.

Central Brooklyn. This area of more than 500,000 people is made up of three communities—almost all-black Bedford-Stuyvesant, two-thirds blacks and one-third Puerto Rican; Brownsville; and the more varied East New York, which has a large Puerto Rican and Italian population. The area covers 5,119 acres, almost 10 percent of the total land in Brooklyn. The population is continually decreasing, and the number of whites has been cut rapidly since 1960. Nearly half the white population is 65 years or older. Change is rapid. East New York, for instance, was 85 percent white in 1960 and is 20 percent white in 1972. About 75 percent of the housing is deteriorated. Unemployment is more than double the city average. Forty-two percent of the work force does not make a living wage. In 1968 only 220 youths out of a potential of 25,000 were going to college. And an estimated 120,000 people here do not receive adequate medical care.

History

General. Mayor Lindsay wanted to get a jump on the nation's Model Cities Program, so he pledged city funds early to get planning started and to begin housing construction in the Model Neighborhoods. His request for $25 million of city funds to start the construction of a projected 5,050 units of Vest Pocket housing in Central Brooklyn was approved by the Board of Estimate in September 1967. This is how the Model Cities Program in New York and Vest Pocket housing became closely linked and dependent on each other. This key program figured influentially in Model Cities' impact on the community because of its slow progress and the bitter feelings it engendered in residents.

In November 1967, Mayor Lindsay set up a planning committee and the Model Cities (central) Committee with a $238,000 HUD planning grant. Former city HDA official Eugenia Flatow was appointed executive secretary of the committee, which was made up of city commissioners but no community representatives.

It was not until June 1968 that the year-long planning period began and the central office started making attempts to set up local committees in the three Model Neighborhoods. During the next several months, intensive efforts were made at the central and community level to work out some agreements on first-year plans. Planning went more rapidly in Brooklyn than the other two communities, which were held back by the inability of conflicting local factions to work out compromises on membership and control. Primarily, disputes centered around power struggles by local organizations and community corporations, often along lines that separated Puerto Ricans and blacks. Although the programs eventually got funded, serious conflicts ensued into the second action year, with little progress toward project implementation. Flatow understood the role of Model Cities was to create a "partnership" with the neighborhoods, but it turned out that local groups became dominant and pressured Flatow into demanding things the city did not want. During this period the city did not impose programs on the community, and there were few innovations and little impact on the bureaucracy. Flatow was about on the same level of authority as that of a neighborhood director— not very impressive to agency heads.

Shortly, after his reelection in 1969, Lindsay contracted with the McKinsey Consulting firm in November to develop a new Model Cities management plan and organization. To save the programs, the mayor felt it necessary to move it in the direction of city hall, face up to the strong community opposition that had developed, and strongly direct bureaucratic city agencies to cooperate. However, dissatisfaction was growing even in Brooklyn, which had been fairly docile. Several Brooklyn projects had been ready to move but encountered lengthy delays of red tape at the central Model Cities office and some of the city departments already mentioned: Budget, Real Estate, Personnel, and Investigations. As a result, the entire Brooklyn committee was led by the staff and accompanied by several elected officials in sitting in at City Hall for two days in December 1969. The protests centered around the Brooklyn complaint that they had been able to spend only a fraction of their alloted $29 million, even though the first action year was nearly half over. The other two MNs were in worse shape.

The sit-in created a noisy stir in the press, embarrassing Lindsay. There were several meetings between the mayor and community groups to speed the process. Acting on McKinsey recommendations and the suggestions of mayoral aide Gordon Davis, to give the program stronger central direction and lessen local delays, Lindsay removed Flatow and Bronx head Anibal Asencio shortly thereafter. Soon afterwards in April 1970, the mayor abolished the original central committee and created the Model Cities Administration, to be headed by Joseph Williams, a black judge and former Liberal Party supporter of Lindsay. Community power was to be reduced further, and the local Policy Committees were made answerable to a Central Policy (advisory) Committee, consisting of two representatives from each local policy committee and a majority of agency, business, and civic people. The central committee met only once in its first year and only once or twice in its second. Needless to say, it has had little influence and for all practical purposes is defunct. Occasionally, Williams may call on individual members for advice and support, but a formal relationship does not exist. The main thrust of these changes was the underlying belief that the program had been held up by community input and the lack of central office clout with other agencies. On the other hand, community residents contended that there was insufficient community input and too much bureaucratic delay. Evidence shows unusual delays in both sectors.

By January 1971, over a period of 18 months, the program had spent only $30 million of its first $65 million, and the press began to focus negative public attention on the program. The mayor defended it and requested HUD to make an evaluation. A quick review was done by Marshall Kaplan, Gans and Kahn Associates. Their evaluation was positive, calling the program "overprotected" but one of the better ones in the nation. Some progress was evident. A $288,000 Community Legal Services Program in Harlem was announced, along with a $1.9 million training program in Brooklyn to be operated by the New York Port Authority. Also, HUD approved the city's second $65 million in March 1971, although the initial grant was still not entirely used up. This two-year total plus $110 million from the city's capital budget, earmarked for site clearance and new housing construction, constituted almost $250 million of Model Cities money.12

At the same time, the program was gearing up for Model Cities elections, which had been announced in March. Little public attention was focused on the elections because of lack of knowledge about the program and general apathy. Election guidelines limited the number of "povertycrats" who could serve. But only part of the existing policy committees were obliged to run, and many of the rest were representatives of poverty programs. In addition, many new candidates who were put forward and elected represented official board members and officers of poverty boards. This has meant the continued, though lessened, presence of "povertycrats" on the policy committees. It has also meant the creation of two power structures in poor communities—the antipoverty program and Model Cities. Many criticized this as duplication of effort and waste of money, but dual programs were operating in almost every participating city in the country.

Only 5,000 voters turned out for the elections in the Model Neighborhoods, whose total populations added up to well over a million. Few community leaders had expressed interest in the elections, and most of those elected were previously unknown. Reruns were held the following week in the Bronx and Brooklyn with only a few hundred voters turning out citywide. Some polling places recorded fewer than 10 voters.

Eventually, Administrator Williams's leadership abilities were felt, especially during the last months of 1971, and by spring 1972 money was being spent almost at a level equivalent to appropriations. Most program components were in operation, and the administration began to look for ways to cut the number of projects and to concentrate on fewer, more productive priority areas. By spring 1972, the third action year plan was approved.

Bronx. The Bronx program began with the appointment of Neighborhood Director Asencio in March 1968. By October an election had been held (half of the membership was elected and half appointed for each of the Policy Committees) with a total of 4,300 persons recorded as voting, nearly as many as had voted in all three model areas in later elections in 1971. The neighborhood directors were never able to assert their power over the committee, although Bronx has had three directors—Asencio, who was not a community resident; Augustus Davis, a black and an ally of Congressman Herman Badillo, who is Puerto Rican; and Victor Marrero, a 29-year-old Puerto Rican Yale Law School graduate and mayoral aide who was appointed in March 1970. Marrero is much stronger than his predecessors and has been able to guide the committee more positively, although some community residents consider him an agent of Lindsay and not a community advocate. "We tolerate him," said one. But Marrero is effective and making progress. His staff is also relatively independent from the central staff, designing much of its own programs and priorities.

The policy committee has been dominated by Ramon Velez, founder and head of the $7-million-a-year Hunts Point Multi-Service Center. The facility has declined in power of late, recently losing HUD funding because of irregularities and resulting in a considerable loss to its basic $12 million budget. Velez exerts power over several antipoverty agencies including Model Cities by placing center employees in key positions on boards of directors and the policy committee. He lost a bid in 1972 for a congressional seat, and his power has been declining. But his initial thrust in the Hunts Point area caused a triplication—Hunts Point Multi-Service Center, CAP community corporation, and Model Cities—and jockeying for primary recognition of citizen power. These three independent structures have made it difficult for Model Cities to develop comprehensive planning or achieve a reasonable degree of coordination. Moreover, the area has undergone a severe black/Puerto Rican split, with the Puerto Ricans gaining the upper hand in influence and jobs. During the summer of 1969, several persons were killed in antipoverty feuding. And the split caused the temporary closing of the South Bronx Community Corporation in 1970.

Harlem. In summer 1968, director John Edmonds was appointed. There was always severe friction between Edmonds and the policy committee, to the extent that his and the committee's offices were maintained at separate addresses. Friction was also caused because the committee was run by a Puerto Rican, while Edmonds is black. Another black, John Sanders, was appointed in the latter part of 1970. He displayed strong personality and worked well with the policy committee, but few programs got implemented. The appointment of directors in Harlem has always been on a temporary basis. This in itself has diminished Policy Committee confidence in them and reduced their effectiveness with staff.

For a long time, residents felt Model Cities programs had virtually no impact on them. When Williams took office, he made wholesale changes in the staff and commenced hiring competent professionals in place of patronage appointments. Some projects began to show promise in the second action year, and almost all were in operation in the third year.

By the summer of 1972, the Harlem neighborhood office had improved communications with operating agencies, developed fuller job descriptions, and resolved fund shortages and purchasing discrepancies with the central office. Harlem staff was still reporting a backlog of work because of what it called personnel shortages and low employee morale. The Office of Management Information and Evaluation (OMIE) reports that clerical and line staff have received no salary increases after as many as two years of employment, although administrative staff have received annual increments. In addition, the office complains of unreasonable demands for weekly submissions of project monitoring forms and monthly manpower forms. There are even difficulties in identifying the operating agencies of some projects. But the program has become more responsive, and administrative costs have been cut slightly.

Another blow hit Harlem in October 1972. Sanders was found not to have reported a disbarment for reasons of mishandling client funds and was dismissed. He was replaced by a central staff deputy assistant administrator, Geneva McRae, another temporary appointment, but a blessing to the program because projects and general efficiency show marked improvement and staff morale has risen. The program and staff are now more closely tied to Williams because of the tighter relationship with central staff member McRae.

Brooklyn. In September 1967, the central Model Cities Committee sent out 2,000 letters to influential residents of the area requesting their assistance in selecting a local director and setting up planning committees. However, the local organizations responded by setting up a nine-member personnel committee representing the three communities in the area. Although Flatow told the committee to submit three suggested names, they submitted only one, Horace Morancie, who was sworn in reluctantly by Lindsay in January 1968. Morancie, a West Indian (as are several members of his staff), had been an engineer with the Port Authority and is reported to have political designs. He has been able to expedite programs more rapidly than other directors and exerts strong control over the policy committee. Usually his recommendations are accepted, and it appears that the recent centralization of power at headquarters has not affected his operation very much because of extreme staff independence from central staff and because committee members have always been fairly isolated from local decision-making anyway.

Earlier, in March 1969, Morancie began to form his committees. Each area would be represented by 25 persons, divided into five committees—physical development, economic development, sanitation and safety, multiservices, and education. The chairmen of the committees comprised the Policy Committee representing the three communities of the area. The process went relatively smoothly in East New York and Bedford-Stuyvesant. In Brownsville, however, residents resisted the format of committees based on function and for a time insisted on geographical divisions. According to the Brooklyn first action year plan, "the difficulty encountered in the formation of committees arose because of a preference for full control over a small operation rather than shared power over a much larger program."

From March through January 1969, the committees worked on weekends and evenings to prepare their first-year plan. In June, they met for a weekend retreat with city and HUD officials, who ostensibly explained the program. At the same time, the local office was opened.

By December 1968, ground was broken for the first Brooklyn housing, an event that was to become a bitter memory because of the rapid demolition and lack of construction. Relocation was already 71 to 81 percent complete. However, only 31 percent of the dislocated residents were placed in public housing, and the rest disappeared into other slums or went to abandoned houses because of a lack of decent housing.

In January 1969, a final retreat was held to finalize the Brooklyn package. However, according to State Senator Waldaba Stewart, who played a major role in creating the program in Brooklyn, the central office had "physically" lost the Brooklyn package and produced its own version, which was visibly different. Residents had only two days to approve or reject the plan and felt betrayed by city hall. Stewart feels this was the beginning of the program's problems in Brooklyn. He further claims that Lindsay used his staff to influence community meetings in order to lessen local resistance to central office policies.

In July 1969, the first action year had started. A second groundbreaking was held for a $20.9 million, 622-unit housing project. But bureaucratic problems stalled many programs. In September 1969, friction broke out with the area's community corporations because of the collapse of an agreement to distribute to them $1 million in Model Cities funds. This money was intended to soften any resistance from CAP to Model Cities programs as they were introduced to the area. But it was later announced that HUD guidelines prevented dispersal to OEO-funded groups. By then it was too late for CAP to have any direct control over Model Cities programs. To have any influence, CAP people would have to become members of the policy committee, and they thus felt betrayed.

In December 1969, the policy committee and staff sat in at City Hall to protest the red tape the program had encountered. By June 1970, the end of the first action year, several programs were under way, including a Summer Academy, the purchase of ambulances, fire and police cadet programs, training for television production, and licensed practical nursing. Some new programs were added in 1971, but the total of projects for the 1971-72 action year was reduced from 50 to 25.

Citizen Participation in Model Cities

General. Citizen participation has taken a backseat since Model Cities was made into a superagency. Administrator Williams has taken a strong hand in directing the agency, a move believed necessary by many, in order to get the program moving. The Central Policy Committee has been used too infrequently to be meaningful. On the other hand, the three Neighborhood Policy Committees have gained some importance again because of the ineffectiveness of the central committee and because the neighborhood bodies have been legitimized through formal elections. They have become somewhat more effective by experience and the development of better procedures between them and the central staff. Nevertheless, power is centered in the administrator.

Policy Committee Membership. In the beginning, only half of the local policy committee members were elected; the other half were appointed by the executive secretary of the central committee. The method of election was devised by each community. But the whole process proved unsatisfactory because its legitimacy and representativeness were continually challenged. There were frequent changes in the number of members and in the members themselves, making it difficult to tell who really represented the community or with whom city officials should deal. Moreover, powerful spokesmen dominated most of the committees, making it difficult to achieve genuine or widespread resident participation.

One of the reasons new elections were held in the spring of 1971 was to secure more representative bodies, by hopefully wresting control away from the opportunists. The elections were administered centrally by Model Cities staff, and voting took place in the neighborhood offices of the Legal Service Agency. Election guidelines excluded staff members and limited persons already serving on antipoverty boards to three on each policy committee. To provide continuity, each policy committee was permitted to choose 12 incumbents for the first year only, and the Model Cities administrator was authorized to appoint one person from a list of five names, submitted by residents, from each of five groups: business, education, health, religion, and social welfare. The elected members hold a majority of 18 of the 35 total. In addition, ex-officio membership is granted to the city councilman, assemblyman, and congressman of each district, and full membership to each community corporation in areas where they operate. Consequently, policy committees vary in number from 35 to 41 persons. They are also designed to have broad representation in order to lessen the likelihood of domination from any single age group; therefore, categories include youth, adults, and senior citizens. The only qualification is Model Neighborhood residency—and not length of residency.

Importantly, one-third to one-half of the membership face election or appointment annually. Annual elections are necessary not only for injection of new blood but for coping with the problem of migration. The Model Neighborhoods have experienced high emigration, as residents move out to seek better conditions. The influx of more poor people is also significant.

Committee Power. Policy committees never have had final decision-making power but did possess an informal veto through their ability to hold up projects they did not like. Their role has diminished in favor of greater central authority. Their responsibilities now consist principally of the following: representation on the central committee, review of programs, authority to approve new housing and rehabilitation sites, development of relocation plans, and voice in the selection of neighborhood directors. In the choice of directors, for example, a list of five names is presented to Williams from each committee for his choice of one. In some ways, the committees have become more sophisticated and skilled in incorporating their perceptions into Model Cities policy but do not have the strength for informal vetoes they once had. They can only stall action or exert force through large pressure groups. And knowing the importance of keeping the program moving, Williams says, "If they fail to act, we won't wait for them." He is also taking a stronger role in the appointment of neighborhood directors.

Citizen participation is good in terms of numbers of policy committee and task force meetings (functional subcommittees). The Brooklyn Policy Committee, for example, is subdivided into three areas—Brownsville, East New York, Bedford-Stuyvesant—and meetings are held as often as three times per month. But most meetings of the policy committees are informal, and public minutes are not kept. Few Model Neighborhood residents attend, despite the fact that they are paid $50 per month to do so.

Some projects are still developed by the policy committees, but staff has overridden them in several cases, such as in the clerical skills training program, a methadone project in Brooklyn run by the Narcotics Addiction Research Corporation, and a program involving the Brookdale Hospital in Brownsville. On the other hand, Williams is trying to develop a proper balance between citywide priority projects and favorite local ones. Mainly, the staff, not policy committees, develop programs.

Committee strength or weakness depends a great deal on the personality and ability of the neighborhood director. Morancie is powerful and very knowledgeable about New York's program; therefore, he is convincing to his policy committee. Bronx Director Marrero exerts less strength but directs a fairly smooth program in spite of a committee that is outspoken and insistent on many things. Harlem's former director Sanders worked closely with his policy committee. He did not hire anyone until citizens screened candidates. His policy committee also chose sites for day-care centers and housing rehabilitation projects and made other significant decisions. In general, neighborhood directors have to get a job done within a limited time frame and many times end up manipulating their committees in order to keep things moving. The excuse of having to bow to a strong central administrator only assists their role.

Policy committees have a certain degree of inherent power. They are relied upon when city agencies need help to gain community consensus. In the Bronx, former Deputy Director Jorge Baptista felt Model Cities had more clout than any other city agency because it could muster 200-300 people to go to Board of Estimate or city council meetings. "They never would have put 10,000 units of housing in this area without Model Cities support," he said. And this strength is broadened through 30-member planning committees in six Model Cities subareas. All three policy committees are used to qualify clients for programs to decide which families have priority for health and rehabilitation services. For example, HDA used Model Cities Committees to approve recipients under the Municipal Loan Program. The committees are a vehicle to enable city officials to reach residents and gain their support. When used properly, they have been effective.

But too often they have been dominated by special-interest groups or individuals. The first-round committee membership in the Bronx experienced strong influence from persons in the antipoverty programs. And the Harlem and Brooklyn Committees consisted of members with little or no real constituencies of their own. In the beginning, struggles were numerous. Many members resigned from policy committees because of heated arguments both internally and with the city. There were few grass-roots or professional members, and many responsible members chose to leave because of the emergence of "strongmen." In Brooklyn, for example, one member (with an extensive criminal record) threatened people and boasted of his threats against Williams. Others also have damaged the image of the boards, but the city has tried to rectify this through improved election procedures, which have been only partially effective.

Hunter College Analysis of Citizen Involvement. A May 1970 report prepared by Seymour Z. Mann, Chairman of the Department of Urban Affairs of Hunter College, described policy committee participants mainly as the older middle class or middle class oriented, leaders of poverty programs, church groups, political clubs, education groups, and other special-interest bodies. Most belong to several organizations, and their primary motivation for participation has been economic and power-related. To a large extent, those who ran for election were unsuccessful in getting on Community Corporation Boards. Distrust of the administration was prevalent; therefore, members wanted their own staffs to do local planning, much of it secretive and some of it designed to test the CDA with demands over issues of control. In the process, power passed to the city, and the unequal partnership threw many members into a state of hostility, apathy, and resignation. A closer relationship developed with the Community Corporations and Community Action Agency (CAA) staff as Model Cities bodies looked to them as natural supporters in their common fight with city officials. Yet, this whole experience built another clique jealous of its powers and resulted in greater intracommunity conflict.

Mann relates that during the first two years of the program, almost none of the programs were implemented, and city agencies even stopped many of their activities in Model Neighborhoods for fear of being accused of promoting programs without community approval, resulting in further deterioration of the environment. Although the central staff continued to battle the bureaucracy in favor of the communities, it had low visibility and residents looked upon the CDA as their agency. "The result was a colossal series of misunderstandings in which the CDA saw itself as working in behalf of communities, but communities perceived their efforts as being either inhibiting or hostile toward them" Mann states.

In conclusion, the report reveals that participation had little effect on the implementation of programs during these first two years (planning and first action year) but that it did result in a number of procedural and institutional changes, including (1) decentralized planning; (2) CDA task force operation and better coordination of city agencies; (3) coordination by Model Cities Committees; (4) greater coordination between CAA and CDA at the local level; (5) earmarking of funds for Model Cities area as a priority matter; (6) greater consideration given to combining related programs under one roof, as multiservice school programs, for example; (7) changes in union and civil service rules allowing residents to be hired and run their own programs; and (8) greater skills in the CDA in dealing with the partnership relationship and in changing rules and procedures to open up opportunities for residents.[13]

Model Neighborhood Resident Employment. Citizen participation can also be measured in terms of Model Neighborhood employment in the program. The employment of MN residents (MNRs) varies among agencies, but by August 1972 only 56 percent were employed in Model Cities projects and in administration, as shown below. The percentage rises substantially to 89 percent when those residents near the MNs (PMNRs) are included. The picture is also improved for MN residents in training programs but appears weak in relation to objectives, taking into the fact that account over 400 trainees are not living in the MNs. Of 1,447 positions managed by New York City agencies, 88 percent are MN residents, for an over-all percentage of approximately 76. This analysis indicates that it may be unreasonable to limit services and employment to only MN residents and that a citywide or at least a somewhat broader approach is preferable.[14]

August 1972 Employment of Model Neighborhood Residents

	MNRs	PMNRs	Other Areas	Total
1. Central and neighborhood staff	352 (42%)	337 (40%)	132 (18%)	821
2. Core staff	7 (16%)	6 (14%)	31 (70%)	44
3. Projects operated by NYC agencies	860 (67%)	353 (26%)	16 (7%)	1,229
4. Projects operated by third-party (outside) contractors	113 (42%)	88 (32%)	71 (26%)	272
5. Projects that are lump-sum-funded	21 (66%)	8 (25%)	3 (9%)	32
	1,353 (56%)			2,398

Administration

Office of Administrator. In the first two years of the program, Model
Cities central administration was weakly organized, with an executive
secretary on about the same par as the three neighborhood directors,
each acting independently and pressuring city hall for change. Neighborhood staffs worked in isolation as well. But its reorganization
into a superagency changed these roles and the position of executive
secretary became that of administrator, with single authority and
clear lines of command.

In order further to grasp hold of this separatist agency and to
remain personally on top of problems, Administrator Williams, after
brief experimentation, ordered most key Model Cities officials to
report directly to him. At first there existed the position of deputy
administrator, designed to absorb much of this feedback. Robert
Carrol served in this slot for about seven months in 1971 but resigned
because he found himself estranged and without a significant role.
To Williams, the position was a bottleneck to smooth lines of authority.
And at this stage, he prefers to deal directly with staff even below
the assistant administrator level because this method keeps him in
closer touch with the program and has made his presence widely felt.
The five assistant administrators—from Program Development and
Implementation (PDI), Staff Operations, and the three neighborhood
directors—have recognized the importance of this mobility (See Chart
9).

The neighborhood directors use both titles interchangeably (sometimes signing memoranda with both titles), perhaps indicative that
their roles have not changed very much, despite superagency terminology. The most important way Williams has been able to secure
tighter lines of authority and loyalty with neighborhood directors has
been by changing personalities, not titles, as he did by appointing
McRae in Harlem. The question has always existed whether it was
necessary to create a superagency at all or simply change personnel
and get rid of a defunct central committee. But taken in its political
context—to diminish the community's role and demonstrate new
leadership—the creation of superagency status may have been the
best intermediate step.

Program Development and Implementation. PDI has turned out to be
one of the best listening posts for Williams. He put it together in
early 1970, after he first took office. At that time some 121 projects
were in a log jam and in need of a unit like PDI to implement programs
quickly and effectively. Three deputy assistant administrators were
appointed to this division, in charge of physical, social, and economic
programs. An assistant administrator, Julio Vivas, was placed in

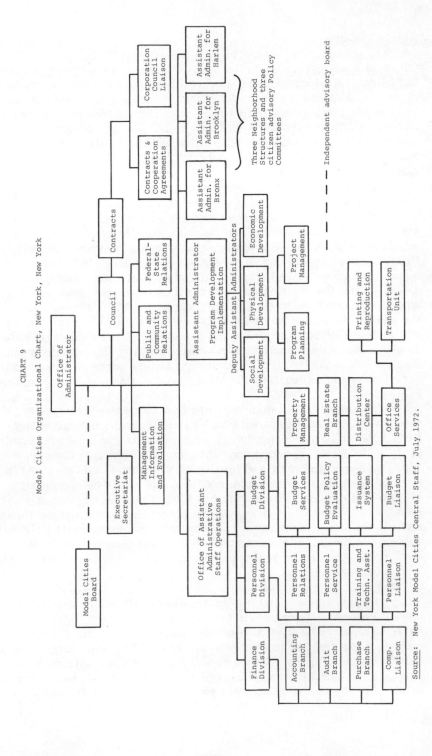

CHART 9

Model Cities Organizational Chart, New York, New York

Source: New York Model Cities Central Staff, July 1972.

360

charge of the entire division in January 1971. By May, 69 programs were in operation and, in early 1972, 89 were operational and another 12 eliminated as ineffectual. Implementation of at least two dozen other programs is still pending. But the whole operation was streamlined and its "shot gun" approach drastically changed, when some 300 programs were condensed to slightly more than 100. Almost all small-impact projects (those under $50,000 and some in the $100,000 range) were eliminated.

With almost all programs operational, PDI relinquished its implementation role, except for 10 citywide projects, in the summer of 1971, to the three neighborhood offices and began on-site monitoring. Implementation and technical assistance are still part of its function, particularly where citywide coordination is necessary. But monitoring is its chief activity now; and it has reviewed over 20 projects so far. Monitoring for PDI involves a number of elements: cost-benefit analysis, reviewing work loads, comparing projected timetables and implementation dates, correlating objectives with achievements, structural analysis, and client interviews. The most frank and comprehensive review of projects has come out of this office.

Office of Management Information and Evaluation. In a broader sense, the Office of Management Information and Evaluation, headed by James Fukumoto, an experienced analyst, performs most of its evaluation by analyzing and reporting the over-all impact of projects on the economy, city, and region. It assesses what progress has been made against Model Cities strategy: its major issues and programatic developments, citizen participation and resident employment, the information system, nonsupplemental funding sources, and the city's capacity and commitment to get the job done. These two divisions are so closely intertwined that many believe they should be one. If they were united, certainly better coordination and staff utilization would result. In this respect, Williams has already indicated one of his chief priorities is to restructure OMIE into a more useful component. Lately, OMIE began monitoring and evaluating individual projects.

Some feel monitoring should simply be a component of OMIE. It is presently confusing to many whether PDI is between OMIE and the neighborhood or OMIE is between PDI and the neighborhood. Moreover, the heads of each of these components report directly to Williams, who wishes to see monitoring reports firsthand. On the other hand, some would like to see monitoring placed at the neighborhood staff level and PDI simply used as an implementation unit.

There is little question, if programs are to be continually improved, that local staff and residents should be involved in in-depth evaluation. Many officials believe that the almost useless role of

OMIE in preparing quarterly statistical reports—which consume almost all of its time—ought to be trimmed to dispensing annual reports and its role broadened by integrating it with PDI to monitor systematically all projects. They feel the federal government ought not only to cooperate but to welcome this reduction in paper shuffling, treating New York more like a Planned Variations city.

Another problem, not only between these two staffs but among most divisions, is that information does not flow freely and is difficult to get. Divisions do not know exactly what others are doing. Policy committees do not have access to monitoring reports, and PDI and other departments do not regularly see quarterly evaluation reports, perhaps attesting to the reports' uselessness. Yet certain information—particularly, detailed monitoring reports—would be valuable to all components and would also encourage policy committees in efforts at evaluation. A central information system has not yet been developed, although such steps are being taken by OMIE. When it is developed, the proper distribution of information will be very important.

New Studies and Structural Change. To improve information and other problem areas, OMIE, with the support of HUD's regional office, has contracted with a private firm for the undertaking of a macro-management study of the entire agency, to be completed sometime in 1973. Its objectives are to strengthen information flows and management processes and ultimately improve service delivery. It will assess moving the program at an acceptable rate of speed, developing the means to measure progress, strengthening information flows between neighborhood offices and the central office, creating a well-trained staff to deal with systems, and clarifying roles and improving agency coordination and operation methods between Model Cities and other agencies.

The third action year also calls for an Operations Division, which will first engage in six studies covering manpower training and employment, early prisoner work release, a community accountability system, educational achievement (through educational contractors), neighborhood indicators of change, and health and drug treatment. Model Cities has already conducted a comprehensive over-all analysis of health and crime. Moreover, in an attempt to treat and bring more ethnic groups into the program, OEO has granted Model Cities $250,000 for an ethnics study. All studies will be made available to city officials in anticipation of improving over-all city management and also neighborhood quality of life.

Important current changes include the development of major institutes or task forces (somewhat like the task forces that were operating at the beginning of the program to help coordinate agencies and act as trouble shooters). An institute has been put into operation for manpower, and others are under development for criminal justice, health, and housing. Besides resolving problems, the primary task is to coordinate related agencies. For example, the Manpower Institute is coordinating efforts with the Manpower and Career Development Agency, Youth Services Agency, and other manpower and job development projects having an impact on the Model Neighborhood. Moreover, in order to improve coordination and expedite process, certain Model Cities personnel have been assigned as part of the core staff of other agencies, such as in the Department of Purchases and Real Estate, Comptroller's Office, Bureau of the Budget, and in each of the offices of the presidents of the three boroughs where the program functions. These special full-time Model Cities employees, working only on Model Cities processes, have had some beneficial effect on speeding up the bureaucracy.

Furthermore, to expedite neighborhood programs, Williams has appointed "community interest groups," whose members are from five categories—special services, education, religion, health, and business—and are designed to provide a broad range of expertise to policy committees in planning, developing, and monitoring programs. These groups are likely to do one of two things: make policy committees more effective or reduce their role even more. What happens depends much on what the administration feels is a good balance to keep the program moving.

What is evident from these changes is that a more coordinated and direct attack on problems is to take place, with much more expertise imposed on communities. There is also considerably stronger interest from the mayor and his chief appointees about the impact Model Cities can have on other agencies, if used properly as a catalyst for change.

OMIE Evaluation Process. OMIE has begun to develop base data and procedures for project-by-project, cost-benefit analysis. In most cases, however, Model Cities does not have direct control of productivity levels because projects are in the hands of separate operating agencies, limiting its role primarily to monitoring and planning. Also, goals are broader than those for other agencies—stressing basic job training and quality of life, for example—which again limits how far it can pursue productivity objectives. In almost every project, for example, extra staff is built in, not necessarily to operate the program but to gain training and experience for the purpose of improving future employability. This automatically raises budgets and cost-benefit ratios.

Nevertheless, some valid comparisons can be made with Model Cities projects in other cities and among the three Model Neighborhoods, even though neighborhood conditions and certain other factors

vary from neighborhood to neighborhood. They can also be usefully
related to programs from other public and private agencies, by comparing long-term costs and allowing for base differences. OMIE
chose to concentrate its analysis on 12 projects because they operate
in all three MNs and have citywide impact.

It has grouped these projects under three headings and has projected highlights, described below, for the 1972/73 fiscal year as compared to the 1971/72 fiscal year:

Training and Delivery of Service Programs	Training Programs	Delivery of Service Programs
Community Service Officer (Police)	Health Careers Work Release	Ambulatory Detoxification Ambulance Decentralization
Housing Authority Community Service Officer		Housing Maintenance New Housing Construction
Fire Prevention		Emergency Repair
Sanitation		Recreation/Culture

1. Training and Delivery of Services Programs

It is anticipated that trainees in all four programs
will increase.

Trainee increases far outstrip planned increased
staffing in the Housing Authority and Fire Prevention Programs.

The Sanitation Program has the largest number of
trainees and trainee-graduates of any single Training and
Delivery of Services Program. This may explain the large
staff increases relative to new trainees.

Trainee productivity output may subsequently increase in terms of patrol, lectures/demonstrations,
escort services, and refuse collection as they graduate
to higher levels in these programs.

2. Training Programs

It is anticipated that Work Release trainees will
increase in greater proportion than staff.

Health training enrollees and graduates are expected to significantly increase during the current year.

3. Delivery of Services Programs

It is anticipated that the Ambulatory Detoxification
Project, which plans to open another clinic in 1973, will

be able to treat substantially more beneficiaries with a proportionately lower increase in staffing.

The numbers of beneficiaries served are also expected to increase above Second Year levels for Ambulance Decentralization, Recreation, and Housing Maintenance.

Emergency Repair and New Housing Construction reported continuing efforts in alleviating Model Neighborhood Housing conditions. Housing Construction plans to complete many dwelling units begun during its previous operations to date.[15]

OMIE Cost Benefit Data. In addition to these projects, OMIE has at least started, although crudely constructed because of lack of data, a cost-benefit analysis of all ongoing projects. Its information (output measures) is drawn from routine project reporting forms and, as yet, has not been carefully audited. It also does not include benefits from more than one type of output, again mostly because of lack of available data. For example, results are based on primary and secondary measures of productivity, such as tons of refuse collected, numbers of people attending a demonstration, or some other single prominent factor, without regard to the interaction of factors.

Table 10 provides an example of project measurement from one of the MNs. It shows cumulative budgets and expenditures, number of trainees who have participated since project inception, other output measurement (such as number of clients, repairs, and complaints), and the cost per trainee or other output measure (derived by dividing total money spent by output measure). Where a project has both trainees and other outputs, the area in which the project placed the greatest emphasis was used. Certain figures show a fairly accurate assessment of costs, such as the cost of community service officers' salaries, administrative expenditures of $10,313 per trainee in Brooklyn, and housing maintenance costs of $2,000 per unit in Harlem. But the short- and long-term results of officer training or the quality of housing maintenance are not evaluated. In some cases, the output measure has no valid relationship to expenditures, such as in the Brooklyn Educational Television Project, where the $1,031,000 expenditure shows a $2.83 per unit cost by assuming that the entire MN population of 364,000 is the viewing public and that each person derives a benefit.

OMIE does not contend these are accurate measurements and insists it will refine them as time and capability permit. The process has some utility because it provides information on budgets, rate of expenditures, number of trainees, and other general data. However, an accurate, in-depth analysis of each project is what is needed. Such evaluation has been started for some projects.

TABLE 10

Brooklyn Model Cities Cost to Beneficiary Analysis
(First Action Year to May 11, 1972)

Project	Total Budget (in dollars)	Total Spent (in dollars)	Total Trainees	Total Other Output Measure	Cost per Trainee (in dollars)	Cost per Other Output Measure (in dollars)
Housing						
Emergency Repairs	7,088,000	4,083,000	35	10,264[a]	—	397.80
Public Housing	1,677,000	671,000	—	3,000	—	223.67
Construction Subsidy (Underground Parking)	1,162,000	193,000		[b]	—	—
Transportation-Communication						
Educational TV	2,054,000	1,031,000	9	364,446[c]	—	2.83
Satellite Radio	818,000	425,000	61	364,446[c]	—	1.16
Crime-Delinquency						
Police Dept. CSO	2,627,000	1,186,000	115	—	10,313.04	—
Work Release	1,644,000	776,000	—	559	—	1,388.19
Housing Authority	1,733,000	904,000	75	—	12,053.33	—
Delinquency Control	301,000	103,000	—	2,400	—	42.92
Manpower and Job Development						
Clerical Training	184,000	91,000	250	—	354.00	—
Job Training	7,282,000	3,217,000	1,319	—	2,438.97	—
Health Careers Training	5,592,000	1,934,000	374	350	5,313.19	—

[a]Repairs made.
[b]Subsidized construction programs in Model Neighborhood.
[c]Serves the entire community.

Source: Office of Management Information and Evaluation, Model Cities, New York, May 1972.

Administrative Costs. A more revealing analysis of costs is derived
from looking at administrative costs. OMIE reports accumulative
program and administrative expenditures from July 1, 1969 to March
31, 1972 as $70,984,000 and accumulative administrative costs as
$12,656,000 for the same period, or 17 percent. This is high when
compared to operations of certain other agencies and many private
operations. However, if based on total appropriations rather than
expenditures, administrative costs drop to 9 or 10 percent. They
could reach this in the future, as new projects are started and money
is spent on time. It would be unfair to include Model Neighborhood
housing construction costs (as distinguished from seed money and
other funds used to assist projects) as part of the total budget because
they are administered by HDA, although a large sum is usually expressed as part of the Model Cities Program.

Of these costs, the central office accounted for $5,868,000 and
the neighborhood offices $6,788,000. The following shows program
and administrative expenditures for each neighborhood accumulative
for two different periods of time, indicative of some decline in administrative costs.[16]

	Program Figures (millions)	Adminis- tration Figures (millions)	Cost to Administer $1 of Program by Area
Harlem/East Harlem			
9/30/71	$ 5.914	$1.294	$0.22
3/31/72	10.993	1.900	0.17
South Bronx			
9/30/71	11.780	1.583	0.14
3/31/72	17.760	1.875	0.11
Central Brooklyn			
9/30/71	21.016	2.360	0.11
3/31/72	29.375	3.013	0.10

Administrative costs of 10 to 17 percent for the three neighborhoods are high. When the central office costs are added, the total
averages 17 percent. Also, when normal overhead costs of other city
agencies (such as Budget, Legal, Purchasing, and Real Estate) are
added, costs rise higher. On top of this, there are the administrative
and overhead costs of each project, since Model Cities is simply a
dispenser of funds—other agencies operate the programs. These
costs add from 5 to 10 percent more to each project, with some projects revealing lower costs and some exceedingly higher.

    Furthermore, training residents on projects has raised costs
well above normal in relation to the services delivered. For example,
in Emergency Repairs there are 305 regular personnel plus 110 trainees, and in Sanitation there are 100 regular personnel plus 265 trainees. To correct this disparity, many believe training and service
aspects ought to be separated, so that service can be provided to the
bulk of citizens at reasonable costs.

Staff Operations. Staff Operations handles finances and budgeting,
auditing, purchasing, personnel, training, real estate, and office services (transportation and reproduction). F. William Ling was appointed
as its assistant administrator in mid-1970 and has played an important
part in achieving several important changes: (1) It took months to
gain clearance and hire people due to normal city personnel procedures.
Now Model Cities may hire managerial personnel first and get clearance later, speeding the process considerably (to about three weeks)
and encouraging more competent people, who are in demand, to apply.
Also, people can now be hired above minimum salary levels and un-
classified personnel given cost-of-living increases. (2) The number
of purchasing steps have been reduced from 82 to 32. (3) The number
of days needed to get approval for budget expenditures has been cut
from 64 to 16. And (4) the time necessary to secure permission from
the Department of Real Estate for rentals and leasing has been minimized, although it is still too lengthy.
    In addition to the above, the requirement for high school gradua-
tion was dropped by the City Department of Personnel for the promotional position of paraprofessional Relocation Aide and Community
Specialist, because of convincing arguments presented by Model Cities.
Model Cities also requested that certain tests be given in Spanish as
well as English, since many residents are Spanish-speaking. City
Personnel compromised and has agreed to give an alternative version
of the test with 60 percent of the items in Spanish and 40 percent in
English, another Model Cities victory.
    In regards to the problem of spending money on time, Model
Cities is now spending funds fairly close to target, at the rate of $4.6
million monthly in 1972, or about $500,000 per month less than pro-
jected. All but $9.8 million of its full allocation of $130 million was
spent up to February 1972, a considerable improvement over its less
than 50 percent expenditure rate earlier.
    Tight control over Model Cities expenditures, particularly close
audit by the city comptroller, has been welcomed by most officials
in order to lessen the possibility of fund misuse. The shortening of
expenditure approval time has made the process more acceptable.
Nevertheless, some Model Cities personnel feel that the program
will have to be almost entirely independent of city bureaucracy to

expedite processing effectively. Too many things have to be done twice—once by Model Cities, then again by an appropriate city branch.

On the other hand, Model Cities itself needs streamlining and clarification of regulations and procedures. Personnel are quick to quote regulations but are unable to find them. A codification of regulations, widely distributed, would be an asset to the organization.

PDI reports the most prevalent problem is moving paper through the Model Cities Administration. The difficulties are not so much within each unit (budget, legal, and so on) as with the interaction of multiple functions, such as relationships among budget development, contract modification, site selection, acquisition, remodeling, personnel selection, and payment of vouchers for materials. To correct this problem, PDI has successfully instituted a staff of expediters to review and "walk through" documents pertaining to program clusters. These program specialists are familiar with all appropriate city and state agencies. At the same time, they have developed better agency relationships and are also assisting in the monitoring of programs.

Division of Federal/State Relations. A special unit, Federal/State Relations, was formed in July 1970, and a special assistant to the administrator was appointed as its head. The first head, William Toby, Jr. was highly qualified to fill the assignment, having been special assistant to the HEW regional director. Although staff in the Budget Bureau performed part of this role, the additional component was deemed necessary because New York City was not getting all the funds it was entitled to.

This unit is charged with coordinating resources and acting as liaison with all levels of government, determining impact of HEW projects on the MNs, disseminating information about federal grants-in-aid that go through the state, and making the best use of supplemental funds for matching purposes.

One of its first actions was to analyze HEW funds granted to the state. It was determined that New York State received $23,952,948 in 1970 and New York City only $2.5 million (18 percent) of that amount, when it had 70 percent of the state's educationally disadvantaged, 62 percent of the economically disadvantaged children, 58 percent of all high school dropouts, and 50 percent of all the jobs in the state. The 1968 Vocational Education Act amendments are specific in their guidelines for grant distribution. Grants are supposed to be based on priorities to areas of high rates of unemployment, number of school dropouts, and other disadvantaged requirements. Besides this difference, when the amount is added to the state allotment, New York City was getting only 10 percent of a total of $47 million—a significant disparity.

In meetings with state officials, Model Cities tried to get New York City funds increased. However, the assistant commissioner for occupational education in the State Department of Education identified several reasons for New York City's low allotment: (1) federal funds should be used to support only new projects and should be funded for only one year at a time; (2) nothing compelled the state to distribute funds according to any special formula; and (3) New York City Board of Education had not developed the administrative apparatus or arrangements necessary for a sound vocational education program.

With these facts in mind, further meetings, and local congressional help, New York City received an increase from $2.5 million to $4.5 million for fiscal year 1971.

This example of the work of the Division of Federal/State Relations demonstrates its effectiveness. In this case, it was able to draw attention to a funding imbalance, bring the chief actors together, and attain a significant increase in funding.[17] This division had had a series of successes in seeing that the city gets its fair share of funds.

Model Cities Projects

General

In New York, as in a number of other cities, many officials have looked upon Model Cities as merely another source of funds or a place where problems could be dumped. Model Cities has been trying to change this of late. Its underlying strategy is to continue the consolidation of operating projects and concentrate administrative energies in "fewer and bigger projects" so that the effect of each is strengthened and the program becomes more manageable.

With the reduction of programs from 300 to about 100, concentration is now on 10 major projects. The Model Cities Administration believes these programs have reached satisfactory levels of success and has encouraged each Model Neighborhood to adopt all of them, as well as maintaining other hopeful programs. The third action year stresses a coordinated offensive through five priority functional areas—unemployment, crime, health, housing, drugs, and alcoholism—and expansion of the ten major projects: (1) emergency repair, (2) sanitation, (3) work release (counseling, training for ex-convicts), (4) project children (day care), (5) medical transportation, (6) education (scholarships, career training), (7) alcoholic outreach, (8) drug addiction, (9) police training, and (10) fire (personnel) training.

In the following pages, each Model Neighborhood is discussed separately; however, attention is directed to Brooklyn because it is the largest and has been the most active program area. Primarily, the most significant projects are discussed, but lesser ones are mentioned in order to give the reader an idea of the scope and comprehensiveness of the program. Budgets are shown to provide a concept of the size of projects and where expenditures are going, and they reflect annual expenditures, in most cases for the third action year. The Federation of Addiction Agencies Project in Brooklyn is discussed in some length as a case study of the kinds of problems that have confronted the total Model Cities Program.

Where sources are not indicated, information was provided by Model Cities staff and neighborhood residents through interviews. Where specific data are mentioned without sources, material was derived from Quarterly Evaluation Reports of the Model Cities Office of Management Information and Evaluation, particularly the 12th and 13th Quarterly Reports. Information was also gathered from Division of Program Development and Implementation memoranda.

Where not indicated, evaluation covers the period of the second action year (which ended June 1972) and part of the third action year. The intention of this review was not to evaluate individual projects in-depth but to provide an over-all view of the program. Some local investigation was conducted, but for the most part, where administration data and evaluation were not available, no further information could be provided.

Brooklyn

Manpower and Job Development

1. Community Service Officers (CSO) Project and Fire Cadet Training and Service Project. These programs seek to get Model Neighborhood residents on the civil service career ladder. In May 1971, there were 22 Model Cities citywide career-ladder projects under way, with a total of 775 trainee slots filled, out of an allocation of 1,062 (542 for Model Neighborhood residents). These projects are priorities, but in August 1972 there were only 120 trainees in the CSO project in Brooklyn and 330 citywide, although the program started in December 1969. The first action year budget for the police project was $559,089, second year $1,233,000, and third year $1,491,000. The first year showed an unexpended balance of $323,000 because of project delays. But delays were not caused by the police department administration.

The Fire Cadet Project has moved more slowly. There are 40 cadets in training; the first year budget was $249,000, second year $826,000, and third year $1,196,000. In addition, there are 49 MN residents in training for Fire Salvage (water protection) with a budget of $634,000. OMIE reports that this and the Sanitation Project (described later) are not operating well because of inadequate facilities. And high school education equivalency has not yet been made available, although this is an integral part of the program.

Trainees in both programs are on provisional civil service status and may have to go through the standard civil service process as a result of a state supreme court decree March 8, 1972, which struck down as unconstitutional a special city-sponsored examination for aides for police, fire, and the Housing Authority. Justice Samuel J. Silverman invalidated qualification tests given to more than 3,000 Model Cities residents in October 1971. About 825 aides were to be hired. Silverman stated that special examining "may be a very desirable thing to do" but that the program was selective in purpose and disregarded state civil service regulations that make appointment to the uniformed forces solely a matter of competitive examination on the basis of "merit and fitness." He said, "If the Civil Service requirements are unfair, they should, of course, be corrected by appropriate changes in the examinations. But I do not think this justifies imposing residence requirements."

The Patrolmen's Benevolent Association and Uniformed Firemen's Association complained in the suit filed September 1971 that the plan gave "preferential treatment" and "competitive advantage" to the blacks and Puerto Ricans living in the Model Neighborhood. The PBA was also against the creation of a separate "aide" category on the forces. Justice Silverman wrote:

> I do not think it can rationally be contended that a person who has lived in the area all his life and moved to an adjoining area the day before the test is less sensitive to, understanding of or experienced with the problems of the area than a person who has never lived in the area but moved in the day before the test; yet the latter is qualified to take the test and the former is not.[18]

The proposal advocated entrance examinations for training at lower salaries and, after 15 months, second tests to qualify for regular positions. Earlier, state supreme court judge Paul Fino (an arch conservative and former civil service commissioner), issued an injunction preventing administration of the tests. The appellate court lifted the injunction, allowing the examinations, but prevented training until a final court ruling on the issues. The unions argued that the testing would be prejudicial to the 8,000 already on waiting lists, that it provides advantage based on race, and that lower qualifications will hurt the service. The city's corporation counsel is appealing the decision. Moreover, the final decision will have an important impact on the whole Model Cities Program because similar career ladders are being developed for positions in emergency repair, mental retardation, education information, satellite radio, TV education, housing authority security, licensed practical nursing, X-ray technician, and clerical areas.

Nevertheless, without civil service changes, job opportunities are being improved because trainees are being developed to a level where a higher percentage can pass regular examinations and other related tests. For example, in one test in the Bronx, all 26 residents under the Model Cities training program secured positions on the fire cadet list. And candidates are being recruited for positions with state and city corrections departments. About 30 public community service officers passed the City Correction Officers test, 10 passed the State Correction Officers test, and 86 passed the City Correction Aide test. Also 38 housing CSOs and 74 fire cadets passed the Correction Aide test. In addition, New York Model Cities is awaiting results of a Hartford Police Department examination, which 27 CSOs took.

2. Clerical Training Project. The New York Chamber of Commerce Educational Foundation is operating a Clerical Training Project designed to train 350 residents from the three Model Neighborhoods on typists and stenographers during a 23-week comprehensive course. The Department of Labor is funding 88 percent of the $1,875,000 budget and Model Cities $276,000 of it. The Chamber is to find jobs for all graduates.

3. Job Training Project. The Job Training Project began operating in March 1971 and is run by the Port of New York Authority, designed to train 1,665 MN residents in drafting, heavy vehicle driving, general maintenance, electrical appliance service, air conditioning and refrigerator repair, oil burner repair, and basic office practices. A day-care facility for 55 children is included. The project was funded for $3,583,000 in the second action year and $4,334,000 in the third action year. As of December 31, 1971, 953 trainees had been enrolled from the beginning of the project, 322 were in training, 363 had been graduated, and 132 had been placed in gainful employment. To date, the program has been a failure based on the criterion of job placements and less than satisfactory based on numbers trained and graduated. The cost-benefit ratio is completely out of line with results.

New York City's poor job market certainly had had a negative effect on the program, but other problems such as extensive use of drugs by trainees has also hurt results. PDI reports that drug use has been sharply reduced, but counseling is inadequate because personnel are required to perform many other tasks, such as taking urine samples and developing jobs. The teaching staff is rated high by the PDI monitor, but teaching equipment is faulty.[19] PDI monitoring reports "ineffective job development; procrastination in processing site relocation, acquisition and remodeling; and insensitive counseling procedures."[20]

Another site was under renovation for the third action year. Some improvements are in progress, such as dropping programs with low job placement potential and those that attract little interest. Most importantly, negotiations are under way to change the operating agency, possibly to the Opportunities Industrialization Center (OIC), Training and Development Corporation (TDC), or Joint Apprenticeship Training (JAP). But as of September 1972, an operating agency or a suitable training site had not been found. This project has seriously held back the progress of New York's Model Cities Program.

4. Health Careers Training Project. Health and Hospitals is operating the Health Careers Training Project, designed to train 544 persons in 1972 as nurses, X-ray technicians, medical services assistants, health administrators, dental assistants, and mental health counselors. The second action year budget was $1,820,000, with 150 trainees; the third action year $3,341,000, with 179 trainees. Although only one class of 30 had graduated at the time this book went to press, hiring is taking place, and the potential in these job categories looks good.

5. Sanitation Training Project. Under this program, sanitation trainees are paid $6,000 to $6,450 annually. The second action year budget was $3,309,000 and the third was $3,715,000. Trainees take regular civil service tests given in the neighborhood. A second civil service list is maintained for trainees. There were 157 trainees in the first year, 127 in the second, and 283 in the third. But there are no official figures as to how many have successfully completed the program or have become full-time regular employees of the Sanitation Department. Absenteeism is high, averaging 67 per week. And there is little job satisfaction.

Early in the program, the Brooklyn Policy Committee took issue with the Sanitation Department and threatened to withhold funds because the department was operating with the same number of trucks, although money was provided for additional equipment. Eventually the Sanitation Department consented to comply with the agreement. Also the Sanitation Union has resisted the program. For example, it will allow trainees to carry refuse to the curb only and has forced many of them into cleaning sidewalks and vacant lots, hardly positions requiring training. In addition, the union has pressed litigation to prevent civil service employment for MN residents who were hired as trainees under the second civil service list, which is designed to by-pass regular personnel procedures.

Health Programs. A $1,171,000 Group Practice Medical Center will be operated by the Health and Hospitals Corporation (a unit of the Health Services Administration) to provide comprehensive family-oriented routine medical and dental diagnostic and treatment services. But renovation of facilities has delayed the project.

374

Also, Health and Hospitals operates an ambulance/ambulette service consisting of 26 vehicles and 68 employees at an annual cost of $883,000. So far, three ambulances and 34 personnel are being utilized. Over 15,000 emergency calls have been answered, and the program seems well received by the community. However, based on the number of ambulances and personnel, costs are extremely high for the number of calls being made.

Crime and Delinquency. One of the most innovative and successful programs, Work Release, is operated by the Department of Corrections with an annual budget of $892,000. Inmates from the Model Neighborhood, serving the last few months of their sentences, are released to a residential facility, which prepares them to reenter society. Detainees are referred to as residents, and the atmosphere is relaxed and informal. Through extensive counseling and guidance, 51 percent have been placed in jobs within one to three weeks after arriving at the center. A total of 438 clients used the facility since its inception in February 1970. Its capacity at any one time is 60 but is being increased to 100. As with other projects, this one was initially stalled by powerful union and bureaucratic interests but got into operation in time to show successful results. There is evidence of a considerably lower recidivism rate for this group. The Commissioner of the Department of Corrections appears pleased with the program and has initiated an annual award ceremony for the participants making the most progress.

Also under the crime and delinquency component, a $100,000 Delinquency Control Service, operated by the Protestant Board of Guardians (nonprofit agency created by probation officers and judges of children's court), has treated over 500 youths with 50 percent satisfactory adjustment rate. Work continues on those who need continued service. About 1,000 youths are expected to receive counseling.

Closely related to the above, the Brooklyn Businessmen's Committee for the Employment of Ex-offenders is now operating a $62,000 Project Second Chance, which is to find jobs for 500 ex-offenders.

In addition, the Legal Aid Society will operate a $358,160 Community Defender Office. These are all third action year programs.

Education

1. Academic Opportunities. A Summer/Winter Academy assists junior high and high school students in their regular curriculum and helps prepare them for college work and for the transition to college academic and social life. The Brooklyn Polytechnic Institute operates the program (although Model Cities operated it directly the first year) and enrolled 425 students the summer of 1969; 1,900 in 1970; 1,500 in 1971; and 4,175 in 1972, at 17 different colleges and universities for

375

an eight-week period. Stipends of $350 are awarded after completion of the program, but a first-year winter project enrolled 215 students without stipends. As interest spread, an expanded 1971-72 Winter Academy enrolled 993. College scholarships are also awarded to graduates based on need and academic record. In 1971, over 300 students were on scholarships, ranging from $600 to $1,500. The total budget and scholarships for the academy was $5,569,000 in 1972.

Also in 1972, a Summer/Winter Academy Parents Association was formed to involve parents. In addition, residents are members of the Scholarship Board, which makes awards. OMIE's preliminary evaluation in August 1972 was inconclusive. It stated, "Outcome data to measure the educational achievements of the summer students through standardized tests (before and after) which have been administered, along with follow-up data, on credits awarded by the Board of Education, are essential to any judgment about the effectiveness of this major program."21

Nevertheless, the academy has sparked the public school system, is providing genuine educational opportunities, and is reported by Model Cities monitors to have widespread community appreciation. Clarence Whittington, administrator of Summer Academy of Southhampton, believes the program is a huge success, saying, "Our kids, for the first time, accepted the fact that college was not outside of their reach."

2. Television and Radio Project. This Model Cities project is the only one of its kind in the nation. By early 1972, over $2.7 million was spent on training residents in broadcast skills, establishment of a community communications system, and community programing for community consumption. Under the program, residents are to be trained to produce 20 hours of weekly programing by cable TV, Ultra High Frequency broadcast, or closed circuit television. Forty trainees were selected for the radio program, 25 for engineer technician class, and 15 as reporter-writer apprentices—all at $100 a week stipends under the direction of the Brooklyn College faculty.

Donald Singleton, in a New York Daily News article of November 10, 1971 wrote, "The only visible output of the television project has been a single half-hour show which was aired once on WNYC-TV, UHF Channel 31. There has been no audible output from the radio project—in the winter of 1971, the satellite radio station consisted of several unpacked crates of expensive electronic equipment in a building at 1251 East New York Avenue in the Brownsville section of Brooklyn."22

Singleton said the television project began with acquisition of almost $700,000 worth of equipment to modernize the black-and-white facilities in the Brooklyn College Television Center. He stated the new equipment, with full color capability, is so ultramodern that only one of the three national-network commercial stations in New York—WNBC—can match it; and he argues that few trainees were actually Model Neighborhood residents, that some were already skilled in broadcast areas, and that many dropped out of the program when it failed to develop anything. Singleton also contends that the program spent about $100,000 in the recent Model Cities election to attract voters but ended up convincing so few that it cost approximately $200 per vote.

Neighborhood Director Morancie responded to these charges by saying, "If all we wanted was to train people, we could have done that by giving them scholarships to existing schools. But we have an end goal of a communications station, a radio station and television station that will be operated by the community, and will employ the people we've trained."

The radio/television project was one of Model Cities' most ambitious. Richard Starkey, a former NBC newsman who is one of the two teacher consultants in the program, believes it may be grandiose but a farsighted effort. And Dr. Donald MacLennan, codirector of the Television Center of Brooklyn College, feels that by the end of the five-year Model Cities program there will definitely be something to show. In general, officials feel this has been the most publicly embarrassing example of Model Cities programing in Central Brooklyn. Besides its administrative and program weaknesses, it appears to be technically unsound. It is difficult to break easily into so complex a field, and prospects do not look good. However, at this stage, the system is broadcasting, and it will be curious to see how many residents are truly interested in the programing.

Housing

1. Housing Development Programs. In May 1971, Brooklyn opened the nation's first low-income public housing development built under the Model Cities Program. The $5.9 million development contains 160 apartments and received a $750,000 Model Cities grant. The buildings, as specified by the Policy Committee and other community organizations, are designed to blend with the four-story structures in the area. Model Cities also opened its first completed middle-income project, located near a public housing project in the East New York section. A coalition of church groups sponsored the $3.6 million, 142 units of vest pocket housing.

The Model Cities plan calls for 789 units of public housing, of which 622 are now under construction or completed, and 406 units of middle-income housing, of which 396 are now under construction or completed. There are 125,000 existing units in Central Brooklyn, of which 75,000 require rehabilitation and 20,000 demolition. An additional 5,000 a year deteriorate to the extent of needing replacement. Plans also call for construction of 11,400 other units. As of

January 1971, 9,993 low-income units and 669 moderate-income units were under construction, and another 4,100 units of low-income and 7,300 units of moderate-income were planned. In addition, rehabilitation was in progress on 1,031 units, and 321 units were completed. Another 2,400 are proposed for rehabilitation.

In the Brownsville Model Cities area, often described as the "slum-of-slums," there was not a single housing start by January 1972, moderate or low income. However, some units have been started under Brownsville Urban Renewal. The lack of progress is mostly because of politics and jockeying for position among Policy Committee leaders to determine who will control development.

In the Marcus Garvey Urban Renewal Area, the largest single urban renewal area in the city and possibly the nation (50 city blocks), there has not been one unit of new construction. For three years, the area has been subjected to massive city acquisition, mismanaged maintenance and relocation, and widespread demolition and abandonment. Model Cities has approved this process step by step, despite enormous community pressure for changes in the acquisition and management policies of the New York Housing Authority.

The only construction funds Marcus Garvey has received was for rehabilitation of 110 units of housing under the city's troubled Municipal Loan Program. Their builder, George Jaffee, was recipient of $5 million of Model Cities approved municipal loans (all for Central Brooklyn) and was one of the chief contractors against whom charges were placed. Jaffee, once the largest "slumlord" in Brownsville, got all his rehabilitation projects pushed through the Policy Committee by its powerful vice chairman, Bill Wright. Wright has been on Jaffee's payroll, first as a labor consultant at $225 a week, then as the manager of some of his housing projects. The current manager of some of Jaffee's Brownsville projects is Gloria Boyce, the chairman of the Brownsville Policy Committee.

Boyce and Wright allegedly influenced the awarding of contracts to Jaffee in exchange for jobs and management benefits. A disturbing paradox is that some of Jaffee's Brownsville output was torn down by city demolition crews only months after the city rehabilitated them. They were demolished to make room for the only other housing development in Brownsville, the mobile home park. Fifty-seven mobile homes were placed on two vacant square blocks in the middle of the blighted Marcus Garvey Urban Renewal Area. This is a New York City Housing Authority experiment for temporary emergency relocation housing.

The principal delay in development of Marcus Garvey was a year-and-a-half hassle over the use of modular housing on the site. The Brownsville Policy Committee, and in particular Gloria Boyce acting in conjunction with Bill Wright, attempted to deliver the entire

Garvey area to the Development Corporation of America, a Boston-based modular housing firm. They wanted one community sponsor for the entire site, namely Boyce and Wright, incorporated as the CBMC Housing Development Corporation.

In regards to Model Cities and housing, Bedford-Stuyvesant's State Senator Waldaba Stewart, a favorite of Democratic Party leader Meade Esposito, has played a major role in creating the program in Brooklyn and speaks out frequently. In an early 1972 interview, he stated: "They [city establishment] have intentionally allowed the program to fail. Then they turn around and accuse blacks of not being together. The program was sabotaged. They have built some houses and will be building more. But blacks have not shared in the overall involvement. When the smoke clears, $500 million will have come through the Model Cities area and blacks will not have been appreciably helped.

"It has been 50 percent successful. Housing is going up slowly but this was supposed to be a package involving training and economic development. In that sense, it has not been successful. I sometimes suspect that it is because the city administration has no commitment."

And Frank Emerson, Community News Service reporter covering Central Brooklyn, stated about the same time: "I'm most intimately familiar with housing. Some of their most ambitious projects have yet to get off the ground. I can't single out one particular program that has really been valuable. Model Cities has shown a definite political connection, to its detriment. There is too much collusion with city agencies. I wouldn't blame Model Cities too much for that because they have to deal through the city agencies."

2. Emergency Repair Program. Model Cities entered this program well after its design by the city's Housing and Development Administration and after it had been in operation for several years. Model Cities wishes to use it to employ Model Neighborhood residents, leading to career ladder positions. In Brooklyn, the annual budget is $2.8 million, almost all for personnel except $137,000 for repair contracts and $51,000 for materials. HDA money also is used for materials. Initially, there were 237 personnel, about half Model Neighborhood residents, all under provisional civil service trainee status. Civil service career ladders have not come about. Recently, the program was trimmed to 141 staff and 35 trainees.

The program has not helped Model Cities' image. A bribery scandal of major proportions resulted in the arrest of some of the program's staff (part of which were selected by the Brooklyn Policy Committee). Under the program, HDA hires contractors to repair private buildings not meeting minimum standards. Costs are to be eventually recovered from owners of the buildings, but the city has failed to do an adequate job of collection. City Councilman Bertram

Selford (D-Bronx) has charged that the city has failed to recover 90 percent or about $6.5 million of the repair costs and that immense emergency repair bills were charged to buildings without protest from owners because the owners were abandoning them anyway. He said that the program, designed to help tenants, has largely benefited dishonest contractors because the city paid for thousands of repairs that were never made.

Citywide, the program has received over 93,000 complaints and completed 28,000 repairs. But Assistant Administrator Vivas states in the Quarterly Report that the program has been damaged because of "the indignation of a community made cynical by press reports of corruption and their personal experience with delay, inaction and futility."[23] PDI relates "the program lacks coordination . . . . and cost-benefit ratios showed exhorbitant administrative costs."[24] In fact, four PDI monitoring reports have delineated extensive problems, including exorbitant costs, slow service, public dissatisfaction, and need for increased supervision over field offices.[25] Despite the problems, Model Cities has forced the Emergency Repair staff to concentrate on the most critical housing and the worst offenders. Also, the program has been trimmed, and the administration is taking steps to make it more efficient and eliminate corruption.

3. Other Housing Projects. In the third action year, several other projects were started: structural improvements to existing public housing units and tenant education ($1,100,000); small home renovation and realtor training ($339,000); and construction subsidy for the Industrial Homes for the Blind ($38,000).

Economic Development. A budget of $1,237,000 has been set for a Business Assistance Project designed to create new enterprises for MN residents, provide entrepreneur training to minority contractors, and provide loans and financial assistance. An operator was still being sought in the middle of the third action year. A Business Training Project was also seeking an operator. In addition, a Vest Pocket Industrial Development Project, with a $991,000 budget, was in the process of hiring staff during this period.

Social Services. There are several projects under social services. The $757,000 Day Care Assistance Project is operated by the Human Resources Administration. A $50,000 Human Rights Complaint Center opened in January 1972.

The Health Services Administration operates the $383,000 Ambulatory Detoxification Program for drug addicts. This project treats residents with methodone until they are capable of receiving long-term therapeutic care. Recently, gonorrhea testing for females was added to the standard series of medical tests. The project has treated over 2,600 patients. None of these services have been evaluated by Model Cities to date.

Recreation. Recreation projects expend $889,000 annually for playground sites, community theaters, and a broad range of group activities. The primary operator is the Parks, Recreation and Cultural Affairs Administration.

The Mobile Theater Project ($278,000) has had a history of difficulties between the operator, Bedford Stuyvesant Theater, and the neighborhood MC office concerning authority for operating and administering the project under established guidelines and in accordance with the co-operation agreement. No performances were given between January 1972 and September 1972. OMIE concluded that the operator failed to carry out two critical components: "training and scholarship activities. Failure to do this lessened the value and contribution toward cultural benefits to the residents."26

Transportation. The Polytechnic Institute of Brooklyn completed a $326,000 transportation study, which has been in demand by numerous agencies and is being utilized by the New York City Planning Commission, New York City Taxi Commission, and the New York City Transit Authority. Its conclusions recommended rerouting some bus lines and establishing free transfer areas; improving subway and bus station facilities; and providing services where lines are deficient, such as to employment areas, hospitals, clinics, day-care centers, shopping areas, and senior citizen centers. Some 20 miles of mini-bus routes, to compliment existing routes, were also recommended. There seems to be general agreement that the study has made an important contribution to the Model Neighborhood.

The Federation of Addiction Agencies and Brooklyn
Model Cities

The following more detailed discussion of one program is presented in order to highlight the kinds of problems that confronted not only Brooklyn,but also the other MNs. The Federation of Addiction Agencies Program provides such an example and shows how the new Model Cities Administration, under Judge Williams's leadership, has taken steps to solve the problems. How far the city administration is willing to go to eliminate those at fault and perhaps step on the toes of powerful groups may determine the success of the total program.

In the summer of 1970, community groups within the central Brooklyn area came together to form a loose confederation, built on the theory that drug abuse could best be dealt with at the community level. Several drug programs were already operating within the Central Brooklyn area, specifically the Community Organization of Narcotics Education and Services Inc. (CONES) and Self Help Unit on Narcotics (SHUN), both operating agencies of the city's Addiction Services Agency (ASA). Newly formed groups such as Your Own Thing and Nat's Comin' were just beginning to develop. CONES and SHUN were both successful programs with ongoing day-care and residential treatment centers. Faced with the need to increase drug programs in the central Brooklyn area, Model Cities chose to do so through a cooperation agreement with ASA, awarding ASA over $1.4 million to supervise the programs. However, instead of increasing the funding of ongoing projects like CONES and SHUN, ASA and Model Cities chose to form the Federation of Addiction Agencies. This decision was essentially influenced by strong local action.

The decision to fund the federation resulted from a series of what an ASA spokesman now describes as "thug-actions" by the leaders of Your Own Thing and Nat's Coming'. Ted Baptiste, a self-declared Moslem prophet, roamed the central Brooklyn area for months with an entourage of turban-clad toughs, disrupting meetings and intimidating officials. He styled himself a reincarnated Nat Turner, pronounced drugs as the only problem of the community, and created his own program with a $25,000 director's salary. Baptiste was a principal proponent of the federation. Also supporting it was Charles Dorner, founder of Your Own Thing and a vice chairman of the Central Brooklyn Model Cities Policy Committee. Dorner was a close ally of Bill Wright, also Policy Committee vice chairman. Local sources allege that Dorner and Wright, the two most powerful individuals on the committee, agreed to divide the Model Cities spoils between them. Dorner was to control the federation and Wright the housing programs. Wright and Dorner, from the Model Cities side, and Baptiste, essentially from the ASA side (where he applied a great deal of pressure), forced funding of the federation. CONES and SHUN, the only operating parts of the federation at its inception, became subordinate in budgetary terms to the decisions of Wright and Dorner. At a meeting shortly after the funding of the project, Baptiste and one of his partners were shot. Wright and Dorner fled the meeting, but Dorner was subsequently stabbed in the back and hospitalized. While in the hospital, he was arrested for the attempted murder of Baptiste. However, Baptiste, after being released from the hospital, left New York altogether, and Dorner never came to trial. With Baptiste's disappearance, Dorner and Wright controlled the federation absolutely.

Understanding the power of these individuals is crucial to understanding the problems this and other programs faced and still confront. Model areas are in tough neighborhoods where needs are dramatic

382

and the means to meeting them often crude. Wright and Dorner, veterans of poverty programs, recognized that federal money was shifting out of "community action" and into drugs and housing. They shifted with it. And by controlling the Model Cities' weak and apathetic citizen participation structure, they could force funding into directions from which they could profit. Dorner remained on the Policy Committee while employed at $17,000 a year by the federation as its assistant director. He intimidated Policy Committee members by bringing a group of armed men to the meetings (eye witnesses have reported that these men passed guns among each other during policy meetings). To avoid a conflict of interest, Dorner would leave the policy meetings whenever the federation was discussed, leaving his entourage and, of course, Bill Wright. Eventually, Dorner, with no professional or active experience in the operation of a drug program, was appointed acting director of the federation, controlling $2 million in program funds. At this point, the city's corporation counsel ruled that Dorner must step down from the Policy Committee. In late 1971 he did.

The decision to fund the federation, meaning Dorner and Wright, rather than expanding other programs was the first in a series of tragic errors. The roots of that decision can be traced to an earlier practice of allowing Policy Committee members to profit from the programs they approve.

It was determined that ASA would contract to the federation rather than operate any programs directly, which meant that ASA lost control of even the functioning CONES and SHUN programs. In a contract prepared and approved by Model Cities, the federation received the entire $1.4 million (and a subsequent state grant through ASA of $600,000), and it budgeted certain amounts for all the federated groups including CONES and SHUN. This device ensured Dorner budgetary power and was adopted in the name of community control, on the theory that a truly community-based program could only be generated if ASA, a citywide white agency, would step out of the picture and not directly operate anything. ASA acceded. In fact, it bent over backwards to keep clear of the federation. Model Cities, highly sensitive to the power of Wright and Dorner, let the program slide with no effort to evaluate or monitor it.

ASA assigned two people to monitor the programs, but both were budgeted under different functions and had other obligations. It did not fulfill its monitoring for contract compliance requirements. Repeatedly ASA requested that Model Cities fund a position or two at ASA for independent monitors of federation programs, but Model Cities continually declined. Finally one of the ASA monitors was transferred and the other position dropped. ASA and Model Cities were thus left in the position of funding a $2 million project without any independent monitoring.

In the summer of 1972, there were still no statistics available as to the number of patients treated or rehabilitated for most of the facilities. Some projects admittedly operated without patients. Money disappeared for illicit or nonexistent contracts and rentals. High salaries were paid for unskilled employees and in some cases employees who did not work. ASA seemed incapable of exercising any control.

For example, in a program to train federation personnel, federation staff failed to appear for the training sessions, and finally ASA training staff refused to return for future sessions unless ASA administration could get some cooperation. They could not and the sessions ended. Perhaps more serious were the series of financial advances ASA granted the federation. In early 1972, the federation still existed on ASA advances and had been operating without a contract since September 1971.

Changes are now taking place. The project is being centralized to both Model Cities and ASA. Central Brooklyn has abdicated any responsibility for it, and Administrator Williams is taking it directly under his wing. He has called meetings involving the federation and ASA without including Brooklyn Model Cities and has ordered establishment of a community board of directors. He has granted ASA seven Model-Cities-funded positions for a monitoring staff for ASA-Model Cities programs and has tightened up audit and evaluation procedures. Most importantly, Williams and ASA have put together a new organizational structure for the federation, with a new administrator at the top and Dorner relegated to an associate directorship. Williams has refused to re-fund the federation until he is satisfied that the changes are working. Williams can terminate the program at any time, and Dorner knows this. Dorner and his associates also know that the abuses in the program have been kept quiet, and he would like to keep them that way.

Despite all these difficulties, the federation has opened 14 drug facilities. In recent months, it has made facility-by-facility progress reports to ASA. During the reporting period May 1 through May 31, 1971, the federation reported 83 persons receiving 24-hour care in three residential centers and 395 receiving attention in day-care programs. By summer 1972, a total of 671 addicts were receiving treatment each quarter in the four centers of East New York, Bedford Stuyvesant/East, Bedford Stuyvesant/West, and Brownsville. Virtually all of the federation's critics agree that some of the programs, particularly CONES, are effectively reaching addicts. The federation has also stimulated innovation. It is a fully black project, and all clients, directors, and clinicians are residents of the community. And it has advanced a new approach to treating the addict: ego-affirmation through nationalism, rather than the more traditional approach of egodestruction and reconstruction.

One ASA staff member says, "Drugs is a problem without an answer, not therapeutic or medical. Decentralization is a means of sharing the blame, not advancing an unknown solution. With a decentralized drug program, we can concentrate on issues like bad administration and stealing and ignore the fact that no one, not the community, not the professionals, have any answers." Many observers now believe that decentralization in residential therapeutic treatment centers is the most effective approach to the drug problem.

ASA will spend $117 million on drug programs in 1972. It will be important to see whether any lessons have been learned. The latest OMIE evaluation of the program states:

> Although this project is not operating at its maximal effectiveness, in view of the important need which might not otherwise be served, the Evaluation team has recommended a conditional and qualified continuation of this program. This recommendation is subject to making significant changes in operations and service delivery as well as the implementation of continued program effectiveness evaluation.[27]

Harlem-East Harlem

Education. The Youth Scholarship/Career Skills Project ($810,000) dropped its Career Skills component when teachers and students lost interest and failed to attend classes. On the other hand, Youth Scholarship has made it possible for over 500 students to attend college, with scholarship awards from $500 to $3,000. Other projects include the Paraprofessional Program ($109,000), which is training MN residents for job upgrading, and Youth Tutoring Youth ($138,000), which utilizes a maximum tutor-to-student ratio of 1:4. Parent Leadership ($40,000) is operated by City University of New York and Research Foundation CUNY and has successfully completed one 10-week training cycle and will eventually include 140 parents for the project year.

Liceo Hispano Inc. ($100,000) was designed to provide a comprehensive planning document for a community school and international library. OMIE reports that it did not carry out the intent of the initial six-month contract. Instead, a more ambitious and massive proposal was substituted containing 35 separate proposed projects. Thus, the viability of the new expanded plans must be weighed against the original intent and purposes of the authorizing contract. In this case, there is serious doubt about the viability of continued funding. The assessment is being reviewed by the city administration. On the other hand, some Model Cities officials feel that what has been done by the local community is an excellent start for a viable, effective program. A new look at its objectives is needed.

Health

Treating Physicians provides pediatric, adolescent, and adult medical care at three medical facilities—Mt. Sinai, New York Medical School, and Italian Hospital—during day and evening hours ($361,000). Program Development and Implementation (PDI) states that all three programs operate well but that Italian Hospital is underutilized and all three components need expanding. Furthermore, hospital staffs express considerable irritation concerning delays in communicating decisions about contract extensions—a further verification of central administration bottlenecks.

Alcoholic Outreach services part of the estimated 30,000 alcoholics in Harlem ($238,000). Residential treatment is provided for only 12 persons, communication and coordination are poor between HSA and the neighborhood office, and there is insufficient staff, equipment, and materials. There need to be increases in group therapy, recreational therapy, vocational rehabilitation, and dissemination of information to the public. Needless to say, the project is not fully operational.

Social Services

Senior Citizens Work/Care Program ($131,000) is operated by the New York City Office for the Aging and provides many levels of assistance to persons over 60, including daily midday meals for approximately 100 persons. However, PDI reported in early 1972 that the program "has not scratched the surface of its original goal—to be a comprehensive approach in attacking the many problems that confront elderly residents in the community." PDI believes the budget for all three MNs is too small and that "the need for increased and coordinated services is documented." Priority areas of need have been identified as (1) meal service for the homebound; (2) Walk-N-Meal service; (3) housekeeping service; (4) escort service (outreach service for the homebound of all kinds is reported to be lacking); and (5) nursing homes.[28]

Crime and Delinquency

The Community Service Officer ($850,000) project is similar to the Brooklyn project. There is $703,000 for housing Authority CSOs. In the latter program, there are complaints about lengthy procedural steps and "red tape." The PDI monitor states, "Whatever has been accomplished to date is due to a high level of enthusiasm and desire on the part of the program staff." A high school equivalency program had not yet been implemented as part of the program but is considered necessary for long-term job security for CSOs.

Manpower and Job Development

The Clerical Skills ($92,000) project is operated by the Chamber of Commerce Educational Foundation and provides training for 350 persons. Some recommendations made in early 1972 by the PDI project manager for improving career skills programs in Harlem are generally as follows:

1. There is a gross overlapping of commercial skills training programs, which are located in the same building as the Model Cities Program and are directed toward the same group of Harlem residents. Students change rapidly from one program to the other without any restrictions.

Another operating agency should prove more feasible. This would also eliminate having the same teachers for two programs— and their motivation and/or loyalties to Model Cities Program and residents would not be questionable. Their salaries would not consume approximately 80 percent of the yearly budget, as is currently the case.

2. At present, there are no provisions for any course of study designed toward college pursuits. Therefore, it is recommended that the program details be revised to include study towards obtaining the high school equivalency diploma. There is no place in Harlem where a resident can sit down (at ease comfortably) to take the high school equivalency examination given by qualified persons from the neighborhood.

3. It is recommended that the drafting course be dropped, unless it can be proven more relevant to the community, and replaced by advanced typing, IBM key punch, and stenography skills. This would allow for upward mobility for the students, both in employment and in academic pursuits.

4. The Iowa Achievement Test should be reevaluated. The California Adult Reading Test has been validated on various "poverty groups" throughout the country. This test has been proven to have more input-output results.

5. It is recommended that a course in office practice be a part of the over-all curriculum. This time would be geared towards instruction in office procedures, such as filing, proper telephone services, office decorum, and general office management. Many of the students are presently employed full time and come for a short time in the evenings to "brushup" on their skills. They, too, need this office training, as do those who have never worked in an office setting. Instructions in the above category would prove most beneficial.

Housing

A Revolving Fund ($351,000) is administered by the Association of United Contractors of America (AUCOA) to assist minority contractors and small neighborhood businesses with capital so they can compete for government contract bidding. But PDI reports that up to April 27, 1972, the fund was used only three times and then only by members of AUCOA. There is poor communication between AUCOA and Model Cities and poor dissemination of information to the business community. This program, which could do so much to help local businesses, has hardly scratched the surface of its potential.

<u>Comments</u>. Projects in Harlem did not get off the ground until the second action year, and then only a few began operation. In the third year, almost all projects were operational, but evaluation is limited because they have been functioning for such a short period of time. Model Cities officials themselves criticize the program, and some city officials when asked to comment on progress simply say, "Well, that's something else again."

During the second action year, Charlayne Hunter, a New York <u>Times</u> Bureau Chief, said in an interview:

> What program? It's difficult to say when it was its most chaotic, but it was getting there for a while. The major part of the problem was a lack of clear cut understanding of what the program was supposed to be on the part of all concerned on every level. Local residents, some of whom had jobs in the program, had come from the poverty program and they felt it should operate like that. There were limited amounts of technical assistance on the local level and nobody to explain to the people that this wasn't the way the program worked.
>
> The critical question to ask is are the programs out? They had the money and they weren't spending it. I don't see anything happening, anything of any major substance. Most people don't even know it's there. The last election proves that.

About the same time, Robert Yin, of the RAND Corporation, said that he believes it would be better to stop the program and start fresh:

> Model Cities is nonexistent in Harlem. The Bronx got a little further. The problem is that, after the poverty program in which the city didn't have the power of the purse, it s hard to go to the community and say now we control it, not you. But at least they're providing jobs.

As stated previously, the program has picked up under its third director, McRae, and staff morale has improved. However, it appears a long way from providing the services residents were led to believe they would receive.

Bronx

Education
Around-the-Clock Community Schools ($692,000) is operated by the Board of Education to keep selected schools open evenings and weekends for educational, cultural, and recreational opportunities for children and adults. In 1971-72, 1,500 residents were served in 12 schools.

Youth Tutorial ($349,000), operated by the Board of Education, was judged effective in the achievement of its objectives by the Human Affairs Research Center of New York. Reading skills increased an average of 0.8, and more positive relationships developed among students and tutors toward the school system.

Health
Community Mental Retardation ($53,000) is operated by Hunts Point Multi-Service Center and provides vocational counceling services to adults and out-of-school mentally retarded youths. It has been rendering services at a reduced level because Model Cities funds have not been made available as of the middle of the third action year.

Social Services
Early Childhood Day Care ($439,000), operated by HRA, was discontinued in favor of state-operated centers, which are being readied. Some Model Cities funds are being used as seed money. In this case, PDI states the program was crippled by state delays and that only three of the nine local operators approved by the Policy Committee were rated "feasible," yet 11 other sponsors exist that could receive state assistance.

Drug Abuse Centers ($869,000), operated by the Addiction Services Agency, treats over 150 addicts per day. A good attempt is being made to coordinate all drug programs through the centers.

Ambulatory Detoxification ($419,000), operated by HRA, is functioning with one center, and a second will be open soon. About 50 drug addicts per day are served by the present clinic.

The Human Rights Complaint Center ($50,000) is similar to those in other MNs.

Recreation and Culture
Camping ($606,000), operated by HRA, had the participation of 2,400 children in a two-week summer camp and 1,200 in fall and winter programs.

Open Space ($300,000), operated by HDA, has had three operating agencies and, therefore, considerable delays. It has cured much of the problem by finally creating its own Local Housing (Development) Corporation to channel funds and has recently signed contracts for 18 play lots.

Manpower and Job Development

Clerical Skills ($92,000) and Health Careers ($541,000) are similar to previously described programs. Results of the Health Careers programs are encouraging. Forty paraprofessional trainees completed two training cycles, and 25 were placed in permanent jobs. Five entered college to continue advanced work, three are still in training, and seven resigned.

Housing. Emergency Repairs ($2,628,000), Housing Assistance ($3,547,000), and Housing Maintenance ($3,427,000) are similar to programs already described but have not made much head way up to this time because of the absence of a local housing development corporation, which has only recently been created.

The nonprofit South Bronx Community Housing Corporation (SBCHC) will act as a conduit for housing construction, rehabilitation, management, and maintenance programs and building community facilities, such as day-care and multiservice centers, parking facilities, and open-space and recreational facilities. Its objectives are to construct 2,000 housing units, rehabilitate 1,500 units, and convert 500 units to cooperative ownership properties. It will provide private investment counseling to community groups, create a viable relocation program, and implement the Tenant Education Program. It also will foster community economic development by assisting minority and local builders and achieve better coordination by a working alliance with the Neighborhood Self-Help (Sanitation) and Emergency Repair Programs.

Environmental Protection

Fire Aides ($877,000) and Sanitation ($1,869,000) are similar to other Model Cities projects of this type. Residents appear satisfied that clean-up work is having a salutary effect in their neighborhoods. Effectiveness here contrasts sharply with the Brooklyn and Harlem programs, where performance is inadequate. PDI cities South Bronx for good operating agency relations, good community relations, and good decentralized operations. However, the project in all three MNs suffers from inadequate equipment and clothing; slow administrative processing through central MCA; low pay; and limited promotional possibilities.

Comments. In general, programs in the Bronx have been more effective and productive than those in either Harlem or Brooklyn. Policy Committee disputes and struggles over control, in particular, held up programs in the beginning. But Marrero has been on top of most programs once they are operational. And the Policy Committee has been able to coordinate plans fairly well with the city and boroughs because two of its members are also on the Community Planning Board and attend sessions of both bodies regularly.

Marrero was able to introduce R-72 zoning (which permits increased housing development in designated zones by allowing the closing of streets), which has allowed more comprehensive community development planning and more economical use of space (42 percent of city land is streets). His staff also convinced the Board of Estimate to allow exemptions from regular city bidding procedures to give advantage to certain local firms in order to improve the neighborhood economy.

Moreover, Bronx Model Cities is making up the difference of high construction costs by providing a partial capital outlay subsidy on over 1,000 housing units. Jorge Baptista, former director of physical development in the Bronx, believes this program has gained at least a year on housing development and that units would not be under construction now without Model Cities assistance. In addition, staff has developed on accelerated design concept. As soon as sites are acquired, a Model Cities fund provides for design so that bids can be obtained earlier to speed the process and save on construction and finance costs. About $4 million is in the revolving fund, which is continually replenished from mortgages and should allow full reimbursement to Model Cities. Model Cities also believes that use of "start-up money" to secure land options, obtain sites, and hire architects for 20 day-care centers moved this program ahead several years. Where Model Cities could not give money to local day-care sponsors, it hired its own architects and loaned them to the sponsors.

Systems and computerization in the Bronx are far ahead of the other two Model Cities areas and even most city agencies, according to local staff. The Fire Department's data bank is being used to process information from several agencies so for the first time, housing, fire, police, social, and other statistics are available to all departments. In this sense, Model Cities has made some progress in the coordination of agencies. The system is now being developed for the other MNs and may eventually contribute to the development of a citywide data bank.

Analysis and Recommendations

Reasons for Delay of Program

New York's Model Cities Program has had a more difficult time getting started than most other Model Cities programs, and it continues to experience serious operational problems well into its third action year. The program has been considerably improved under new direction, but it is doubtful whether it can make up for time lost.

Although the Model Cities Program received a HUD planning grant in November 1967, it was not until June 1968 that committees were formed and the year-long planning period actually began. The first action year started July 1969, but it was well into the second action year before most projects got started; and less than half of the funds were expended on schedule during this period.

Community Delays. Initial delays were primarily the result of disputes among power groups in the three Model Neighborhoods, each vying for control and disagreeing on representation and program policies and priorities. The Central Policy Committee, composed of city commissioners, took little interest in the program, often sending subordinates to meetings. Indeed, most city agencies showed little interest. Although it appeared that city hall wanted to see citizens fail in their new experience at planning and running programs, the "hands-off" policy was in fact a desire on the city's behalf to let residents make local decisions. Contradictions in federal policy did not help matters. HUD's regional office stressed a partnership relationship between the city and citizens, while the Washington, D.C. office told citizens to appeal to it "if they didn't get what they wanted." Thus, uncertainty and confusion reigned.

Eventually, in desperation and in opposition to community groups, Mayor Lindsay was forced to order plans pulled together and some kind of document created and sent to HUD—not dissimilar to how some other mayors handled the problem. His action was correct, for New York could not afford to lose several hundred million dollars of innovative funds over the following five years. No responsible leader could have done otherwise.

Lack of Official Interest. However, city leadership had already taken a back seat. When Lindsay and his commissioners were needed to resolve differences in the communities, they did not actively participate. Citizen participation never meant that residents would do everything on their own without the benefit of professional help or political and administrative leadership. The Model Cities "partnership" concept stressed working together rather than independently. But the city failed to do this, partially because officials felt they would be imposing themselves unwillingly upon residents. Yet the overwhelming membership of the community Policy Committees were not first-layer grass-roots residents, but, rather, sophisticated persons who, for the most part had headed other community groups or were employed in other social service programs. An open yet constructive exchange with residents would have been beneficial. It has always been a city responsibility to monitor and intervene, when appropriate, to save programs.

Bureaucratic Delays. After these initial planning delays, agency bureaucracy was more to blame for delay than anything else. Agencies were not particularly interested in the success of Model Cities or in changing their own priorities and methods of operation. Red tape has been unbelievable: for example, (1) it took several months to gain key personnel background clearances before an employee could be hired; (2) there still exist inflexible civil service rules and union restrictions, which have, in many cases, prevented the creation of meaningful jobs; (3) a total of 82 steps were needed to purchase items; (4) two months were necessary for expenditure approval; and (5) it took three to six months to secure approval for property rental or lease. These conditions merely highlight New York's laggard bureaucracy. It is doubtful there is any other American government, not even at the federal level, where red tape is as prevalent or serious. Unfortunately, this bureaucracy has been built layer by layer, year after year, and it will be difficult to change without some basic institutional modifications. Although most of the bottlenecks mentioned above have been lessened, some persist, with Model Cities as one of the victims. One measure of influence of the administration and the bureaucracy on Model Cities is the level of success of Model Cities projects.

Projects

Insufficient Progress. Model Cities has experienced some well-run programs that valuably serve their clients; but, in too many cases, projects have been mismanaged and unsuccessful, not effectively serving the residents they were designed to reach. On the other hand, consistent progress is being made in improving the quality of programs. Reducing the number of projects from 300 to 100 has made the total program more manageable and has made it easier for the city to concentrate its efforts on about 10 priority areas of concern. Almost all projects are under way now, and changes in top administrative staff, particularly in the directorship of the Harlem program, and cleaning house generally, in Harlem and some other individual projects, are significant advances. It appears that programs will continue to be improved under the new management and direction.

Yet it has taken so long for the program to get off the ground that it is doubtful the remaining life of the program will allow sufficient time for it to generate any comprehensive and lasting success in project implementation. So far, success is primarily in procedural changes and in demonstrating where problems exist and possibly how to handle them in the future. These lessons could be a most valuable contribution if they are learned.

Model Neighborhoods Differ. Success has varied from one Model Neighborhood to another. Until recently, the Harlem program has virtually been a waste of funds. It is only now getting started under the aggressive leadership of a neighborhood director trusted by Judge Williams. It is doubtful that much was learned here or that competent staff was developed during the first several years of bureaucratic maneuvering and make-work conditions. Recently, however, staff morale has been raised, and one can point to a few successful projects.

In Brooklyn, the largest and most comprehensive program, projects did get under way, even though it took until the end of the first action year. Many of the projects are successful; yet too large a number have been mismanaged. There has been the continued presence of a corrupting influence from several board members; staff has been strongly independent and oblivious to what is happening in the rest of the city; and, in addition, the package of projects has not had much influence in changing the system or on the quality of life in the neighborhood.

The Bronx program is better managed, with several competent administrators in charge of programs, but it too has been absorbed in local power battles and delays and has not reached sufficient clients for the time and effort expended. However, it has stimulated changes in city management and procedures. Perhaps the most important achievements have been in compiling and computerizing, for the first time, valuable data that can be utilized by other agencies, and also in creating innovative changes in zoning laws and in housing and physical development. As a consequence, the other Model Neighborhoods are beginning to use these ideas.

Career-Ladder Development. It is perhaps unfortunate that Model Cities and the city administration placed so much of its chances for success on developing career ladders in various city services. Difficulties in changing unions and the law make this approach dubious. One court suit has already been lost, and it appears unions will continue to battle what they call favoritism to special resident groups. Meanwhile, morale and faith in career-ladder advancement are at their lowest, and thousands of trainees have been engaged in mostly meaningless work and millions of dollars have been wasted when the same point could have been demonstrated with several small, pilot projects.

An important consideration is that unemployment will not be solved by putting some Model Neighborhood residents to work from a separate civil service list. Unemployment is a citywide problem that cannot be lessened by limiting changes to several small geographic areas. Basic inequities, resulting from testing, minority cultural differences, and forms of favoritism in establishing the city's basic personnel list, have to be remedied. Skirting these problems will not solve long-range unemployment problems. Moreover, creating special categories for the disadvantaged might very well relegate minorities to a status of second-class citizens. The disadvantaged need extra help but not special and permanent characterization.

In most cases, where trainee aides are being used in Model Cities training programs, they are not integrated into the system or given proper supervision. Sanitation aides spend months training on the job for work that requires only a few days to learn, and in many instances, they simply make work easier for already underproductive regular crews. Unquestionably, a great deal of training is needed—for regular crews, too—in motivation and good work habits, but not in useless, simplistic job watching.

On the other side, the major clean-up programs have been highly beneficial, but this kind of effort will have to be part of the regular system if it is to be meaningful over the long run, and certainly the $17,638,000 expended for special sanitation programs (by the third action year) cannot be justified by clean-up alone. At the end of 1972, Model Cities monitors themselves reported that the training component for this program was inactive; interagency cooperation and communication between Model Cities and the Departments of Sanitation and Health—particularly in the follow-up of health violations—were extremely poor; the vacancy rate for trainees was 24.5 percent and for staff 16.6 percent; substantial amounts of heavy equipment purchased by Model Cities went unutilized; trainees lacked proper working gear; and community education programs were ineffective, primarily because of lack of funds to disseminate information and because of the loss of public input due to the inability to correct violations. The one bright spot is that the decentralization of operations to field offices has resulted in constructive and improved relations with local residents.

In other training programs, police aides are treated mostly as residents to be tolerated so they can retain employment but not to be given much responsibility. Although the aides are put through the police academy, the program would be more effective if the police commissioner planned and administered it according to the needs of the department and genuinely treated aides like regular career officers. In another area, the need and respect for community service officers working in Housing Authority projects are felt more strongly by the community because they fill a vital function. Also, the fire inspectors' program is above average because firemen see the need for building inspection and fire prevention demonstration programs and are happy to get assistance in an area that many fire fighters do not find rewarding.

Manpower Programs. Manpower programs, the prime emphasis of
Model Cities, have been generally ineffective. Health Careers Training
has the greatest potential of success because it is training for meaningful jobs where openings exist. However, since its inception, only
60 percent of the enrollees have stayed in the program, and it has
only graduated 100 trainees—a small effort toward solving the unemployment problem.

Clerical training, operated by the New York City Chamber of
Commerce, has had some success because of its "built-in" placement
features, whereby trainees are hired even before they enter training.
Nevertheless, the dropout rate has been excessive. Out of 842 accepted for training, only 94 remained in the program by the end of
1972.

The manpower project with the biggest expenditure and perhaps
the fewest results is Job Training. It was budgeted for a total of
$7,917,000 for its first two years of operations (cotermious with
Model Cities second and third action years) but graduated less than
400 trainees and placed less than 150 by the end of the first year.
This is an extremely high cost-benefit ratio, especially for job placement, even taking into account costs for capital improvements (which
are mostly scheduled to take place during the second year). Although
the program projects training 1,555 persons during the second year,
it is having serious difficulties in finding a reliable operator, and it
appears that it will not have much greater success in the second
year. Certainly, few Model Cities staff appear optimistic about it.
There is greater optimism about the job training operated by the
Urban Coalition in Harlem, which is reported by the monitors as
efficient and effective; however, there is also serious question here
about permanent job placements. One good result is that those who
have been trained under Job Training have been trained well and by
good instructors.

Health. In other Model Cities projects, there is mixed success. The
Ambulatory Detoxification project is beginning to show results. It
has detoxified over 8,000 drug addicts since its inception through the
operation of seven clinics. It reports reductions in drug use and
crime. But it still has serious problems locating doctors and getting
backup service from hospitals. And as pointed out earlier, the Federation of Addiction Agencies program is in serious difficulty. It
has failed to audit and evaluate dozens of antiaddiction programs and
has been influenced by unscrupulous elements. It is still under intense
review by the administration, and there is question of continuance
under its present leadership and organization.

Dental programs are well received by the public. Model Cities
monitors praise the doctors and staff for diligent work but, at the

same time, express serious need for more funds and help to increase facilities and its three-day-per-week operation.

Model Cities still says day care is in dire trouble mostly because of delays caused by the state and the New York City Agency for Child Development. At this time, not one of the 52 applicant groups has been certified or declared qualified.

Education. In educational endeavors, the most successful programs are the Summer/Winter Academies and Youth Scholarships. Success has been greater where funds have been provided to advance students to already proven institutions of higher learning. On the other side, perhaps the weakest element in education has been the inability to reach the undereducated, to provide basic education toward the attainment of high school equivalency accreditation, needed particularly for career-ladder pursuit.

The Consumer Protection and Education project is showing highly satisfactory results, having reached large numbers of persons in the home and through community meetings. On the other hand, the Educational Television project, already discussed in detail, is just beginning to show a Thursday evening television program after one year and seven months of delay and high costs.

Criminal Justice. In criminal justice programing, Work Release seems to be holding together, having shown a good record in job placement for ex-offenders; however, it lacks effective orientation and security measures in relation to its clients.

The delinquency projects are fairly successful, registering a little over 50 percent acceptance from clients, staff, and judges. The geographic jurisdiction of this program needs to be expanded citywide for greater effectiveness.

Housing. Housing programs have only scratched the surface for meeting shortages, with only a few projects off the ground. In comparison to other cities, new construction figures appear huge—some 6,000 housing units completed since 1969—yet they are not satisfactory for meeting New York's needs. Over 11,000 units are on the drawing boards, and 40,000 are being planned. However, housing construction and rehabilitation funds have mostly been from sources other than Model Cities. Nevertheless, Model Cities has acted as a catalyst to speed up some of the housing starts.

The Emergency Repair program, which has mostly benefited unscrupulous contractors and has been called a "disaster" by Model Cities members, is slowly being corrected of faults. On the credit side, it has served many needy residents. Of about 75,000 complaints to date, 28,532 repairs have been completed. However, the quality of much of this work is questionable, and it appears unlikely that the city will recover its costs from owners.

Recreation and Culture. The recreation and cultural programs have only experienced limited success. Camping and general recreation programs have been serving large numbers of youth, but more specialized endeavors—Drum and Bugle Corps, senior citizen centers, therapeutic projects—are not fully operational. And most of the cultural programs are not meeting their objectives to train artists, coordinate group efforts, or gain community support for program continuance.

Summary of Project Success. In short, the vast sums put into New York's Model Cities projects have reached only a small portion of their potential effectiveness because of inadequate city leadership, poor Model Cities program administration, agency disinterest, community delays, incompetent and inexperienced direction of a large number of projects, and too much selfish consideration and attempts at personal gain by a few board members and staff. Administrator Williams is making headway in clearing up these problems, but it is too late to save monies already wasted. The best that can be done is to take bold steps to improve projects as much as possible for the remaining two years of the program and to gain from the experience so that future projects will be planned and implemented properly.

Model Cities as a Superagency

Leadership Strengthened. Confronted with a slow start, bad publicity, and inability to spend funds, Mayor Lindsay shifted Executive Secretary Flatow out of Model Cities and appointed Judge Williams administrator of the new Model Cities superagency—not yet legally sanctioned by city council but, in practice, operating as one of 10 administrations. The executive abilities of Williams and his prestige as a prominent black judge—working with considerably increased mayoral support— have immeasurably improved the program and convinced more agency heads to cooperate.

Moreover, recent neighborhood elections have changed the make-up of local Policy Committees somewhat, so that new members are willing to accept their roles as more advisory than decision-making. In addition, Williams is able to mediate or make direct decisions involving any local power conflicts. With these new ingredients, which allow Policy Committees to function more smoothly, it seems appropriate to continue a reasonably strong role for committees in planning and developing programs and to delegate to them increased responsibility in monitoring and evaluating local projects.

Representatives of Policy Committees should also serve on any city-wide committee to ensure an opportunity for greater neighborhood input. And local committees should be given the choice of whom they wish to represent them.

Citywide Orientation and Need for a Genuine Coalition

There appears to be little need for a central committee to co-ordinate and make decisions broader in scope than that which may come from the three Model Neighborhood committees because of the multiplicity of existing citywide committees. The mayor, for example, has appointed citywide task forces in many functional areas, and community action and other groups operate in broad areas. The Civic Assembly is composed of representatives of over 100 of the city's major organizations and deals with many of the problems typically associated with community development programs. Rather than create any additional, overlapping citywide committees and to add strength to the Civic Assembly, it seems appropriate to revise the assembly to include representation from officially established community councils. One of its 15 committees could be assigned the responsibility of dealing specifically with community development and Model Cities matters and given official authority to plan, coordinate, and review policies of local bodies so that goals and objectives are compatible with the city's. In addition, this close interrelationship of residents and other civic persons should tend to get more people involved in the type of problems associated with Model Cities and other local programs—a relationship lacking to date.

One of the city's administrative problems is that it has too many relatively independent agency operations, not effectively brought into the total city process, including the Model Cities Administration itself. Coordination and administration of the agencies is poor; there is widespread overlapping of programs, particularly in Model Cities and Human Resources; communication between most agency staffs is superficial (even among many of the principal figures) so that in Model Cities programs, for example, most other agencies do not know the effect or purpose of projects or that certain ones even exist; and staffs are not geared toward common objectives. These problems are more likely to exist in a large bureaucracy like New York's than in smaller cities, yet certain steps can be taken to improve this condition.

City Administrator Needs to Be Strengthened. Much of the coordinating difficulty can be alleviated by assigning the bulk of this responsibility to one office. Organizationally, the Office of City Administrator was envisioned as fulfilling this role. But this responsibility was not given to City Administrator Costello. He was delegated a secondary role, primarily involving special studies and management services. His staff had little idea of what was happening in Model Cities. Under Deputy Mayor Edward Morrison, conditions are about the same except that his office has been given increased responsibilities, such as revitalizing the Civic Assembly and coordinating certain other management service functions. In effect, the city administrator is Edward Hamilton, who has been given such responsibility through budget control and planning, centralized management and budget techniques, and full analytical staff capacity to monitor agency heads. In addition, his personality and competence lend credibility to his role.

Consolidating City Offices. Now that a rather clear distinction has been made as to who the city administrator is, all available management tools ought to be placed at his disposal. Certainly these include the management services, administrative studies, and community involvement projects of Morrison's office. Moreover, this function ought to be beefed up by placing the Office of Neighborhood Government and other experiments at community decentralization under Morrison and allowing the major city-initiated community support elements to feed into one office.

Any citywide coalition needs neighborhood support, which it can better obtain by permitting neighborhood board members to serve on it. Besides this integration, the policy arm of Model Cities and Council Against Poverty ought to be meaningfully included in its membership so that common and realistic objectives can be formulated. Moreover, it makes little sense to have the human-resource philosophies of HRA and Model Cities acting separately. The policy-makers of these two major humanistic programs ought to be brought together as one board and their input effectively integrated into the Civic Assembly or an effective coalition of public interest groups and individuals.

City Administrator's Control over Model Cities. Besides integrating policy boards into one, more functional, unit, the operations of some units need to be placed under more appropriate direction. The most important change concerns Model Cities, which most logically should fall under Morrison along with other management experiments and decentralization demonstrations. Model Cities would then simply be an operating division—like the Office of Neighborhood Government— with its own director but responsible to Morrison. The justification for this change is that Model Cities has always been slated as a demonstration program, an innovator for existing institutions, a catalyst for change, and a program that was to achieve better coordination among all city agencies and levels of government. This can best be achieved under the deputy mayors who oversee all agencies.

Hamilton—through Morrison—could make the best possible use of
Model Cities as an innovator and community supporter. It would
mean integrating some portions of Model Cities administrative and
evaluation staff with Morrison's staff and the transfer of certain other
Model Cities functions to other appropriate agencies. With the possible advent of special revenue sharing, similar steps will be necessary
anyway. Furthermore, it makes more sense functionally even without
national program changes.

In addition, the use of some Model Cities funding citywide has
a greater chance of achieving institutional changes. For example,
increasing the basic planning and technical staff capacity of some
agencies (as was done in the Police Department with Police Foundation
funds) provides a better opportunity for permanent change throughout
the city, including the Model Neighborhoods. If such fundamental
changes are not made, Model Cities will have little effect in its neighborhoods anyway because the much stronger forces and bigger budgets
of the agencies tend to dominate services. Furthermore, institutional
changes will come primarily from the insistence and support of the
mayor and other elected officials because of citywide responsibilities.
It is too difficult to arouse widespread public opinion for changes in
civil service or unions or the bureaucracy if they are only to affect
a limited geographic area. Changes might come about in a smaller
area, only if such an area were truly given decentralized authority.

Model Cities Administration Unnecessary

It is difficult to justify a separate Model Cities Administration
as it is presently constructed. Now it is merely pieces and parts of
a community development agency; and its recent policy to concentrate
on manpower and career-ladder development further limits its scope
of activity. Moreover, it is a bureaucracy that has developed too
top heavily and would be better dismantled rather than letting it evolve
into a comprehensive community development agency charged with
major housing and related physical and human resource functions.
New York City is already too heavily bureaucratized. It needs not
a Model Cities bureaucracy, but rather a Model Cities philosophy
influential to the city administration.

Shifting Model Cities Responsibilities. In the event of special revenue
sharing legislation, federal funds would come to New York (and some
1,200 other cities and counties) on a formula basis, including money
originally allocated to Model Cities. The bulk of Community Development funds will involve physical development. Social amenities would
be concentrated under Human Resources Special Revenue Sharing.
However, with or without special revenue sharing, it is logical to

shift Model Cities programs to more appropriate superagencies: social projects to HRA (since it is already cumbersome, some new elements might be shifted to HDA or EDA), physical to HDA (which might appropriately be the community development administration), criminal justice to police, economic development to EDA, and so forth. And, as already indicated, the Model Cities coordinating role, chief executive review (and Annual Arrangements process), inter-agency and intergovernmental responsibilities, institutional change, and leadership roles would have a better chance for success under the deputy mayors, where most of the authority is concentrated. And at no time should the Model Cities role of innovation and community participation be minimized. It is important to have citizen input into the office of administration and into programs through an effective method of communication with neighborhoods; otherwise, new ideas and new leadership may not develop.

Integrating the Planning Commission, Community Boards, and City Administrator. It is also important to bring the Planning Commission and its staff and community boards into the mainstream of adminis-trative direction and coordination. The Planning Commission chair-man (executive director) ought to be directly responsible to the city administrator. To create an effective and comprehensive planning process, it is necessary to make the diverse planning staffs report through a chain of command directly to a single administrator. It is also desirable to integrate various citizen boards, such as Com-munity (Planning) Boards, Neighborhood Action Councils, Model Cities Policy Committees, and community action and certain other general planning boards. Community corporations and certain other operating bodies should be retained close to their present form in order to sustain innovation and instigate better methods of service; however, a single citizen group should do the over-all planning for each decentralized district in order to minimize confusion and to create a more reliable source of information for elected officials and administrative staff.

Decentralization

The whole concept of decentralization and citizen participation needs to be streamlined. The city is already decentralized into a multiple of resident decision-making bodies. It is now up to city officials to make the mechanism effective. Only one general govern-ment citizen group should officially represent all the residents of a district, and it should have sufficient power to get things accomplished; otherwise, confusion will continue to reign and community councils will simply be additional layers of bureaucracy. In order to avoid

the informal arrangement of the presently structured Neighborhood
Action Councils (weakly designed to avoid any conflicts with unions),
community councils must be given genuine and specific authority by
the city charter.

Authority of Councils. Each community council should, at the least,
encompass the authority of the council it replaces. Also, responsibility
should be given in areas of local budget review and priority setting,
department and project evaluation, participation in the hiring and
firing or principal district personnel, and in-depth involvement in
the development of a community comprehensive plan. Preferably,
community councils, much like Model Cities Policy Committees,
should not operate programs unless it were necessary to revitalize
absolutely hopeless projects. Many innovative projects should be
subcontracted to reliable community corporations or other successfully tested operators who are responsive and capable. Furthermore,
basic and routine administrative and fiscal matters ought to be handled
by city government. Overindulgence in administration and operations
takes too much time away from primary objectives of local councils
and relegates them to a degree of effectiveness no greater than central
government in the ability to administer neighborhood affairs. In
short, community councils should basically concentrate on developing
plans and policies and monitoring and evaluating programs and personnel. Existing agencies should continue to operate services, except
where they have failed to do so effectively. Local councils should
not be created as wholly autonomous units of government but should
be ultimately responsible to citywide officials who are elected legitimately under the principle of one man, one vote. However, specific
authority should be delegated for hiring of the board's staff and
certain other local personnel, project and budget priority determination, and problem areas particularly relevant to each community.
Also, a basic, independent budget should be affixed to each council,
which cannot be taken away except if illegally used.
    Autonomy can lead to greater proliferation of governmental
units and unfair economic distribution, discrimination, service duplication, and frustrated attempts at coordination. However, the meaningful sharing of government power with neighborhood groups is a
worthy and important contribution to better government.

Success and Failures. A more effective balance of power is needed—
one that will allow local councils to make a difference in service
performance and genuinely feed into the system and at the same time
create new leadership. Failure and frustrations with school decentralization should not detract from the pursuit of effective, general
government decentralization. The latter deals with a broader range

of city functions and involves deeper citizen concern with the most serious of urban problems. The lack of success of any decentralized movement has had more to do with how the system was guided than anything else. And one has only to look at the bitter fights that take place among councilmen to see that it is a common occurrence for members of groups to argue, regardless of whether the particular project fails or succeeds. Only with maturity and effective guidance will the majority of local councils succeed. But if they close the service gap, reduce alienation, and improve communication, decentralization will be worth it. Delays may be common at first, but as demonstrated in most Model Cities communities, after a period of board training and resolution of issues, projects are usually expedited. This is especially true with urban renewal, highway, and other long-range planning projects where citizens tend to object if not brought into the planning process early. But it is also true with short-range projects.

Model Cities Policy Committees. New York's Model Cities Policy Committees have not succeeded as well as those in some other cities. There has been a tendency for boards to be dominated by a few persons, some with selfish interests. At first, board membership was to be held to 18 but ended up ranging from 56 to 82—hardly manageable numbers. The new elections helped to bring in more young and old persons and a better cross-section of representation, yet few residents participated in the election. For example, of 2,000 voters in Brooklyn, reportedly half were Model Cities employees. The authority of the Policy Committees has been limited to planning and some monitoring and approval of personnel transactions—insufficient to test the concept of decentralization. Their most effective moments perhaps have been when they had to demonstrate and otherwise pressure for change, something that is not as pronounced under Williams as it was under Flateau, because of the reduced role of the new committees.

Lessons of Decentralization. Model Cities, Community Action, and school decentralization have not demonstrated the effectiveness of decentralization. They have only taught some lessons. And as Annmarie Walsh has noted, there are some pet myths about decentralization. She is correct in saying that structure alone does not guarantee vast social, economic, and political changes and that urban government cannot be run by town hall meetings. However, more effective organization can help. Moreover, no one advocates operating government by mass assemblies. Properly elected or appointed boards of reasonable size can effectively communicate what residents believe in and how they can go about gaining support for better services.

No major urban government today can operate effectively without some form of citizen participation. It is not a matter of finding out what system works elsewhere but what works for New York. Basically, New York needs a single, representative citizen body for general government in each area, with sufficient authority, a generous budget, and genuine support and guidance from elected officials if it is to achieve success.

Improving General Government

Strengthening City Council. Improving the concept of decentralization is only one of the lessons learned from Model Cities. One goal of the national Model Cities Program has been to improve all of government through better coordination, full professional staff, and assistance from state and private agencies. Our discussion has already brought out the need to strengthen the city council and make it an effective legislative branch. Increasing the power of the Board of Estimate would weaken city council and the mayor, diminish the importance of neighborhood councils because of the additional layer of borough government, and bring into sharp question the one-man, one-vote principle, because of the disproportionate balance of borough voters compared to the greater equality of councilmanic districts. City council's recent action designed to increase minority council representation brings out the importance of this difference even more. Because of the ambiguity and diffusion of councilmanic power, there is perhaps more confusion and delay than would exist under a system of community councils and well-established councilmanic authority. Today borough government is an anomaly since a highly mobile population tends to by-pass borough life and identify with its neighborhoods and key features of the city at large. No one can really accept the argument that borough presidents should be made strong county executives at the same time that they are powerful legislators. Even now, only the political strength of the borough governments keeps them alive.

Mayoral Power. The mayor would also be in a stronger position if he were working with a more effective legislative body and community councils that could lend strong support for needed changes in civil service, union regulations, bureaucracy, and all areas of bargaining. His highly fragmented authority could very well be consolidated with the support of community councils for common city objectives—for it has been more common for mayors and residents to agree than disagree on the issues and improvements needed in government. For the most part, they have formed common defenses against incompetent and lackadaisical systems.

405

Logic of Superagencies. As mayoral power may very likely gain strength under an effective system of neighborhood government, it can also sustain vitality through the continuance of the superagency structure. Two objectives of Model Cities are to achieve more effective coordination and to consolidate overlapping functions. The consolidation of the city's 62 departments into nine administrations has done this better than any other prior system, conserved central staff, and effected a more reasonable span of control for the mayor. As a result, his cabinet functions better, a good deal of duplication has been eliminated, agencywide standards and productivity goals can be established, and the city is ahead of most others in being prepared to accept federal grants under special revenue sharing because its alignment is similar to the new proposals. And recent steps to decentralize superagency authority by allowing administrators to make their own budget and personnel decisions have further strengthened these administrations. Moreover, superagencies can be compatible with community councils, which have limited authority, as described here, more effectively than under a concept of autonomous neighborhood government. The superagency structure should be retained but made much more responsive to residents by means of community councils with authority over specified district operations.

Administrative Decentralization. Present experiments with administrative decentralization are meeting with disappointing results, mostly because the district managers are merely coordinators of local superintendents. The concept of administrative decentralization is excellent and is working in a number of cities, even in New York to some extent in police administration. But to be effective, managers must be given direct authority over district superintendents and a voice in their hiring and firing. In addition, community councils should be allowed to participate in the process of managerial selection and evaluation, along with agency heads.

Lessons of Model Cities

Model Cities is only one actor in a large governmental process. The system itself needs fundamental tax restructuring, massive housing development and transportation changes, bold new employment and welfare programs, and full support from state and federal government if any significant difference is to be made in the quality of life. Interestingly enough—by the very nature of its comprehensive mandate—Model Cities has touched upon many of these issues. However, it is almost unbelievable that $250 million could be expended without extensive evaluation of projects. But Model Cities has demonstrated a number of vital factors: (1) the need to restructure and guide the progress of citizen councils; (2) how to change procedures to reduce bureaucratic red tape; (3) the ineffectiveness of a Model Cities Administration not integrated into the system it wishes to change; (4) lack of coordination and information flow throughout the city system; (5) projects too independent to have effect on the total city system; (6) the need to tackle most problems citywide if any lasting results are to be obtained; (7) the difficulty in breaking through organized labor and civil service; (8) the effect of employee interest and morale on the success of programs; (9) the need for innovation and support of community leaders to help make programs effective; and (10) the difficulty in reversing trends without state and federal leadership and resources.

In short, Model Cities has not made a noticeable difference in the quality of life, nor has it demonstrated an ability to get things done or make programs successful, but it has alerted—if only inadvertently—the city administration and elected officials to many of the city's problems and archaic procedures. Consequently, the city has a better base of knowledge and considerably greater experience as to how to go about improving the system. Hopefully, it will use this experience to good advantage.

Notes

1. Bruce Kivner, "101 Signs That the City Is Not Dying," New York Magazine, February 7, 1972, pp. 31-40.

2. C. Lowell Harriss, "Tax Issues in New York City," New York City Almanac (Center for New York City Affairs) 6, 5 (February 1972): 1.

3. Ibid., pp. 2-10.

4. From "Financing the City Government," in Academy of Political Science, Governing the City: Challenges and Options for New York (New York: Columbia University Press, 1969), p. 76.

5. Wallace S. Sayre, Great Cities of the World, "New York" (Beverly Hills, Cal.: Sage Publications, 1972), vol. 2, p. 702.

6. New York Times, April 24, 1972, p. 34.

7. Citizens Union of the City of New York, "The City Council Committee System in 1972," Spring 1972, pp. 1-5.

8. David Rogers, The Management of Big Cities (Beverly Hills, Cal.: Sage Publications, 1971), pp. 1-45.

9. Ibid., pp. 57-59.

10. New York City Council, Hearings on Construction Union Hiring, 1972.

11. Rogers, op. cit., p. 167.

12. Sylvan Feldstein, "Financial Management of New York's Model Cities," Municipal Finance Officers' Association Special Bulletin, September 1, 1971.

13. Seymour Z. Mann, Participation of the Poor and Model Cities in New York City: The Impact of Participation and Has Participation Made a Difference (New York: Department of Urban Affairs, Hunter College, May 1970), pp. 30-39.

14. Model Cities Administration, 13th Quarterly Report, pp. 40-43.

15. Ibid., pp. 17-19.

16. Model Cities Administration, 12th Quarterly Report, p. 45.

17. U.S. Department of Housing and Urban Development, Local Strategies to Affect State Plan Allocation of Federal Funds, Community Development Evaluation Series No. 3, January 1972, pp. 13-19.

18. In Walter H. Wagener, "Slum-Job Tests Voided as Biased," New York Times, March 8, 1972, pp. 1 and 55.

19. Program Development and Implementation (PDI), Quarterly Report, op. cit., p. 10.

20. New York Model Cities Administration, Division of Program Development and Implementation, "Monitoring Report for Quarterly," February 24, 1972.

21. Model Cities 13th Quarterly Report, op. cit., p. 72.

22. New York Daily News, November 10, 1971, p. 7.

23. Model Cities 11th Quarterly Report, Submitted by Administrator Joseph B. Williams, New York City, March 15, 1972, pp. 12 and 16.

24. PDI Quarterly Report, op. cit., p. 11.

25. Model Cities, 12th Quarterly Report, op. cit., p. 31.

26. Model Cities, 13th Quarterly Report, op. cit., p. 71.

27. Ibid., p. 70.

28. PDI Quarterly Report, op. cit., p. 8.

PART

III

SUMMARY

PART

III

SUMMARY

1. The Model Cities Program has been the single most effective instrument for providing local officials with the means and motivation to give the broadest range of services to disadvantaged areas and to improve local government operations. It has had a more profound effect on changing local government operations than other federal programs because it has primarily worked within local government systems and has brought strong resident influence with it.

2. Contrary to the belief of many, Model Cities has been the federal program with the least federal interference in local problem definition and priority setting. It has given local officials and citizens in 147 cities almost complete discretionary authority over the types of programs and the amount of money to be spent. It is doubtful whether special revenue sharing or other forms of block grants will in themselves provide greater opportunity for local decision-making. However, they will extend this ability citywide, as has been done through Planned Variations, which is an expansion of Model Cities concepts citywide in 20 cities.

3. The federal commitment—in resources and the talent necessary to fulfill the goals and objectives of the program—was never realized. The limitation of funds was greatly accentuated because of the requirement to develop comprehensive plans. Too little federal money was spread among too many cities, and funds in almost every city were spread sparingly among too many programs. The effect has been failure to reach massive impact in any functional program area.

4. Although comprehensiveness contributed to underfunding, it has been useful because it has required city officials to experiment with new programs and expand proven programs in almost every functional area, such as health, employment, education, criminal

411

justice, social services, and municipal services. Because of its usefulness in helping to achieve more effective coordination and to develop whole information systems, comprehensiveness should be retained as a planning requirement, and there should be continued emphasis on local experimentation (project innovation and demonstration) in all program areas. Rather than comprehensive systems being eliminated, they should be improved to collect and maintain accurate human resource data in a central municipal source so that planning technicians do not continually have to estimate prevailing conditions and so that projections may be improved.

5. The requirement to use all resources in disadvantaged areas has been beneficial to the poor; however, it has restricted the ability to coordinate programs and has hindered the development of citywide objectives and cooperation from the community at large. Planned Variations is a more desirable approach: first, to continue concentration of the majority of resources in the most needy areas but, second, to apportion funds citywide to help solve the city's broad problems and to develop sound management techniques and service effectiveness for the entire city. Community development legislation should require that the majority of funds be spent for the benefit of the most depressed areas in each city and county. Without such stipulation, it is doubtful whether the problems of the poor will ever be addressed adequately. It is not enough that distribution formulas allocate money to whole cities and counties based on poverty factors. Legislation should make clear the priorities of need within localities as well.

6. Budgets for the proposed Better Communities Act and other community development legislation now before Congress will have the effect of maintaining the status quo for most urban areas, reducing funds for others, and increasing funds in some newly participating communities. Because of the great needs of cities and counties, funds should be not only kept at present levels in all localities that are using them properly but increased in many. The formula for the distribution of funds should be based on need and reflection of the real conditions of poverty. The distribution formula in the Better Communities Act does not reflect the truest poverty indices and would have the effect of passing money to some communities that have a low priority for community-development-type activities. The expenditure of community development funds should reflect national priorities. The amount each community gets should be based not only on need but also on plans that localities submit of how they intend to meet community goals and national priorities.

7. "Maintenance of effort" should be required in any new community development legislation so that cities and counties do not replace local tax effort with federal money and thus merely maintain

the status quo. In addition, there should be some state and local matching requirements for community development funds so that local interest and commitment are maintained. This should also have the effect of increasing the amount of money expended for community development purposes in contrast to more traditional uses.

8. Excessive red tape and paper-work requirements have been a principal fault of the Model Cities Program, although Planned Variations has reduced this burden by as much as two-thirds. Block grants, minimum application and reporting requirements, and post-audits would have the effect of reducing requisites to tolerable levels. However, officials should not regard the development and maintenance of comprehensive plans, information systems, and evaluation as synonomous with delay and red tape. These are natural parts of any community's realistic planning and goal setting and are best designed to reduce costs and prevent delays over the long run.

9. The excellent experience of evaluating projects in the Model Cities process should be expanded to all community development activities. Many local and federal evaluation techniques need improvement. Yet there are many that have proved valuable. Local government has not made a regular practice of evaluating all local services, except by means of a more superficial budget review process. The Model Cities evaluation experience should be passed on to other city county departments. Furthermore, federal evaluation of local government should carry more stringent guidelines for enforcement and compliance with stated community objectives.

10. In many cases, Model Cities initiated successful steps toward improving intergovernmental cooperation and program coordination. Representatives from private and state agencies have joined to discuss community goals and to prevent overlapping and duplicate programing. In a number of cases, standing intergovernmental task forces have been formed, sanctioned by laws or executive orders and composed of top state and regional officials. Nevertheless, there are extreme jealousies among agencies, and much more formalized and effective coordinating mechanisms are needed. Federal regional councils are helping to achieve federal coordination. State regional councils with authority to plan and allocate resources are also needed in the more complex urban areas. Model Cities, from its small geographic area, cannot be expected to achieve a high degree of coordination. Planned Variations will not succeed much further without full state cooperation.

11. There has been a notable lack of cooperation from private groups, particularly business and unions. This has resulted from the inability of these groups to identify their memberships and organizational objectives with the needs of the inner-city poor. There has also been discouragement by militant and self-interested "community spokesmen" and simply lack of encouragement from local Model Cities

officials. The maturing of the citizen board process and greater concern for citywide objectives are encouraging more private response. Model Cities experience has shown that private initiative and resources are necessary to develop fully the community's potential.

12. Model Cities has operated largely under the guidance of local general government in varying degrees of partnership between Model Neighborhood residents and city officials. This process has had greater effect on influencing operations and changing established procedures of local government than have programs that have operated largely outside general government. It has caused local government to evaluate seriously many of its programs, change city hiring practices, expand regular services to disadvantaged areas, institute social service planning, and become a leader in coordinating other agencies. And Planned Variations has taken this process a step further by going citywide.

13. Processes such as A-95 (local clearing house for federal programs), Annual Arrangements (priority and resource determination), Chief Executive Review and Comment (CERC, a strengthening of the chief executive's review authority), Planned Variations, integrated (federal-local) financial and information systems, consolidated funding, and other management improvements have been natural evolutions from the Model Cities experience. Although Model Cities has not been able to take more than the initial steps and although it will not have the opportunity to do so in its present state, it has been the principal catalyst. This is evident from the fact that few cities outside the Model Cities Program have made advances in these techniques.

14. The flexible use of Model Cities funds has been one of its chief assets. The ability to "buy into" other agencies (under contractual arrangements), by offering funds for new or expanded programing, has enabled Model Cities to secure important changes in agency operations. Moreover, any block grant program should not be so stringent that it eliminates the advantages of the flexible and catalytic use of federal money.

15. Model Cities has achieved some degree of innovation and institutional change. Innovations have included such things as model schools, nonprofit corporations, neighborhood health centers, multiservice centers, decision-making by the poor, less restrictive hiring procedures for minorities, increased employment of minorities in local government, new and improved services to disadvantaged areas, improved city management techniques, and an increased involvement of elected officials in the problems of the poor. However, Model Cities has only taken the first few steps, and further action along these lines is essential.

16. Perhaps Model Cities' most notable achievements have been in improving the processes of local government, including

414

management, coordination, citizen involvement, and planning techniques. Yet there have been improvements in product as well. Services have been improved in most model areas. And the number of clients using facilities is gradually increasing. Better programing and public acceptance have meant an improved cost-benefit ratio. Although Model Cities has not reached its high "quality-of-life" goals and many individual programs are failures, this situation does not call for the flat abandonment of all programs but rather for careful analysis, elimination of unsatisfactory projects, and improvement of the others.

17. Citizen participation has been perhaps the most innovative force in the Model Cities Program and in local general government. Its innovation has been not so much in programing but in changing the attitudes of local officials and the ways they make decisions and in alerting other community groups to the need to involve themselves in governmental decision-making. Although some citizen boards have delayed or damaged some projects, others have improved government service, communication, and community development. The good far outweighs the bad. Because some cities have not been able to develop a satisfactory participation process does not necessarily mean that meaningful citizen involvement is impossible but rather that city officials have not yet found the correct ingredients for success. In this regard, community development legislation should require active citizen participation and provide the necessary resources for it. It should permit neighborhood groups not only to participate in decision-making but to operate some programs. The operation of programs has the effect of increasing citizen board interest, responsibility, and longevity.

ABOUT THE AUTHOR

GEORGE J. WASHNIS is director of municipal studies for the Center for Governmental Studies in Washington, D.C. Prior to this he was chief administrative officer for the city of East St. Louis, Illinois for seven years; assistant city manager for Evanston, Illinois; and held two managerial positions in private industry. He received his MGA (Master of Governmental Administration) from the Fels Institute, Wharton School of Business Administration, University of Pennsylvania.

Mr. Washnis has had extensive experience in public administration and has been a consultant to cities and national governmental organizations. In Evanston he held a variety of governmental positions and instituted innovations in personnel selection and performance. In East St. Louis he was largely responsible for bringing to the city and developing a number of programs, such as community action, model cities, comprehensive planning, computerization, and general improvements in the capacity of government. In his years of service in the St. Louis area he served on 47 committees, including seven regional committees concerned with mass transit, comprehensive health, human resource programs, economic development, and general regional government.

During the past four years Mr. Washnis has studied programs and been a consultant in more than thirty U.S. cities and states, and has reviewed general local governments in over twenty foreign cities. He has written numerous articles and reports. His recent book, Municipal Decentralization and Neighborhood Resources (Praeger Publishers, 1972) was chosen as a selection of the Library of Urban Affairs book-of-the-month club. Mr. Washnis has served on and assisted the International City Management Association (ICMA) Task Force on Sense of Community and Neighborhood Identity and also the Task Force on Management Criteria. He has also served on the National League of Cities United States Conference of Mayors Finance Committee and made presentations in a number of their conferences and workshops. He is a past president of the St. Louis Chapter of the American Society of Public Administration (ASPA) and has continued to work and serve the national organization.

RELATED TITLES
Published by
Praeger Special Studies

GOVERNING URBAN AMERICA IN THE 1970s
Edited by Werner Z. Hirsch and Sidney
Sonenblum

MUNICIPAL DECENTRALIZATION AND
NIEGHBORHOOD RESOURCES: Case Studies
of Twelve Cities
George J. Washnis

NEW STRATEGIES FOR REGIONAL
COOPERATION: A Model for the Tri-State
New York-New Jersey-Connecticut Area
Edward N. Costikyan and Maxwell Lehman

PLANNING AND MANAGING THE ECONOMY
OF THE CITY: Policy Guidelines for the
Metropolitan Mayor
Joseph Oberman, with a contribution by
Robert Bingham

PLANNING FOR THE LOWER EAST SIDE
Harry Schwartz, assisted by Peter Abeles

RESTRUCTURING THE GOVERNMENT OF
NEW YORK CITY: Report of the Scott
Commission Task Force on Jurisdiction and
Structure
Edward N. Costikyan and Maxwell Lehman

URBAN PLANNING IN THE 1960s: A
Design for Irrelevancy
Marshall Kaplan